Historical
Studies and
Literary
Criticism

Historical Studies and Literary Criticism

Edited, with an Introduction, by
Jerome J. McGann

The University of Wisconsin Press

Published 1985

The University of Wisconsin Press
114 North Murray Street
Madison, Wisconsin 53715

The University of Wisconsin Press, Ltd.
1 Gower Street
London WC1E 6HA, England

First printing

Printed in the United States of America

For LC CIP information see the colophon

ISBN 0-299-10280-7

Contents

IV. Defining a Context: The Example of Women's Studies

Contributors

HANS AARSLEFF is Professor of English at Princeton University.

NINA AUERBACH is Professor of English at the University of Pennsylvania.

MARILYN BUTLER is Fellow of St. Hugh's College, Oxford University.

TERRY EAGLETON is Tutorial Fellow in English at Wadham College, Oxford University.

SANDRA M. GILBERT is Professor of English at Princeton University.

SUSAN GUBAR is Professor of English at Indiana University.

CECIL Y. LANG is the Commonwealth Professor of English at the University of Virginia.

MARJORIE LEVINSON is Assistant Professor of English at the University of Pennsylvania.

LAWRENCE LIPKING is the Chester D. Tripp Professor of Humanities and Director of the Program in Comparative Literature and Theory at Northwestern University.

JEROME J. MCGANN is the Doris and Henry Dreyfuss Professor of the Humanities in the Division of the Humanities and Social Sciences at the California Institute of Technology.

SUSAN MORGAN is Associate Professor of English at Vassar College.

BARBARA CLARKE MOSSBERG is Associate Professor of English at the University of Oregon.

BRUCE A. ROSENBERG is Professor of American Civilization and English at Brown University.

JOHN SUTHERLAND is Professor of English at the California Institute of Technology.

Acknowledgments

THANKS ARE due to the California Institute of Technology and to the Weingart Foundation for providing the funds and the facilities for the fourth annual Caltech-Weingart Conference in the Humanities, which was held at the Caltech campus in the spring of 1984. Special thanks are due to David Grether, chairman of the Division of Social Sciences and Humanities at Caltech, for his aid and support. Finally, there is Betty Hyland, who administered all the important details of the conference; neither this book nor the original conference would have been possible without her kindness, skill, and tireless work.

Historical
Studies and
Literary
Criticism

Introduction: A Point of Reference

Jerome J. McGann

THE ESSAYS in this book represent such a variety of viewpoints and critical strategies, and cover such diverse subject matters, that their common ground can be easily lost sight of. For all the differences— they are many and important—these essays share a commitment to explore the social and historical dimensions of literary works. More than this, the writers of these essays are all extremely self-conscious about their sociohistorical interests, and about the academic context in which their work has been initiated and pursued. The essays here are antithetical, in several respects, to the (equally various) tradition of formal, structural, and text-centered literary studies which have been so influential in the academy for two generations. In the present essays one sees at work the recently emergent effort to reconstitute sociohistorical methods and interests as the heart of literary studies.

Some of these essays are explicitly critical of formalist traditions, others implicitly so; and all exhibit, in different ways, a positive debt to the various strands of immanent critical traditions. What will not be found in these essays, however, is the assumption, so common in text-centered studies of every type, that literary works are self-enclosed verbal constructs, or looped intertextual fields of autonomous signifiers and signifieds. In these essays the question of referentiality is once again brought to the fore.

The concept—and the problem—of the referential aspects of literary works is so central to an adequate literary theory and critical practice that I want to take it up here by way of introducing this collection of essays. Two things may be initially observed. First, referentiality appears as "a problem" in formalist and text-centered studies precisely by its absence. Though everyone knows and agrees that literary works have sociohistorical dimensions, theories and practices generated in text-centered critical traditions bracket out these matters from consideration, particularly at the level of theory.[1] Second, referentiality appears as a problem in historically grounded criticism because such criticism has thus far been unable to revise its theoretical grounds so as to take account of the criticisms which were brought against it in this century,

3

and in particular the criticisms developed out of the theory of literary mediations. Involved here is the view, pressed strongly on various fronts in the past fifty years, that language and language structures (including, perforce, literary works) are modeling rather than mirroring forms. They do not point to a prior, authorizing reality (whether "realist" or "idealist"), they themselves *constitute*—in both the active and the passive senses—what must be taken as reality (both "in fact" and "in ideals"). To the extent that traditional forms of historical criticism have not been able to assimilate or refute such a view, they have been moved to the periphery of literary studies.

In recent years, however, textual and intertextual approaches have begun to yield up their own theoretical problems, and literary studies have witnessed a renewed interest in various kinds of sociohistorical critical work. Marxist and Marxist-influenced criticism has been an especially important factor in this development, largely, I think, because the questions it poses are founded in a powerful and dynamically coherent tradition of critical inquiry. Feminist studies have also done much to expose the sociohistorical dimensions of literary work. Because both of these critical approaches necessarily practice a hermeneutics of a repressed or invisibilized content, both have found no difficulty in assimilating the basic poststructural programmatic. At the same time, the traditional methods of historicist philology have also begun to reappear in interpretive studies. Bibliography, manuscript studies of various kinds, analyses of the forms, methods, and materials of literary production: these materialist and empirical branches of learning have been experiencing a renascence and at the same time have begun to rediscover their theoretical ground. Hermeneutical studies are increasingly realizing that the symbolic discourse which is literature operates with and through many forms of mediation besides "language" narrowly conceived. The price of a book, its place of publication, even its physical form and the institutional structures by which it is distributed and received, all bear upon the production of literary meaning, and hence all must be critically analyzed and explained.

When we speak of the referential dimensions of literary work, therefore, we have in mind several different things. In the first place, literary work can be practiced, can constitute itself, only in and through various institutional forms which are not themselves "literary" at all, though they are meaning-constitutive. The most important of these institutions, for the past hundred fifty years anyway, are the commercial publishing network in all its complex parts, and the academy. The church and the court have, in the past, also served crucial mediating functions for writers. Literary works are produced *with reference to* these mediational structures, are in fact embodied in such structures, and criticism is therefore obliged to explain and reconstitute such structures in relation to the literary work. As we now realize more clearly than ever before, criticism must factor itself and its own mediations into its explanations. In the final accounting, "the work" and its mediations are as inseparable as are "the (original) work" and its (subsequent) critical explanations.

Historically considered, the problem of referentiality first appeared not as a fault line in empirically based critical studies, but much earlier, in the Kantian response to the philosophic grounds of empiricism. Derrida's influential account of the textual dynamic ("the joyous affirmation of the play of the world and of the innocence of becoming, the affirmation of a world of signs without fault, without truth, without origin, offered to an active interpretation")[2] recalls nothing so much as the opening of Kant's *Critique of Judgment*, in which not only is the radical subjectivity of the esthetic event founded, but it is founded via an explication of the judging subject rather than the "work of art." Coleridge's important variation on this Kantian move was to emphasize even more clearly the "ideal" content which the poetic text constitutes. Poetical works do not "copy" the phenomena of the external world, they "imitate" the ideal forms which we know through the operations of the human mind.[3] As a good recent critic of Coleridge has put the matter: "The 'reality' that poems 'imitate' is not the objective world as such, but . . . the consciousness of the poet himself *in his encounters with* the objective world. . . . the poet's only genuine subject matter is himself, and the only ideas he presents will be ideas about the activity of consciousness in the world around it."[4] Coleridge's critique of the insistently referential aspects of Wordsworth's poetry—what he calls its "accidentality" and its "matter-of-factness"—is merely the critical reflex of his positive position: that "poetry as poetry is essentially *ideal*, [and] avoids and excludes all *accident* [and] apparent individualities."[5]

Coleridge is himself an impressive historicist critic, as his commentaries on the biblical tradition show. Nevertheless, his theoretical ground would eventually be appropriated by those idealist and subjectivist forms of criticism which emerged out of twentieth-century linguistics and semiology. If "poetry as poetry" has reference only to a field of subjectivity, then the criticism and interpretation of poetry which pursue the accidentalities and matters-of-fact of philology will themselves be necessarily misguided.

Coleridge's view is recapitulated, in a variety of ways, by all twentieth-century practitioners of purely immanent critical methods. C. S. Lewis's remarks in "The Personal Heresy" in 1934, and Cleanth Brooks's in *The Well Wrought Urn* (1947), typify the New Critical position on the matter of poetry's relation to sociohistorical actualities.[6] That is to say, while the New Criticism was a vigorously antihistorical movement, and consciously in reaction to the philological and historicist methods which had come to preeminence in literary studies during the eighteenth and nineteenth centuries, it always made practical provision for certain "extrinsic" materials in the poetic product. The position is epitomized in Wellek and Warren's widely used handbook *Theory of Literature* (1947), where the concepts of "intrinsic" and "extrinsic" interpretation are enshrined. Equally characteristic are formulations like the following by Brooks, who means to have an organic-intrinsic idea of the poem, but cannot altogether evade the informational-extrinsic dimensions of the text: "If we see that any item in a poem is to be judged only in terms of the total effect of the poem, we shall readily grant the importance for criticism of the work of the linguist and the literary historian."[7]

In short, the intrinsic and text-centered approaches of the early and mid-twentieth century made certain tactical accommodations and compromises in their critical programs and arguments. Indeed, it was precisely this compromised status of their theory which brought them to ruin at the hands of their ungrateful children, the deconstructionists. For the latter had no difficulty in showing that New Critical strategies were based upon an illusory and mystified form of the very empiricism which those strategies were consciously designed to displace. The idea of "the poem itself," of the stable (if paradoxical) object of critical attention, was swept away in the aftermath of structuralism. "De-ferral," "de-stabilization," "de-centering," "de-construction": the history of the emergence of these ideas during the 1970s is well known and needs no rehearsing again here. Nor will it be necessary to point out what is equally well known, that the deconstructionist movement was (and of course is) a form of immanent criticism's twentieth-century wilderness.

Two important aspects of these late forms of immanent criticism do need to be attended to, however. The first is the extremity of their antihistorical position. None of the earlier twentieth-century text-centered critics ever spoke, as Hillis Miller has spoken in one of his most celebrated essays, of "the fiction of the referential, the illusion that the terms of the poem refer literally to something that exists."[8] This bold pronouncement offers a final solution to the problem of the social actuality of poetical work, and it is quite typical of (at any rate) the American deconstructive establishment. The repudiation of referentiality is made, as Miller says, "according to the logic of a theory of language which bases meaning on the solid referentiality of literal names for visible physical objects."[9] Here Miller intends to dispose once and for all of that Great Satan of so many humanists, "empiricism," by dismissing at last the supposed "theory of language" on which it rests.

In making his attack, however, Miller unwittingly exposes another important aspect of his critical position. That is to say, he reveals his assent to a particular concept of referentiality. A "solid" correspondence of "literal names for visible physical objects" is certainly *an* idea of referentiality, but it is manifestly an impoverished concept. This idea of how language "refers" to the actual world where those language forms called poems operate may reflect the view which someone (besides Miller) has held at some time or other. It is not, however, characteristic of the thought of the great traditional philological and historical critics. When Miller dismisses this concept of referentiality, then, he is trying to cast out a mere phantom. His dismissal thus fails to confirm his own critical practice.

Of course one can, with some searching, find other critics besides deconstructionists like Miller who have subscribed to excessively simple concepts of referentiality. When Daniel Aaron, for example, says that "the historian who writes about the past might be likened to a naturalist as he observes and analyzes specimens in a museum or perhaps animals caged in a zoo,"[10] his words betray a concept of referentiality that is quite comparable to Miller's. One is tempted to reply merely that this is not a persuasive idea, and that it runs counter to the lines of historical thought which have dominated critical thought for almost three centuries. But one might do better to quote, for example, Vico's stronger thought, that "human history differs from natural history in this, that we have made the former, but not the latter."[11] Indeed, it is Miller's sympathy with Vico's thought which has helped to set him, along with so many other recent literary critics, in opposition to "referentiality."

What is necessary at this juncture, therefore, is not to bracket the referential dimensions of poetry out of critical consideration on the basis of an impoverished theory of language and literary reference. Rather, we should be trying to recover and reformulate the idea of referentiality which underlies the thought of the great historical critics of the recent past. Only in this way will the full significance of Miller's excellent critical work — and the work of many other immanentist critics — be revealed. The American line of Derridean thought, in particular, would do well to recall the following passage from Derrida himself: "A deconstructive practice which would not bear upon 'institutional apparatuses and historical processes' . . . , which would remain content to operate upon philosophemes or conceptual signified[s], or discourses, etc., would not be deconstructive; whatever its originality, it would but reproduce the gesture of self criticism in philosophy in its internal tradition."[12] When Miller, in his essay "The Critic as Host," speaks of "deconstructive strategy" as "going with a given text as far as it will go, to its limits," he echoes Derrida, as he does when he goes on to add that all criticism, including deconstructive criticism, "contains, necessarily, its enemy within itself."[13] But the fact is that American deconstructionism does not go to those limits and does not expose its internal fault lines. On the contrary, it hides and obscures them at every turn. The enemy which deconstructive critics like Miller will not face is history, and the fault line of such criticism appears as its elision of the sociohistorical dimensions of literary work.

At the beginning of his first book, *L'épithète traditionnelle dans Homère* (1928), Milman Parry consciously set his work in the line of the great tradition of modern historical scholarship.

> The literature of every country and of every time is understood as it ought to be only by the author and his contemporaries. . . . The task, therefore, of one who lives in another age and wants to appreciate that work correctly, consists precisely in rediscovering the varied information and complexes of ideas which the author assumed to be the natural property of his audience.[14]

Parry is quick to observe that this scholarly project of "reconstructing that [original] community of thought through which the poet made himself understood" is a task "so complex as to be impossible of realization in an entirely satisfactory manner."[15] Nevertheless, the project must be pursued if we are to hope to have any reliable understanding of the culture of the past.

The twentieth-century attack upon the historical method in criticism, initially focused on the so-called intentional fallacy, soon became a broadly based critique of genetic studies in general. John M. Ellis's *The Theory of Literary Criticism: A Logical Analysis* (1974) has summarized and completed this line of critique. His argument is not merely that genetic studies cannot recover the "original context," but that the human meaning of literary works does not lie in that context. Rather, it lies in the context of immediate use: "If we insist on relating the text primarily to the context of its composition and to the life and social context of its author, we are cutting it off from that relation to life which is the relevant one."[16] In addition, genetic criticism limits and shrinks the dynamic potential of literary products by reducing their meanings to "static" forms, and by suggesting that certain "information" can supply "the key to the text" and its meaning.[17] Poststructural critics like Miller would merely take this (ultimately Nietzschean) line of thought to a more extreme position. Genetic criticism is the epitome of all critical forms which seek after the "univocal reading" of a text.[18] For deconstructionists, it does not matter whether the finished reading stands as an "originary" form to which criticism seeks to return, or an accomplished form which criticism makes in its own rhetorical praxis. All are unstable and operating under the sign of *différance*. Thus, "Nihilism is an inalienable alien presence within Occidental metaphysics, both in poems and in the criticism of poems."[19]

Ellis's view that criticism justifies itself in its social praxis is important and will be reconsidered below. Before taking up that matter, however, we have to inquire into the idea that genetic criticism offers static and univocal meanings for literary works. In fact, all the great historicist critics were well aware that their method could not do this. The ideal of reconstructing the originary material and ideological context, even if fully achieved, would provide the later reader only with what "the author assumed to be the natural property of his audience." The method does not offer static and univocal readings, it attempts to specify the concrete and particular forms in which certain human events constituted themselves. The "meanings" of those events, whether for the original persons involved or for any subsequent persons, are themselves specifically constituted events which can and will be reconstituted in the subsequent historical passage of the poem. The "reading" and the "criticism" of poems and the human events they represent set what Blake called a "bounding line" to human action. In this sense criticism — and historical criticism paradigmatically — does not establish the "meanings" of poems, it tries to re-present them to us in "minute particulars," in forms that recover (as it were) their *physique* in as complete detail as possible. Thus Parry says, of the historical reconstruction which his criticism brings about: "I make for myself a picture of great detail,"[20] *not* "I translate for myself and my world the meaning of the ancient texts." The originary "meanings" (Parry's "complexes of ideas which the author assumed") are themselves concrete particulars, not concrete universals; and their complexity involves diverse and often contradictory lines of relations. Historical criticism's great critical advance lay in its ability to reconstruct, in methodical ways, the differential and contradictory patterns within which poetical works constitute themselves and are constituted.

Parry and those like him understood very well that texts and the criticism of texts labored under various destabilizing forces.

If I say that Grote's account of democracy at Athens is more revealing
of the mind of an English Liberal of the nineteenth century after Christ,
than it recalls what actually took place in Athens in the fifth century before Christ, and then go on to admit that the opinion which I have just
expressed about Grote may in turn reveal even more my own state of mind
than it does that of Grote (indeed, I know that I am expressing this thought
here because I came across it about two weeks ago in one of the essays
submitted for the Bowdoin prize essay contest and it struck me)—even
in that case I am still doing no more than to try to attain a more perfect
method for the historical approach to the thought of the past.[21]

This is Parry's version of "the critic as host," and it explains why he
will state the following basic paradox of historical method: that by it
"we learn to keep ourselves out of the past, or rather we learn to go
into it."[22] Historical method in criticism clarifies and defines the differentials in concrete and specific ways for the originary and the continuing past, as well as for the immediate present (and the as yet uncon-
structed future).

These passages are taken from Parry's great essay "The Historical
Method in Literary Criticism" (1936), where Parry also expresses "a certain feeling of fear" that this method will "destroy itself."[23] His fear recalls Nietzsche's critique of philological studies expressed in *On the Advantage and the Disadvantage of History for Life*, and anticipates the
antihistorical arguments of the immanentist critical methods which, in
the early 1930s, were just beginning to gain force and prominence. "I
have seen myself, only too often and too clearly, how, because those
who teach and study Greek and Latin literature have lost the sense of
its importance for humanity, the study of those literatures has declined."[24]
What Parry proposes is that scholars "create their heroic legend" of the
importance of the historicity, not merely of truth, but of the search for
truth: "Otherwise they will be choosing a future in which they must
see themselves confined not by choice, but by compulsion, to be forever
ineffective, if they would not be untruthful."[25]

In fact, however, historical criticism—at least as it was practiced in
the Western academy—did not go on to fulfill what Parry called for.
This failure occurred, I believe, because historicist criticism always tended
to conceive its terms in a recollective frame. Thus "referentiality," in this
program, tended to be construed as bearing upon persons and events
which lay behind us, in a completed form of pastness. It is true that
language "refers to" particular actualities. But if no historical critic of
any standing ever understood this referential connection in the simple
empiricist terms laid down by Miller, neither, on the other hand, did
they explore the full theoretical implications of some of their most important historicist principles.

"I make for myself a picture of great detail." This is the heart of the historicist program. But the traditional historicists—even late figures like Parry—tended to "read" this picture with their gaze turned backward. Parry knew perfectly well that the picture he made for himself contained historical layers (himself, Grote, fifth-century Greece, as well as many intervenient distances), but when he actually *made* the picture for his audience, the layers and intervenient distances tended to disappear into the outlines of the originary picture. This blurring of the palimpsest seems most obvious to us, now, in the picture's avoidance of its projected future details. These we now call, in general, the "prejudice" (after Gadamer) or "ideology" (after the Marxist tradition) of the critical account.

Any present deployment of historical criticism will have to renovate the original program along such lines. The picture which the historical critic makes is one which includes a future as well as a present and a past, which includes, perhaps, several pasts, presents, and futures. Historical criticism can no longer make any part of that sweeping picture unselfconsciously, or treat any of its details in an untheorized way. The problem with Parry's brief anecdote about fifth-century Greece, Grote, and himself is that he was unable to incorporate the shrewd insight of this anecdote into his explicit programmatic scheme. As a result, the anecdote stands apart, an ancillary sketch which would not find its way into a single, larger picture of great detail.

In this context we can begin to reconstitute the idea of "referentiality" and even sketch the outlines of a renovated historical criticism. We begin with what Parry called the "detail." For a properly historical criticism—which is to say, in my view, a dialectical criticism—those much-maligned matters of fact are the postulates of a critical discourse. The historical particularity of a poem by Wordsworth or a novel by Austen have to be clearly specified in the act of criticism if that act is to preceed dialectically, i.e., if that act is not simply to project upon "the work" its own conceptual interests. Such elementary particulars establish the ground for a whole system of critical differentials that stretch across the continuing social life of a literary work from its point of origin to its current operations.

These matters ought to be clear enough. What also needs to be said, however, is that the "referent" of any discourse—whether the "original" creative discourse, the intervening discourses of the work's reception, or the immediate discourses of current criticism—cannot be conceived simply as an empirical datum. The matters-of-fact which poems and criticism embody (or constitute) are not—to borrow Coleridge's phraseology—"objects as objects"; rather they are objects-as-subjects, objects which have been (and continue to be) a focus of important human interests.[26] The poems themselves, because they are "social texts" and events, are also objects as subjects, but the poems acquire this character because they "have reference to" the larger (human) world of social interactions. Literary works represent, and are representative of, that larger world.

All this does not mean, however, that the task of criticism is a historicist reconstruction or glossing of a particular work's originary referential field. The critical ideal must be a totalizing one, for literary "works"[27] *continue* to live and move and have their being. The referential field of Byron's *Don Juan* is by no means limited to the period 1789–1824, though that is the explicit frame of the poem's narrativization. *Don Juan* " has reference to" a larger share of the past than the period of its immediate focus. Indeed, that focusing period, as reconstituted through *Don Juan*, is revealed to be itself a vehicle (or system of mediations) by which history is rendered up for human use. In the end, what we must see is that works like *Don Juan* have reference to—make use of and assume an interest in—some more or less comprehensive aspects of the past, and the present and the future as well. Because critical activity shares in that work, it too operates with its own various, and more or less explicit, sociohistorical interests.

To recover the concept of referentiality, we might well begin by reminding ourselves that "facts" are not mere data, objects, or monads; they are heuristic isolates which bring into focus some more or less complex network of human events and relations. As such, "facts" always have to be reconstituted if those networks are to be clarified and redeployed. One of the special graces of poetic works—probably their chief social value—is that they are conceptual forms which operate at a high level of generality, on the one hand, and at an equally high level of particularity on the other. The particulars, the "matters-of-fact," are subjected to a general organizing structure which precisely *does not* reduce those particulars to conceptual finishedness, but instead preserves them in a state of (as it were) freedom. The particulars are grains of sand in which the world may be seen—may be seen again and again, in new sets of relations and differentials.

It may be useful to recall at this point the more traditional theory of literary imitation. Sidney's *Defence of Poesie*, the finest English representation of the Aristotelian doctrine of mimesis, concerns itself principally with what he calls "right poets," that is, those poets who in their art of imitation "borrow nothing of what is, hath been, or shall be; but range . . . into the divine consideration of what may be and should be."[28] When Coleridge, in the *Biographia Literaria* and his related essay "On Poesy or Art," distinguishes between what he calls "imitation" and "mere copying," he is recollecting the Aristotelian tradition.[29] In this view, what the poet imitates are not simply matters of fact or accidentalities or minute particulars; the poet imitates the essential qualities of his subject, human beings or individual persons in their generic distinctiveness. As a consequence, since human life — in contrast to the natural world — is distinguished by its spiritual or moral dimensions, the object of poetic imitation will have to be a re-presentation, via a judicious selection of phenomenal details, of noumenal realities.

The authority of this theory of imitation, along with its related concept of referentiality, began to be undermined with the development of eighteenth-century empiricism and modern historical thought. The rise of the novel is connected to the emergence of what we now call "realism," in which accidentalities and matters of fact are crucial to the deployment of a new type of poetic imitation. Among poets, Wordsworth has the distinction of being the first — in the Preface to the *Lyrical Ballads* — to intimate the relevance of these new ideas. Minute particulars of time, place, and circumstance gain in importance (for artists as well as for people in general) when the character of human morals is seen to be a function of social and political processes. Erstwhile "noumenal" realities are *functionally* related both to the determinations of given phenomenal circumstances, on the one hand, and, on the other, to the manipulations of current human perspectives and engagements. Briefly, it came to be believed that if one wanted to understand "human nature" in general, one had to proceed along two dialectically related paths: along the path of a thorough sociohistorical set of observations, and along the path of the (now so-called) "sciences of the artificial."[30] For "human nature" was not (is not) "made" by God; it was (and continues to be) artfully, artificially, constructed by human beings themselves in the course of their social development.

What art "imitates," then, what it "has reference to," is this totality of human changes in all its diverse and particular manifestations. Since the totality neither is nor ever can be *conceptually* completed, however, art works must always intersect with it at a differential. That is to say, art must establish its referential systems — including its reference to the totality — in the forms of dynamic particulars which at once gesture toward the place of these particulars in the ceaseless process of totalization, and also assert their freedom within the process. Such freedom is relational, and it illustrates a key element in the maintenance of the process of dynamic totalization: that the particulars which are to count in art, the particular acts, events, circumstances, details, and so forth, along with the textualizations through which they are constituted, are those which in fact *make (and/or have made) a difference* — particulars which will be seen to have been (and to be still) positively engaged in processes of change. Whether these processes offer themselves as progressive or conservative does not in itself matter; in either case the reader's attention will be drawn, via such details, to the socially located tensions and contradictions, as well as the responses to such things, which poetry imitates and participates in. In art and poetry these particulars always appear as *incommensurates:* details, persons, events which the work's own (reflected) conceptual formulas and ideologies must admit, but which they cannot wholly account for.

In this context one may see the emergence of a new theory of representation that has modified the traditional Aristotelian theory. Modern idealist and deconstructive attacks on literary referentiality, and hence on any criticism which presupposes such a concept, assume—as the traditional theory had assumed—that no natural relation exists between "what is, hath been, or shall be," and "what may be and should be." (In traditional theory, the relation between the two is supernatural, whereas in the poststructural model the relation is at best arbitrary and at worst illusory.) Sociohistorical criticism, however, argues that "what may be and should be" is always a direct function of "what is, hath been, or shall be," and its theory of representation holds that art imitates not merely the "fact" and the "ideal" but also the dynamic relation which operates between the two.

In addition, sociohistorical criticism will both assume and display the *determinate* character of this dynamic relation. This emphasis upon the determinate is fundamental if "what is" is to stand in a *natural* or scientific relation to "what should be." But because knowledge is a project rather than a possession, it always falls short of a complete grasp of its objects. The determinate relation between "what is" and "what should be" is what Shelley had in mind when he spoke of "something longed for, never seen." The determinate is—in the alternative sense of that word—what exists by acts of determination. Knowledge as a project is knowledge grounded in a Platonic Eros, which is in the end both determined and determinative, in every sense of those two terms. Kant's "categorical imperative" is an analogous concept, though it seems to me that subsequent readers of Kant have misleadingly emphasized the categorical rather than the imperative salient in his thought.

This is the framework in which we are to understand the idea of the "incommensurate" in poetry and art—the "irrelevant detail," the "accidentalities," all those arresting particulars of fact, language, text, and event which seem to escape both the ideologies of the works themselves and the ideologies of criticism. Poetry aims to establish a holistic and totalizing act of representation, but this project or purpose can be achieved only in the dynamic condition of the work itself—which is to say that it must look to have, like the human life it reflects, an *actual* rather than a conceptual fulfillment, a completion in the continuous deed and event which are the poetic work. Accidentalities and incommensurates in art localize this permanent discontinuity between (as it were) "the consciousness" of the poetical work and its complete if unrealized self-understanding. The deep truths that poetry knows are, as Shelley observed, "imageless" even in the poems themselves; and that tension in the unrealized desire of the images points toward the absent totalization. The entire process was captured, in the most witty and understated way, by Pope when he spoke of poetry as "what oft was thought, but ne'er so well expressed."

In sum, poetical work epitomizes the referentiality of communicative action. Criticism moves in constant pursuit of the text's lost and unrealized points of reference—all the verbal and eventual matters of fact which constitute the work's complex symbolic networks, and without which criticism cannot hope to *re*-constitute those networks. That reconstitution is not achieved, however, as some factive historicist reconstruction of the "original context" of the work. Poetry operates a form of finishedness, but that form cannot be finished in conceptual fact. On the other hand, when purely immanent criticism condescends to the historicist and philological effort to reestablish an image of some originary form of a poetical work, it has missed the point of why criticism must pursue referential particularity and concreteness. The project of historicist work, its insistence upon matters of fact and accidentalities, is a critical reflection (and redeployment) of poetry's incommensurable procedures. Far from closing off poetic meaning, factive reconstructions operate such an array of overdetermined particulars that they tend to widen the abyss which is the communicative potential of every poem. It is as if, reading Wolf on Homer, or Driver on Genesis, one were able to glimpse, however briefly, the deep and totalizing truth in and toward which literary works are always moving, and to feel as well how and why their images have preserved an imageless and referential import, and their significance has remained in process of realization.

The essays in this collection were all presented as papers or lectures at a recent conference entitled "Historical Studies and Literary Criticism."[31] Each was written for one of the four defined topic areas which make up the four sections of this book. Needless to say, the topics do not begin to cover—even in a schematic way—the main lines of a comprehensive sociohistorical criticism. To have sought for this kind of comprehensiveness was judged impossible, given the relatively small size of the conference and the current state of literary critical practice. The conference instead sought, first, to elicit papers from a number of scholars who work out of very different sociohistorical methodologies and presuppositions; and second, to arrange those papers under topic areas which would promote discussion of a wide variety of the most important theoretical and practical questions. It seemed important, for example, that Marxist and Marxist-influenced critical procedures be displayed, but that more traditionally grounded philological methods (both materialist and otherwise) be represented as well. Feminist studies are equally crucial, perhaps even the most crucial, since—in the United States at any rate—this is the critical line which has most vigorously pursued a hermeneutics of repressed sociohistorical contents. Finally, since the institutions of criticism incorporate the history—and therefore the meaning —of the discipline itself, it was felt that questions about the institutionalization of critical meanings would have to be addressed if the conference was to have a concrete frame of reference within which its own activities could be self-consciously pursued.

The variety of these papers reflects my own belief about what is needed at this juncture: a wide and diverse exploratory program in sociohistorical theory and method. That purely immanent critical procedures will no longer do is apparent to all, even to those who have done most to establish and develop such methods.[32] What is not apparent is precisely how we should best advance the resocialization of literary studies. My own conviction is that what will have to be achieved —*methodologically*—is a criticism which joins together work that is at once empirically comprehensive and hermeneutically self-conscious: a conjunction, let us say, of what one finds in Robert Darnton's *The Business of Enlightenment*, on the one hand, and Frederic Jameson's *The Political Unconscious* on the other.[33] Such a criticism will also have to incorporate, in an antithetical way, the entrenched forms of purely immanent critical procedures, from New Criticism to the latest forms of intertextual studies.

Elsewhere I have set forth, in a brief way, my view of how such a critical program ought to proceed. The schema is based upon the "dialectic between the work of art's point of origin, on the one hand, and its point of reception on the other":

> Although writing verse is itself a social act, only when the poem enters social circulation—in MS copies, in private printings, or by publication —it begins its poetic life. Once born, however, a poem opens itself to the widest possible variety of human experiences.
> To determine the significance of a poem at its point of origin demands

that we study its bibliography. That subject is the *sine qua non* of the field, for in the study of the poem's initial MS and printed constitutions we are trying to define the social relationships between author and audience which the poem has called into being. It makes a great difference if, for example, an author writes but does not print a poem; it also makes a difference whether such a poem is circulated by the author or not, just as it makes a very great difference indeed when (or if) such a poem is printed, and where, and by whom.

The expressed intentions, or purposes, of an author are also significant for understanding a poem. At the point of origin those intentions are codified in the author's choice of time, place, and form of publication —or none of the above, by which I mean his decision *not* to publish at all, or to circulate in MS, or to print privately. All such decisions take the form of specific social acts of one sort or another, and those acts enter as part of the larger social act which is the poem in its specific (and quite various) human history.

What we call "author intentions" all appear in his particular statements about his own work. Those statements may be part of a private or even a public circulation during his lifetime, but as often as not they only appear later, when (for example) conversations or letters or other ephemeral writings are posthumously given to the world (an event that likewise occurs under very specific circumstances). All publications of such material are of course social events in their own right, and they always modify, more or less seriously, the developing history of the poem.

Once the poem passes entirely beyond the purposive control of the author, it leaves the pole of its origin and establishes the first phase of its later dialectical life (what we call its critical history). Normally the poem's critical history—the moving pole of its receptive life—dates from the first responses and reviews it receives. These reactions to the poem modify the author's purposes and intentions, sometimes drastically, and they remain part of the processive life of the poem as it passes on to future readers.

From any contemporary point of view, then, each poem we read has —when read as a work which comes to us from the past—two interlocking histories, one that derives from the author's expressed decisions and purposes, and the other that derives from the critical reactions of the poem's various readers. When we say that every poem is a social event, we mean to call attention to the dialectical relation which plays itself out historically among these various human beings.

The traditional function of historical criticism has always been taken to involve the study and analysis of these past sets of relations. Roy Harvey Pearce's famous essay "Historicism Once More" shows this quite clearly. But the historical method in criticism, to my view, involves much more, since every contemporary critic, myself at this moment included, focuses on something besides a poem written, read, and reproduced in the past.

The critic focuses as well on the present and the future, that is to say on the critic's audience, in whom he discerns the locus of his hopes for the project which his criticism *is*. Any reading of a poem that I do is a social act not primarily between myself and (say) Keats's work, but between myself and a particular audience.

Since this is always the case, the same sort of historical awareness which we would bring to bear on the past history of a poem must be introduced into every immediate analysis. In this case, the analysis must take careful account of all contextual factors that impinge on the critical act. Most crucially, this involves the need for precise definitions of the aims and the limits of the critical analysis. Like its own object of study ("literature"), criticism is necessarily "tendentious" in its operations. The critic's focus upon history as constituted in what we call "the past" only achieves its *critical* fulfillment when that study of the past reveals its significance in and for the present and the future.

I should add that everything I have noticed here is always involved in every critical act, whether the critic is aware or not that such matters are involved in his work, and whether the critic is an historical critic or not. (A person may, for example, give a reading of "La Belle Dame Sans Merci" in total ignorance of the poem's bibliographic history. Students do it all the time, and so, alas, do some scholars. Nonetheless, that history is always *present* to a person's critical activity despite his ignorance of that history, and even despite his ignorance *of* his ignorance. It is simply that the history is *not* present to his *individual* consciousness.) One of the principal functions of the socio-historical critic is to heighten the levels of social self-consciousness with which every critic carries out the act of literary criticism.[34]

A more detailed outline of these procedures can be found in a related paper.[35] I offer this here not as something which any of the writers in this book would approve or endorse, but simply as a model against which others interested in these questions may react. An adequate program will emerge, however, only when literary students are once again moved to initiate a related series of practical and theoretical studies that correspond to what was produced in the great philological renascence of the late eighteenth and nineteenth centuries. That many of those studies now seem to us the epitome of academic Dryasdust does not mean — as it once seemed to mean — that sociohistorical studies are peripheral (rather than central) to literary studies; it signifies merely that such modes of work have to be retheorized. Were it otherwise — were sociohistorical methods actually marginal to hermeneutics — we would be able to dispense with literary scholarship altogether and simply "read" our texts.

We cannot do this because scholarship — the sociohistorical acts by which criticism preserves and reconstitutes the past for immediate use — is the ground of every form of critical self-consciousness. We cannot know the meaning of our own current meanings without setting our work in a reflexive relation with itself and its history, including the history of which we are ignorant. And we cannot know that history outside its documentary and otherwise material forms. This is why historical criticism must also be material and sociological. It will be, finally, dialectical because the pasts reconstituted by present literary studies are established for *critical* purposes: to expose to itself the mind of the present in order that it may be better able to execute its human interests and projects for the future.

Notes

1 The antihistorical line of the New Criticism and (generally speaking) of its structuralist aftermath is well known. The same limitation applies to the principal work of the deconstructionists, at least in America: see *The Yale Critics: Deconstruction in America*, edited by Jonathan Arac, Wlad Godzich, and Wallace Martin (Minneapolis, Minn., 1983) especially the summarizing "Afterword" by Arac. See also the similar critical exposition in Suresh Raval, *Metacriticism* (Athens, Ga., 1981), pp. 209–38, especially p. 220.

2 Jacques Derrida, "Structure, Sign and Play in the Discourse of the Human Sciences," in Richard Macksey and Eugenio Donato, eds., *The Languages of Criticism and the Sciences of Man* (Baltimore, 1970), p. 264.

3 *The Collected Works of Samuel Taylor Coleridge. Biographia Literaria*, ed. James Engell and W. Jackson Bate (Princeton, 1983), 2:72–3 and n.

4 C. M. Wallace, *The Design of Biographia Literaria* (London, 1983), p. 113.

5 Coleridge, Biographia Literaria, 2: 45–46.

6 See C. S. Lewis and E. M. W. Tillyard, *The Personal Heresy in Criticism* (Oxford, 1934), especially Essay 1 and Cleanth Brooks, *The Well Wrought Urn* (New York, 1947), Appendix 1.

7 Brooks, *Well Wrought Urn*, p. 227.

8 J. Hillis Miller, "Stevens' Rock and Criticism as Cure," *Georgia Review* 30 (1976): 29.

9 Ibid., pp. 28–29.

10 Daniel Aaron, "The Treachery of Recollection," in Robert H. Bremner, ed., *Essays in History and Literature* (Athens, Ohio, 1967), p. 9.

11 Quoted by Marx in *Capital* (New York, 1967), 1:372.

12 Quoted by Godzich in *Yale Critics*, p. 39.

13 J. Hillis Miller, "The Critic as Host," *Critical Inquiry* 3 (1977): 443, 447.

14 Milman Parry, *The Making of Homeric Verse: The Collected Papers of Milman Parry*, ed. Adam Parry (Oxford, 1971), p. 2.

15 Ibid., pp. 3, 2.
16 John M. Ellis, *The Theory of Literary Criticism: A Logical Analysis*, (Berkeley, Ca., 1974), p. 136.
17 Ibid., pp. 137, 154.
18 Miller, "Critic as Host," p. 458.
19 Ibid., p. 447.
20 Parry, *Making of Homeric Verse*, p. 411.
21 Ibid., p. 409. We are aware, of course, particularly from the work of Hayden White, that the construction of a "picture" by historians is a narrativizing act which imbeds in itself an interpretive structure. But the "great detail" which underlies this narrativizing whole always exercises a countermovement of more or less extreme resistance. The best historians, and historical critics, insist upon the significance of these details and matters of fact. See below for a discussion of incommensurate detail.
22 Ibid.
23 Ibid., pp. 410, 413.
24 Ibid., p. 413.
25 Ibid.
26 The most complete analysis of the structures of human interests operating in culture and its products is set forth in Jürgen Habermas, *Knowledge and Human Interests*, trans. Jeremy J. Shapiro (Boston, 1971); see especially chapters 3, 8, and the appendix.
27 Throughout this Introduction the distinction between poetical "works" and poetical "texts" is being preserved. The former refer to cultural products conceived of as the issue of a large network of persons and institutions which operate over time, in numbers of different places and periods. "Texts" are those cultural products when they are viewed more restrictively, as language structures constituted in specific ways over time by a similar network of persons and institutions. Barthes's critique of the concept of the poetical "work" was a salutary move against the naive idea of poems as stable and defined objects. His related effort to install the concept of "text" in literary discourse has much less to recommend it, since this concept—while it has promoted certain forms of dialectical thinking in criticism—has also broadened the gap between the empirical and the reflective dimensions of literary studies. See Roland Barthes, "From Work to Text," reprinted in Josué Harari, ed., *Textual Strategies: Perspectives in Post-Structuralist Criticism* (Ithaca, 1979), pp. 73–81.
28 Sir Philip Sidney, *An Apology for Poetry or The Defence of Poesy*, ed. Geoffrey Shepherd (London, 1965), p. 102.
29 Coleridge, *Biographia Literaria*, 2: 72–73 and n.
30 Herbert A. Simon, *The Sciences of the Artificial* (Cambridge, Mass., 1969).
31 At the conference, the order in which the papers were presented was slightly different: see the appendix. Two (those by Eagleton and by Gilbert and Gubar) differed from the essays here; all were revised for publication.
32 See Geoffrey Hartman, *Criticism in the Wilderness: The Study of Litera-*

ture Today (New Haven, Conn., 1980), p. 259, as well as Michael Sprinker's critique of the contradictions in Hartman's call for a resocialized criticism in "Aesthetic Criticism: Geoffrey Hartman," *Yale Critics*, pp. 43–65, especially pp. 58–60.

33 Robert Darnton, *The Business of Enlightenment: A Publishing History of the Encyclopédie, 1775–1800* (Cambridge, Mass., 1979); Frederic Jameson, *The Political Unconscious* (Ithaca, 1981).

34 Jerome J. McGann, "Keats and the Historical Method in Literary Criticism," *MLN* 94 (1979): 993–94.

35 The related paper is Jerome J. McGann, "The Monks and the Giants: Textual and Bibliographical Studies and the Interpretation of Literary Works," in *The Beauty of Inflections: Literary Investigations in Historical Method and Theory* (Oxford, 1985), part 2, chap. 1.)

I.

Historical
Methods and
Literary
Interpretations

Against Tradition: The Case for a Particularized Historical Method

Marilyn Butler

AMONG THE critical issues that have been debated over the past decade and a half, none is more urgent than how we are to write historical criticism. Much the greater part of the material we work on is literature written in the past. Yet, since literature became a discrete subject of academic study, most of the prestigious fashions or critical New Waves, ever since romanticism, have been modernist, formalist, esthetic, ahistorical—in a word, have declined to address themselves to, or even to acknowledge, the intellectual problems facing those who have to read outside their own culture and sphere of intuitive understanding. The past, the historical point at which a particular book was produced, is *different* from the present, in which it is being read. How fully should our theory (or, for my purposes, more urgent) our critical practice allow for that fact?

The quarrel of the Ancients and Moderns, which has been around since the seventeenth century, is in a flourishing state at present. The extremes of each position are familiar. On the one hand, Moderns such as Barthes, Derrida, De Man, and "il n'y a pas de hors-texte"; on the other hand, a confused band of old New Critics and tunnel-vision close readers, largely inarticulate and thus grateful to such theorists as can be found to represent them, like E. D. Hirsch, who began with a somewhat dogged and extreme goal of retrieving the (past) author's intention. Even more familiar than the extreme position is the caricature of it cherished by each side. The Modern is perceived by opponents as subjective, self-indulgent, narcissistic, and motivated either by personal ambition, or by the desire to bring down Western society as we know it; the Ancient as autocratic and either insincere or deeply stupid, since he clings to the notion of his own objectivity, the impossible possibility of arriving at the truth about the past, or of escaping from his own prejudices and self-interest. But the potency of caricature is such that it comes to be accepted by both sides as having at least something in it. As usual with rhetoric, the negative points work better than the positive, and we all begin to notice what is wrong with our own position rather than what is right, or what admittedly fallible premises still enable us to do. After a decade and a half in which the running has been made by modernists, the historical critic has his or her back to the wall. The problem with the discussion to date is not only that it is polarized, simplified, and caricatured; it is itself profoundly unhistorical. A debate led by Moderns focuses upon the philosopher's restricted field of interest, what is being said or thought; the historian wants to know how and why it came to be said, what the local circumstances were, what previous statement or question it was an answer to. Even when he is arguing for the death of the author, the end of the writer's tyranny over his text, the theorist deploys professional devices to cover up the circumstances surrounding his own performance, for which he means to claim as much authority, disinterestedness, and even objectivity as he can. Though he may be preaching deconstruction, his rhetoric totalizes, making assertions which are absolute truths or nothing.

But the historian feels the need to break down this essentialist and universalist discussion. We must do so, for example, if we are to grasp just what it is in the word "history" that has currently given such offense. For the history of history is, like all histories, shifting and complex; just what it connotes, and whom it challenges or disadvantages, varies greatly from culture to culture and from time to time. Historiography is a composite text for which no critic, not even the most univocal, would claim a single stable reading. Quite often in the 1970s and 1980s the literary antagonist of "history" is a young professional academic lampooning the practice and assumptions of older professional academics. The rhetoric of Barthes and Derrida makes more sense when it is perceived as a rejoinder to the sterile academicism of received French practice in the humanities, including the French variant of literary history, than when it is matched against an Anglo-American or especially a British empiricism.

Even when criticism of the prevailing history becomes more recognizably historical, as it does with Goldmann and Foucault, it is nevertheless only some history that is at issue, and not necessarily the history that the American or British reader was brought up on. Habits which have attracted much hostile attention are, for example, those of the nineteenth-century German classic school of philosophical, politically motivated historians—Niebuhr, Mommsen, Ranke, Weber, Meinecke—whose line begins at the end of the Napoleonic Wars, in the Europe of the restored autocracies and the rising nation-states. There is nothing new about criticizing the kind of history written in Hegel's generation, and in those succeeding, for an overt bias, a doctrinaire commitment to the purposes of the state, and a willingness to parallel and extend the operations of autocracy. This is precisely Marx's "German Ideology," and it is also the tyrannical history with which Nietzsche declared the creative individual will to be at war.

No one proposes as a matter of historical fact that philosophical history, or the literary history that rose in parallel with it, survived unchallenged even to the end of the nineteenth century; it was superseded by positivist history, which introduced its own practices and its own problems into literary history.[1] Yet, perhaps largely for polemical reasons —because right-wing totalitarian history is an easy target—German nineteenth-century classics continue to cast a long shadow over current debate. They remain the showcase examples for history's critics. Hayden White's *Metahistory* (1975), for example, and Edward Said's *Orientalism* (1978) both generalize about the ideological purposes of all history out of examples from this period when Europe, including of course Britain, was at the height of its wealth and power. It was the heyday of bureaucratizing liberal democracy at home and of aggressive expansion abroad. Given these nationalist cultures, it is easy to represent literary historians and historians in general as tools of the state's purposes. An ample past lies at their feet to be mastered, like Africa and Asia.

Whatever the objectionable practices of the nineteenth century, there is no justification for attributing them to another period, which might put the individual writer in a quite different situation, and history in a quite different role. Students have no inhibitions about transferring favorite "radical-historical" insights from one set of circumstances to another, and in the ahistorical climate scholars seem increasingly willing to do the same. In a recent intelligent psychoanalytical study of some classic books written allegedly for children, *The Case of Peter Pan*, Jacqueline Rose makes some derogatory observations about the eighteenth-century interst in primitive man—a favorite topic of that era's universal historians, of Rousseau, and of Rousseau's English follower Thomas Day: "Seeing these distant communities as one stage of our own historical development is one way of subordinating them to us."[2] "Is one way" sounds at first like a qualification, but it isn't: the motives of eighteenth-century primitivists are being fairly and squarely impugned. But doesn't the eighteenth-century anthropologist commonly represent the present condition of advanced society not as a development from the primitive world, but as a corruption?

Rose writes as if the historian inevitably flatters the modern state, rather than holds its institutions and practices up to critical scrutiny; to conceive of the social role of history as unvarying is itself uncircumstantial and unhistorical. Her remarks on the school of Rousseau are interestingly countered by Lionel Gossman's summary of "the transformations of history": "the Enlightenment practice of history as a crucial activity in the struggle against traditional legitimizing stories; the post-Revolutionary romantic attempt to construct a new history reconciling science and religion, criticism and myth, as a legitimation of the national state; and the retreat, after 1848, to a chastened view of history as positive knowledge in opposition to philosophical and religious speculation."[3] Rose's diagnosis fits Gossman's description of "legitimating" post-Revolution historiography well, his description of delegitimizing Enlightenment historiography not at all. It is repeating the authoritarian practices of nineteenth-century history to impose modern, anachronistic interpretations indiscriminately on earlier writing, rather than to make separate analyses of modes which played a part in their own series. Eighteenth-century primitivists idealised distant communities as part of their challenge to modern oligarchies, the established church and the centralized state. By foregrounding the savage in their work, while suppressing the rhetorical uses to which he was put, Rose makes the Rousseauists more banal than they were, thus doing to them what she says they did to the savage and the child. Reading even the iconoclasts of the past as less enlightened than ourselves is also "one way of subordinating them to us."

In mitigation of the tendency of Said and Rose to generalize and to patronize, it has to be conceded that, unlike eighteenth-century history, nineteenth-century history is still with us as a current method. And it needs the aggressive scrutiny which Said and Rose bring to it, since the literary history which emerged in the nineteenth century as a subdivision of history proper not only reproduced most of the dubious practices of the parent form, but brought in a few more of its own. In fact a new order of problem arises when the large-scale chronological narrative, aiming first at establishing a correct sequence, second at a total view, deals not with events but with books and ideas. When, in history writing, event *B* follows event *A*, the reader infers that *A* caused *B* to happen. Post hoc has never officially meant propter hoc; yet historians, and, after them, literary historians, are taught to strive for an effect of coherence, and linearity or sequence contributes massively by its apparent explanatory function. But in what sense does an earlier book— often by a different author, sometimes in another culture—"cause," or partly cause ("influence"), a later book? What is the process of transmission? Doesn't it matter if writer *B* has never heard of writer *A*, or can't speak his language? Why is writer *B* so impressible, receptive, and amazingly attentive to the good books he's supposed to have read (far more so than the students you and I meet, and *they* have been disciplined for years by regular examining), and so amazingly *in*-attentive to other stimuli? For most influence criticism ignores minor writing, reviewing, newspaper articles, the intellectual ambience which is the actual seedbed of intellectual discussion. Scholarly editions of great poetry—often repositories of influence criticism—pick out similar-sounding lines in previous great poets, and silently block alternative possibilities: that another book, obscure now, was the source; that the phrase was "in the (nonliterary) air"; that it occurred to writer B independently.

The linear format adopted from narrative history by nineteenth-century critics has given us practices which convey a very odd view of the mind of the writer. The syndrome traditional literary historians work with—book fixation—is unknown to psychology. Their descriptions of cultural transmission are implausibly steady and rational: though they claim to give an account of "thought," neither they nor the rest of us know actual people who think this way. Their notion that ideas, attitudes, "world view" somehow derive from those books that fellow academics deem great may be professionally convenient, but it finds no support in empirical data-based work by political scientists or sociologists, who see ideas and attitudes transmitting themselves through socializing, as the individual becomes aware of membership of a group with its own group interests. Of course there's nothing final about the hypotheses of any specialists, but influence isn't a hypothesis so much as a work practice that has grown up. No one ever specifically *argued* that writers acquire their views by a uniquely rational and unsocial method, in a laboratory inhabited only by other writers.

An embarrassing amount of professional time is spent at literary history in its received form: forging links between earlier and later books by authors A and B; identifying allusions and echoes; source hunting. Linear literary history has enjoyed a revival in English studies since the thirties, especially since World War II, probably largely because of the influx of scholars educated on the Continent in the German scholarly tradition. The malpractices of nineteenth-century literary history recur in two of the most ambitious and prestigious types of academic book, the survey or morphology of a given theme (say utopianism or numerology) over time, and the large-scale literary history of a period. These five-hundred-page, loose, baggy monsters are physically so impressive that it's easy to overlook the shakiness of their assumptions and the degree of pressure exerted subliminally by their structure upon our thinking.

One distinguished example is M. H. Abrams's morphology of romantic criticism, *The Mirror and the Lamp* (1953), a rich and elegant illustration of the paradigm at work, the modern structure of thought imposing itself upon a body of past writing. The book's title alludes to Abrams's two images for criticism, the "Before" and "After" which measure the romantic revolution in thought. Eighteenth-century estheticians saw literature as reflecting reality, like a mirror; those of the nineteenth-century, as shining out like a lamp. These images convey Abrams's own partisan preference for the later phase; like most literary historians, he is a decided believer in that characteristic nineteenth-century liberal tenet, the Whig Idea of Progress. Literary historians dealing with the period after 1780 commonly see the past as a smooth, uphill rise toward the eminence on which they are standing. As it happens, Abrams's subjects, his supposed romantic critics and poets, prove fairly recalcitrant: he doesn't find many out-and-out "Lamps" till the 1830s, which in an account of English romanticism seems oddly late. Mirrors are more plentiful in the Age of Johnson, but they present problems of another type. Some explanation is being given for the Lamps, of a contemporary, contextual kind: they oppose or correct the Mirrors. But how to account for the doctrines of the Mirrors, arid and arbitrary as they seem? Who are their immediate contemporaries and precursors, who are their readers, whom are the writers for and whom are they against? In addition to the Englishmen Johnson, Reynolds, and Hurd, Mirror-critics include the Scotsmen Blair and Beattie, members of the first British group of university teachers to specialize in literature; they had a special interest in isolating the study of literature from that of culture and general society, in developing the autonomy of esthetics. *Their* writings on the arts should not be treated as neutral or innocent, or as representative eighteenth-century writing on the arts; they turn away from other writing which is more historical and social, more worldly, or in the political sense more opinionated.

Abrams (who has no section for Enlightenment historical criticism) might reply that all he ever meant to give was an account of a change within esthetics; but that would not justify withholding information that enables us to read esthetic changes within the context of their own time. Esthetics have become a formalized university discipline; at the moment of inception that is something they cannot have been. What questions or problems of that time, then, did the new esthetics as a code of practice respond to?

Abrams's book is an example of its genre at its best and most apparently open; it is less aggressively paradigmatic than, for example, René Wellek's *Romantic Age* (1955), the volume in his *History of Criticism* covering the same ground. Armed with strong, German-centered definitions of the preoccupations and techniques he deems romantic, Wellek is able to bring a line of dead English writers shuffling to the bar like felons, and to send many of them down for transgressions of laws they did not know existed. Abrams's book sounds more flexible than this, and less autocratic in tone, yet he, like Wellek, has written from an internal professional perspective which prevents the reader from placing or criticizing either his group of writers or romanticism as an entity (let alone from denying that it is one).

The most drastic solutions to the shortcomings and absurdities of literary history in its received form are those of the Moderns with whom I began. What is doubtful about the structuring of Abrams and Wellek is solved at a stroke by deconstruction. But in any case modernist opinion is broadly antihistorical, not necessarily in the cause of the post-structuralist's radicalism and skepticism. Northrop Frye in *Fearful Symmetry*, for example, releases authors from their sequential chains into a timeless zone where they are all contemporaries and stateless persons, Blake coexisting with Isaiah.[4] Frye's procedure ignores the author's intention and the probable meaning for the informed first reader, and instead makes the text yield an archetypal or universal meaning, unavailable in Frye's formulation before the twentieth century. At its most general, the modernist case is that we can speak only for ourselves, not for dead readers and writers; that both original intention and contemporary meaning are largely irrecoverable, and always were; that the most painstaking efforts to restore vocabulary, in its widest sense, and context, in its most meaningful sense, will still be contaminated by modern preconceptions. All of which would be deeply troubling if it were not too absolute and too interested. Who knows a "text-only" critic who lives by his precept, and wholly ignores what is outside the text, or really writes as though there is nothing? And who has not noticed causes and beliefs emanating from the wider world making their reappearance, once history has been got out of the way? The critic of Frye's type passes from being a skeptic in the historical exercise to being a true believer in the religious sphere; the claim to know what is timeless and universal in a text, which cannot in any case be substantiated, is ultimately a preference for idealist thinking rather than materialist thinking.

Viewed from a historical perspective, the modernist case against historical criticism looks very vulnerable. The modernist generally works to cast himself or herself as a pure professional, working on timeless material (literature) in a desocialized space (the seminar room). But the erasure of the contexts of time and space, which the modernist critic rhetorically demands, is challenged by the historical critic, who proceeds to restore the circumstances and the covert interests, professional and ideological, which modernist abstraction is designed to hide. It is curious to see historical criticism singled out as biased, by those practicing a method which either disguises the writer's interests, or defends subjectivity. It is also odd to find historical criticism labeled especially coercive, when the modernist's method allows the cavalier dismissal of the viewpoint of past writers, and the appropriation of their work for someone else's purposes.

More helpful, because more qualified and discriminating, is the case against "positivist" literary history made from within the historical ranks by Marxists: the observation that a supposedly neutral style and a modest limitation to empirical fact also convey values, though they purport to be value free; that the approach flatters the professional by making him believe in his own objectivity; most cogent of all, that the practice of treating literary history as an autonomous series, or works of art as purely esthetic entities, prejudges all the important questions of meaning and of value. Much of what Marx himself said about the arts in *The German Ideology, The Eighteenth Brumaire of Louis Bonaparte*, and briefly in the Preface to *The Critique of Political Economy* must command quite wide assent from non-Marxists. (The excellence of Marx as a critic derives, for one of a historical turn, from his seizing the oppositional role at a period when right-wing academic orthodoxy supplied a monolithic target—as a somewhat differently constituted orthodoxy did for an earlier generation of intellectual mavericks, the philosophes.) Unfortunately, if we are thinking of the *method* of historical criticism and of the problems entailed in actually writing it, Marxists at the moment are not offering a clear, practical lead. At least, it seems at present as though in Britain their practitioners and theorists are heading in two quite different directions, and as though one left hand does not know what the other left hand is doing.

A type of historical criticism flourishes in Britain at the moment which is radical not by virtue of its method but by virtue of its subjects. The University of Essex has called a series of conferences, for example, on "critical historical moments"—1642, 1789, 1848, 1936. In the journal *Literature and History*, edited by the Marxist Peter Widdowson and others from Thames Polytechnic, many topics similarly cluster around historical moments and issues with radical appeal, such as Puritan influence in Stuart theater, pro-French Revolution writers like Blake and Godwin, noncanonical writers and works, occasionally popular culture. Since Raymond Williams's *Culture and Society* (1958), and even more since *The Country and the City* (1973), attention has also focused on "problematical" aristocratic forms like pastoral verse. It is significant that the connection between this spate of articles and Williams is with an earlier phase of his work, which has been described as "left-Leavisism," rather than with his later tendency to write more theoretically and on less specific literary topics. Though not using avant-garde methods, or indeed displaying much critical ambition at all, these researchers function as challengers of dominant critical ideas, by bringing to light neglected writings, and by uncovering the political interest of literature. Their work parallels much of the modestly scaled historical work being done, to similar ends, by feminists. The premises of this type of criticism, seldom explicitly spelled out, are that the writing of the past needs to be more fully, or less selectively, recovered and more disinterestedly explicated, and that subsequent readings of it, above all the ones we have been taught in the academy, should be viewed as partial and not authoritative.

This seems in principle unexceptionable, but it is also very localized, so much so that unsupported it has little chance of making much impact on the profession as a whole. The topics are too small, and too easily dismissed as special cases. Besides, research findings like these, often the products of many hours in a scholars' library, can't be offered as models to the average undergraduate. The editors of *Literature and History* seem uneasy about the confined scale of many of their contributions, and it is noticeable that in the work they commission themselves—the reviews—a specific theoretical element is either encouraged or required. Confronted with two styles of work that barely interact, localized examples and "theory," they apparently incline to the latter, though it is also plainly true that the tendency of "theory" to be systematic and doctrinaire makes it of limited use to the genuine researcher.

In various locations, Terry Eagleton has explained the relations between literature and history as the intelligent Marxist sees them:

> Marxist criticism is not merely a "sociology of literature," concerned with how novels get published and whether they mention the working class. Its aim is to *explain* the literary work more fully; and this means a sensitive attention to its forms, styles and meanings. But it also means grasping those forms, styles and meanings as the products of a particular history. The painter Henri Matisse once remarked that all art bears the imprint of its historical epoch, but that great art is that in which this imprint is most deeply marked. Most students of literature are taught otherwise: the greatest art is that which timelessly transcends its historical conditions.[5]

This is excellent, in theory. It's pleasing that all the better British Marxist critics, like Jameson in America, repeatedly say that they, following Marx, allow for the complexity of art and avoid any simple mechanical correspondence between economic conditions and art forms, or base and superstructure. The problem is that this is not something that should be merely stated; it has to be shown in the criticism of specific works of literature. And there is a real shortage of good, sensitive, applied Marxist historical criticism — a fact which leaves H. R. Jauss still free to write of the brutal simplification that arises from forcing literature into parallelism with economics, and of the Marxist critic's tendency to explain literature "as a merely reproduced reality":

> Literature, in the fullness of its forms, allows itself to be referred back only in part and not in any exact manner to concrete conditions of the economic process. Changes in the economic structure and rearrangements in the social hierarchy happened before the present age mostly in long, drawn-out processes, with scarcely visible caesurae and few spectacular revolutions. Since the number of ascertainable determinants in the "infrastructure" remained incomparably smaller than the more rapidly changing literary production of the "superstructure," the concrete multiplicity of works and genres had to be traced back to always the same factors or conceptual hypostases, such as feudalism, the rise of the bourgeois society, the cutting-back of the nobility's function, and early, high, or late capitalist modes of production.[6]

Raymond Williams has tried hard to meet such accusations by urging his fellow historical critics to explore the "structure of feeling" appropriate to each work in its circumstances. He wants a particularized cultural hypothesis that derives from evidence about how the factors intrinsic and extrinsic to the work have interacted: "It is intrinsically less simple than more formally structured hypotheses of the social, but it is more adequate to the actual range of cultural evidence. . . . It is the reduction of the social to fixed forms that remains the basic error. Marx often said this, and some Marxists quote him, in fixed ways, before returning to fixed forms."[7] This is fine, but one wishes Williams had also made the point more memorably by example: he has written about individual works of literature, not often poetry, in a somewhat wooden, predictable style, and even his best book of applied criticism, *The Country and the City*, is put-down-able. John Barrell of King's College, Cambridge, who has developed Williams's work on the pastoral mode by giving it a needed depth of scholarship, has failed to shed the woodenness, along, indeed, with the unwanted economic determinism: as so often with applied Marxist criticism, the key factors shaping literature, in Barrell's case the poetry, painting and novels of the eighteenth and early nineteenth centuries, turn out to be broad impersonal social and economic factors, such as class.[8]

Terry Eagleton, who writes with a wholly un-Williams-like wit, panache, and clarity, may have escaped this contagious predictability by writing very little about individual texts since his book on the Brontës,

Myths of Power (1976): nowadays, when he does engage with, say, *Clarissa*, he does so in a modernist, ahistorical manner. There is no question of Eagleton's setting out in *The Rape of Clarissa* (1982) to recover the discourse or structure of feeling in Richardson's group, or to address himself analytically to the interaction between the writing of the novel and the particular historical circumstances. When in the last chapter of *Literary Theory: An Introduction* (1983), Eagleton recommends the use of rhetoric, the works he means to analyse are not primary but secondary—modern critical interpretations, in which he means to track latent political concerns. Though a staunch subverter of the literary canon on principle, in practice Eagleton is obliged to stick to it if he mentions texts at all, since he professes an equally firm contempt for the antiquarianism and pedantry needed to recover "minor" or hitherto disregarded writers. He thus successfully sidesteps the methodological problems general to historical critics, and the rigidities common to Marxist ones, at the large cost of not writing as a historical critic at all.

With or without the practical example of the leading Marxist theoreticians, historical criticism seems to be on the point of a marked advance. It is noticeable that a great deal is now being written by young scholars in Britain and America which is specific without being limited to issues like Eagleton's derisory "whether they mention the working class." In Britain, Jacobean and Stuart drama has become a topic as likely to be debated by historians as critics, thanks to recent books by Margot Heinemann, Jonathan Dollamore, Martin Butler, and others; the later eighteenth century has become another growth area, with interesting books by Barrell, Heather Glen, and Olivia Smith already out, and a study of Godwin's intellectual and social milieu by Mark Philp shortly to appear. The "theoretical" case for their procedures has been slow to clarify, since most historical critics are naturally more inclined to justify their methods within a historical discourse than within a philosophical one. It was a theorist who first launched the notion that philosophy and theory are metadisciplines, capable of judiciously examining all methodologies; theorists have their own axes to grind, their own professional and ideological biases, their own *history*. Nevertheless, it is reassuring to those practicing a reformed historical method, self-evidently critical of what has passed for literary history, to find theorists increasingly looking for a way out of the modernist/historicist impasse.

Some of the most interesting writing on the topic is coming from Germany: from Robert Weimann in *Structure and Society in Literary History* (1969), from Hans-Georg Gadamer in his important *Truth and Method* (1972), but also, at first sight most practically, from Gadamer's pupil Hans Robert Jauss. The title of one of Jauss's essays, "Literary

History as a Challenge to Literary Theory," promises great things. Most of its seven theses are helpful—that the literary work can be viewed in the historical moment of its appearance; that the expectations it would have met make an objectifiable system, superior to subjective "interpretation"; that, by reconstituting this "horizon of expectations," the critic can uncover the questions the text gave an answer to; that he can thus correct "the unrecognized norms of the classicist and modernist understanding,"[9] thus giving a far more precise critical role to "context" than was ever supplied by an abstraction like "the spirit of the age." But the concluding pages of Jauss's article, and his last two theses, are surely disappointing: he ends by proposing a vast effort to study a work's reception, in order to replace the old linear narrative of literary history with an endlessly proliferating series of case studies showing how the same work has been received by different readers over time. Quite apart from its impracticality and almost certain tedium, each work sustaining its own teeming colony of parasites, the Jaussian method seems gravely defective on principle. First, though Jauss expresses opinions as critical of formalists as of Marxists, he is here clearly bent on retaining their belief that literature has its own distinct history, which evolves in an autonomous series within the study or the academy, rather than in society at large. Second, he has borrowed what was initially a democratic tactic, giving the text to the reader to remake, and he has formalized and institutionalized it, so that it is all too clearly the critic or professor whose authoritative readings we are to study. This would surely in practice turn out to be an unskeptical, conservative reconstituting of literary history.

Jauss is most acceptable and most practical before he gets specifically to the "reception theory" for which he is now known. In his first approach to the book's context his argument resembles that of a group of historians, headed by Quentin Skinner, John Dunn, and J. G. A. Pocock, who want to write history of ideas, and find themselves caught between systematizing, overcontextual social scientists, and ahistorical, single-text philosophers.[10] In his article "Meaning and Understanding in the History of Ideas," Skinner proposes to approach the author's meaning by exploring his immediate context, which he defines as his vocabulary, discourse, or linguistic and mental ambience. Such a definition allows in nonliterary elements, including the sociology of the writer's world and its ideological crosscurrents, but Skinner is also careful to note that some elements in a work have already been mediated in writing or literature—George Herbert or Jane Austen takes up a genre with its own language, which the ideal first reader already has practice in interpreting. As a notion of context this has the advantages of being workably limited, and well suited to support supple literary discussion. Thinking of context as a language is better than thinking of it as historical facts or events (the Civil War, the French Revolution, the rise of the bourgeoisie, commoditization).

Skinner's word "meaning" sounded overconfident and seems to have become a stumbling block in further discussion, but in fact his definition promises something reasonably modest—the categories shared by a group, the counters they used when they interacted. Moreover his historical methodology has elements in common with Williams's, and with E. D. Hirsch's recent formulation. In *Validity in Interpretation* (1967), Hirsch was searching for the author's intention, as deterrent a term for many as meaning, but he now offers a semiotic translation, which incidentally appears to demote the author from sole authority for his text: "Instead of referring an interpretation back to an original author, we could just for a moment refer it back to an original code or convention system. Let us say that the historical interpretation is the one that applies an earlier code-system to the text."[11] Hirsch, Williams, Jauss, and Skinner make up no coterie. A method each has arrived at independently could be the formula a lot of people are looking for.

If so, it is not before time, because ours is proving to be the age not merely of modernism, or of a type of literary history that should be dead but won't lie down: it is also a breeding ground for a peculiarly insidious pseudohistory, the belief that there is something readily knowable called "tradition," to which we can attribute explanatory power.

Tradition looks at first sight like a stylization and simplification of literary history. But it is really far older than literary history in its nineteenth-century format: traditions are features of all regularized practices in all societies, for they are a basic tool of selecting and ordering the past in order to validate activities, and people, in the present. The literary critic calls on tradition when he draws up a genealogy or family tree of writers, some modern or near modern, others from the past and remote past. Transmission down the line is usually described as easy and harmonious, though there is often a gap, which tends to occur near to the present day. Against the odds, the spark jumps across it; on the far side the current flows back more smoothly toward, and even into, prehistory. Renaissance writers were thus inclined to dismiss whole centuries of the Middle Ages as unimportant, while they identified their true forebears among the Greek and Roman classic authors. In the eighteenth century, Thomson and Collins wrote odes in which they imagined the muses fleeing from imperial Rome, along with political liberty, touching down lightly in the fourteenth century in the Italian republics, taking off again to overfly the Europe of the autocrats, and in the present coming to rest in enlightened, constitutional Britain, seat of a new, individualistic Atlantic commonwealth. Contemporary with this picture was a localized, purely British version, which approved of only Milton and Spenser among relative moderns, left out the feudal Middle Ages, and picked up earlier—perhaps in Anglo-Saxon England, home of pure language and liberty, perhaps in the oak groves of the Celtic Druids. This last version, which not only belittled degenerate modern institutions like the church and state, but also made an expensive upper-class training in the classics redundant, was particularly congenial to an autodidact like Blake.

The eighteenth and nineteenth centuries were a period of new scholarship and of the founding of scholarship and scholarly institutions in their modern forms, but they were also a heyday for traditions. The historians E. J. Hobsbawm and Terence Ranger have edited a collection of essays, *The Invention of Tradition* (1983), which describe, often hilariously, the "discovery" of such British eternal verities as the Scottish past, the Welsh past, and the ritual, customary side of royalty. It was rather after the mid-eighteenth century that Scotland became the haunt of kilt and sporran, bagpipe and clan tartan, while Wales acquired an Archdruid and took to calling itself the Land of Song. A Welshwoman like myself has been brought up to hear massed male choirs extolling the unique merits of "gwlad beirdd a chantorion": ours is the land of bards and singers, says the third line of our national anthem (composed in 1856). It comes as a shock to find that Welsh "traditional" music appears to be no more than a bastardized version of the pop tunes of the 1700s, which in their actual origins were Italian, German, or, much more unfortunate, English.

What is the function of this manner of arranging the past? Hobsbawm defines the traditions his historians have analyzed as "a set of practices, normally . . . of a symbolic nature, which seek to inculcate certain values and norms of behaviour by repetition—which automatically implies continuity with the past." He observes that though the invented tradition may invoke an actual historical past, may indeed unearth genuine evidence about parts of the past, the claim to *continuity* with that past is spurious. Tradition has to be distinguished on the one hand from the more prosaic routine, which lacks the ritual, symbolic, ideological dimension; on the other, from custom, which has an element of vagueness that permits flexibility. "The object and characteristic of traditions, including invented ones, is invariance; the past, real or invented, to which they refer imposes fixed (normally formalised) practices."[12]

There is something wrong with the phrasing here: what does Hobsbawm mean by the real past, and by his hint that some traditions are not invented? There is also something dubious about the assumption, though many share it, that the traditionmonger is always conservative, nostalgic, and regressive. The chapter in the book by Prys Morgan on Wales refutes Hobsbawm's generalization, by uncovering the intention and meaning in eighteenth-century Welshmen's sustained and imaginative reinvention of a past that could be specifically theirs, not centralized bureaucratic London's. By linking themselves to an earlier race of poets, bards, Druid-priests, they gave themselves linguistic and literary priority over the English, and insinuated that their literary authority was ultimately religious authority. We talk about historical antiquarianism and about romantic nationalism as though they were fashions any literate contemporary might take up, but they were patchy and local, and this is part of their meaning. In Britain and in France, upper- and middle-class readers before 1800 were more likely to be internationalist. Passionate antiquarianism in the form of the recovery or invention of local roots tends to be a relatively poor man's occupation (Stukely, Ritson, Blake); it's commonly radical, and in Britain in the late eighteenth century it takes off, not in the sophisticated cities or in a countryside run by landed aristocrats, but in the new industrial cultures of the Newcastle region and the Glamorgan coalfield. It is only later, in the nineteenth century, that antiquarianism becomes an assured middle-class pursuit, a nostalgia which cultivates primitive, pastoral worlds precisely because they are not industrializing and thus not disturbed by modern social and political conflict.

The basic structure of these historical myths betrays their origins, as counters to other myths; whether they are conservative, therefore, depends on the circumstances, and on the antagonist. An acute concern to establish one's legitimacy implies some threat to it, that the inventor's status or his group's status is dubious in *someone*'s eyes, and the fuzziness about the present and recent past indicates the whereabouts of the enemy. Inventing a tradition maintains your legitimacy, and someone else's lack of it; your mythical past is your defensive strategy in a real present. So traditions stand in a dialectical relationship to other practices they don't describe at all, a literary or intellectual actuality which the traditionmonger seeks to block or bypass, and which the alert tradition reader needs to restore. Though the invented tradition loudly insists on its own authority, it must be taken, not as authoritative, but as a polemic with particularly strong motives for hiding the circumstances which brought it into being.

As the Hobsbawm and Ranger book implicitly testifies, traditionmongering flourished around 1800, perhaps as a symptom of the heightened sociological awareness of that age: groups acquired group identity, and adopted the vocabulary and practices needed to sustain themselves at the expense of others. They included poets writing for the market in England, and academic critics, historians, and scholars in Germany and Scotland—two groups whose collective interests are not identical, though regularly merged and confused in the construct we call romanticism. Early and mid-eighteenth-century opposition writers in Britain employed a common rhetoric against centralized power and authority, a government perceived as unduly centered on London and unduly dominated by rank and wealth. Against Court and City, diverse polemicists (Fletcher, Addison, Bolingbroke, Toland, Smollett, the gamut from Jacobites to Jacobins) posed a notional Country, which might at its most naive be an affecting landscape or a pastoral retreat, but at its most rigorous would describe better systems of social ordering. Homeric Greece, republican Rome, Druidic Britain all served as reminders that a society could be more individualistic, egalitarian, organic, and happy than eighteenth-century Britain. Broadly, then, this "Country party" rhetoric has a political function, and in harder specimens, by, say, Rousseau, Ferguson, Macpherson, and Gibbon, the case then being made against centralized power still shows through. In softer specimens, such as certain poems by Collins and Wordsworth, the rhetorical counters are much the same as in the oppositional poet James Thomson, where Collins probably found them, but the poet's target has become not so much covert as more limited: no longer the public question, who rules, but concerns that are either personal to the man, or professional to the writer. Collins and Wordsworth represent writers, especially poets, and signal that they do by taking the writing of poems as their main subject. They also construct a specialized tradition, with room in it only for poets—a pointed revision of the Country party pantheon of oppositional intellectuals, which had room for Milton, but also for Algernon Sidney, Hampden, and Bacon.

The point for us is that a notion of tradition which for Wordsworth was antithetical and provisional has become a fixity, absolute rather than relative, an answer to a question which is no longer heard. Leslie Stephen, T. S. Eliot, Yeats, and Leavis all accepted, as though it were historically verifiable, Wordsworth's account of a moment of loss of vision somewhere in the mid to late seventeenth century. They also picked up Coleridge's pejorative term for the eighteenth century, "mechanistic," though less partisan observers would perhaps have noticed that a new literary intellectual had a vested interest in making the public think "Imagination" a good thing, and science and technology very inferior things. Thus, detached from the circumstances which gave birth to them, traditions lose their original adversarial force. They turn into a form of pseudohistory maintained to perform certain professional functions, which include defining the literary type of intelligence so that it sounds more elevated and perhaps rarer than the scientific kinds of intelligence. And the fact that twentieth-century formulations of tradition do not differ markedly from those of 1815 warns us that Hobsbawm could be right about the way traditions now generally function: they appeal in the present day to what their friends would call continuity, and Hobsbawm calls invariance.

The model of tradition which prevailed from the 1920s to the 1940s was summed up by René Wellek in an article of 1978 on the New Critics (in which he called their view of tradition, incidentally, "literary history properly conceived" and "a philosophical view of history that permitted evaluation"). According to Eliot, Ransom, Tate, Brooks, Warren, and others, says Wellek,

> There used to be once a perfectly ordered world, which is, for instance, behind Dante's poetry. This world disintegrated under the impact of science and scepticism. The "dissociation of sensibility" took place at some time in the seventeenth century. Man became increasingly divided, alienated, specialized as industrialization and secularism progressed. The Western world is in decay, but some hope seems to be held out for a reconstitution of the original wholeness. The total man, the undivided "unified sensibility" which combines intellect and feeling, is the ideal that requires a rejection of technological civilization, a return to religion or, at least, to a modern myth and, in the Southern critics, allowed a defense of the agrarian society surviving in the South.[13]

This model seems tendentious rather than philosophical. It is still designed to demote nonliterary types of intellectual, who are, we notice, alienated, secular, and specialist, while the literary thinker remains religious and whole. The strange assertion that Dante's world *was* "perfectly ordered," rather than that Dante for various analyzable reasons chose to render it as ordered, betrays the partisan anxiety of these traditionalists to uphold some cause in the modern world—here, for example, the agrarian society of the South. The puzzle is that scholars who can write with great sophistication, or (some of them) display a concern for evidence, seem unabashed at using a device they recognize as transparently fictitious in an Irish historian who has George III descending from Milesius, or a Tudor historian who has Henry VIII descending from Arthur and King Priam of Troy.

Modern American romanticism first set itself up as a countermove to the Eliot and New Critical schema of tradition. Bloom said so in 1971 when, in a new introduction to *The Visionary Company*, he deplored Eliot's Tory and Anglo-Catholic tradition, declared it wrong to let students come to Milton by C. S. Lewis's Anglican way, and proclaimed that the romantics had descended from the left wing of England's Puritan movement.[14] Geoffrey Hartman, writing in 1965 in praise of Frye, one of the first rediscoverers (inventors?) of the romantics, connected that achievement with ridding literature of "the spell of the priest-interpreters."[15] The challenge wasn't lost; in the same year, the New Critic W. K. Wimsatt sharply drew a connection between the new romantic "prometheans," with their telltale preference for the radicals Blake and Shelley, and a growing disorder on the streets and on the campus: they [the romanticists] were "not likely to suffer from absent-mindedness regarding the lovely colors of combustion, the fiery permanent discontent which may be generated by contemplating the gospel of contraries."[16]

Yet this new school has proved addicted to the noncombustive practice of tradition building, perhaps more so than even Eliot was. Frye, Bloom, and Hartman remain orthodox in their view that the eighteenth century constitutes a chasm, over which they thrown a frail rope bridge, the slender oeuvres of William Collins and Christopher Smart. On the far side of the chasm they see, as traditionalists commonly do, a better-populated territory. Bloom's roll call of precursors has become programmatically Jewish: the Kabbalist Isaac Luria, the Alexandrian Gnostic Valentinus, the Old Testament J-poet, and he has recently claimed sweepingly that "British Protestant dissent . . . has roots in normative rabbinicism."[17] Frye puts more emphasis on the apparent diversity of the doctrines he cites, though his aim is ultimately to syncretize them; an opponent once accused Frye of perversely incorporating "idealist, irrationalist and obscurantist doctrines from the whole of Western tradition."[18]

Bloom and Frye are in some respects eccentrics, but it is the current orthodoxy to fit a much-simplified and unified romanticism into a tradition—for which, of course, there is neither historical evidence, nor authority except the critics' own. A very similar paradigm occurs in M. H. Abrams's *Natural Supernaturalism* (1971), which interprets romantic politics and literature as "a displaced and reconstituted theology," "an endeavor to salvage traditional experience and values," "a return to a hereditary wisdom."[19] What is this wisdom calling to agnostic poets? The learned, allusive, allegorical, mystical tradition of Neoplatonism, Christian hermeticism, Christian and Jewish gnosticism, all of which, Abrams claims, went underground in the rational, skeptical eighteenth century, and had to be revived around 1800 by poets and critics. Abrams's tone and vocabulary have become more noticeably exalted and religious than in *The Mirror and the Lamp*: he has kept in step with the marked drift of American critical writing in the past decade and a half toward theology, not necessarily all that displaced. *Natural Supernaturalism* builds upon the alleged link with Alexandria, insisting upon the resemblance between English romantic poetry and Plotinus so literally that it becomes world hating, a poetry of spiritual quest. Abrams's constructed tradition functions to block out the view he's afraid of—that the period is diverse, variously critical, and more often than not antireligious. A more mixed, skeptical account would find better corroboration in, say, prose fiction and nonfiction, journals, minor poetry—but that is to look much wider than is customary among the high-romantic arguers. Many leading neoromantic critics were trained in comparative literature, and they readily overlook circumstantial evidence as parochially British, not archetypal and not international enough to fit their preconceptions. Unfortunately you cannot omit the local circumstances and retain a sense of the rhetorical function of a work, how it fitted into the literary discourse, what questions it answered. It is for want of this specificity that the present academic image of early-nineteenth-century British literature has readily accommodated itself to the prevailing mood of the 1970s and 1980s. In fact, British romanticism has become more harmonious, syncretizing, responsible, and respectable than at any time since it was written.

What then should we do? Not, surely, abandon history: the literature of the past has been so little pursued of late on its own terms that a genuinely historical criticism should have all the appeal of a radical new departure. I am interested in that radicalism, and especially in exposing the partisanship of writers and critics, but I do not think that historical criticism of itself belongs to left or right. A method, like a style, has no innate politics; the politics of a work are to be elicited by exposing its function in its own literary series, by revealing the question or questioner it is answering.

The method, which might be put to any ideological use, would incorporate the following principles:

1. The writings of the past ask for an educated reading, as far as possible from within their own discourse or code or cultural system. Texts have their specific and localized contexts, which include, but are not limited to, the literary context of an established genre and the linguistic context of a vocabulary at a certain stage of evolution. Intellectual issues and preoccupations also make up the language of a given group, as does the vaguer and broader concept, ideology. By looking

at these systems, by which the material world and society are already selected and mediated, we can learn something, though not everything, of the language appropriate to a particular text. It follows that most of the best historical criticism is localized in respect of time and place, and directed to the understanding of specific works.

2. The definition of literature, what we choose to call interesting, should not be exclusive. Ideally, the scope of the subject takes in what is written: for a hierarchy or canon of great works is no more beyond question than a tradition.

3. The relationship of a work to its literary predecessors, what is loosely conveyed by the word tradition, is all-important, but complex. Many works counter other works, without necessarily alluding to them directly; authors are forced by market conditions to be competitors, and they may be more stimulated by disapproval than by admiration; a debt generously acknowledged is often to a long-dead author, seldom to a live competitor. Literary works proceed in a series which is neither smooth nor autonomous, though writers themselves since the mid-eighteenth century have usually represented it as both, and the two practices of standard literary history and tradition building portray the relations between writers as unrealistically harmonious.

4. The modern critic should acknowledge his own position as similar to that of all writers, bound in time and place. Historical criticism, like other modes of criticism, is a modern discourse. The aim is not to reconstruct the past, which could not be done innocently, even if it were worth doing at all. It is to understand how writing functions in its world, in order to understand writing, the world, and ourselves. Certainly there are respects in which it is easier to understand writing of the past than writing of the present: more evidence might be available about the genesis of a work by a dead writer than is commonly available for a work by a living writer. But what can be gained in richness of documentation and clarity of perspective is lost if we do not recognize the pastness of the past, the fact that its languages and its purposes are distinctive. The intentions and attitudes which are embedded in past writing can interrogate our own, if we will let them. It is a common feature of the modernist position and of the pseudohistorical practices — literary history and tradition building — that they all protect the modern critic from interrogation on equal terms by an author of another time and culture.

5. A genuinely historical perspective discourages dogmatism, by obliging us to foreground the difference between our circumstances, aims, and language, and those of the past. This acknowledgment runs counter to the practice of those critics who use the teaching of literature to uphold their own doctrines, which may be anything from religion or hu-

manism to feminism or world revolution. The monism of the proselytizer seems incompatible with the heterogeneity of historical material; and vatic criticism is a contradiction in terms. Unlike Paul de Man's and Nietzsche's modernism, which is a willed "forgetting," the obliteration of the steps which brought us as writers to our present position,[20] history asks us to declare our interests, whether personal, national, or professional. It is an antihistorical tendency which asks us to attend to fellow critics and scholars as though they were prophets. A better analogy has legal as well as theological connotations; we are all witnesses, and thus, however able and honest, can see only as far as our particular vantage points will let us.

A list of principles looks dismayingly like a set of rules to the empirically trained mind, especially when they are numbered. But a meditation on method is not a rule book, either for its author or for anyone else. It is almost reassuring to see how Skinner and Pocock, the former especially the author of trenchant criticism of old-style linear history of ideas, have not let their own theory inhibit their practice. Skinner's *Foundations of Modern Thought* (1978) and Pocock's *Machiavellian Moment* (1975) are not localized, but "morphologies of ideas" on a large historical scale, and they each represent ideas passing, by the old bad unexplained process, from one Great Thinker to the next.

Perhaps we should try harder than this to avoid linearity; and, above all, to introduce into both our structure and our style a stronger consciousness of the historical relativity of our own position. Carl Schorske's *Fin-de-Siècle Vienna: Politics and Culture* (1979) sets a good example, by opening with a discussion of the late-twentieth-century American taste for turn-of-the-century Vienna. The book would be profoundly less intellectual shorn of that introductory chapter, if it began instead with the first of its case studies of Viennese art and intellectualism around 1900. Then the presentation of the past would have been rigid and two-dimensional, and the author's and reader's angle of vision unspecified. As it is, the book is both an open series of discrete studies and a train of thought, which takes its cue with humility from Burckhardt's observation "History is what one age finds worthy of note in another."

Historical criticism, which is skeptical and analytic, teaches a healthy distrust of all forms of history writing. There is a role there for reception theory, in uncovering a long series of exemplary misreadings.

Notes

1   "Positivist literary history . . . borrowed the methods of the exact natural
    sciences. . . . The application of the principle of pure causal explanation

to the history of literature brought only externally determining factors to light, allowed source study to grow to a hypertrophied degree, and dissolved the specific character of the literary work into a collection of 'influences' that could be increased at will." Hans Robert Jauss, *Toward an Aesthetic of Reception*, trans. Timothy Bahti (Minneapolis: University of Minnesota Press, 1982), p. 8.

2 Jacqueline Rose, *The Case of Peter Pan; or, The Impossibility of Children's Fiction* (London: Macmillan, 1984), p. 54.

3 Lionel Gossman, program for seminar at Folger Institute, 1984–85.

4 "All imaginative and creative acts, being eternal, go to build up a permanent structure, which Blake calls Golgonooza, above time, and when the structure is finished, nature, its scaffolding, will be knocked away and man will live in it. . . . And the artist who uses the same energy and genius that Homer and Isaiah had will find that he not only lives in the same palace of art as Homer and Isaiah, but lives in it at the same time." Northrop Frye, *Fearful Symmetry* (Princeton: Princeton University Press, 1947), p. 91.

5 Terry Eagleton, *Marxism and Literary Criticism* (London: Methuen, 1976), p. 3.

6 Jauss, *Toward an Aesthetic of Reception*, p. 12.

7 Raymond Williams, *Marxism and Literature* (Oxford: Oxford University Press, 1977), pp. 132–33.

8 John Barrell's books are *The Idea of Landscape and the Sense of Place: An Approach to the Poetry of John Clare* (Cambridge: Cambridge University Press, 1972); *The Dark Side of the Landscape: The Rural Poor in English Painting, 1730–1840* (Cambridge: Cambridge University Press, 1980); and *English Literature in History, 1730–1780: An Equal, Wide Survey* (London: Hutchinson, 1983).

9 Jauss, *Toward an Aesthetic of Reception*, p. 28.

10 See, for example, Quentin Skinner, "Meaning and Understanding in the History of Ideas," *History and Theory* 8 (1969): 3–53; John Dunn, "The Identity of the History of Ideas," in *Political Obligation in Its Historical Context* (Cambridge: Cambridge University Press, 1980); J. G. A. Pocock, "The History of Political Thought: A Methodological Enquiry," in *Philosophy, Politics and Society*, 2d ser. (Oxford: Blackwell, 1969); and a critical survey of the controversy, D. Boucher, "New Histories of Political Thought for Old?" *Political Studies* 31, no. 1 (1983): 112–21. Though treated here as a group, these scholars are not always in agreement: Skinner, for example, puts much more stress than Pocock on recovering the author's intention. Other historians, furthermore, with no overt ties with the Skinner group, have developed similar lines of thought; cf. the collection of essays on nineteenth and twentieth-century radical movements by Gareth Stedman Jones, *Languages of Class: Studies in English Working-Class History, 1832–1982* (Cambridge: Cambridge University Press, 1984).

11 E. D. Hirsch, Jr., "The Politics of Theories of Interpretation," *Critical Inquiry* 9 (Sept. 1982): 239.

12 E. J. Hobsbawm and T. Ranger, *The Invention of Tradition* (Cambridge: Cambridge University Press, 1983), p. 2.

13 René Wellek, "The New Critics," *Critical Inquiry* 4 (1978): 616. Wellek's continuation confirms his sympathy with this general view of tradition, and adds detail of much interest: "The basic scheme has a venerable ancestry: Schiller's *Letters on Aesthetic Education* (1795) was the main source for Hegel and Marx. In the American critics, particularly in Tate and Brooks, the scheme is drawn from Eliot's view of tradition. In Eliot the "unified sensibility" comes from F. H. Bradley, who knew his Hegel. Brooks is confident in focusing on Hobbes as the villain; Tate singles out Bacon, Gibbon, and La Mettrie as the destroyers of the old world view. Ransom puts out a different version blaming "Platonism," which means presumably any generalizing abstracting view of the world. Tate praised Spengler's *Decline of the West* (*Nation* 122 [1926]: 532) and gave the scheme a peculiar twist in his practical criticism. He was most interested in poets who come at the point of dissolution of the original unity, who dramatize the alienation of man: Emily Dickinson and Hart Crane in particular. Tate sees poems always within history and echoes Eliot saying, in 1927, "My attempt is to see the present from the past, yet remain immersed in the present and committed to it" (*The Literary Correspondence of Donald Davidson and Allen Tate*, ed. John Tyree Fain and Thomas Daniel Young [Athens, Ga., 1974], p. 189)."

14 Harold Bloom, *The Visionary Company*, rev. ed. (Ithaca: Cornell University Press, 1971), pp. xvii–xviii.

15 Geoffrey Hartman, "Ghostlier Demarcations," in Murray Krieger, ed., *Northrop Frye in Modern Criticism* (New York: Columbia University Press, 1966), p. 115.

16 W. K. Wimsatt, *Hateful Contraries* (Lexington: University of Kentucky Press, 1965), p. 21.

17 The syncretizing tendency apparent in this remark is confirmed by another observation in the same review article, which fits rebels and angels into a single grand design: "the counternormative tradition of the Jews and Judaism was as important a continuity as the rabbinical tradition, and indeed the two frequently could not be distinguished from each other." Harold Bloom, in *New York Review of Books*, Jan. 19, 1984, p. 31.

18 Pauline Kogan, *Northrop Frye: The High Priest of Clerical Obscurantism* (Montreal: Progressive Books and Periodicals, 1969), p. 56.

19 M. H. Abrams, *Natural Supernaturalism* (New York: Norton, 1971), pp. 65, 69, 146.

20 Paul de Man, *Blindness and Insight* (New York: Oxford University Press, 1971), pp. 145–51.

Wordsworth's Intimations Ode: A Timely Utterance

Marjorie Levinson

IN HIS great essay "English Romanticism: Spirit of the Age," M. H. Abrams exposes the profoundly political interests of a group of poems which, in their mythic ideality, appear to refuse categorically topical analysis. Abrams explains that the English poets of the 1790s employed the panoramic procedures of epic and ode—procedures closely associated with Milton's political visions and invoked under that aspect —by way of focusing contemporary political meanings.

In a second landmark essay, published in 1965, Abrams defines the apolitical character of a central Romantic form which he designates the greater Romantic lyric.[1] My adjective, "apolitical," isolates the leading tendency of Abrams's implicitly contrastive formal description. The greater lyric—a private meditation born of the speaker's nonspecific, existential malaise—reaches articulation through his response to a present, particular, and precisely located natural scene. The meditation concludes with the production of a consolation which is valorized by the private and disinterested character of its motivation and development.

Abrams includes in this category a number of odes and odal forms unrelated in his analysis to the panoramic odes of the nineties. He derives poems such as the Intimations Ode and "Dejection" from the eighteenth-century local poem and, further back, from the seventeenth-century religious meditation. The Romantic lyric is said to lack, however, both the "historical and political" dimension of the former and the "public symbolism" of the latter. To describe the "crisis" upon which the lyric turns, Abrams uses the language of the Intimations Ode; it would seem that he regards Wordsworth's poem as exemplary of the form inasmuch as the lyric's motivation and procedure are so closely aligned in his analysis.

In several important ways, however, the Intimations Ode, read in the spirit which it and most of its readings recommend, fails to approximate Abrams's model. One cannot by any stretch describe the pastoral landscape of the Ode as "particularized and localized," nor is the narrator developed as a historically determinate authorial presence. The dominant stylistic mode of the poem is that of sonorous, lofty oratory, just about the opposite of Abrams's "fluent vernacular." The Ode's verbal resources consist of stylized iconographic representations and generic, typologically resonant allusions. The syntax fails to effect that blending of subjective and objective moments which distinguishes the Romantic lyric; it vigilantly discriminates perceiver and perceived and their respective loci: psyche and nature. Finally, the Ode features a discursive intellectual speculation which is not qualified by a fiction of spontaneous overflow nor offered as an enabling surmise.

I enumerate these discrepancies not to undermine Abrams's model but to illuminate the Ode by an observation Abrams himself advances in the earlier essay "Spirit of the Age." There, he notes that the great Romantic poems, most of which were written in the post-Revolutionary period of "disillusionment or despair," exhibit "in a transformed but recognizable fashion" a number of terms developed in the activist, republican period, terms which "assume a specialized reference to revolutionary events." Among these leitmotifs, Abrams includes "the dawn of glad day [and] the awakening earth in springtime." Although Abrams discusses the place of another such figure ("hope") in Wordsworth's so-called quietist or post-nineties period, he does not remark the occurrence in the Intimations Ode of the first two topoi, perhaps because he formally classifies the poem in a way inconsistent with a topological and a topical reading.[2]

To my mind, Abrams's oversights signify his respect for the rhetorical instructions encoded in the poem. For while the Intimations Ode, like the panoramic or nineties ode, introduces "history, politics, [and] philosophy," it does so to expose them as apparitional and to denounce the apparitions as mental enthrallments.[3] Hence the greatly transcendent and interiorized character of the poem. One may, however, account for the Ode's resemblances to the politically interested nineties ode without violating that lofty character by proposing that the object of the poem is precisely to pose and answer political questions at the level of abstract idea, and thus to command formally as well as intellectually a disturbing political prospect. Or, the Intimations Ode carries out its repudiation of politics on two levels, the level of argument and the level of style.[4]

These procedures and objectives are not unique to the Ode. As Jerome McGann has argued, they locate the center of the Romantic ideology, one of whose chief illusions is the triumph of the inner life over the outer world. Where the Ode *is* unusual is in its adoption of a representational style closely associated with that outer world: that is, with the particular history the poem refuses. This is to say that the idealizing action of this poem is a two-handed engine; it develops a determinate, topical polemic and, at the same time, veils that polemic in clouds of glory. Early-twentieth-century criticism seems to have grasped something of the Ode's referential character. One encounters in the literature wayward attempts to anchor the poem's generalized and ideal allusions to objects and events that figured or might have figured in Wordsworth's life and thought.[5] This scholarship was not fruitful because the concept of referentiality on which it was based was, as we shall see, too narrow. The Ode offers a historical rather than a naturalistic particularity; its topography is ideologically and emblematically specific; and the speaker voices the unique but collective experience of a generation. The place to look for the meaning of Wordsworth's Tree or Field is not in a universe of natural objects but rather among ideas of Nature, ideas structured and colored by contemporary conditions and obtaining for Wordsworth as for others of his time, place, and position. Rather than ask of the text, "which Tree?" one might instead try to reconstruct the nexus of associations informing that image and word for the poet and his early readers.

This procedure is familiar to students of *Coopers Hill* and *Windsor Forest*. Critics of these poems explain the ways in which landscape compositions represent not just or primarily particular persons and events but the ideas and values which inform and, as it were, occasion that topical material. One reason these ratios are, to most readers, nearly imperceptible in the Ode is that Wordsworth sets them under the sign of conflict and incommensurability rather than harmony.

The allegorical methods of the meditative and local poem as well as the political odes of the nineties derive, of course, from an analogical concept of the order of things: an assumption of systematic (i.e. motivated) symmetry obtaining between moral and phenomenal Nature. This concept was not simply unavailable in the central Romantic period, as Abrams suggests; in the case of the Intimations Ode, its "evanishment" is the poetic subject.[6] What is harder to see is that the narrator attributes his reluctant skepticism—a very personal dereliction and dismay—to a very public, an ideological treachery. A doctrine which had identified Nature with mankind's best interests had been seen to engender an irremediable catastrophe in human affairs. The results of that political, moral, and semiotic betrayal are depicted in the Ode, stanzas 1 and 2, a "paysage *de*moralisé."[7] Throughout the poem, Wordsworth uses the devices of allegory to discredit that form's projection of an analogically organized universe, confirming in this way the terrible vision of stanzas 5–8: the morbidity of Nature and history.[8]

What makes the Ode so Romantic a poem, then, is not that it lacks

the public symbolism which Abrams attributes to its formal precursors, but that it repudiates that publicity *which it introduces* through
its images and allusions. In Wordsworth's poem, history acquires its
meaning through its bearing on one man's life. The failure of the French
Revolution is represented as exclusively the poet's loss, and as a strictly
emotional, epistemological loss: "To me alone there came a thought of
grief." The meaning of this representation resides in its originary function: to transfer ideologically *possessed* material from public to private
domain.

Hazlitt, whose comments on the Ode imply that he construed the
work as an allegory addressed to the intellectual powers, provides us
with a convenient point of departure. Here is an excerpt from his review of *The Excursion*:

> But though we cannot weave over again the airy, unsubstantial dream,
> which reason and experience have dispelled,
> "What though the radiance, which was once so bright,
> Be now for ever taken from our sight,
> Though nothing can bring back the hour
> Of glory in the grass, of splendour in the flower" [*sic*]: —
> yet we will never cease, nor be prevented from returning on the wings
> of imagination to that bright dream of our youth; that glad dawn of the
> day-star of liberty; that spring-time of the world . . . when France called
> her children to partake her equal blessings beneath her laughing skies;
> when the stranger was met in all her villages with dance and festive songs,
> in celebration of a new and golden era; and when . . . the prospects of
> human happiness and glory were seen ascending . . . in bright and never-
> ending succession. The dawn of that day was suddenly overcast; that sea-
> son of hope is past; it is fled with the other dreams of our youth. . . .⁹

Hazlitt's quotation of the Ode in the context of an explicit political reflection, and his pronounced stylistic imitation of the poem, suggest that
he read in it a commentary on the French Revolution and its metamorphoses. In Wordsworth's description of an abstract and timeless Innocence, Hazlitt found a reference to that "bright dream" of his own and
of Wordsworth's youth — a social and political dream. In Wordsworth's
generic and greatly estheticized May jubilee, Hazlitt discerned the rural
fete which figured so prominently in the early days of the Revolution
and in Wordsworth's experience of it.¹⁰ In a characteristically telling
analysis, E. P. Thompson identifies phrases from Hazlitt's review as "stale
libertarian rhetoric" cast into "nostalgic rhythms."¹¹ In that the passage
self-consciously imitates Wordsworth's Ode, Thompson effectively un-

derlines the conventional and political character of the odal materials as well. Of course, Wordsworth's own description of his sojourn in France and her politics—"Bliss was it in that dawn to be alive, / But to be young was very Heaven!"—should amplify the political overtones of the Ode's celestial nostalgia and of the metaphysic thereby introduced, as should the following excerpt from *The Prelude*, where the poet, recalling the glad dawn of the Revolution, observes the present political twilight:

> . . . the sun
> That rose in splendour, was alive, and moved
> In exultation with a living pomp
> Of clouds—his glory's natural retinue—
> Hath dropped all functions by the gods bestowed,
> And, turned into a gewgaw, a machine,
> Sets like an Opera phantom
> (*The Prelude*, 1850: bk. 11, lines 363–69).

When Hazlitt described his own enthusiasm for the Revolution by way of evoking the spirit of the nineties, he again adopted the idiom of the Ode, from which he again quoted:

> . . . at this time the light of the French Revolution circled my head like a glory, though dabbled with drops of crimson gore: I walked comfortable and serene by its side—"And by the vision splendid / Was on my way attended."[12]

Here, too, Hazlitt indirectly but unequivocally identifies Wordsworth's "vision splendid" as a reference to the worldly renewal heralded by the French Revolution.

To suggest that Wordsworth's general theme—the terrors and *longueurs* of Experience—gets focused through a topical issue is not to trivialize or in any way depreciate that high theme. The Ode *is* about the inevitable loss of that celestial light which makes of everyone's childhood a "visible scene / On which the sun is shining." I propose only that the archetypically radiant state of Innocence remembered and recreated in stanzas 1–4—a touchstone for the Ode's emotional and intellectual argument—was embodied for Wordsworth and his readers in the memory of a briefly enlightened epoch in human history. When the odal narrator observes, "There was a time," a reader such as Hazlitt may have recalled the opening phrase of Coleridge's "Religious Musings"—"This is the time"—itself an echo of Milton's "This is the month." In Coleridge's ode (1794), the phrase designates the millennium once glimpsed in the French Revolution. To read Wordsworth's general elegiac lament against Coleridge's (and Milton's) fiercely specific proclamation is to identify the occasion of that lament as the passage of a *particular* time, say, 1790–93.

The poet's nostalgia, then, for a vivid experience of Nature, must be the reflex and expression of his nostalgia for the particular idea of Nature which informed the Revolution and its philosophic discourse. The Nature addressed as a *dea abscondita* in stanzas 1–4 (and demystified in 5–8) is the concept personified in eighteenth-century libertarian art: fierce goddess of the Revolution, incarnation of freedom, ground of sociality, and guarantor of the meaning of mundane experience.[13] It is, moreover, and as I argue below, the Nature conceived by Holbach and the philosophic school he exemplified. The Child Wordsworth addresses in the strophe as a lost power—the power to feel Nature's meanings—is a displacement of the poet's own young manhood with its unconflicted attachments to Nature and mankind. And the child he celebrates in stanza 8, "best philosopher," is a negation of the ratiocinative methods and analytic values so famously associated with the French *philosophe*—implicitly, "worst philosopher."

Mary Moorman has remarked Wordsworth's habit of "telescoping" incidents which occurred at different times, and her metaphor aptly describes the method of the Ode.[14] There, in a single field of vision, Wordsworth interweaves his and his generation's political and philosophic disillusion with his private memory of a season of "glad animal spirits." These two themes—the one derived from a recent, specific, and social experience, the other an eternal, existential fact—meet in Wordsworth's awareness that by negating the structure of ideas which had formed his young manhood, he renounced as well the vital self which he had experienced through that conceptual structure and in the era of its social hegemony.

By reconstructing the occasion, private and public, of this awareness and its expression, I hope to elucidate the function of the vision elaborated in stanzas 5–8, a vision sharply inconsistent with Wordsworth's canonical statement, as the poet himself acknowledged in 1843.

The first extrinsic factor to address is the immediate compositional situation. The odal strophe (stanzas 1–4) was written on a day of national significance, March 27, 1802, the day which concluded the negotiations for the Peace of Amiens. Wordsworth could not have known *on* the twenty-seventh that the peace with Napoleon was achieved that day, but the press had been full of the business for months. On March 15, the dispatches from Amiens arrived by special courier and the cabinet council hastily convened to examine them. The papers were returned for signing as reported in the *Times* of March 17, and, on the thirtieth, the arrival of the definitive treaty was proclaimed.[15] Wordsworth, an avid reader of the *Times* could not have been ignorant of the imminent conclusion to the negotiations. The perfect coincidence of national events with Wordsworth's poetical calendar is sheer serendipity. But the fact that the Ode was conceived in mid to late March 1802, the season of the final talks, strongly urges a causal explanation. The ode is, of course, the traditional formal choice for a poem on the occasion of a major national event.

The treaty officially marked the end of the season of conflict for Wordsworth, the season which began in 1793, when he could hope only for a divorce between "him who had been" and "the man to come."[16] With the end of hostility between his two early allegiances, Wordsworth could begin to reintegrate his experience. The treaty, which vastly favored France's imperialistic regime, underlined the perfidy of the Revolution and the faultiness of its guiding principles. (Sheridan called the treaty "a thing of which every man must be glad but no man can be proud.") Thus while the Peace brought to Wordsworth a welcome end to his divided loyalties, it also impressed on him once and for all the error of his "first affections."

Moreover, spring 1802 was the season of Wordsworth's projected marriage to Mary Hutchinson and of his visit to and emotional divorce from Annette Vallon.[17] Wordsworth had, of course, given up Annette long before 1802; he had also emerged from his Jacobin enthusiasm at least two years before he began writing the Ode. But it is one thing to "pass insensibly," as it were, from one position to its "contrary," feeling all the while that "things revolve upon each other."[18] It is quite another to find that not altogether perspicuous decisions and/or circumstance have enjoined upon one a position sharply antithetical to a former structure of belief. Wordsworth's engagement to Mary not only cast the involvement with Annette as a digression from what had come to seem his domestic destiny, it officially marked the period of the romantic phase of the affair.[19] In the same way, the Peace of Amiens, by formalizing France's role as imperialist aggressor, had to figure a major breach in the poet's carefully integrative self-chronicle. The closures thus defined for Wordsworth by the peace and by his betrothal could well have compelled him to revise more deliberately than he had yet done his sense of the past.

By 1802, Wordsworth was well established in the country of his boyhood and in the domain of a remembered Nature associated with eternally recurrent revolutions, as opposed to violent, political, and singular

Revolution. He had engaged to marry an old family friend, a country-woman. At such a time, the gap between Wordsworth's childhood and his present maturity would have seemed especially wide. The closing of that gap—which is to say, the reinterpretation of those "noisy years" of political passion—is a major objective of the Ode, as its headnote implies:

> The Child is Father of the Man;
> And I could wish my days to be
> Bound each to each by natural piety.[20]

Hence, I suggest, the indirection of Wordsworth's ideological revisions, by which he avoids the discontinuity of a recantation in the style of Coleridge's "France: An Ode" (1798; reprinted October 1802).[21]

The poems written in closest proximity to the Ode—"To the Cuckoo," "The Rainbow" ("My heart leaps up"), and the Sonnets Dedicated to Liberty—betray Wordsworth's preoccupation with what seemed to him the fragmented condition of his life, a condition foregrounded by personal and political developments. In the two little lyrics, the narrator, who inhabits a bleak and tedious Experience, seeks through the agency of the natural mnemonic, bird and rainbow, to enrich his present being with feelings from "that golden time" of childhood, when Nature was a living sacrament.

The Sonnets to Liberty, most of which were written in 1802–3, many of them based on Wordsworth's 1802 visit to France, articulate in full voice some of the themes which are rendered *sotto voce* in the Ode. Whereas "To the Cuckoo" and "The Rainbow" treat abstractly of existential discontinuities, the sonnets anchor these sensations to the dispiriting view of Napoleonic France. In that several of the sonnets contrast England's moral decline to the glorious era of *her* Revolution, readers have associated the republican rhetoric of the series with a lofty Miltonic eloquence. This rhetoric had, however, become the stylistic exponent of the Jacobin position, and, in terms of referential priority, the French Revolution clearly took precedence over the Puritan. Moreover, the preponderance in both the sonnets and the Ode of certain key words and verbal effects evoking the classical naturalism of Enlightenment rhetoric strongly imputes to the Ode the political themes developed in the sonnets.[22] When one reads in Sonnet 11, "Inland, within a hollow vale, I stood; / And saw, while sea was calm and air was clear, / The Coast of France . . . "—prelude to a depressing political reverie—it is difficult not to think of the *meta*-physical prospect seized by the narrator toward the end of the Ode:

> Hence in a season of calm weather
> Though inland far we be,
> Our Souls have sight of that immortal sea
> Which brought us hither,
> Can in a moment travel thither,
> And see the children sport upon the shore,
> And hear the mighty waters rolling evermore.

To attend that echo means historicizing the Ode's ideal and imagined scene by associating the narrator's indefinite *accidie* with the spiritlessness infecting all those children of the Revolution who lost their Innocence and their Eden when France lost her virtue.

The third sonnet of the series, with its extended depiction of France's political springtime, presents some suggestive parallels to the pastoral festivities represented in the Ode. Wordsworth describes the French countryside, 1790, as "like the May / With festivals of new-born Liberty" (1837 revision). "The antiquated earth / Beat like the heart of Man," and the narrator recalls the joyous expressions of this new rhythm: "songs, garlands, mirth, / Banners, and happy faces." Then, reductively and in rueful retrospect, he acknowledges the irrecoverability of "these things." Here, as in *The Prelude* (books 6 and 10) and the Ode (stanzas 1–4), Wordsworth elegizes that perfect harmony of man with Nature, singular with social existence, which defined for the poet and through his experience of "the gorgeous festival era of the Revolution" the meaning of that tremendous event.[23]

Wordsworth's style ultimately tells us more about his referential universe than do his representations per se. Moorman, in characterizing the Ode's pastoral landscape as that of Spenser, Shakespeare, and Milton, evidently observed that the Nature depicted in stanzas 1–4 differs significantly from the intimate, particular, and impressionistic landscapes far more frequent in and typical of the Wordsworth canon.[24] The landscape of the Ode is a stylized, static, and ideal affair. Wordsworth's manner clearly invokes a tradition; Moorman emphasizes the literariness of that tradition whereas Hazlitt's extrapolation (and Wordsworth's epigraphic allusion to Virgil's Fourth Eclogue, see below) highlights for us the political motives of the pastoral. The Ode, like "To the Cuckoo," "The Rainbow," and many of the Sonnets to Liberty, features a figurative mode best described as abstract and emblematic; commonplace and general nouns are pressed into service as lofty, even mystical and numinous universals. The Cuckoo, the Rainbow, "Fair Star of Evening," "Rising Sun in May"; these naturalistic materials function in the sonnets and lyrics as classical and biblical emblems denoting transcendent ideas that are nonetheless accessible to human understanding and capable of influencing historical development. Abrams, in a discussion of the *Lyrical Ballads* preface, identifies "the essential, the elementary, the simple, the universal, and the permanent" as Wordsworth's controlling norms. Marilyn Butler, who has discriminated the political meaning of these qualities in the work of Blake, Gillray, and the *Lyrical Ballads* Wordsworth, exposes the modishness of these effects in certain contexts.[25]

The simplicity of the Ode is, then, quite unlike the experiential and idiomatic inflection of "Tintern Abbey," despite the initial tonal and thematic resemblances. The Intimations Ode develops an austere, monumental, and self-conscious simplicity—a *philosophic* simplicity denoting the purity of a language and iconography purged of the topical, the local, the particular, the adventitious.[26]

Consider, with reference to the history of styles and their ideological meanings, Wordsworth's portentous isolation of common—and commonplace—nouns (Rainbow, Rose, Moon, etc.); the pointedly archaic, hieratic pronominalization (thy, ye, thou) and phrasing (and cometh from afar, behold the Child); the oratorical expressions of pathos (stanzas 1 and 2); the conspicuous use of parallelism; the idealized simplification of Nature.[27] In his work on the art of the Revolution, D. L. Dowd has described the character of David's painting as follows:

> The form . . . was "classical". . . . [or] characterized by an emphasis upon line rather than color, upon static composition rather than movement, and upon the imitation of Greek and Roman sculpture. On the other hand, the treatment of his subject matter was highly "realistic" in its imitation of nature. Finally, the content of his art was essentially romantic, if by "romantic" we mean . . . an admiration of an enviable and idealized past, and an emphasis upon an emotional message.[28]

To read these comments in the light of the Ode is to recognize in the opening movement of that poem the look of a particular painterly school. It is to materialize the *meaning* of Wordsworth's style: the pictorial but highly abstract representation of an ideologically charged object (the organic community) focused through emblematic tableaux (babe leaps up, children culling flowers) and suffused with nostalgia for an enviable and idealized past.

Wordsworth not only organizes his imagery in an ideologically specific fashion, he draws his denotative and iconic materials from the dictionary of eighteenth-century libertarian discourse. Rather than gloss these materials individually, let me bring out the relevant correspondences by sketching the argument developed allegorically in the Ode. There was a time when Nature, conceived as goddess of the Revolution, was instinct with providential omens signifying human fulfillment in time. During this season and by virtue of a certain widely held belief structure, the common was sublime and quotidian life a recurrent sacrament. The individual felt himself to be a member of a vast human family: then, "joy of one / [was] joy for tens of millions." The pastoral community so poignantly portrayed in stanzas 3 and 4 gives us the displaced representation of that defunct ideal. Those "things" (line 9)—the dreams of a particular time, place, and culture—have vanished. The narration *does* imply that man's power to perceive existing realities has also fallen off, but it presents that cognitive debility as the *result*, not the cause, of a more primary and a political disillusion. The syntax of the first two stanzas is clear, even insistent, about this: "The things which I have seen"; "There hath past away a glory from the earth." The lines unambiguously denote an external depletion.[29] Nature, the product of a historical moment and its modes of perception, no longer houses the glorious meanings which had endeared physical and social reality. The narrator faithfully records the presence, even in an unhallowed Experience, of illuminations, most of them secondary or reflective sources: rainbow, moon, glittering waters, stars. The conceptual and therefore organizing effulgence, however—the light of Reason and Nature as kindled by the Enlightenment, that "master-light"—has faded, rendering all other sources of light dubious, unreliable, or simply insufficient.

The word glory, so hardworking a noun in the Ode, seems to have been something of a code word during the Revolutionary era. Hazlitt, in both the excerpts quoted above, employs the word, and, in the idiom of the day, glory apparently signified something like the classical and Renaissance *virtù*. Brissot, leader of the Girondins, the party which briefly won Wordsworth's loyalty, proudly exclaimed, "j'ai prodigieusement aimé la gloire." Marat, describing the ancient Greek republics, asserts that "glory, that fruitful source of whatever men have done that is great or beautiful, was the object of every reward."[30] In "France: An Ode," Coleridge adorns his personification of Revolutionary France with "clustering wreathes of glory," and, in his *Lectures on Politics and Religion*, he refers repeatedly to that "small but glorious band" of thinking and disinterested Patriots," a theoretically defined Jacobin group.[31] In a substantial passage of *The Prelude* treating of Wordsworth's involvement with the Revolution, that interval is designated "a glorious time, / A happy time" (bk. 6, lines 754–55), and in two major passages, from *The Excursion* and *The Prelude*, the one somewhat sincere in its remembered political enthusiasm, the other openly derisive, the narrator recurs to the word glory.[32] Finally, Wordsworth's decision to render his phrase "great and glorious birth"—a phrase describing France's upsurge of Revolutionary energy—as "lovely birth" in his revision of "Descriptive Sketches" argues his sensitivity to the political nuance of the word.[33] When the narrator of the Ode recalls, then, "the glory and the freshness of a dream," he remembers that vision of individual, social, and natural harmony which was the ideological center of the Revolution. ("Dream," here, is used in its high-Romantic, realized character.) When he laments, "there hath past away a glory from the earth," he observes Nature's lack of personal meaning to him now that its public and ideological meaning has been discredited.[34]

The explanation of Wordsworth's original epigraph—"paulo majora canamus"—seems to reside here, in the poet's memory of a golden age in its dawning. The quotation is the first line of Virgil's Fourth Eclogue. The eclogue is generally assumed to have been composed "to announce the Peace [of Brundisium and] to anticipate the natural and desired consequences of the wedding of Antonius and Octavia." The Peace of Amiens, and Wordsworth's recent betrothal to Mary Hutchinson, might seem to present a debased or parodic occasional analogy (or a particularly egotistical sublime), but the resonance is not implausible. In the Fourth Eclogue, Virgil ushers in a new era, a golden age, "to be fulfilled or at least inaugurated by a child soon to be born," the child of an actual Roman father and matron. Or, Virgil's "child of destiny" images a spiritual regeneration effected through the political actions of a temporal leader.[35]

By transforming the "golden hours" of the Revolution (*Prelude*, 1850, bk. 6, line 340) into a psychic and metaphysical postulate, Wordsworth adapts to his purposes the pre- and trans-figurative logic so often applied to Virgil's celebrated eclogue, but he suppresss the militant, apocalyptic thrust of that traditional reading. (The dynamic which the Ode dramatizes is Abrams's "paradox of spiritual quietism.") Moreover, the Virgilian allusion situates the whole business of temporal and spiritual renovation in the discourses of poetry. The French Revolution and the Roman wars both begin to look like leitmotifs. Thus the Ode's epigraph supports its transcendental and interiorizing themes and, at the same time, identifies the factual original of those themes, in this, operating in much the same way as the poem's other images and allusions.[36]

The fiction of stanzas 1–4 is that the narrator's own inevitably evocative utterance reminds him how concrete a thing his loss is. His attempted escapes into poetic pastoral ("Now, while the birds thus sing . . .") repeatedly fail, and he is compelled to confront the form and meaning of his despair. "To me alone there came a thought of grief." That grievous thought, so emphatically particularized, announces the narrator's recognition of the occasion of his *angst:* his memory of a vision of earthly delight, a vision which was political in both the widest and the narrowest sense of that word.

The strangely specific allusion to a "timely utterance" is usually glossed as a reference to one of the two lyrics written on March 26, "To the Cuckoo" and "The Rainbow." The narrator's cryptic reassurance of recovery from his thought of grief—as I have suggested, a political memory—implies a political antidote. The narrator confesses that the conception of Nature developed in "To the Cuckoo" and "The Rainbow"—healer of existential breaches and eternally available mnemonic system—"solves" the historical problem: the invalidation of the Enlightenment idea of Nature. Yet as the narrator strives to consolidate experientially this ahistorical notion, symbols of that other, ideological Nature intrude, giving us a peculiarly Wordsworthian *et in Arcadia ego.*

"But there's a Tree, of many, one, / A single Field which I have looked upon, / Both of them speak of something that is gone." Of all the symbols generated by the Revolution, none was more prominent than the Tree of Liberty. Wordsworth was, of course, familiar with this commonplace symbol; in the passage from *The Excursion* cited above, the Solitary paraphrases the "prophetic harps" as follows: "Bring garlands, bring forth choicest flowers, to deck / The tree of liberty!" Wordsworth spent the summer of 1790 enjoying the Federation, a month of celebration to be encountered throughout France.[37] "C'est probablement vers les premiers jours de l'année 1790 que l'on commença dans les campagnes à planter des mais que l'on appela arbres de la liberté." Wordsworth was back in France, in residence, during the great Federation Feast, July 1792. Carlyle, in *The French Revolution*, describes the feast: "There are tents pitched in the Champ-de-Mars; . . . There are eighty-three symbolic Departmental Trees-of-Liberty; trees and *mais* enough." He describes the great *mai* in the 1790 celebration: "All lamplit, allegorically decorated; a Tree of Liberty sixty feet high; and Phrigion Cap on it."[38]

By associating Wordsworth's Tree and Field (Champ de Mars) with the emblems and events of a glorious and irrecoverable era, one is in a better position to explain the abrupt intrusion of these images and the disproportionate emotion which the narrator brings to them, as well as their extreme specificity. The narrator thus indicates that his attempt to liberate the fond, pastoral memory from its original, political context ("There was a [that is, *some, any*] time . . .") has failed. The historicity of the imagery is as a return of the repressed.

In the Revolutionary context, Tree and Field had signified an apocalyptic idea and its imminent fulfillment. In the Ode, these natural objects assume, for a moment, their former and symbolic character; they remind the narrator of something that is gone. With that loss, all those

natural objects which had been raised into social symbols through the
corporate conviction that Nature meant Liberty and a culture redeemed,
lapse back into the unhallowed commonplace.[39] Wordsworth's blazon,
stanzas 1 and 2, is a cold pastoral, enumeration of signs denoting va-
cancy where once there was meaning. The Pansy that had risen to prominence by virtue of an "analogically meaningful" notion of Nature becomes in stanza 10 "the flower." The subsequent designation, "meanest
flower," a negative valorization, suggests the christological and other-
worldly tendency of "the philosophic mind." The narrator protests that
nature yet lives for him and by his redemptive acts, but he also confesses
that Nature—the historical idea which had endeared the Creation by
binding mankind's happiness to her tutelage—is dead and cannot be
resurrected.[40]

What emerges from the elegiac strophe is the narrator's reluctance
to yield up the mental categories of the Enlightenment along with their
content. The project which the Ode takes up in its antistrophe (composed in 1804) is that of emptying those structures—Nature and Reason
—of their inherited, perfidious meanings. By endowing them with a
new content, Wordsworth could heal the breach defined for him by the
events of March 1802.[41] Stanzas 5–8 bespeak the poet's unequivocal
interest in devaluing historical experience. These stanzas have always
been read across an ideology: Platonic and Stoic. It is important, however, to identify the immediate object of Wordsworth's critique and thus
the stanzas' primary ideological commitment. By representing life in
time as irremediably and radically circumscribed, inimical to man's happiness, and spiritually degenerative, Wordsworth exposes the Enlightenment as a misconstruction of the very order of things. Against Rousseau's proposition "I saw that everything was radically connected with
politics, and that . . . no people would ever be anything but what the
nature of its government made it," Wordsworth sets the perniciousness
of man's investment in the structures that shape his mortal life.[42] To
read the following proposition from Holbach's *Système de la nature* in
the context of Wordsworth's antistrophe is to see that section of the Ode
as a far more pointed statement than it appears.

> The source of man's unhappiness is his ignorance of Nature. The per-
> tinacity with which he clings to blind opinions imbibed in his infancy
> . . . renders him the slave of fiction, . . . [and] doom[s] him to continual
> errour. He resembles a child destitute of experience. . . . Let us then raise
> ourselves above these clouds of [errour and] prejudice, . . . let us consult
> Nature, . . . let us fall back on our senses . . . let us . . . examine the visi-
> ble world, and let us try if it will not enable us to form a tolerable judge-

ment of the invisible territory of the intellectual world: perhaps it may be
found that there has been no sufficient reason for distinguishing them.[43]

Holbach's treatise includes a long section entitled "The Soul and Its
Faculties," and another "The Doctrine of Immortality"—both, of course,
materialist critiques. Wordsworth had certainly read Holbach (a copy
is listed in the catalogue of his library) along with Godwin, his English
counterpart.

Tenet by tenet, phrase by phrase, image by image, Wordsworth deconstructs the Enlightenment's "vision splendid."[44] To each of the *philosophes'* idols—freedom, individuality, joy, progress, Reason, illumination, Nature—Wordsworth opposes a bleak other: imprisonment,
uniformity, sadness, accommodation, degeneration, memory, darkness,
mind.[45] To suggest that our greatest power, clearest amplitude was in
a past we can barely recall, much less recover, is to set a regressive ideal
for mankind. Politically, the Ode advances a radical conservatism; ethi-
cally, a doctrine of consolation and compromise; intellectually, a curriculum grounded in memory. When, in the epode, the narrator gives
thanks for those "obstinate questionings / Of sense and outward things,"
he celebrates his inability to see those "things" of stanza 1, a reference
to the material expressions of the Revolution and to his own believing
endowment. This is to say, Wordsworth constructs his counterfaith from
the very materials of Enlightenment thought.

A serviceable formulation of the negated position might go as follows. We are born into the light of Nature, a light we perceive by our
inner light, Reason, which participates in that visible light; our earthly
experience can be a progressive exercise in self-enlightenment rewarded
by enhanced vitality and worldly control. Against this program, Wordsworth develops a vision of mankind not just as Nature's "foster" (rather
than "natural") children, but as Inmates of her indomitable "prison-
house," a phrase which, eighteen lines preceding a reference to "that
imperial palace," must bring to mind the Bastille. The prison, we learn,
is life itself; Nature, which had meant Liberty in the context of the Enlightenment, is represented in the Ode as the supreme jailer. In characterizing mankind's native dimension (its being's heart and home) as an
imperial palace, Wordsworth not only appoints the protective enclosure
over imaginative expansion (so-called Romantic Nature), he adopts the
language of the Royalist position. Although he undercuts the elitism of
the phrase by representing this mansion as a universal source, univer-
sally inaccessible, the allusion identifies Wordsworth's vision as a critique of the Revolution's millennial thrust. Likewise, the epithet "Nature's priest" at once inscribes and negates the Revolutionary program.

As we know, a great deal of Wordsworth's poetry and that of his contemporaries develops its Edenic, Experiential, and Paradisal visions with reference to the Child, symbolically and naturalistically invoked. This is not to rule out, however, more topical uses and derivations of the image in particular poems. In the Intimations Ode—as we can now see, a very timely utterance—the representation of childhood draws its meaning from several contrastive relationships. In the context of 1807, apostrophes to a Child could not but conjure Rousseau, he who *made* the child father of the man. The Rousseauvian child, empowered by his ignorance of the coercive categories of social life and by his undefended instinctual life, was, of course, a political as well as a psychic postulate. The construct of a former (but historical) sublimity serves in Rousseau as sanction of a future, and a historical, renaissance.

It is under this politicized aspect that Wordsworth presents his *Lyrical Ballads* "wise child," an essentialist, Enlightenment figure. In the ballads, this figure typically converts a complacent (read, "conservative") narrator to a perception of a universe instinct with apocalyptic energy. The *Lyrical Ballads* child seizes the authority traditionally (paternalistically) accorded to age; his unclouded intellect grasps the simple, subversive truths which we are toiling all our lives not to find.

The wisdom with which the odal Child (a far more sublime and generalized representation) is credited is that of the removed seer. He is the passive possessor of a vision "into the life of things"; his metaphysical penetration is incommunicable and, but for the pleasure and memories it yields him, without effect. Whereas the *Lyrical Ballads* child, something of an *enfant terrible*, performs a monitory (and minatory) function, the odal Child develops a critique of pure reason which amounts to a lesson in "wise passiveness." There is a devilish irony in all this. The French *philosophe* had invented the child as a symbol of unfettered Reason, powerful to see and to act on its clear visions. Wordsworth not only restricts this power to a period of physical and political impotence, but enlists it in the service of Enlightenment critique.

> Childhood is the cornerstone of the philosophy of [Wordsworth's] great Ode. The child's joyous acquiescence in the free spirit of life and his indomitable instinct for the unseen and eternal make him humanity's best philosopher.[46]

This observation by Helen Darbishire may sound dated, but its substance would not be rejected by most modern Romanticists. Once we appreciate, however, the extent to which the Ode is informed by political associations and anxieties writ large elsewhere in Wordsworth's canon and illuminated by the discourses of the day, we perceive the developmental and psychological themes as a device for (dis)figuring a specifically treacherous vision.

The dark determinism of the mythic stanzas is reinforced by the suggestion that active resistance to Nature's deadening influence only hastens the inevitable enslavement. Since self-affirmation implies acquiescence in the categories, hence the reality of natural life, even Prometheanism ultimately constitutes a self-betrayal: betrayal of the eternal by the earthly self. The Enlightenment commitment to exertion in the service of personal, intellectual, and social liberty is opposed in the Ode to the spiritual freedom passively realized by the Child in his possession by the immortal Mind, which is to him "a Master o'er a Slave."

The Ode associates "delight and liberty"—the "simple creed" of the Revolution—with the nonreflective condition of childhood. According to the Ode, adult wisdom, such as it is, begins in the memory of an Edenic infancy, proceeds by inference (intimation) to the hypostatis of a more blessed, prenatal state, and concludes in the certainty that "natural life is the history of the acceptance of loss."[47] This is an epistemology based upon normatively contrastive acts; present perception and historical memory live, move, and have their being through shadowy recollection of a noumenal world.

This scheme is what is meant by "thoughts that do often lie too deep for tears." The phrase divests 'philosophic thought' (rational, inductive problem solving: a communicable process and product) of the supreme value it had acquired during the Enlightenment. Such thought—Reason in its most, or least, exalted mood—had failed Wordsworth dramatically. In the Ode, he develops a context wherein to redefine Reason, thereby preserving a shade from his past. The canceled passage (lines 121–24) where the narrator postulates an intellectual life in death was more clearly in the service of this de- and re-valuation—a salvaging action.

Those grand and pitiful concluding lines ("To me the meanest flower that blows can give / Thoughts that do often lie too deep for tears") are not nearly so devoid of polemic as they seem. With this announcement, Wordsworth denies a correspondence essential to the whole structure of Enlightenment rationalism: a consensus correspondence between objects of thought (meanest flower) and the conceptual object (thought). Wordsworth clearly intends this denial; the expected phrase is "feelings" too deep for tears. The narrator's affirmation brings out his independence of Nature, any indifferent piece of which "means" insofar as it awakens a private memory of a consecrating past. Moreover, a thought that lies too deep for tears is also too deep for words. One might observe that a thought which cannot be formulated cannot be disconfirmed and, further, that such thought is the stuff of ideology. With the final line of the Ode, Wordsworth installs a definition of thought not just independent of Reason and Nature but inimical to them.

In sum, Wordsworth's myth of the soul, a pragmatic narrative never assimilated into his thinking, situates his grief over the failure of the Revolution and the invalidation of its ideology within a vision so vast and impersonal as to disappear that pain. Those "noisy" or politically passionate and "restless" years are contextualized by the sobered narrator as but "moments in the being / Of the eternal Silence."[48] The "truths" to which mankind should cling are those, we learn, "that wake, / To perish never," decidedly *not* those which were born of historical immediacies and which maintain their relation to those lived truths. Wordsworth celebrates the sort of truths that no amount of "listlessness, nor mad endeavour"—one might say, no attempts at implementation—can destroy. History is exposed in the Ode as an unworthy object of human interest and involvement, its challenges nugatory. "Another race hath been, and other palms are won"; there are victories, the narrator's Pauline allusion suggests, far greater than those once anticipated from the French Revolution. Rather than grieve over those mundane losses, the reader is exhorted to set his sights on those other and spiritual palms. The heroism that Wordsworth ultimately defines is the capacity to live in the absence of a "consecrating dream," a "dream of human life"—by the end of the poem exposed as a belle dame sans merci.

In place of that treacherous dream or "gleam," the narrator recommends the "soothing thoughts that spring / Out of human suffering." By this substitutive reemphasis, Wordsworth rejects the hectic, hopeful fellowship promoted by the Revolution. He derives the authentic human community from a common pathos, which is to say, from a shared knowledge of irremediable human defect and deficiency. The object of Wordsworth's Ode is, like Gray's, to "teach [us we] are men."

Let me ask, once again, the question framed at the outset: why would a writer concerned to empty out history structure his statement by way of political allegory? I have argued that a dominant motive of the Ode is to expose the fallacy of those analogical assumptions which had governed Enlightenment thought and Revolutionary action. By his allegorical efforts to bridge the abyss separating Nature from Mind ("clouds" from "colour," "meanest flower" from "thoughts"), Wordsworth at once defines that abyss and identifies Mind as the source and stuff of Nature's meaning.

In that the Ode develops a metaphysics of absence punctuated by individual projective acts:

> Not for these I raise
> The song of thanks and praise;
> But for those obstinate questionings
> Of sense and outward things,
> Fallings from us, vanishings;
> Blank misgivings of a Creature
> Moving about in worlds not realized,

it behooves us to notice the tension between the poet's "act of mind and the material acted upon."[49] Of course, the narrator's triumph in the Ode is his concluding, symbolic act: his vision of a "paysage consacré," its meanings ineffable and consubstantial with its appearances. Since, however, the value of this achievement is predicated on its factitiousness —on the special motives and acts that produce it—we read most sympathetically by refusing the symbolic, the Romantic option.

This is one reason why I have elaborated here a "knowledge of the text"—what Terry Eagleton has defined as a reconstruction of "the conflicts and dispositions of its specific historical codes . . ."[50] I agree with Eagleton that this is not always and necessarily the most important thing to do. But with a poem like the Ode—one which has been so securely seized as "literary," which has been "detached by a certain hermeneutic practice from its pragmatic context and subjected to a generalizing reinscription"—it does seem to me most important right now and for the politics of Romantic scholarship to nudge the work toward a less literary register.[51]

Notes

1 This essay, "Structure and Style in the Greater Romantic Lyric," and the above in Harold Bloom, ed., *Romanticism and Consciousness* (New York: Norton, 1970), pp. 90–118, 201–29.

2 Above quotations from Abrams, "English Romanticism: The Spirit of the Age," in Bloom, *Romanticism and Consciousness*, p. 107.

3 Abrams, "English Romanticism," p. 103.

4 For an extended definition and critical history of this phenomenon, see Jerome McGann, *The Romantic Ideology* (Chicago: University of Chicago Press, 1983).

5 McGann, *Romantic Ideology*, p. 88.

6 Abrams, "Structure and Style in the Greater Romantic Lyric," pp. 210, 211.

7 Ibid., p. 209.

8 Hegel knew Romantic art by its indifference to "the sensuous externality

of form" which assumes in the work an "insignificant and transient" character. ("Introduction to the Philosophy of Art," in *Hegel Selections*, ed.
and trans. J. Loewenberg [New York: 1929], pp. 326, 327). What we observe
in the Ode is the deliberateness of this indifference and this assumption.

9   William Hazlitt, "On Mr. Wordsworth's Excursion," in *The Collected Works
     of William Hazlitt*, ed. A. R. Waller and Arnold Glover, vol. 1 (London:
     Dent, 1902), p. 119.

10 Charles Cestre, *La révolution française et les poètes anglaises* (Paris:
     Hachette, 1906), p. 29. "Ils [Wordsworth and Robert Jones] arriverent à
     Calais la veille du jour où fut célébrée dans toute la France cette fête splen-
     dide, qui sembla exalter la nature humaine au-dessus d'elle-même, la Première
     Fédération, la fête de la fraternité. Ils virent 'dans un petite ville et chez
     quelques-uns comme les visages deviennent radieux, quand la joie d'un seul
     est la joie de dix millions.' . . . Tout le long de la route, ils trouvèrent des
     vestiges de la grande fêtes, des guirlandes, et des arcs de triomphe, et ils
     assistèrent aux réjouissances de la liberté . . ."

11 E. P. Thompson, "Disenchantment or Default? A Lay Sermon," in Conor
     Cruise O'Brien and William Dean Vanech, eds., *Power and Consciousness*
     (London: University of London Press, 1969), p. 178.

12 Hazlitt, *Collected Works*, 12: 236.

13 I refer to such artists as Peyron, Barthélemy, Jeaurat de Bertry, painters of
     allegorical works wherein topical and ideological argument is developed
     by a specifically charged classical style. I trace my line of thought on this
     subject to a lecture by Tim Clark, Swarthmore College, 1980. For an apt
     literary representation of Liberty in the 1790s, see "Invocation to Liberty,"
     anonymous, in *The Watchman*, March 25, 1796, in *Collected Works of
     Samuel Taylor Coleridge*, ed. Lewis Patton and Peter Mann, *The Watch-
     man*, vol. 2 (London and Princeton: Routledge and Kegan Paul and Prince-
     ton University Press, 1970), p. 130.

14 Mary Moorman, *William Wordsworth: A Biography. The Early Years,
     1770–1803* (London: Oxford University Press, 1957; rpt., 1968).

15 This research executed by Rick Halpern, Department of History, Univer-
     sity of Pennsylvania.

16 Moorman, *Early Years*, p. 223.

17 Wordsworth became engaged to Mary Hutchinson probably during mid-
     November 1802; they planned a spring wedding (Moorman, *Early Years*,
     p. 518). Toward the end of March, however, two or three days after com-
     posing the strophe of the Ode, Wordsworth decided to take advantage of
     the peace and visit Annette at Calais. The rapidity with which the visit
     was conceived and executed suggests that Wordsworth had cherished the
     idea for some time, presumably while he was conceiving the first part of
     the Ode. We do know that on March 22, Wordsworth heard from Annette
     and resolved both to see her and to visit Mary (Mark Reed, *Wordsworth:
     The Chronology of the Middle Years, 1800–1815* [Cambridge: Harvard
     University Press, 1975], p. 155). According to Moorman (p. 518), "a long
     exchange of letters with Annette Vallon occupied the spring months." The

sojourn with Annette interfered with Wordsworth's marriage plans; the wedding was postponed until October 1802. One cannot know, of course, but one could confidently surmise that the engagement to Mary and the interest in renewed contact with Annette were not unrelated.

18 William Wordsworth, "Essay upon Epitaphs" in *The Prose Works of William Wordsworth*, ed. W. J. B. Owen and Jane Smyser, vol. 2 (Oxford: Clarendon Press, 1974), p. 53.

19 Wordsworth maintained a correspondence with Annette until the war interrupted it again. Upon the marriage of his and Annette's illegitimate daughter, Caroline, Wordsworth settled £30 a year upon her until 1834, when he gave her the sum of £400 (Moorman, *Early Years*, p. 565). The closure I discern in Wordsworth's relationship with Annette (as prompted by his marriage to Mary) refers to an internal, intellectual and emotional shift rather than to an active expression of detachment.

20 The headnote was added in 1815, and it replaced the Virgilian epigraph. The new extract, with its existential generalities, obviously discourages the sort of pointed, politically sensitive reception invited by the original epigraph. The substitution suggests Wordsworth's interest in deemphasizing, even obscuring, the Ode's topical and allegorical dimension. The emergence of this interest, or its gradual ascendancy, is consistent with what we know of Wordsworth's political and social development.

21 Spoken by the Solitary: "Such recantation had for me no charm, / Nor would I bend to it." Like the Solitary, Wordsworth would not declare, with others, "'Liberty, / I worshipped thee, and find thee but a Shade!'" or "dream" (*The Excursion,* bk. 3, lines 776–79). He did, however, say *just* that in the Ode, but through a subtler language than, say, Coleridge's.

22 "Star," "splendour," "glory," "Man," "hope," "master-spirit." Of course, the most elaborate metaphor in the Ode is that of light, and the political resonance of this word and image would have been obvious to Wordsworth's early readers. Here is Paine's celebrated elaboration of the figure: "The revolutions of America and France have thrown a beam of light over the world, which reaches into man . . . when once the veil begins to rend, it admits not of repair . . . the mind, in discovering truth, acts in the same manner as it acts through the eye in discovering objects; when once any object has been seen, it is impossible to put the mind back to the same condition it was in before it saw it." Thomas Paine, *Rights of Man*, ed. Henry Collins, (New York: Penguin, 1979), p. 140. James Boulton, in his *Language of Politics in the Age of Wilkes and Burke* (London: Routledge and Kegan Paul, 1963), p. 206, quotes Priestley, *Letters to Burke*: "Prejudice and error is only a mist, which the sun, which has now risen, will effectually disperse." For additional examples of these and related, shared metaphors of the day, see Boulton, *Language of Politics in the Age of Wilkes and Burke*, pp. 75–249.

23 "Wordsworth, it is well known to all who know anything of his history, felt himself so fascinated by the gorgeous festival era of the Revolution . . . that he went over to Paris and spent about one entire year between that

city, Orleans, and Blois." De Quincy, quoted in Leslie Chard, *Dissenting Republican: Wordsworth's Early Life and Thought in Their Political Context* (The Hague: Mouton, 1972), p. 70.

24 Moorman, *Middle Years*, p. 23.

25 M. H. Abrams, ed., *Wordsworth: A Collection of Critical Essays* (Englewood Cliffs: Prentice-Hall, 1972), p. 1; Marilyn Butler, *Romantics, Rebels, and Reactionaries: English Literature and Its Background, 1760–1830* (Oxford: Oxford University Press, 1982), pp. 11–68.

26 "But if I am to tell the very truth, I find . . . the great Ode not wholly free from something declamatory." Thus does Arnold distinguish the Ode from Wordsworth's best and most characteristic poems, those which "have no style." Matthew Arnold, "Wordsworth," 1879.

27 These also define the Pindaric ode. The "Intimations Ode is, however, predominantly Horatian in its private, contemplative, and tranquil character. One could think of the poem as representing an attempt to marry the two traditions, but this is to treat the work as an academic exercise, or to situate it in a rather narrow esthetic space. I have been trying to ascertain the meaning of particular styles and formal decisions during a particular interval.

28 David Lloyd Dowd, *Pageant-Master of the Republic: Jacques-Louis David and the French Revolution*, University of Nebraska Studies, no. 3, (Lincoln, June 1948), p. 22.

29 The received readings of this stanza indicate, more than any other single fact, the idealist character of so much Romantic criticism. The lines which conclude the first and second stanzas of the Ode—"The things which I have seen I now can see no more" and "There hath past away a glory from the earth"—are typically taken as statements of spiritual exhaustion, perceptual debility, and decrease in personal power to consecrate the objective contents of vision. The literal meaning of these lines—the expression of an external and imposed impoverishment—is consistently overlooked.

The language of several critics, however, seems to expose unacknowledged associations and assumptions of the sort I have isolated above. Mary Moorman describes Wordsworth's political disillusion in 1795 (viz, the increasingly unmistakable reign of violence in France): "Then came the great crisis; the human tragedy breaking into the bright vision of his youth; the sharp suffering, and the desperate search for a philosophy that would make life possible again" (*Early Years*, p. 279). Moorman's metaphors as well as her psychological reconstruction ("search for a philosophy") appear to derive from the Intimations Ode. One might observe that Moorman's phrase "bright vision" refers not to Wordsworth's childhood but to his young manhood with its political and social visions. Cestre, in his *Révolution française*, characterizes Wordsworth's post-Revolutionary resolve as follows: After the crisis of the Revolution, Wordsworth hoped to project upon reality "une lumière de rêve" (p. 548). More recently, Clifford Siskin discerns in the Ode the essentially revisionist and dehistoricizing procedures I address here: "This strategy is most familiar to us as enacted in the "Intimations Ode"; the poet becomes philosophic hero as change felt as loss is transformed by revision into intimations of the unchanging . . . the apotheosis of the 'Poets' entails the repression of history under the weight of transcendent continuities." Siskin, "Revision Romanticized: A Study in Literary Change," *Romanticism Past and Present* 7, no. 2 (1983): 1–16. And George Watson, while he offers no critical observations, characterizes the period in question as follows: "Wordsworth had lost two paradises by . . . the years between 1799 and 1805: a political paradise in revolutionary France, and a sensory paradise of youth as well. He is a twofold Adam." Watson, "The Revolutionary Youth of Wordsworth and Coleridge," *Critical Quarterly* 18, no. 3 (Autumn 1976): 57.

30 Harold Parker, *The Cult of Antiquity and the French Revolution* (New York: Octagon Books, 1965), pp. 47, 48.

31 Samuel Taylor Coleridge, "A Moral and Political Lecture" and "Conciones ad Populum," in *The Collected Works of Samuel Taylor Coleridge. Lectures 1795 on Politics and Religion*, ed. Lewis Patton and Peter Mann (Princeton and London: Princeton University Press and Routledge and Kegan Paul, 1971), pp. 12, 40.

32 From *The Excursion*, bk. 3, lines 711–26.

> Fell to the ground . . .
> A golden palace rose, or seemed to rise,
> The appointed seat of equitable law
> And mild paternal sway. The potent shock
> I felt: the transformation I perceived,
> As marvellously seized as in that moment
> When, from the blind mist issuing, I beheld
> Glory—beyond all glory ever seen,
> Confusion infinite of heaven and earth,
> Dazzling the soul. Meanwhile, prophetic harps
> In every grove were ringing, "War shall cease:
>
> .   .   .
>
> Bring garlands, bring forth choicest flowers, to deck
> The tree of liberty."—my heart rebounded . . .

From *The Prelude*, 1850, bk. 11, lines 236–44.

> How glorious! in self-knowledge and self-rule,
> To look through all the frailties of the world,
> And, with a resolute mastery shaking off
> The accidents of nature, time, and place,
> Build social upon personal Liberty,
> Which, to the blind restraints of general laws
> Superior, magisterially adopts
> One guide, the light of circumstances, flashed
> Upon an independent intellect.

The derisive excess evident in the passage above measures Wordsworth's early investment in that "dream of human life"; his rude awakening from that millennial dream figured to the poet a second Fall.

The narrator of Sonnet 15 ("Great men have been among us") reflects upon France's decline by way of comparing the character of her Revolution to England's redemptive revolt, the Puritan Revolution. The English "master-spirits" taught us how rightfully a nation shone / In splendor." "They knew how genuine glory was put on." One might observe that beyond the shared diction, the sonnet and the Ode develop the concept of a "glory" which is not the necessary expression of an inalienable nobility ("glory" in its religious and painterly connotations) but the historical manifestation of an elevated and conditional state of the soul: a majesty assumed, "put on," an "apparel." As James Chandler has argued ("Wordsworth and Burke," *English Literary History* 47, no. 4 [Winter 1980]: 741–71, 756), Wordsworth, as early as 1799, had adopted Burke's wryly literal characterization of "habit" or prejudice as moral clothing. "Burke's related figure of reason's 'nakedness' also appears in the 'Essay' ('bald and naked reasonings') as well as, more prominently, in *The Prelude*." Chandler argues that "such figures are properly called Burkean . . . because, though Burke did not invent them, he did invest them in the 1790s with an ideological power distinctly his own." To accept Chandler's very sound reasoning is to read the Ode's representation of Nature and the Child—respectively appareled in celestial light and trailing clouds of glory—across Burke. Again, like Burke, Wordsworth characterizes the condition of the strictly rational creature—which is to say, he who has lost his "intimations"—as that of a nakedness signifying poverty and weakness. "Not in entire forgetfulness, / And not in utter nakedness." To learn that Wordsworth recommends the healing properties of memory and that he celebrates the habitual, instinctual character of childhood wisdom is no surprise. But the Burkean polemic of these moves—the denigration of a particular and politicized idea of Reason—is a less commonplace critical inference.

33   Abrams has set Wordsworth's famous account of the imagination (Simplon Pass episode) against his earlier, political "prophecy of a new earth emerging from apocalyptic fires," by way of establishing the poet's post-nineties "spiritual quietism." Abrams isolates from the passage the leitmotif, hope, and centers his contrastive analysis on that word ("English Romanticism," p. 109). I would add to Abrams's discussion that in the Simplon Pass section, it is individual imagination which rises up and, "awful Power," assumes a "glory"—not Liberty and not a militant populace.

34   Nature's fall into historicity is explicitly represented in the Sonnets Dedicated to Liberty as the result of a historical treason: the failure of the French Revolution. The Ode's representation of an abruptly profane experience of Nature can be illuminated with reference to that theme in the sonnets (see Sonnet 19).

35   Peter Manning, "Wordsworth's Intimations Ode and Its Epigraphs," *Jour-*

nal of English and Germanic Philology 82, no. 4 (October 1983): 526–40.
And see Sir Ronald Syme, *The Roman Revolution* (Oxford: Oxford University Press, 1939), pp. 218, 219 (on the Peace of Brundisium and Virgil's Fourth Eclogue). Manning takes an interesting psychoanalytic approach. I thank Mac Pigman, California Institute of Technology, for identifying the classical, political meanings embedded in Wordsworth's allusion.

36 As I noted above, Wordsworth's 1815 decision to replace the Virgilian epigraph with a headnote quotation from "The Rainbow" suggests his wish to suppress the originally political burden of the Ode, and to emphasize the priority of what has been treated here as instrumental: the metaphysical, psychological argument. In the absence of the new headnote, stanzas 1 and 2 need not be construed as a reference to childhood. Although the indeterminacy of the phrase "there was a time" conjures a mythical past, the line could have been read as a reference to the Revolutionary era; the new headnote makes such a construction more problematic.

37 Alan Liu, "Wordsworth: The History in Imagination," *English Literary History* 51, no. 3 (Fall 1984): 505–48.

38 Thomas Carlyle, *The French Revolution*, 2 vols. (London: Dent, 1906), 2: 102; 1: 285. See Abbé Henri Grégoire, *Essai historique et patriotique sur les arbres de la liberté* (Paris: n.p., [1794]).

39 Nature meant Liberty and accordingly, when Liberty in its historical incarnation proved itself a false god, Nature too was emptied out. The clearest expression of the symbology which married Nature and Freedom is Coleridge's "France: An Ode." The poem, prompted by France's invasion of Switzerland, 1798, was published in that year and later reprinted in the *Morning Post*, October 14, 1802, with the addition of a note and Argument. Coleridge explains that "the present state of France and Switzerland give it [the Ode] so peculiar an interest at the present time that we wished to re-publish it." The poem was originally titled "The Recantation: An Ode."

David Perkins (ed., *English Romantic Writers* [New York: Harcourt Brace and World, 1967], p. 423) summarizes the thought of the first stanza: "That natural objects ceaselessly inculcate the idea of liberty." Thus, the great disillusion addressed by Coleridge in his ode (and by Wordsworth in his), rendered Nature, which had been a semiotic system promoting specifically humanitarian meanings, a chaos. One of Wordsworth's Sonnets Dedicated to Liberty crystallizes the sentiment: "I find nothing great: / Nothing is left which I can venerate; / So that a doubt almost within me springs / Of Providence, such emptiness at length / Seems at the heart of all things" (Sonnet 12 on Independence and Liberty). In order to sustain his libertarian posture and, more important, to preserve Nature's meaningfulness in the face of this ideological earthquake, Coleridge locates "God in Nature." Wordsworth's strategy, far more radical than Coleridge's pantheism, is first to denounce Nature as a great confiner (and thus oppose the literary and political association of Nature with Liberty) and then to divest Nature of all public or consensus meaning. When the narrator asserts, "I love the Brooks which down their channels fret, even more than when I tripped lightly as they," he not only characterizes Nature as a private amour, he attributes his love to the "vanishings" which Nature inscribes and which invite his valorizing acts.

40 He implies, moreover, through the changes he rings upon the word "dream," that the death of that idea calls into question the fundamental mechanism and thus all the products of human vision. In stanzas 1–4, "dream" denotes either a preview of reality or the essence of reality (that is to say, "dream" in its high-Romantic, subjectivist character). When the narrator asks, "where is it now, the glory and the dream," he refers to, in Keats's phrase, an "existence." Specifically, he remembers the Revolutionary vision of a collective and liberated imagination. This Blakean premise, however, is quite literally discredited in the Ode's antistrophe. Here, "dream" ("a sleep and a forgetting," a "dream of human life") assumes its more pedestrian and prudential aspect: the delusive, fantastic, and dangerous escape from or ignorance of the real. An apposite usage occurs in *The Prelude*, 1850, bk. 11, line 125; "Fed their childhood on dreams" (i.e., of the Revolution).

Hazlitt, in the passage quoted on p. 51, professes his sustained belief in the essential truth of that "airy, unsubstantial dream" of his youth. He implicitly characterizes the fictive status of that dream as conditional, a vision of reality in that finer tone man will one day experience directly. For Wordsworth, apparently (from the evidence of the Ode and, more important, of his political evolution) the despair induced by the failure of his Enlightenment dream was too profound for any response but total abjuration. "Hence, perhaps, the flatness of the word 'Flower'—Wordsworth does not even give the daisy its specific name—which may be taken to signal the intuition that we may as well give up trying to find the *word* which does ample justice to the *thing*, and points us back to the immediacy of an experience outside language, which language at its most efficient can only tentatively indicate." David Simpson, *Wordsworth and the Figurings of the Real* (London: Macmillan, 1982), p. 25. Simpson's subject here is Wordsworth's "The Daisy." The "intuition" with which he credits the poet can be detected as well in the Intimations Ode and in the same device: the abstention from concrete and particular designation (Pansy to Flower). In the Ode, however, Wordsworth's intuition seems a more interested or motivated determination whereby he reinforces his critique of reason (the intellectual processes which transform perception to communicable thought) and of Nature, which, in her necessarily specific and fixed manifestations tends to reduce and immobilize imagination.

41 This might remind one of Coleridge's advice to Wordsworth, 1799: "I wish you would write a poem in blank verse addressed to those who, in consequence of the complete failure of the French Revolution, have thrown up all hopes for the amelioration of mankind, and are sinking into an almost epicurean selfishness, disguising the same under the soft titles of domestic attachment and contempt for visionary *philosophes*" (from E. P. Thompson, *The Making of the English Working Class* [New York: Pantheon, 1964], p. 176). In one major passage of *The Prelude*, Wordsworth responds spe-

cifically to Coleridge's analysis. Here, he articulates what one scholar has called the "moral depression, not to say hopelessness . . . which weighed upon Englishmen not only up to the beginning of the Peninsular war but . . . until the English successes in Spain attracted the attention of the whole world. This spiritlessness [was] caused by the continued triumph of Buonaparte." A. V. Dicey, *The Statesmanship of Wordsworth* (Oxford: Clarendon Press, 1917), pp. 72–73. But it is the Intimations Ode which explores that cultural depression and which describes by enacting a way to transcend without trivializing that collective and personal despair. At the same time, Wordsworth both implements and subverts Coleridge's rebuke to those who would offset their bitterness and rationalize their self-centeredness through "contempt for visionary *philosophes*." Wordsworth *assumes* that mantle in the Ode—for what are stanzas 5–8 but a philosophic vision—but in such a way as to repudiate its historically specific character. Wordsworth's myth of the soul is a pointed rebuttal of the doctrine, program, and methods associated with the French philosophy—in the poet's phrase, "pestilential philosophism" ("Convention of Cintra").

42   Jean-Jacques Rousseau, *Confessions,* quoted in Kenneth Eisold, *Loneliness and Communion: A Study of Wordsworth's Thought and Experience,* Romantic Reassessment, Salzburg Studies in English Literature, vol. 13, (Salzburg: Universität Salzburg, Institut für Englishe Sprache und Literatur, 1973), p. 7.

43   Baron d'Holbach, *The System of Nature*, trans. H. D. Robinson (New York: Burt Franklin, 1868; rpt. 1970), pp. viii, 15.

44   Two years intervened between the composition of the strophe and that of the antistrophe. One might conjecture that in 1802, Wordsworth's emotional commitment to "the vision splendid" and to his quondam involvement in it was still too intense to permit the thoroughgoing repudiation enacted in stanzas 5–8. The admission of loss was candor enough. By 1804, Wordsworth was more firmly consolidated in every way; whereas 1802 found him on the verge of marriage, by 1804 he had been established with Mary for two years. Moreover, Wordsworth's return to France on "Buonaparte's natal day" in 1802 and the bitterly ironic pall cast over that lengthy visit, as well as the resumption of the war soon after, had to destroy any lingering attachment to France, or it had to sever once and for all in Wordsworth's mind the France of 1789–92 from Napoleon's France.

In the eight weeks following Coleridge's departure for Malta, Wordsworth wrote the "Ode to Duty," completed the Intimations Ode, and books 3, 4, and 5 of *The Prelude.* He had originally planned *The Prelude* as a five-book work, ending with his return to Cambridge at the end of his first long vacation (described in book 4), *before* his momentous sojourn in France. Wordsworth's sudden decision to include his experiences in France argues his achievement of a sufficiently dispassionate attitude toward those experiences and their meanings as to permit their esthetic resolution. That distance could well have been the chief factor in Wordsworth's decision to resume work on the Ode.

45 Although I lacked the opportunity to read Ronald Paulson's recent study, *Representations of Revolution, 1789–1820* (New Haven: Yale University Press, 1983), before or during the composition of this essay, I would like to note here its consonance with my line of argument, and its confirmation of some local matters (see pp. 22, 24, 27, 46, 47, 149–50, 190, 192, and 206).

46 Helen Darbishire, ed., *Wordsworth: Poems in Two Volumes, 1807* (Oxford: Clarendon Press, 1952), p. xlvii.

47 Eisold, *Loneliness and Communion*, p. 130.

48 Truths "do rest" upon the child, whereas the man vainly "is toiling all [his] life" to recover those early wisdoms. He is restless in pursuing them and the more desperate his pursuit, the more he estranges himself from its object. "Restlessness," in the context of Wordsworth's canon, denotes political anxiety, the condition which came to a head in Wordsworth's London experience, 1793.

49 Simpson, *Figurings of the Real*, p. 113.

50 Terry Eagleton, *Walter Benjamin; or Towards a Revolutionary Critique* (London: Verso and NLB, 1981), pp. 122, 123. And see pp. 6–10, 22, 117.

51 Eagleton, *Walter Benjamin*, p. 123.

Reconstructed Folktales as Literary Sources

Bruce A. Rosenberg

A CRITICAL analysis of *Beowulf*, published in 1969, argued that the character of Unferth was a necessity within the epic tradition of its culture; the author's methodology was not only that of the literary critic / historian but that of the traditional folklorist as well. In outline, the argument proceeded as follows: Narrative structural similarities between *Beowulf* and the folktale type designated by Aarne-Thompson as "The Three Stolen Princesses" (A-T 301) invites comparison between the two. But Beowulf's challenge by Unferth when he first arrives at Hrothgar's court has no counterpart in the folktales. Similarly, while nearly all of the folktales begin with an *enfance* of the hero (in the subtype "The Bear's Son"), the old English epic introduces a young but mature warrior and commander. Some form of the folktale antedates the epic (probably composed during the eighth century, written down around 1000), and it is unlikely that the character of Unferth would appear in any of them. His (presumed) absence in the folktales suggests that he is the creation of the *Beowulf* poet; but since accounts of the hero's youth are "missing" from the epic, it is likely that in replying to Unferth about his youthful escapade with Breca in the North Sea, Beowulf recounts the adventurous *enfance* which is in the folktales. To conform with Germanic epic tradition, the *Beowulf* scop relocated the story relating the hero's youth from the beginning of the narrative to a more convenient point when it could be evoked, in retrospect.[1]

This comparison between an epic, which has devolved to us in manuscript, and a folktale which has never been collected and must therefore be only hypothecated, is predicated on several assumptions. They are basic ones, so basic to some folklore research—especially as it relates to literary texts—that ignorance of them permits an unbridgeable chasm to exist. Much that will be discussed later in this essay depends on an understanding of these folklore methodologies and how they are applicable to literary, historical criticism.

For much of the past century, the system used to define the components of folk narrative has been the legacy of Finnish folklore; but the clearest definition is Stith Thompson's, "the smallest element in a tale having a power to persist in tradition."[2] Narrative elements are meant—of three kinds: the actors within a tale; descriptive items in the background of the action; and, the most populous kind of motif, single incidents. By current standards this is rather nebulous; but despite all the problems involved in this definition and the analytic system based on it, the influence of the Finns has been so pervasive that folklore narrative study is barely possible without reference to them.

"A type," Thompson also has defined, "is a traditional tale that has an independent existence."[3] Though a type may occur in oral tradition with one or more other types, it does not depend upon them for its meaning. Independent existence is the sole criterion for the determination of a type. But, perhaps confusingly, a single motif may exist independently in tradition and thus be considered as a type. The theoretical problem with these concepts is obvious enough, but as it is often the case the system has been manageable in practice—most of the time. And it may be, considering the directions being taken by American folklorists today, that the motif indexes (dictionaries of motifs arranged by content) are of more value to literary scholars who are trying to establish relations between oral narratives and written. The hero who encounters a monster, defeats it, and follows it to its lair in the lower world, the heroine who marries a nobleman and whose promise of constant obedience is put to the test when the husband pretends to have her children killed, or the husband who wagers with a stranger on his wife's chastity, are all collected (and listed) motifs. The scholar desiring to know whether these aspects of *Beowulf*, the Clerk's Tale, or *Cymbeline* have folklore counterparts or not (they all do) can quickly make that determination in *The Motif-Index of Folk Literature* (1955–58).[4]

In order to establish the relationship, if any, between a literary narrative (in this example *Beowulf*) and a type, a paradigm abstracted from many versions of the latter is compared with the text. Examples of authorities taken from the geographic region of the manuscripts' home are also compared. If the researcher is lucky enough to have a transcript of the precise oral narrative involved, the task is greatly simplified; but such good fortune is extremely rare. Folktales were not collected, per se, until the nineteenth century, and it has not been until this century that electric or electronic recorders have made their collection very accurate. Almost always the oral narrative is not available; folklorists have therefore turned to paradigms, or composites, of a great many collected tales whose consistency in outline—in the nature and sequence of distributional elements—enables the researcher to group them as "types."

The following composite is Aarne-Thompson Type 301 from the in-

ternational index of folktale types, *The Types of the Folktale*, composed
from folklorists' experience with such tales:

I. *The Hero* is of supernatural origin and strength: (a) son of a bear
who has stolen his mother; (b) of a dwarf or robber from whom the
boy rescues himself and his mother; (c) the son of a man and a she-bear
or (d) cow; or (e) engendered by the eating of fruit, (f) by the wind or
(g) from a burning piece of wood, (h) He grows supernaturally strong
and is unruly.

II. *The Descent*. (a) With two extraordinary companions (b) he comes
to a house in the woods, or (b¹) a bridge; the monster who owns it
punishes the companions but is defeated by the hero, (c) who is let down
through a well into the lower world. —Alternative beginning of the tale:
(d) the third prince, where his elder brothers have failed, (e) overcomes
at night the monster who steals from the king's apple-tree, and (f) follows
him through a hole into the lower world.

III. *Stolen Maidens*. (a) Three princesses are stolen by a monster.
(b) the hero goes to rescue them.

IV. *Rescue*. (a) In the lower world, with a sword which he finds there,
he conquers several monsters and rescues three maidens. (b) The maidens are pulled up by the hero's companions and stolen.

V. *Betrayal of Hero*. (a) He himself is left below by his treacherous
companions, but he reaches the upper world through the help of (b) a
spirit whose ear he bites to get magic powers to fly or (c) a bird, (d) to
whom he feeds his own flesh; or (e) he is pulled up.

VI. *Recognition*. He is recognized by the princesses when he arrives
on the wedding day. (b) He is in disguise and (c) sends his dogs to steal
from the wedding feast; or (d) he presents rings, (e) clothing, or (f) other
tokens, secures the punishment of the imposters, and marries one of
the princesses.[5]

If we allow for a number of variations from this basic "type"—itself
incorporating a number of various possibilities—*Beowulf* is an analogue.
Arguments to the contrary have not been very convincing. Beowulf is
of supernatural origin and strength: his relationship to the bear, em-
bodiment of strength for the Nordic Middle Ages, as his name shows,
has often been pointed out.[6] With companions Beowulf does come to
a house (an impressively royal house) in the woods, where a monster
punishes the hero's companions but is, in turn, defeated by him. The
hero follows the monster through "a hole" into the lower world and there
slays the monster with a sword which he finds on the premises. But he
is deserted—treacherously in the folktales, by mistake in the epic—and
has to reach the upper world without his companion's assistance.

But *Beowulf* varies from the Aarne-Thompson paradigm in one important respect: the folktale's abduction and eventual rescue of the three princesses is so important an element that folklorists identify the tale as "The Three Stolen Princesses." No such ladies have been distressed in the epic. Given the masculine quality of this heroic (and essentially martial) poetry, rescuing women—even princesses—would be out of place. The lady in jeopardy as a suitable stimulus for the hero's risk of life is a later development in European literature—late in the thirteenth century in France, a century later in England. It is almost beneath Beowulf's dignity to risk his life merely to save a princess. Consequently, inevitably, when there are no stolen princesses, part III, there can be no recognition—part VI.

Yet researchers familiar with this method of comparison insist that *Beowulf*'s incorporation of four elements (I, II, IV, and V) of type 301 is sufficient to consider it a variant, and not a randomly similar phenomenon. The matter is not without controversy, even among folklorists. The "type" is based, necessarily, on tales collected during the past two centuries; it is just possible that the tale changed during the millennium before that, and is not accurately definable by recent versions of 301.

Finnish folklorist Kaarle Krohn, who helped develop the original methodology, wrote, "Polygenesis [the independent creation of folktales, rather than the diffusion of a single tale] in the most extreme sense, that every variant was composed separately at innumerable sites, is unthinkable. Usually a single origin is assumed for the traditional forms of one ethnic or linguistic group. . . . But even one single independent reoccurrence of such a complicated form, for example, the Cinderella tale, as the result of the general similarity of human fantasy or pure chance is highly unlikely."[7] In the case of "The Three Stolen Princesses," enough variants which do not have princesses have been found to indicate a tradition of narratives similar (in outline) to *Beowulf*. Such narratives are nevertheless judged to be part of the A-T 301 tradition; they are subsets of it, or, more technically, subtypes.

One of the characteristics of the folktale which makes indices of motifs (the smallest decomposable unit of narrative existent in oral narrative) and tale types possible is stability. Stith Thompson remarks that "the examination of all versions of a tale impresses one with the remarkable stability of the essential story in the midst of continually shifting details."[8] This stability is accounted for, in part, by the (now somewhat arguable) "Law of Self-Correction" formulated by folklorist Walter Anderson. This "law" is in two parts; both indicate reasons why folk narrative retains its "essential story" in travels across continents and over the course of centuries. First, most raconteurs have heard their tales many times, not merely once, from their sources. That repetition helps them to get it "right." Usually, in addition, the teller has heard a particular narrative from a number of different people, often in different locations; listeners in these various audiences often ensure that the teller gets his story "correctly" and often will correct him if he makes a "mistake." The internal logic of a narrative is an element not touched upon by Anderson, but nevertheless it seems to be a factor in maintaining consistency: if "A" happens, then "B" follows: before the horse can be stolen the barn door must be unlocked. This logic cannot be violated.

So basic is the idea of the dogma of monogenesis (or the rejection of polygenesis) that when folklorist (and medievalist) W. Edson Richmond found two ballads whose "differences in phrasing are so great that it seems inconceivable that one could have developed directly from the other," he did not seriously consider the possibility of polygenesis, but concluded that "one must, therefore, predicate a lost archetype in which the same plot as that found in our versions was developed, though the lost archetype need not have had phrases or stanzas common to either of our extant texts."[9]

In cases of literary texts for which no analogous folktales have been, or could have been, collected, one makes a hypothetical reconstruction. We assume the existence of folktales of the type "The Three Stolen Princesses" because the essential story (the chain of nuclei distributional elements) of type 301 is the essential story of *Beowulf*. The folktales cannot be dated exactly; *Beowulf* suggests that analogous tales are at least as old as the composition of the epic, perhaps older. And because we assume the stability of the folktale, we assume that, in outline at the least, "The Three Stolen Princesses" was in the eighth century much as it is today. To a degree, this is an article of faith.

On such assumptions certain otherwise puzzling aspects of *Beowulf* can be explained. Why do his companions sleep in Heorot on their first night there when they have come to Hrothgar's land only to fight a monster known to attack its victims at night? No comment is made by the poet about these warriors, so self-possessed that they sleep on the edge of doom; nor about Beowulf's inactivity when Grendel does appear—having burst vigorously through the door—and proceeds to devour the hero's hand-picked warrior friend, Hondscio. Gwyn Jones, who knows as much about folk narrative as he does about medieval literature, puts it succinctly: these details are "gaunt and unassimilable folktale motifs which the *Beowulf* poet found he could neither reject nor rationalize."[10] In the folktale, we should recall, the hero's friends are punished by the monster before the hero kills him.

Friedrich Panzer's detailed study of *Beowulf* in relation to analogous folktales, while making a number of points which we now take as a kind of intellectual public domain, had methodological weaknesses.[11] One of the chief of these was his failure to give proper weight to those variants of type 301 found in Scandinavia, where *Beowulf* was recited and composed for the manuscript Cotton Vitellius A XV. The *oicotype*, a term first borrowed from botany by the Swedish folklorist C. W. von Sydow, in folklore refers to a geographically or chronologically limited variant. Panzer's study was admirable in that it accounted for nearly all the variants of type 301 that were available; but, it took into account variants that had been collected in regions far away from Scandinavia, regions whose variants differed substantially from *Beowulf* which, though a literary work, can be considered a Baltic oicotype.

A summary of the Finnish method (or, as it is commonly called, the historic-geographic method) is in order at this point in the discussion. Perhaps the classic study in English is that performed by Stith Thompson (and published in 1953), analyzing the American Indian "Star Husband Tale." Thompson sought a tale whose known variants were few enough to make the body of data easily comprehensible, but also one whose geographical distribution was wide enough to allow the Finnish method full scope. A few folklorists in his day had argued that literary versions of any tale were so influential (because widely read and thus transmitted) as to render studies of oral tradition defective.[12] Thompson also chose for a model a tale that was current in a culture "with no possible or likely literary influences."[13] The "Star Husband Tale" was found to be suitable. Thompson presented the following outline:

> Two girls are sleeping in the open at night and see two stars. They make wishes that they may be married to these stars. In the morning they find themselves in the upper world, each married to a star—one of them a young man and the other an old man. The women are usually warned against digging but eventually disobey and make a hole in the sky through which they see their old home below. They are seized with longing to return and secure help in making a long rope. On this they eventually succeed in reaching home.[14]

All of the variants of the narrative under examination are collected and groups according to the location of their discovery. According to standard practices, literary versions would have been handled separately; the Finns paid special attention to them in their own analyses owing to the much greater influence exerted on the tradition by tales in print. Since Thompson did not deal with literary versions, his grouping of Amerind tales was by region, e.g., Eskimo area, North Pacific area, California area, Plains area, Southwest area, Woodland area, and so forth. He then isolated the narrative traits that offered significant possibility for differentiation among the variants. For instance, since the number of women occasionally varied, Thompson symbolized that trait as "A" and used subscript numbers to indicate the number of women present; "A_1" indicated that the tale had only one woman, "A_2" indicated two women (the most common variation), "A_3" three women, etc. Trait "B" designed the "Introductory Action," the means or motivation of transportation of the women to the upper world; trait "C" designated the "Circumstances of Introductory Action"—what the women were doing when the action begins; trait "D" signified the method of ascent, and so forth.

Once all of the tales have been thus decomposed into constituents, and the major narrative elements coded, the entire corpus of tales is compared. Each trait is evaluated in terms of its frequency of occurrence, distribution, and content. Thompson remarks of trait "D" that "it seems clear from its frequency and distribution that . . . the translation to the upper world during sleep is the normal form."[15] Some interpretation is often necessary, as in the case of trait "F" (distinctive qualities of the husband). Of the eighty-six tales used in this model demonstration, Thompson found that only twenty-seven described the star husbands as an old man and a young. But in several other versions the star husbands were also contrasted: in two tales the husbands wore different colored blankets, in two others they were initially seen as a "red star sun" and "white star moon"; and in one plains version, the dim star is a chief, the bright star his servant. Thompson, interpreting, concludes that since all of these versions have "contrasting husbands" they "may well be variants of" the old man/young man polarity.[16]

On the assumption—to simplify, but not to distort through oversimplification—that if a raconteur tells a particular tale to several different listeners, the chances are extremely remote that they will all "get it wrong" in the same way, or that they will all make the same changes or all have the same memory lapses. Therefore, in order to determine the "basic tale," the archetype from which all the others derive, the folklorist employing the historic-geographic method counts each variant of each trait to decide, statistically, which versions dominate. The composite of the predominant traits produces this archetype. For the "Star Husband Tale" Thompson concluded that the archetype had the following traits:

> Two girls (65%) sleeping out (85%) make wishes for stars as husbands (90%). They are taken to the sky in their sleep (82%) and find them-

selves married to stars (87%), a young man and an old, corresponding to the brilliance or size of the stars (55%). The women disregard the warning not to dig (90%) and accidentally open up a hole in the sky (76%). Unaided (52%) they descend on a rope (88%) and arrive home safely (76%).[17]

The actual tales may then be examined to see if their traits match those of this hypothetically reconstructed archetype. Thompson was fortunate in this regard, as about a dozen of the collected "Star Husband Tales" did conform to the statistical model. The tales are then examined according to their geographic distribution to identify subtypes and oicotypes. This procedure can now be performed by the digital computer.[18] In this model study, Thompson found that changes in the archetype came about through the addition of a single item or a narrative unit that required additional changes to maintain consistency. The husband's descriptive polarities, he noted, were found in several groups of tales on the periphery of the main area; he concludes with a basic assumption of the Finnish method, the rationale for the identification of ancillary rather than basic traits: "It seems inconceivable that any one of these versions should have originated the story, for it is beyond all probability that any one trait should be consistently forgotten, and never recur elsewhere."[19]

To return to *Beowulf*: when a comparative analysis reveals that analogous folktales (the appropriate subtype of type 301) in Scandinavia depict the hero's childhood, the methodological assumptions of the Finnish historic-geographic method indicate that the epic is "unusual" and that the statistical norm is to present such a subset of narrative units (the *enfance*) at the tale's beginning. The indication is also that this folktale tradition was antecedent to, as well as coexistent with, *Beowulf*, or else the *enfance* would appear with much lower frequency: if *Beowulf* was the original, then several hundred tellers of the collected versions of type 301 "got it wrong," and all of their tellers added this portion of the hero's life. But the epic does have a recounting of the hero's youthful adventures, of sorts; it occurs when Unferth challenges him about a swimming match he has reportedly earlier engaged in, and Beowulf replies with the true account of that contest. If the folktales were available to those scops who rendered the discourse we know as this Old English epic, and the customs of Germanic epic tradition militated against the strictly chronological placement of the *enfance*, it is not unlikely that such a narrative portion would appear, but later. One of the common features of the Bear's Son's youth is his unpromising conduct; that aspect of Beowulf's early years is not mentioned until after two thousand lines have been recited.

These conclusions concerning *Beowulf*'s relation to the type 301 tales are valid if the Finnish method is valid. But that intricate and elaborate methodology is not without its critics. Primary among folklorists is the complaint that a full historic-geographic study commonly takes between ten and twenty years to complete, dealing as it does with several hundred variants of a single tale (sometimes more than a thousand). Very few researchers have completed more than one in their lifetime; only a few have attempted even one.[20] Most American folklorists, if they work with this kind of material at all, much prefer to deal with a limited number of oicotypes, facilitating a cultural statement that is, after all, one of folklore's prime objectives. Not even the development of a computer program to speed up the comparison of decomposed folktale abstracts, and to identify—almost immediately—subtypes, has increased the popularity of the Finnish method in the United States. But this objection—that of the excessive length of time necessary to complete such a project—is not entirely relevant to our study of folklore and literature.

More to the point are two assumptions on which the Finns, and most other European scholars, have founded this methodology; we should ask whether folktales are as stable as the Finnish method seems to imply, and whether polygenesis is possible. As has long been recognized, it is in the nature of material in oral transmission to vary; this is especially true of folk narratives. Antti Aarne has even made a list of the most likely changes: details are forgotten or added; two or more tales are strung together; incidents are repeated (usually three times); narrative material from other tales is substituted; animal characters may be replaced by humans (and vice versa), etc.[21] Vladimir Propp was to complain, as early as 1928, that these constant changes and shifts made the tale impossible to define by current standards.[22] Yet, despite all these doubts about the folktale's stability, it is consistent enough for our purposes—and in the areas that are the concern of literary scholars of a European tradition. It has long been believed that European tale types evolved clearly, and that they are usually relatively fixed in form, like— to use Thompson's metaphor—inert crystals.[23]

Is polygenesis possible? Certainly, but in the main only in certain circumstances, with certain genres, in international contexts. Single motifs, it has long been acknowledged, can arise independently of each other. And certain tales seem to have analogues in other cultures where direct diffusion cannot be demonstrated. For instance, some European tales seem to have analogues among North American Indian tales: "The interesting parallel between the adventures of Lodge-Boy and Thrown-Away and the medieval romance of Valentine and Orson, both concerned with twin heroes, one brought up at home and the other abandoned at birth, is certainly nothing more than a coincidence. That the American Indians should have known the chivalric romance is almost inconceivable, since it has never been told by Europeans as a folktale."[24] And polygenesis is the likely explanation of the great similarity of dozens of hero tales and heroic legends such as the defeated heroes Saul, Leonidas, Bjarki, Byrthnoth, Roland, Gawain, et al.[25] Heroic legends differ from folktales with respect to the belief of the tradition bearers, the "facts" upon which the legend may be based, and so on, all of which factors may cause them to behave differently in oral transmission. Polygenesis is a common occurrence; the problem is to find out when it occurs, and where.

On net, then, when we take into account the major flaws of the historic-geographic method, it is nevertheless valid in most of the cases that would be the concern of the literary scholar. The folktale is often enough unstable in structure in oral transmission, but in the case of type 301, for instance, it has been shown to be satisfactorily constant: it has been recently collected in Latin America in a form immediately recognizable as of a type with *Beowulf*;[26] and it has been quite stable in the Baltic region, where the *Beowulf* scop performed and heard others perform. And, while some genres appear to have spread polygenetically, the ordinary folktale (A-T types 300–749) has not yet been shown to be subject to independent creation. To return to the argument outlined at the beginning of this essay: given several folkloric assumptions about the nature of oral narratives in transmission over the course of a great length of time, it can be reasonably argued that the flyting between Unferth and the newly arrived Beowulf is a repositioning of the hero's *enfance* commonly found at the beginning of tales of type 301.

This discussion of the Finnish method's applicability to literary studies cannot conclude without reference to one of the most useful of such studies in recent years, and one that is in several ways a model of such approaches. "New Light on the Origins of the Griselda Story," by William E. Bettridge and Francis Lee Utley, compares about fifty variants of "Griselda" (Aarne-Thompson type 887) with the literary versions of Chaucer, Boccaccio, and Petrarch, and arrives at new—and rigorously argued—conclusions.

In the first step in this demonstration, Utley and Bettridge show that the striking similarity of episode and even phrasing between some contemporary folktales of the type 887 and literary versions marks the oral narratives as reflexes: "We cannot doubt that the provenience is ultimately literary."[27] The "Griselda" folktale—that is, one of its type—cannot therefore have been the source of Boccaccio's *Decameron* tale.

The authors next demonstrate that "Cupid and Psyche" ("The Monster/ Animal as Bridegroom," A-T type 425A) is hardly likely to be the source tale either, despite the claims of Griffith and Cate;[28] though the argument at this point does not depend entirely on the Finnish method, Utley and Bettridge maintain that the Griffith/Cate argument is weakened greatly because the subtype of A-T 425 in which the children are taken away has not been found in Italy or the Mediterranean. "No romance oral variants," they remind us, "of the stolen children subgroup exist."[29] Utley and Bettridge insist upon precise oicotyping methods in their literary analysis:

> One is reminded [by Griffith/Cate's guessing at the origin of Griselda's name] of nineteenth-century folktale study, where scholars like Clouston, Frazer, or Lang could take a fragment from India, another from Australia, and another from the Faroes, and from them construct a flourishing tale; . . . One major difference between folklore research a hundred years ago and now is that today the folktale is a recognized set of identifiable and identified documents, most of them well-attested from scientific and accurate collectors, rather than a few exemplars "literated" like those of the Grimms with many a hypothetical "lost source" as intermediary between them.[30]

The positive conclusions of this research tentatively suggest that Boccaccio's source was a Turkish folktale similar to a complex of Aarne-Thompson types which includes type 894 ("The Ogre Schoolmaster"), 707 ("The Three Golden Sons"), and some version of 425. In the final stages of their deliberations, Utley and Bettridge locate nine Mediterranean versions of their tale, listed in the Turkish archives as type 306 ("The Patience of a Sultaness/Princess"). A composite abstract of this tale readily shows its similarity to the Chaucer/Boccaccio/Petrarch versions:

1. A Padishah wants a wife, who has great patience and looks like him.

2. He marries a poor girl and takes away three of her children under the pretext that he will eat them.

3. Then he announces that he will marry another wife.

4. The wedding turns out to be that of his eldest son, and the Padishah explains everything.[31]

But how would Boccaccio have access to a Turkish version? The last element in the Utley-Bettridge research is historical. Corresponding with scholars in Turkey and Greece, they were able to establish the existence in the fourteenth century of a cultural bridge "from Turkey to Greece to Italy" and also in the reverse direction, though one would have been enough. The (tentative) route of transmission then suggested that the tale, of Turkish origin, was picked up by a Greek, in the fourteenth century or earlier, and brought across the Aegean to Zakynthos, whence it found its way to Italy and to Boccaccio.[32] Narrowing the search down to nine tales gave these scholars an easily graspable corpus of material to work with, but also made statistical analysis very risky. Nevertheless, theirs is one of the most thorough, incisive, and learned examinations of this narrative; given the paucity of collected tales available, it is difficult to believe that this study will ever be methodologically surpassed.

And yet the Utley-Bettridge conclusions are only as sound as their methodological assumptions and the corpus of collected tales of the 894/707/425 type. More thorough collecting in the western Mediterranean may someday uncover narratives which undermine their argument. And more rigorous analysis of folktale behavior may one day fatally question the Finnish method, throwing the whole mountain of argumentation onto that academic slag heap where now repose those nineteenth-century theories of solar mythology and of the unitary source of folktales. It just might happen; for just as the folktale can be seen, over centuries, to be evolving, so folktale research is spinning, and at a much faster rate. Utley and Bettridge analyzed *The Clerk's Tale* according to the procedures of a time-honored methodology, but that methodology is not for all time.

Is it even for our time, let alone for times to come? In America the prognosis is not encouraging. To begin with, folklorists are hesitant to commit so much of their time and labor to historic-geographic studies, and dubious of the results. And the present generation of folklorists is wary of literary studies; certainly they avoid any analysis that highlights the text—as opposed to the live performance as communicative event. The folktale of (scholarly/analytical) choice is the Urban Belief Legend. Among literary historians, the Finnish method seems to be of most interest mainly to medievalists, as the folktale is so frequently an analogue or a source of the narratives they study.

The Finnish method incorporates many of the inherent weaknesses and shortfalls of structuralism, and of source studies as a critical mode. Historic-geographic researchers may have difficulty dealing precisely with narrative material that is thought to have existed before the first folktales were collected, since tales from ancient times may have been different from their present configurations and textures. Propp thought that just as astronomers could hypothecate the existence of stars never seen, so folklorists could postulate the existence of tales never collected.[33]

This assumes a great deal about astronomers and their discipline; is such optimism transferable to the study of human-generated stories? That issue may lie at the core of the matter of the Finnish method; we are more skeptical today about our potential to understand human behavior.

Notes

1 Bruce A. Rosenberg, "The Necessity of Unferth," *Journal of the Folklore Institute* 6 (1969): 50–60.
2 Stith Thompson, *The Folktale* (New York: Holt, Rinehart and Winston, 1946), p. 415.
3 Ibid.
4 Stith Thompson, *Motif-Index of Folk Literature*, 6 vols. (Bloomington: Indiana University Press, 1955–58).
5 Antti Aarne and Stith Thompson, *The Types of the Folktale*, F. F. Communications, no. 184 (Helsinki: Academia Scientiarum Fennica, 1964).
6 R. W. Chambers, *Beowulf: An Introduction to the Study of the Poem*, rpt. and rev. by C. L. Wrenn (Cambridge: University Press, 1959), pp. 365–81.
7 Kaarle Krohn, *Folklore Methodology*, trans. Robert L. Welsch (Austin: University of Texas Press, 1971), p. 136.
8 Thompson, *Folktale*, p. 437.
9 W. Edson Richmond, "Den Utreu Egtemann: A Norwegian Ballad and Formulaic Composition," *Norveg* 19 (1963): 75–76.
10 Gwyn Jones, *Kings, Beasts, and Heroes* (London: Oxford University Press, 1972), p. 24.
11 Friedrich Panzer, *Studien zur germanische Sagengeschichte.* 1: *Beowulf* (Munich: C. H. Beck, 1910).
12 Stith Thompson, "The Star Husband Tale" (1953), reprinted in Alan Dundes, *The Study of Folklore* (Englewood Cliffs: Prentice-Hall, 1965), p. 418.
13 Ibid.
14 Ibid., p. 419.
15 Ibid., p. 439.
16 Ibid., p. 440.
17 Ibid., p. 449.
18 Bruce A. Rosenberg and John Smith, "The Computer and the Finnish Historical-Geographical Method," *Journal of American Folklore* 84 (1974): 149–54.
19 Thompson, "Star Husband Tale," p. 450.
20 Thompson, *Folktale*, p. 444.
21 Listed in ibid., p. 436.
22 Vladimir Ja. Propp, *Morphology of the Folktale*, trans. Laurence Scott, ed. Louis A. Wagner (Austin: University of Texas Press, 1968), pp. 3 ff.
23 Thompson, *Folktale*, pp. 390, 447.

24 Ibid., p. 337 n. 21.

25 Bruce A. Rosenberg, *Custer and the Epic of Defeat* (University Park: Pennsylvania State University Press, 1975).

26 Robert A. Barakat, "The Bear's Son Tale in Northern Mexico," *Journal of American Folklore* 78 (1965): 331–34.

27 William E. Bettridge and Francis Lee Utley, "New Light on the Origins of the Griselda Story," *Texas Studies in Language and Literature* 13 (1971): 157.

28 Dudley Griffith, *The Origin of the Griselda Story* (Seattle: University of Washington Press, 1931); W. A. Cate, "The Problem of the Origin of the Griselda Story," *Studies in Philology* 29 (1932): 389–405.

29 Bettridge and Utley, "New Light on the Origins of the Griselda Story," p. 150.

30 Ibid., p. 168.

31 Wolfram Eberhard and Pertev N. Boratov, *Typen turkische Volksmärchen* (Wiesbaden: F. Steiner, 1953), pp. 333–43.

32 Bettridge and Utley, "New Light on the Origins of the Griselda Story," pp. 192, 193.

33 Propp, *Morphology of the Folktale*, p. 114.

II. Scholarship and Ideology

Scholarship and Ideology: Joseph Bédier's Critique of Romantic Medievalism

Hans Aarsleff

JOSEPH BÉDIER was a French medievalist who devoted his entire career to a relentless critique of the methods and foundations of nineteenth-century scholarship. This tradition's chief aspiration was the confident ascertainment of ultimate origins in a distant past beyond the earliest written records. The gap between documentation and essential beginnings was breached by faith in a few powerful romantic doctrines. The Homeric poems were not one man's work, but the late confluence of balladlike oral poetry which was the collective creation of the spirit of the folk. Armed with clouds of facts and evidence, philological expertise shrouded the speculative foundations and made them appear solid. The prestigious methods and procedures of positivism gave faith that the results had the quality of certain knowledge and established truth. In humanistic scholarship romanticism and positivism joined forces in the enterprise of system building.

It became Bédier's aim to break down the fortress of this romantic ideology by attacking it from the realist position to which he was committed. It was a long battle, but his efforts succeeded. Toward the end of his life he stated the basic problem in these words: "Unfortunately, if evidence is said to be 'the criterion of certainty,' the criterion of evidence has never been discovered. What is evident to Peter is not always so to Paul."[1] Though this may sound innocent, it means that objectivity itself is problematical. Issues are decided, not by facts alone, but by the interpretation of facts.[2] The results of scholarship have only relative value because they rest on timebound ideological commitments that have remained unexamined. In his critique of these commitments Bédier explored the relations between scholarship and ideology with exceptional vigor and acuteness. By ideology I mean the set of ruling beliefs, attitudes, and values that give emphases and thrust to scholarship in a direction that is not determined by the material under study. The very mildness of this version of ideology increases the value of the example. Since we still suffer the legacy of much that Bédier opposed, his critique and insights have not lost their relevance.

Bédier was not an outsider. He received thorough training in the solid tradition of medieval studies under the guidance of Gaston Paris, from whom he took over and initially accepted the basic views which he later rejected—change of mind and even rebellion seem to be characteristic of very great intellects. These views included the fundamental doctrines of romantic scholarship: the oral tradition and long reliable transmission of early poetry; the historicity of early epic poems such as *The Song of Roland* and the *Nibelungen*; the distant oriental origins of the European folktale such as the fabliau; and the acceptance of Karl Lachmann's principles for the editing of early texts. These closely related doctrines played a central role in the tradition, and Bédier wrote almost exclusively on them, at length and often. In Gaston Paris he also met the positivist credo which even today enjoys assured academic prestige. This credo looks on discontinuity as a sign of failure in the aims and practice of scholarship. It holds that the weighing of evidence and the disinterested pursuit of truth steadily bring us closer to incontestable and timeless truth with a capital T, that objectivity is unproblematic for men of sound method and right training, that differences of opinion and results are merely temporary anomalies, that there is no straying from the path and no going back to past positions. It trusts the scholarly expert and looks with suspicion on the crossing of established boundaries between the disciplines. These beliefs give confidence in the controlled production of knowledge, and both the process and the cumulative effect are not very different from the oral creation of poetry by the folk soul. The "esprit de système" was the collective scholarly soul of the nineteenth century. Anonymity was a virtue, too great ingenuity a risk, and individuality an impediment to progress.

The credo received classic formulation by Gaston Paris in words that Bédier quoted in the introduction to his doctoral dissertation:

> I profess absolutely and without reservation this doctrine, that scholarship has no other object than truth, and the truth for its own sake without concern for the consequences whether good or bad, welcome or unwelcome, that could result from this truth. Anyone who, in the facts he studies, in the conclusions he draws from them, permits himself the slightest dissimulation or even the smallest alteration is not worthy of having a place in the great laboratory where probity is a title of admission as indispensable as ability.[3]

Bédier remarked that these words could stand as the epigraph to Paris's entire life's work, and in this case he also made them his own, though he may well have read a somewhat different meaning into them. Bédier never failed to mention his teacher with affection and respect, but the quotations from him often assume a curious ambiguity that bares the profound disagreements under the surface of assent.[4] He might also have agreed with Paris that the scholar must bring to his studies "the disposition of mind that is taken for granted in the natural sciences,"[5] but he would never have used those words or the word "laboratory" in the passage above. The total absence of references to the model and authority of science is one of the basic features that distinguish Bédier's realism from the positivism of romantic scholarship. Bédier would not have agreed with Paris that "there are no indifferent, no useless truths,"[6] for he did not share the "nefarious" opinion that every object of scholarship merits equal attention, and he deplored the "common tendency of many erudite men to shut themselves up in their subject without further concern for its importance," while leaving the decision of its relevance and use to others "on the pretext of scholarly disinterestedness."[7] Having little respect for narrowly executed specialist studies because he thought they failed to examine the wider implications and underlying assumptions of their subjects, he boldly crossed borders into such fields as folklore, mythology, hagiography, and history where his contributions were acknowledged with admiration and respect.

Methodical skepticism informs all Bédier's writings except the earliest small publications, in which he showed himself to be the pupil of Gaston Paris. The first major work was his doctoral dissertation, published in 1893, entitled *Les fabliaux: Études de littérature et d'histoire littéraire du moyen âge*. In 1904, having then succeeded his teacher in the chair of medieval literature at the Collège de France, he began to lecture on the French national epics, then commonly known as "les chansons de geste" or "les épopées françaises." Out of these lectures grew his largest and most influential work with the provocative title *Les légendes épiques: Recherches sur la formation des chansons de geste*, totaling nearly two thousand pages and published in four volumes, two in 1908 and two in 1913. Finally, between 1913 and his death in 1938 he published a series of writings, including an edition of *The Song of Roland*, which made signal contributions to the problem of textual criticism and the editing of early texts. These writings were a critique of yet another romantic legacy, the editorial principles associated with the name of Karl Lachmann.[8] In his treatment of these three very large topics Bédier was the critic of Gaston Paris, and in every case he changed the scholarly landscape so completely that future work has been forced to acknowledge his innovations. And in all three topics the central problem was the romantic doctrine of origins. It is justified to see certain large similarities between Darwin's and Bédier's roles in science and humanistic studies. Both of them were deeply indebted to the traditions they revolutionized, both fought current theories about origins and faced the companion problem of essentialism, and both used a sort of alluring rhetoric to attain their ends. But before I turn to Bédier's major topics, let me begin with a booklength study he published around 1900, entitled "Chateaubriand en Amérique: Vérité ou fiction."[9]

This monograph is typical of Bédier's method and radical criticism. Chateaubriand was one of the great figures of French and European romanticism. In his youth in the early 1790s he traveled in America, an experience to which he returned again and again for the rest of his life in writings that gave exciting and vastly influential accounts of the lives of the Indians, of Niagara Falls and the Ohio and Mississippi rivers, and of Louisiana, Florida, the Blue Mountains, and indeed most of the continent east of the great river. These accounts were first written in some form during the 1790s and eventually appeared in *Atala* and *René* in 1801 and 1802, in *Les Natchez* in 1826, in *Voyage en Amérique* in 1827, and in *Mémoires d'outre-tombe* in 1849–50 after his death, but written between 1811 and 1841. The *Voyage* especially was often cited as a reliable source of knowledge about the country and its people, and to these works we largely owe the popular romanticized image of America before the great westward migrations. In his *History of the United States* George Bancroft cited the *Voyage* as a source.

Chateaubriand had covered more ground than any traveler in the New World. Here is his itinerary: from France to Baltimore and Philadelphia, then to New York and Boston and back to New York, from there via Albany to Niagara Falls followed by exploration of the Great Lakes, then via Pittsburgh down the Ohio and Mississippi rivers to Natchez followed by travels in Louisiana and Florida, and finally by way of Nashville and Knoxville to Salem (in Virginia) and from there via Chillicothe (in Ohio) back to Philadelphia, where he embarked for France. In the *Voyage* he allowed about sixteen months to cover these enormous distances, from April of 1791 to July of 1792. In the memoirs he changed the chronology somewhat, in part it seems because he had taken out a marriage license in St.-Malo soon after his return to France. He now said that he had left Philadelphia for France on December 10, 1791, a very substantial reduction of time, but he still kept silent about the date of his arrival at Baltimore. All the same, the memoirs still retained the itinerary of the *Voyage*. In December of 1827 an article in the *American Quarterly Review* raised questions which came to the attention of an obscure author who published his doubts in an equally obscure publication in Fribourg, Switzerland, in 1832. It remained unnoticed except by the voracious reader Sainte-Beuve, who tactfully suggested that something was wrong, but left it at that. It seems likely that

Bédier found the problem in Sainte-Beuve, whom he greatly admired as an unacademic writer with no penchant for system building. Chateaubriand's travels posed the sort of problem that interested Bédier. If it could be shown that they were all or mostly fiction, then one of the great romantic myths would be exploded.

Bédier went to work in his usual style, collecting evidence and facts from a wealth of sources. He pored over timetables and gazettes and even had contacts in America search out small details in local libraries. It is characteristic of his painstaking care that he at one point, in a footnote, cited fourteen travel accounts in which he had found nothing of relevance, to save future students the trouble of looking again.[10] What he found was this. Chateaubriand arrived in Baltimore on July 10, 1791, the date he had never given; thus he had had at most five months for his travels. We need not go into details, but the result is easily imagined. Chateaubriand never went beyond Niagara Falls, and even before that much was fiction, including a detailed account of a visit with George Washington in Philadelphia. The rest and major part was based on clever use of travel books, with romantic rewriting of their descriptions. Some of these books Chateaubriand had mysteriously mentioned here and there, but others he had not. It became evident to Bédier that "the poetical legend of the travels in America presents a perfect example of autosuggestion."[11] After many pages of parallel quotations from Chateaubriand and his sources, Bédier concluded: "It seems that to write he needed the suggestion of a page already written, which explains the information he gave about himself when he said that, unlike Rousseau, he could write only at his desk, pen in hand."[12] It was all a matter of poetic invention.

But while he had destroyed one of the great romantic myths of the century, Bédier had also achieved something positive: he had shifted the emphasis away from Chateaubriand's reliability onto his way of working with texts, to the literary and psychological aspects of writing, or in other words to the spontaneous act of composition and creation. The texts did not reveal a traveler or historian, but a poet. This critical insight was gained by "the technical resources of philology," but Bédier did not wish to suggest that philology was more than the prerequisite for criticism. Instead of depending on an apprenticeship in certain procedures of research, philology is "an intellectual habit, a turn of mind: it is essentially the will to observe before imagining, to observe before reasoning, to observe before drawing conclusions," but a critic worthy of the name is in addition "a philosopher, a historian, a poet, or in short Sainte-Beuve," who was great precisely because he combined the best qualities of the critic with respect for research and philology.[13] Academic scholars would have disagreed with Bédier on both counts, about the limits he set to philology and about the admiration for Sainte-Beuve, who had ridiculed romantic and German scholarship, for instance on the Homeric question. As an interlude between the two major works, the study of Chateaubriand is typical of Bédier's method and ideology.

Les fabliaux is a large work about the literary genre which Bédier unceremoniously called tales that make you laugh—he spurned the essentialist implications of definitions. In the preface to the second edition, published little more than a year after the first, Bédier could list fifteen reviews in France, England, the United States, Germany, and Italy. He also changed the irreverent tone of some portions. He had suggested, for instance, that some scholars would employ their time better in stamp collecting than in scholarship and spoken of a famous German scholar as the Messiah, of the introduction to his great work as the gospel, of his preface as the credo, of his pupils as the apostles, and of the journal that carried his views as the Acts of the Apostles.[14] All this was gone in the new edition, but irony and clever ambiguity remained the delightful vehicles of Bédier's radical skepticism.

It would have been normal for such a work—and especially for a dissertation—to stay strictly within the conventional limits of the subject without doubting the trusted foundations, but "scholarly disinterestedness" and the "idolum libri" were not among Bédier's habits of mind.[15] He explained his transgression in this typical passage: "Just as a phrase gains full importance only in its context, an animal in its class, a person in his historical milieu, so literary facts deserve study only in so far as they, to a greater or lesser degree, deal with more general groups of similar facts, and a monograph is not useful unless the author has clearly understood these relations."[16] As a consequence he devoted more than half of the work to a critique of the three major origins doctrines. The oldest of these held that the folktale was the common creation and inheritance of the Indo-European race; its chief advocates were the Grimm brothers, Adelbert Kuhn, and Max Müller, who was still very active, but this theory was now out of favor. The most recent theory was the creation of Edward Tylor and Andrew Lang within comparative anthropology and folklore, which was then causing much deserved excitement. Bédier had much sympathy for this unromantic theory, and his discussion of it shows his up-to-date and unorthodox interdisciplinary orientation. But Bédier directed his critique chiefly against the orientalist or Indianist theory, which then ruled in literary studies.

The orientalist doctrine postulated that all European tales originated with Buddhist preachers in India and that the tales had traveled westward by different modes of cultural contact in historical times, via Byzantium, pilgrimages, the Crusades, commerce, and the Moors and Jews in Spain. It had first been proposed to the scholarly world by the German orientalist Theodor Benfey in the introduction to a large collection of translated Indian fables and fairy tales. Never missing out on the latest in German learning, Gaston Paris had introduced this doctrine in France in the opening lecture to a course on the fabliau in December of 1874; he remained committed to this theory and expounded it often in later years.[17]

Bédier saw many obvious difficulties, taking great pains to show, for instance, that while he had found eleven themes of the fabliau in oriental sources, he could also locate five in classical literature, a result that was incompatible with the postulated lines of transmission in postclassical times. But the deeper problem was the inherent inability of all origins doctrines to supply documentation for the claims that were being made. To fill in this void, the proponents were forced to distinguish the real and original elements of the tales from the recent and fortuitous accessory accretions. By a sort of essentialist divination, Gaston Paris isolated "the elements that really constitute the tale" from the "accessory traits," which resolved the question of propagation.[18] Bédier answered that, on the contrary, whenever the "real elements" could be determined they were always found to belong to a particular civilization, marked by special customs and beliefs that pertained to a closely localized social group. There were Breton, German, Slavic, and Indian tales, all with their own ethnic bases, but there was no "privileged people that had received the mission to invent the tales that were forever destined to amuse humanity in the future."[19] He could not accept the factless ideology that lends "a certain vague mystique to the idea of popular creation" and attributes to it "an unknown force of collective, anonymous, impersonal invention that is different from the individual and literate invention" of later times.[20]

But let me quote the words of Bédier and his teacher. They were both eloquent, and I think it will become apparent that Bédier had a clever and at times somewhat malicious way with quotation. On one of the early pages of the introduction to *Les fabliaux*, he quoted Gaston Paris:

> Where did the fabliaux come from? Most of them have an oriental origin. By following the path that brought them to us, it is in India that we find the most distant source (even though a good number of them do not originally come from there but have been borrowed from even older literatures). Buddhism, the friend of exempla and parables, collected these tales and also invented some excellent ones. They have come into Europe

by two principal routes, via Byzantium which got them from Syria and
Persia, directly imported from India, and via the Arabs by contact in two
places, in Spain and in Syria at the time of the Crusades.[21]

Paris's spatial and temporal panorama is rather like a breathtaking fantasy. Bédier continued immediately with this characteristic passage:

> Need I say that for a long time the author of this volume did not doubt
> that this was the truth? This theory had in its favor not merely the quali-
> ties of beautiful systems, of amplitude and simplicity, not only the au-
> thority of glorious names . . . but also the irresistible force of current ideas,
> of anonymous ideas received in youth without knowing from whom, from
> everywhere and never discussed. The system was safe, it seemed. After
> so many scholars, there was no more to do than to retrace again the pres-
> tigious journey to the Orient: to travel with each fabliau from a French
> provincial tavern, where a jongleur had rhymed, to Grenada where some
> Spanish Jew had translated it from the Hebrew into Latin; to carry it all
> the way to the court of the caliphs who were Charlemagne's contempo-
> raries; and then, still higher, in Persia into the presence of the Sassanian
> princes, to stop at last on the shores of the Ganges where some religious
> mendicant, preaching the four sublime verities, told it to the masses.[22]

Some pages later Bédier closed the brief survey of his own argument
with these words:

> In short, the oriental theory is true when it is reduced to saying: "India
> produced large collections of tales; it has made its contribution to the
> dissemination of a large number, whether orally or in writing." But these
> are claims that fit any country whatsoever. It is false when it gives India
> a primary role, when India is called "the reservoir, the source, the vagina,
> the hearth, the homeland of tales." This means that the orientalist system
> dies at the precise moment when it becomes a system.[23]

Neither facts nor argument could save the orientalist doctrine. Against
the inherently essentialist monogenicism of the romantic origins theory, Bédier asserted the polygenesis of tales.

Nearly three hundred large pages later came the final conclusion.
In so far as a tale is universal and has found wide acceptance, it belongs
not to history but to psychology, and the only question it raises is about
the universal psychological conditions that have made its popularity
possible beyond its first ethnic locale. To drive home his point, Bédier
used several amusing analogies. The history of art, for instance, can
study the history of styles of particular doors and openings, but the
naked idea of door does not allow the question of origin. Similarly,

philology can study the word *lectum* (which means couch or bed) in the Romance languages and trace it back to other languages, but "it is pointless to seek the origin of the idea of lying down, for it is universal. Likewise, for tales that are as unbounded in space and time as lying down, it is pointless to seek the origin."[24] This is an argument about what Ernst Gombrich has called "essentialist criticism,"[25] and it is not surprising that essentialism is the fundamental issue. The romantic scholarly tradition had folded the psychological and cultural dimensions into the speculative quest for origins, almost as if it was in Adamic pursuit of the ultimate archetype, finding it not in the Garden of Eden but in an idealized, half-real world from which it had come down to us along the channels so confidently mapped out by scholars. Only the method of philological optimism could have remained deaf to the fundamental questions, but the deafness was a sort of nearly congenital idealism. An altogether different ideology was required to pierce the silence. Bédier knew that Gaston Paris would not agree. "He believes it is true," wrote Bédier. "The study of the facts has led me to contrary conclusions . . . I do not express them without trembling; but I express them all the same."[26] There has since been universal agreement that Bédier decisively demolished the orientalist doctrine. The book was also accepted as a significant contribution to the study of folklore.

Bédier was aware that scholarship was not supposed to be merely negative, for it was—and is—part of the academic credo that scholarship which has gained acceptance is like another addition to the firm foundations. Progress keeps adding to the same fortress; tearing it down or beginning to build another structure somewhere else on other foundations cannot be progress. But Bédier defended himself boldly. Here is what he said, again in a very characteristic passage:

> If at the end of these long discussions I am blamed for their too frequent quality of negative polemics, if I am told that scholarship has no business with this agnosticism, I protest with all the energy and sincerity I can muster. It is false to say that refutation is sterile. A refutation is fruitful when it reduces error to nothing. There are, on the other hand, affirmations that are sterile and harmful: the Indianist theory is one of them. There are wrongly formulated problems on which students exhaust their vital forces in total waste, and the problem of the origin and propagation of tales is one of them. There are pointless researches and it is good to say so firmly, for the number of workers in each generation is not so large that they can be permitted to go astray, lured by the prestige of useless scholarship. It is said that each system is good in its time, and that is a great truth, for each system is based on a hypothesis and nothing except hypotheses cause the desire to collect and group facts. But when the group-

ing of facts destroys the very hypothesis which directed the research, we must have the courage to give it up. To demonstrate its falseness, even without replacing it by another hypothesis, is a not merely negative result. True, it is not to make scholarship progress [faire avancer la science]; but if scholarship [la science] is stuck in the mud, it is to get it unstuck. . . . Soon others will come who will move the study of popular traditions away from the swamp in which it was mired down. If we have helped to dry out this swamp, it is enough; it is already a positive result.[27]

Bédier was all of twenty-seven years old when this was published. It was surely potent stuff to use the word swamp about one of the busiest territories of European scholarship. All the same, Bédier made his academic way without difficulty, but then the École Normale (where he was a student, 1883–86) and the Collège de France were not ordinary academic places, and Gaston Paris was an extraordinary scholar and man. Andrew Lang concluded an admiring review with these words: "His work is dedicated to Gaston Paris; it may not convert him from 'Orientalism,' but it must surely convince him that he has not wasted his labors teaching a pupil who is industrious, accurate, and *spirituel*."[28]

When Bédier began to lecture on the Old French epic, it had been the object of an enormous body of scholarship that was built on the same doctrines that he had criticized in *Les fabliaux*. The problem was again the gap between the texts and the postulated origins. It was agreed that no text was earlier than the second half of the eleventh century and that most of the poems were composed during the following centuries, but since the events they described pertained to Merovingian and Carolingian times several hundred years earlier, there was a strong temptation to believe that their few ascertainable historical elements confirmed their general reliability. The battle of Roncevaux is dated 778, but *The Song of Roland* is some three hundred years younger. Since the facts of history could not possibly have been preserved so long in the absence of written records, the oral tradition was once more invoked to close the gap. Among the slightly different solutions, the best known was that of Gaston Paris, which Bédier made the chief object of his critique. Paris argued that short poems—"des chants lyrico-épiques" or historical ballads—had been composed by witnesses at the time of or soon after the events and preserved orally until they flowed into the later epics. Thus the historicity of the epics appeared firmly established even in the absence of factual evidence. Léon Gautier, who before Bédier had written the largest work on the subject, maintained in 1896 that the epic "is in all nations the primitive form of history; it is history before the historians." The historicity of these epic poems was also accepted by professional historians on the authority of their colleagues in literary history.[29]

Bédier's immensely detailed and penetrating examination of the primary literature, including all the epics, did not turn up anything that supported the arguments of his predecessors. The system collapsed once its ideological foundations had been exposed. Much like historical novels, the epics were imaginative works of fiction created long after the events they purported to portray by poets who found their matter along the pilgrim routes. They had received it from clerics, and their aim was not to record history but to call attention to shrines and holy places along these routes. Bédier could not accept the principle "that nothing could be fictive in a chanson de geste and that no one could be so deprived of imagination as a poet."[30] He was baffled by a "method of investigation, which, beginning with a simple fictive work, knew how to restore the dignity of history to apparent fictions and discover the themes of lost epics with surprising precision." The best epics were the creations of good poets, for "a masterpiece begins and ends with its author," not with the "collective, unconscious, anonymous forces" that were used to replace the individual poet.[31] Like the best French linguists of his time, including Michel Bréal and Ferdinand de Saussure, Bédier accepted uniformitarianism as the fundamental axiom in the human sciences.[32] The romantics, on the contrary, had built their doctrines on the assumption that creation in the past followed processes that were radically different from anything that can be observed in the present. *Les légendes épiques* performed a sustained deconstruction of the origins doctrine as well as of the historicity that was based on it. The question was not the origins but, as the subtitle announced, the formation of the old epic poems.

Bédier paid much attention to the history of scholarship, and it is easy to understand why. Having broken with the tradition he had absorbed in his youth, he wished to know its sources. His writings frequently devote quite long passages to this subject, but the most extended treatment came suddenly in the middle of the third volume of *Les légendes épiques* where, in connection with *The Song of Roland*, he launched into a brilliant hundred-page history of the tradition from Herder, F. A. Wolf, the Grimms, and Lachmann to Pio Rajna and Gaston Paris. His teacher's theory of cantilena or "chants lyrico-épiques" was a version of Wolf's and Lachmann's lieder theory, which they had applied both to Homer and the *Nibelungen*, and which Bédier could show had been introduced into France around 1830. He cited a lecture by the old Revolutionary politician Pierre Daunou, who in 1824 had taken it for granted that the epics are the products of their times, of the Crusades and of the new chivalric spirit that began around 1100. Daunou's outlook was entirely that of the eighteenth century, and he was, incidentally, the patron of the young Sainte-Beuve.

Not surprisingly, Bédier found the source in Germany, "in that patriotic mystique which gave birth, during the *Sturm und Drang* and later in the romantic period, to German philology, to German scholarship, and especially to the nineteenth-century systems on the origin of language, the formation of myths, and the formation of the national epics."[33] It was this tradition that since 1800 had made the Middle Ages the most important object of literary and historical studies because much more than learned and academic matters was at stake. The sense of national identity, even of legitimacy and claims to autonomy, demanded possession of a past that was one's own, the older the better. Treasured historical heroes would pale into shadowy figures if the historicity of the early literature was drawn into doubt. Romantic scholarship gave the study of the Middle Ages a vital relevance to the sense of nationhood in the present. In Scandinavia, Danes and Norwegians fought scholarly battles over national heroes and great historic events, and when the break in northern romantic historicism came, Bédier appears to have played an important role. Only this present relevance of its learned subject can explain the astonishing popularity of *Les légendes épiques*.[34]

Owing to this popularity, Bédier could publish 44 percent of the entire work, or some eight hundred pages, in various journals before these chapters appeared in the four volumes. He strategically placed them in several kinds of journals: six chapters in journals of wide and general circulation (*Revue des deux mondes, Revue du mois, Revue de Paris*), seven in the two most important French historical journals (*Revue historique, Annales du Midi*), and five in journals of romance philology (*Romania, Romanische Forschungen*). The record of reviews is equally astounding, and even the journal publications were reviewed. Between 1907 and 1916 there were according to my no doubt incomplete count at least fifty-eight reviews in France, Germany, Italy, the United States, Holland, Belgium, Sweden, and Norway. They appeared in a broad spectrum of journals both general and specialist in major disciplines, and most of them were long and written by very prominent scholars. It is safe to say that both the publication record and the mass of reviews have no parallel.

With very few exceptions the reviews agreed that Bédier's achievement was stupendous. Let me cite a few passages by two historians, the first by Charles-Victor Langlois: "I believe that M. Bédier has expelled romanticism from one of the last positions it occupied in scholarship. That is a service of the first order."[35] In the same year, Ferdinand Lot wrote this assessment of the entire work:

> After reading this series of studies, one reflects with astonishment on the success of the traditional theory of the formation of the chansons de geste, which for nearly a century has imposed itself, not only on philologists and literary historians, but on historians *tout court*. . . . This theory is only a particular example of the romantic and mystical conception of the development of humanity which, born in Germany toward the end of the eighteenth century, has enchanted Europe throughout the nineteenth century. The scholars who today pass their time reconstructing so-called primitive poems are still the victims of this theory, though unaware of it.

Lot later continued that Bédier "has given us more than facts, more than theories, namely, a method. It is an odd thing that this method is the historical method, which consists in explaining the works in terms of their milieu. And it is curious that it is a philologist who has had the idea of applying it in that fashion. This is the work of a master, undoubtedly the most perfect in the literature of the French Middle Ages."[36] Many reviews pointed out that the long investigation of the historicity and formation of the epic poems was carried out in the spirit of *Les fabliaux*. Like that work, *Les légendes épiques* was acknowledged to make weighty contributions to other disciplines, in this case, as we have just seen, to history and also to hagiography, a subject that was then enjoying great attention and success.

Either one of Bédier's two works on medieval literature would have been sufficient to establish a great scholarly reputation, but he did not stop there. From the beginning of his career around 1890 until his death in 1938, he devoted a series of writings to the genealogical method of stemmatic reconstruction that is generally associated with Karl Lachmann.[37] This method was based on the axiom that two copyists working independently of each other do not make the same errors, which entails that manuscripts that repeat errors of another manuscript can be discarded, leaving only the representatives of different versions which then point to the ultimate original or archetype of the text. The results can be graphed on a family tree or *stemma codicum*, which with seemingly mathematical accuracy will define the task of the editor. This method was first applied to a French medieval text by Gaston Paris in his edition of *La vie de Saint Alexis* in 1872, one of the achievements for which he was rightly admired. In 1878 Léon Gautier succinctly stated the aim: "The principle that rules the entire question can be stated in a few words: When we undertake to publish a chanson de geste, we must seek to reconstruct the original text. In other words, the textual critic's task is to recover the form of the work at the moment it left the hands of the author."[38] Once more it was a question of undocumented origins.

This all sounds very safe and scholarly, but Bédier was not so sure. Here briefly is what happened. In 1890 he did an edition of the early French poem *Le lai de l'ombre* according to the Lachmann method, in which he postulated that there were only two manuscript families to work with, or in other words his stemma was bipartite.[39] In a review Gaston Paris argued that the stemma should have been tripartite, a claim taken so seriously by Bédier that he continued to work on the problem. When in 1913 he did another edition of the same poem, he had in the meantime from various editions collected eighty stemma of which seventy-eight were bipartite. From this he deduced the "surprising law" that stemma on which editions were based overwhelmingly tended to operate with only two manuscript families. He even mischievously suggested that scholars who wrote about editions without actually doing them usually created tripartite stemma, and he wondered whether their stemma would have remained tripartite if they had actually done the editions they criticized. The reason, he thought, was that it is much more difficult to work with a tripartite stemma than with one that merely has dual branching, but at the same time he did not find it likely that the tripartite stemma was more plausible than the bipartite. He therefore offered this interpretation of the "surprising law." Since he could not believe that binary division was a fact about text reproduction and transmission, the explanation must lie elsewhere. He saw only one possibility: we are dealing with phenomena that occur in the minds of editors, and in that case an indeterminate but perhaps considerable number of our editions may be based on illusory classifications. Thus Bédier once again cast doubt on the procedures and objectivity of scholarship; what had been presented as historical facts was a projection of illusions that had been shrouded in the deceivingly objective codification of details.[40]

In his new edition of the poem in 1913 he abandoned the Lachmann method and did not attempt a classification of the manuscripts, not because it was too difficult to make one, but precisely because it was too easy. He based his text on a single manuscript of the seven he had because he found that it was on the whole, in purely pragmatic terms, the simplest, most reasonable, and most coherent, with good French grammar and consistent spelling, or in short the manuscript "one is the least inclined to correct." He did not choose it because he felt it was the closest to the original, for he did not presume to know or be able to divine what the original would have been like. Intuition and personal judgment had replaced the old scholarly, objective rigmarole.[41]

In the edition of *The Song of Roland* and later in a series of articles, Bédier argued more strongly along the same lines. Except for the very few emendations that he considered obviously necessary—twenty-five or at most thirty—he followed the Oxford text, and he did not, like several other editors, convert its Anglo-Norman language into proper French, for though "certainly very pure," that would be to put it into a form we do not know it ever had, "a grammarian's language too pure ever to have been spoken anywhere."[42] On the penultimate page of this long article, published after his death, he said he hoped that others would agree that "in matters of textual criticism one must not make it a point of honor to have an answer to everything and that the great secret is, on the contrary, to know where to draw the line that marks the limit of our capacity to know. To say these things is not, far from it, to praise a lazy method."[43] For Bédier the problems raised by the Lachmann method of textual restitution, and by the doctrine of oral tradition behind our oldest texts, were similar. In both cases the trusted tradition of technical scholarship had greatly overestimated its powers to reach ultimate origins by divining the true essence that existed in the beginning. To all this there was no solution except respect for the integrity of the texts and admission that we cannot know all. Since the criterion of evidence has never been found, it is not helpful to say that evidence is the criterion of certainty. Human fallibility cannot be remedied by philological optimism and positivist manipulations.

It is not easy to know what inner springs activated Bédier to engage in his radical critiques of three major creations of nineteenth-century scholarship—so major that they are international. The problem would be simpler if he had shown pronounced religious and political leanings, if, for instance, he had been anticlerical in the French radical tradition. It is said that he was an agnostic in religion, but his works do not give the slightest sign that this stance was more than a private commitment. In this respect he differs from many of his contemporaries among both historians and students of literature. His outlook was narrowly French, and he is said not to have found it possible that one could genuinely understand the literature of another language. He obviously felt little affinity for German thought and scholarship, but he did not except incidentally take the opportunity to oppose Pio Rajna's theory of the Germanic origin of the French epics, though he left no doubt that he rejected it. His dismissal of the oral tradition and historicity took care of that theory without additional effort. It would be easy to cite the familiar Cartesian doubt, but that of course was equally available to other French scholars who did not apply it to the romantic systems.

So far everything about Bédier is neutral except his work. He was a scholars' scholar, respecting all the canons of the trade. Still, he under-mined the foundations of scholarship, and it is this remarkable act that makes his case so interesting, for he was fully aware of what he was doing. This awareness shows in all his writings, in many ways, but most obviously in his sarcastic way with quotations, in his revealing surveys of the history of scholarship, and in his rhetoric. A scholar, so the credo has it, must have faith in objectivity, yet Bédier clearly did not. He was tireless with facts, but since there was no good match between evidence and certainty, he rested his case chiefly on argument about the non-objective portion of scholarship, that is, about the ideology.

Bédier stressed the importance of the milieu in human affairs. It was this steady emphasis that saved his critique of historicity from becom-ing unpatriotic. What he took away he paid back in better coin by mak-ing the old poems the artistic creations of individual French poets. His own milieu explains in part the profile he presented. It included Gaston Paris and the École Normale, which he left with the *agrégation* in 1886. Late in life he praised the freedom of intellectual investigation he had enjoyed there.[44] Throughout the nineteenth century this eminent insti-tution kept alive the spirit of the eighteenth century; it was closed for periods of years during the early decades of the century, and at least until the 1860s its graduates were generally suspected of dangerous radi-calism. But Gaston Paris also had a share in Bédier's intellectual forma-tion, although an ambiguous one, as reflected in this passage: "From him we have all learned the scrupulous and patient but independent and bold research into what is true; the obedience of the worker, not to an external principle of authority, but to facts and to the consequences he discerns in them; the defiance of self, great care in drawing conclu-sions, but, also, when he believes the facts have spoken, the honesty that lies in saying again what they have said."[45] Paris, however, was a man of systems, much wedded to German thought and scholarship, but uncritical of the idealism that was their essence. Gaston Paris was a positivist, Bédier was not.

He had another quality that was the mark of his time. A French historian who attended the École Normale in the 1870s wrote in his memoirs that his youth was the time when realism — le *réalisme* — came into its own as the reaction against romanticism. The century had "de-voted its activity to the question of origins," there was much admiration for "Germanic methods," but the great minds of the day were commit-ted to the spirit of the eighteenth century; "revered by the intellectual public . . . they had broken with romanticism and prepared the com-ing of 'réalisme.'"[46] First introduced in art and art criticism in the 1850s, *réalisme* had by the 1880s become the banner that signaled opposition to romanticism in scholarship. Bédier called himself a realist. Early in the first volume of *Les légendes épiques* he wrote about his admired predecessor on the path he was entering, the Austrian scholar Philip August Becker: "He has made a breach in the romantic stronghold of systems which I batter in turn. If I had not known his books, would I by myself have arrived at the realist position of mind which the reader will see me adopt?"[47] Some pages later he again paid tribute to Becker: "He observes and thinks for himself; he forces you to think. He has the taste for the concrete fact and for realist explanations, combined at the same time with the power to change ideas into facts and to connect ideas systematically. In his robust and luminous books one admires both his great realist sense and his gifts of combination."[48]

Realism was defined by its determination to question the entire romantic tradition in scholarship. It was an attitude, a frame of mind, an ideology. It was not a method. Realism made it plain that romanticism was also an ideology, while romanticism itself had thought it was the truth because it was the mother of modern scholarship, of learned specialization, and of academic institutionalization. With help from positivism, how could one doubt that the product would be truth beyond question, for all time? It has caused and still causes vast confusion in intellectual history and in the history of scholarship to believe that romanticism was overcome and superseded by positivism. This confusion seems to be caused by the odd equation of positivism with natural science and by the still odder belief that scholarship progresses the more "scientific" it becomes. Positivism was a sort of method; it was like the heavy curtains and draperies that shrouded the shape of rooms. Bédier called it seductive; he wanted common sense, clarity, openness, and excitement. For him scholarship was fallible, like humanity; and it could never be more than the product of its time and milieu.

Toward the end of the long history of scholarship in the third volume of *Les légendes épiques*, Bédier concluded that "the theory of the ancient and popular origins of the chansons de geste" had exhausted its own usefulness. "In every epoch general hypotheses must necessarily be formed, for without them erudite researches would come to a halt and fall into senility. Though unaware of it, the scholar who believes himself most impervious to the ideas of theorists works only by their impulse, and the ideas of the theorists are in turn determined, or at the very least conditioned, by the most profound currents, by the directive tendencies, by the great movements of the spirit of the time. A few general ideas intimately embedded in the spirit of the nineteenth century have been necessary and sufficient to create an entire movement of admirable and learned researches," which had been advanced by scholars of the first rank, "but it would be wrong if their ideas should come to be reputed untouchable; on the contrary, what matters is that they do not become immobile; only death is changeless."[49] All systems have their time, and Bédier did not expect his own work to be an exception in the flow of time. It is not accidental that Bédier agreed with Claude Bernard, who had written: "Though I recognize the superiority of great figures, I nevertheless think that in the particular and general influence they have on the sciences, they are always necessarily more or less a *function of their time*."[50]

One cannot write about these things without asking a question which I hope has already occurred to the reader: Does the story of Bédier have any relevance to our present situation in academic scholarship? I believe the answer is yes. It is a telling symptom that the history of scholarship enjoys little favor with scholars, who tend to believe that they themselves best know the true history of their subjects. It is not nice to say and not comfortable to know that continuity is not assured, that objectivity is rare, that past positions can be better than present truth, that progress is an illusion—or in short that scholarship itself is not immune to ideology, that it may suffer its own self-inflicted disabilities. The sciences take a much more relaxed view of history, but when scientists were the guardians of their own history, they wrote textbook preface history. The world of scholarship in the humanities is rigidly positivistic. This view is prominent among deans and academic administrators, who with a sort of bureaucratic positivism guard the disciplinary boundaries that are believed to ensure the production of knowledge and of permanent truth. It is pleasant and even flattering to think that scholarship is about truth. The trouble is that much truth is not interesting, especially not when it is pursued for its own sake. But it is the end of things to be interesting, to be worth talking about, and to create good argument. Interesting argument is the life of scholarship. In the history of scholarship few have been so miraculously lively and interesting as Joseph Bédier; and what would his life and our enjoyment have been had he not had both an ideology to fight against and another to fight for?

Notes

1 "De l'édition princeps de la *Chanson de Roland* aux éditions les plus récentes. Nouvelles remarques sur l'art d'établir les anciens textes. Deuxième article," *Romania* 64 (1938): 160 [145–244].

2 *Les fabliaux: Études de littérature populaire et d'histoire littéraire du moyen âge*, 4th ed. (Paris: Champion, 1925), p. 165: "La question de l'origine des

contes est, comme toute question historique, non pas précisément 'une question de fait,' mais 'une question d'interprétation des faits.' Ce n'est qu'une nuance, mais, seule, la seconde de ces formules admet que l'homme soit faillible." The so-called fourth edition is the same as the second edition (1895).

3   Ibid., p. 23. When Bédier in 1904 began to lecture on the Old French epic at the Collège de France, his opening lecture was a tribute to Gaston Paris. There he quoted the same passage; see Kr. Nyrop, ed., *Philologie française*, 2d ed. (Copenhagen: Gyldendal, 1915), p. 30 [25–53]. Paris's words occurred in an opening lecture at the Collège de France, delivered on December 8, 1870 during the siege of Paris, on the stirring subject "La Chanson de Roland et la nationalité française," printed in Gaston Paris, *La poésie du moyen âge: Leçons et lectures*, 1st ser., 5th ed. (Paris: Hachette, 1903), pp. 87–118 (with this passage on p. 90). In the same lecture, Paris made an example of the revival of German national sentiment and Jacob Grimm. The Germans "ont appuyé en partie la régénération de leur nationalité sur leur ancienne poésie. Jacob Grimm n'est pas seulement le plus grand philologue de l'Allemagne dans ce domaine: il sera toujours cité comme un des véritables fondateurs de la nationalité allemande moderne. . . . Nous n'avons pas eu de Jacob Grimm: il ne s'est pas trouvé chez nous un homme qui joignît à ce degré le génie scientifique à l'amour intense, profond, enfantin de la patrie." Ibid., p. 113.

4   When Pio Rajna in a review had said that Bédier was disrespectful toward Gaston Paris, Bédier indignantly rejected the imputation. See Bédier, "Réponse à M. P. Rajna," *Annales du Midi* 22 (1910): 538–552.

5   Also quoted by Bédier in the lecture on Gaston Paris. See Nyrop, *Philologie française*, p. 29.

6   Cf. ibid., p. 30.

7   Bédier, *Fabliaux*, p. 1.

8   See Sebastiano Timpanaro, *Die Entstehung der Lachmannschen Methode*, 2d enl. and rev. ed. (Hamburg: Helmut Buske Verlag, 1971). Timpanaro shows that Lachmann was not the only originator of the method that is associated with his name.

9   First published in *Revue d'histoire littéraire de la France* 6 (1899): 501–32; 7 (1900): 59–121; a polemical addition came the following year, ibid., 8 (1901): 80–109. The monograph was reprinted in Bédier, *Études critiques* (Paris: Armand Colin, 1903), pp. 125–294 (without the polemical essay). The next in this collection was slightly revised. I am using the original version, but refer also to *Études critiques*.

10   Bédier, "Chateaubriand en Amérique," p. 59; *Études critiques*, p. 195.

11   Bédier, "Chateaubriand en Amérique," p. 532; *Études critiques*, p. 192.

12   Bédier, "Chateaubriand en Amérique," pp. 119–20; *Études critiques*, p. 291.

13   Bédier, Avant-propos in *Études critiques*, pp. vii–xi.

14   See Per Nykrog, *Les fabliaux*, new ed. (1957; Geneva: Droz, 1973), p. xxxii.

15   Bédier, *Fabliaux*, p. 8.

16   Ibid., pp. 1–2.

17 Gaston Paris, *Les contes orientaux dans la littérature française du moyen âge* (Paris: Franck, 1875).

18 Bédier, *Fabliaux*, p. 12. Cf. this essentialist passage in which Gaston Paris talks about the French nation as a mixture of diverse elements (Celtic, Germanic, Romance). To know this mixture "dans son essence, il faut séparer ces éléments hétérogènes; il faut apprécier, autant que nous le permettent nos instruments imparfaits, la part de chacun d'eux dans le composé que nous nous efforçons de connaître." From a lecture delivered at the Collège de France on December 7, 1869, "Les origines de la littérature française," in Paris, *Poésie du moyen âge*, p. 44 [41–86].

19 Bédier, *Fabliaux*, p. 15.

20 Ibid., p. 63.

21 Ibid., p. 3.

22 Ibid., p. 4.

23 Ibid., p. 11.

24 Ibid., pp. 280–81.

25 Ernst Gombrich, *Norm and Form* (London: Phaidon, 1966), p. 88.

26 Bédier, *Fabliaux*, p. 23.

27 Ibid., p. 285.

28 *Saturday Review of Politics, Literature, Science, and Art*, 76 (1893), 272.

29 Léon Gautier, "L'épopée nationale," in L. Petit de Julleville, ed., *Histoire de la langue et de la littérature française des origines à 1900*. Vol. 1: *Moyen âge (des origines à 1500)*, part 1 (Paris: Armand Colin, 1896), p. 49 [49–70]. Gautier's words are a quotation from Godefroid Kurth.

30 Joseph Bédier, *Les légendes épiques: Recherches sur la formation des chansons de geste*, 4 vols., (Paris: Champion, 1908–13), 1:202; hereafter cited as *LE*.

31 *LE* 1:222; *LE* 3:450: "Mais ne tombons pas dans les théories qui veulent partout mettre des forces collectives, inconscientes, anonymes, à la place de l'individu. Un chef-d'oeuvre commence à son auteur et finit par lui." Cf. 4:220: "Ils ne veulent pas que ce roman soit un roman. Il faut, pour le bien de la théorie, qu'il remonte en droite ligne à des 'événements' de l'époque mérovingienne, à des chants carolingiens ou mérovingiens, 'issus de ces événements eux-mêmes.'"

32 On Bréal and Bédier, see Hans Aarsleff, *From Locke to Saussure: Essays on the Study of Language and Intellectual History* (Minneapolis: University of Minnesota Press, 1982), p. 392. See also index under "uniformitarianism."

33 *LE* 3:215–16.

34 On Scandinavian history and Bédier, see the brilliant essay by Rolf Arvidsson, "Källkritisk radikalism och litteraturhistorisk forskning: Lauritz Weibull, Henrik Schück och Joseph Bédier," *Scandia* 37 (1971): 287–339, with résumé in French, pp. 335–39.

35 *Revue critique des livres nouveaux* 8 (1913): 231.

36 *Romania* 42 (1913): 593–98.

37 On editorial practice and its history, see Timpanaro, *Entstehung der Lach-mannschen Methode*, and E. J. Kenney, *The Classical Text* (Berkeley: University of California Press, 1974). There is a good survey by Kenney under "Textual Criticism" in *Encyclopaedia Britannica*, 15th ed. (1974), *Macro-paedia*, 18: 189–95.

38 Quoted by Bédier in "De l'édition princeps de la *Chanson de Roland* aux éditions les plus récentes. Nouvelles remarques sur l'art d'établir les anciens textes. Troisième article," *Romania* 64 (1938): 521 [489–521].

39 See Joseph Bédier, ed., *Le lai de l'ombre par Jean Renart* (Paris: Firmin-Didot, 1913), p. vii.

40 Ibid., p. xxvii.

41 Ibid., p. xli.

42 Bédier, "De l'édition princeps de la *Chanson de Roland* aux éditions les plus récentes . . . Troisième article," p. 492.

43 Ibid., p. 520.

44 Joseph Bédier, "De l'édition princeps de la *Chanson de Roland* aux éditions les plus récentes. Nouvelles remarques sur l'art d'établir les anciens textes. Premier article," *Romania* 63 (1937): 434 [433–469].

45 Bédier, *Fabliaux*, p. 23.

46 Gabriel Hanotaux, *Mon temps*, 4 vols. (Paris: Plon, 1933–47), 2:116; 4:128; 2:499.

47 *LE* 1: Avant-propos, p. 16.

48 *LE* 1:15. On the revival of eighteenth-century thought, see Aarsleff, *From Locke to Saussure*, pp. 308–12.

49 *LE* 3:287–88.

50 Aarsleff, *From Locke to Saussure*, p. 311.

Ideology and Scholarship

Terry Eagleton

THE CONCEPT of ideology is often roughly defined as a set of ideas which, by distorting or mystifying social reality, contribute to reproducing the power of a dominant social class. There are at least two problems with this definition of ideology. For one thing, ideologies are by no means always the property of *dominant* classes. What of revolutionary or radical ideologies such as Jacobinism, the beliefs of the Diggers or the Narodniks? For another thing, not all ideological statements are distorting. The Queen of England, for all I know, is a charming woman, but even if this is true the enunciation of it is almost always likely to be ideological. Not all ideological statements are false, just as not all false statements are ideological. We might conclude, then, that ideology is less an epistemological matter than a question of the actual effects of certain discourses, true or false, within the power relations of particular societies. Yet an important tradition of thought in the theory of ideology has in fact assumed that distortion, systematic exclusion, or mystification of some kind *is* central to the workings of ideologies. Is this tradition merely mistaken, or is there some truth to be rescued from it?

A broader definition of ideology, avoiding both of the problems I have touched on, would be simply: the articulation of discourse and power. This definition is neutral on the issue of what kind of power is at stake — the power, for example, of a dominant or subordinate social group or class — and neutral also on the epistemological question. Its limitation as a definition is that it sidesteps these questions only at the cost of expanding the concept of ideology to the point where it might be thought to lose all political cutting edge. Is every imbrication of discourse and power usefully described as ideological? Are the cries of children struggling over a ball in the street ideological? We might argue, to avoid this embarrassment, that power conflicts are illuminatingly classifiable as ideological only when they somehow engage issues and institutions which we judge, from some political standpoint, to be centrally significant to a particular social formation. A domestic quarrel over what to have for breakfast is not *necessarily* ideological, but if it engages questions of power relations between the sexes then it becomes so. The advantage of such a position is that it assumes that any proposition or conflict whatsoever *can* be ideological, but that whether it is so or not is a contextual or conjunctural matter. Ideology is less an immanent quality of particular kinds of language than a question of language's contextual effects. Not even the statement "Men are superior to woman" is inherently ideological, since it might always be deployed in an ironic or sardonic context which demystifies rather than deludes. And not even the statement "Pass the salt" is inherently nonideological, since one can always dream up contexts in which it becomes a part of centrally significant power struggles.

Some people may feel uneasy with the phrase "centrally significant power struggles," suspecting that it rudely preempts the question of what is central and what is not. Perhaps it is merely a move to marginalize conflicts which have not classically been recognized as important, but which in fact are so. There is no need to feel uneasy, however, as all you have to do is argue for the importance of any power struggle you regard as vital. If you can show that the squabble of children over a ball dramatically foregrounds an antagonism or contradiction of more than ephemeral importance, then you have shown that it is ideological. The problem will be to prevent the concept from stretching to the point where it becomes simply useless or redundant, as has happened with much poststructuralist thinking about power. The Marxist objection to the poststructuralist "expansionistic" concept of power is not that it is false but that it is quite often politically unhelpful: it gives us no indication of whether children's quarrels are more or less important than, say, the struggles of revolutionary nationalist movements. Poststructuralism, at least in some of its variants, is shy of such discriminations because they appear "hierarchical," just as some left-wing thinking about culture is coy about branding Donald Duck as inferior to Mayakovsky for fear of appearing elitist. It is probably unwise to enter into lengthy theoretical argument with someone who views revolutionary nationalism as no more important than a fight over a ball; you just have to ask him whether he is joking. Perhaps, by dint of sufficient irony and ridicule, you might in the end persuade him to become a properly hierarchical thinker.

The importance of the term ideology is, so to speak, performative: it *achieves* something. The term is less a description of immanent devices or qualities than a practical means of discriminating between antagonisms which we judge for the present of more than purely local or casual significance, and those which for the present we do not. This, I would emphasize, does not rule out the possibility that we may all

be drastically mistaken about which is which, just that in practical political terms there is always such a distinction. Those who feel that such
a position is "exclusivist" are quite correct; it is just that they are mistaken to complain about its exclusivism. If the concept of ideology is
to have meaning, then there must be something incompatible with it.
Otherwise the word becomes an empty noise or a swear word; any word
which can mean anything means nothing. People who feel this move
a little authoritarian are rather in the position of those exponents of
situation ethics in the 1960s who, rightly objecting to tightly legalistic
notions of the term "love," ended up by emptying the term of any meaning by arguing in effect that there was no piece of human behavior which
could not, viewed from a certain angle, be judged as compatible with
it. Viewed from a judicious angle, burning babies slowly over fires
could always be made compatible with the term "love." The point is
not whether or not this is true, but that if *any* activity can be described
as "loving" then the word "love" is struck empty. In order to use it mean-
ingfully, you would have to be prepared to point to kinds of behavior
which you judged irreconcilable with it. If there is nothing which is not
ideological, then there is no point in using the word. This argument
does not commit one to believing that there is a particular kind of discourse which is always and everywhere nonideological, as a moral absolutist believes that there are kinds of behavior which are always and
everywhere nonloving; it simply entails that in any particular situation
one must be able to point to what one regards as nonideological for
the term "ideological" to have meaning. The problem with the highly
generalized definition of ideology—as the nexus or articulation of discourse and power—is that it does not allow one to do this, as long as
"power" is taken to include every possible form of human conflict. "Nonideological conflict" then becomes an oxymoron, and we are committed to the implausible belief that disagreeing over how many eggs are
in the basket is always and everywhere an ideological issue. "Expansionistic" notions of power and ideology rightly alert us to the possibility that such a disagreement *may* be ideological; but they do this
only by blinding us simultaneously to the fact that it always may not.
      Ideology, we might tentatively claim, is a set of discourses which
wrestle over interests which are in some way relevant to the maintenance
or interrogation of power structures central to a whole form of social
and historical life. We might want to add, though the question is for
the moment controversial, that though such discourses by no means always involve falsity, distortion, and mystification, it is characteristic of
them that they quite often do so. Those who believe that such epistemological claims are dubious because they draw implicitly on unten-

ably "absolute" notions of truth, which can then be wielded as standards to measure such distortions, behave rather like the moral absolutists who believe that in order to identify a particular piece of behavior as nonloving they have to rustle up absolutist notions of love. Both partners — legalistic absolutists and deconstructionist skeptics — are locked in the same binary opposition, comrades in crime. Few people trust any longer to the myth of a wholly disinterested discourse, not even some quite conservative scholars, and it is a mere waste of energy to lambaste this particular straw target. Those who do so are for the most part no more than inverted positivists, who subscribe spontaneously to absurdly outdated notions of scientificity and then have great fun knocking them down. In order for the concept of "interested discourse" to have meaning, it is not necessary to posit some mythically disinterested discourse; it is merely necessary to claim that some forms of discourse are more objective than others, in particular those forms relating to material situations. To point out that what counts as objectivity is itself defined by specific interests makes no difference to this claim.

I am not arguing, it should be noted, that some forms of discourse are more objective than others because they are more *disinterested*. The delusive bond between objectivity and disinterestedness, part of our Arnoldian heritage, needs to be broken. Anyone who is not "interested" will never "see the object as it really is," if only because he or she, superbly untainted by all whiff of interest, would see no point in looking in the first place. The most simple argument for the relation of knowledge and interest is that if we were not somehow interested we would not bother to find anything out in the first place, not even the kinds of knowledge crucial to our biological survival. The nineteenth-century proletariat had an interest in getting to know how capitalism really was, because without this knowledge it was quite likely to waste away. The fact that its knowledge of the capitalist mode of production was not "disinterested" does not mean that it was "subjective." Nor, of course, does it mean that it was merely "intersubjective." In the *Philosophical Investigations*, Wittgenstein imagines an impatient interlocutor asking him whether he is claiming that truth is merely a question of consensus, and replies: "It is what human beings *say* that is true and false; and they agree in the *language* they use. That is not agreement in opinions but in forms of life." What Wittgenstein means, presumably, is that the criteria of truth and falsehood are generated by and embedded in our material, institutional forms of political life. This is not, at least in the conventional senses of the term, a question of "intersubjectivity"; it is a question of certain categories which could not possibly be successfully challenged without a deep-seated transformation of the way we actually live." It is our *acting*," Wittgenstein remarks in *On Certainty*, "which lies at the bottom of the language game."

Can the term "ideology," then, be extended to cover all the interests embodied in our discourses? Or would this once again be an unduly "expansionistic" sense of ideology which would threaten to void it of content? We tend to restrict the term ideology, I think, to those interests which have a fairly close relevance to the reproduction or interrogation of dominant systems of social power. But our language also embodies other sorts of interests, which yet are constitutive of our whole form of material life. We are interested in distinctions between animate and inanimate, past and present, far and near, and so on. Can these categories too — categories so deeply embedded in our practices that it is literally impossible for us to think ourselves beyond them — usefully be called ideological? Those who are reluctant to say yes no doubt fear that the concept of ideology will become shapeless; those who wish to say yes fear that otherwise the concept will be superficial.

One thing to notice about interests of this fundamental kind is that they do not move at the same level as more "obvious" forms of ideological interest, because they provide the very frame and matrix of these latter forms. Another thing to notice about them is that, without them, the more "obvious" forms of ideological interest could not exist. When Michel Foucault informs us that Marxism is merely of a piece with a historically outstripped mode of nineteenth-century bourgeois rationality (a sophisticated version of one of the most banal upbraidings of historical materialism), he clearly intends the comment as a scornfully dismissive criticism. For a Marxist, however, it is puzzling why Foucault should regard this as a criticism at all. For it is clear that unless Marxism somehow shares the same set of interests as, say, bourgeois political economy — unless, that is to say, it uses words like "capital" and "profit" in roughly the ways that bourgeois political economy uses them — there can be no sense in which it can be said to be a *critique* of such thought and practice. There can be no disagreement or conflict without agreement and consensus: I cannot disagree with you about whether God exists if you think God is a supreme being and I think he is a goldfish. Discourses which are merely incommensurable cannot be said to be mutually antagonistic. I cannot argue with you over whether Donne is a good or bad poet if you do not agree that he is a poet in the first place. It is only because we share certain fundamental interests in common that we are able to collide.

This is not to say, however, that such fundamental shared interests or categories are simply "prior" to more evidently ideological conflicts, in the sense of providing the transcendental forms which "contain" such common or garden variety ideological contents. Such a standpoint would surely be drastically undialectical—the worst form of Platonic structuralism in which a "deep structure" of general interests simply generates a surface of more specific ones, while remaining in itself quite unaffected. Our most fundamental categories of interest are always *imbricated* with more immediate ideological interests, and are always learned in that kind of context. If we were to track our learning of such distinctions as animate/inanimate, past/present, far/near back to their murky roots, we would no doubt find ourselves fairly quickly back at the breast, an object which is hardly ideologically neutral. What does seem true is that such "deep" categories and interests are, if not ideologically neutral, ideologically *polyvalent*: they can be common to a whole range of distinct power systems, and it is only because they can be so that one power system is able to overthrow and replace another. It is not hard for us to imagine a future society in which nobody tortured anybody else, but it is extremely difficult to imagine the behavior of future human beings who had no understanding whatsoever of the concept of injuring another. Whether we could talk intelligibly to such people is a moot point. The point is not that the interest in injuring another which our languages evince is necessarily here to stay, as a fundamental structure which will survive any more particular ideological struggle unscathed; the point is that we do not yet know whether it is here to stay or not, and can find out only by the process of political change. We do not, to put it another way, yet know what the articulations are between two "levels" of social interest: those which structure our social life so deeply that we cannot imagine what it would be like to be without them, and those which we are conscious of as belonging to this particular form of political life and which we could quite easily imagine transcended. As long as we still belong to this particular form of political life, we cannot by definition learn much about this interrelationship of interests: if we could adequately objectify our fundamental ones, then they would cease to be so fundamental; it is the prejudices we cannot by definition be conscious of which are in this respect most crucial. The only space we might create for such objectification to occur is not transcendental but historical: only in retrospect, on the other side of a transformation which emerges from ideological conflict in the narrower sense, would we be able to look back and grasp some of the dialectical interactions now going on between these more and less conscious levels of interest.

Moreover, the extent to which we were able to do this would be an index of whether the transformation which had taken place was truly "radical." A radical social change would be one which altered the present institutions of power so fundamentally that it transfigured the concept of power itself—transfigured it to the point where members of a future society could probably not speak our own power discourses at all, and where there would be genuine doubt about whether a shared conceptual basis existed between us. This would also be the point at which we might discover what "deep" categories we still *did* have in common with the prerevolutionary past, and whether this was so because such categories were in no important sense "ideological" (they had not been central constituents of the former power structure), or because the revolution was still somehow incomplete. To say that it is our acting which lies at the bottom of our language games is equivalent to saying that it is "history" which will in the end—though there is, of course, no end—sort out the problem of what is ideological and what is not, at the more fundamental level of social interests. Any such future society would of course share *some* interests and categories with the past, since if it did not then we would be confronted with some mysterious metaphysical rupture which made it pointless to talk of the past as the past of this particular society; but if we look far enough into the future then the business of predicting what these categories will be becomes chancy. When Marx, in *The Eighteenth Brumaire*, sketches in a new kind of political semiotics by imagining a future socialist society in which, as he says, the "content goes beyond the form," he is providing us with an index of "authentic" transformation as against the farcical tendency of the bourgeois revolutions to enclose their contents within the recycled forms or clapped-out semiotics of the past. But, so Marx implies, those who "take their poetry from the future" cannot articulate much more than this: if you take your stand in prehistory, then there is little you can predicate about history proper other than what social reorganization would be necessary for it to begin.

The distinction between more specific and more general senses of social interest, then, is among other things a distinction between the short term and the long term, historically speaking. This is also, one might claim, what is involved in the much criticized classical Marxist metaphor of base and superstructure. We can best distinguish between these two "levels" not "vertically," as the model itself misleadingly suggests, but "horizontally"—a matter, so to speak, of time scale. To say that the changes you have effected in a particular form of social life are only "superstructural" is less a philosophical doctrine that a political warning and reminder: it is to argue that you have not yet run up against that outer limit or horizon which will prove most resistant to transformation—for Marxism, the property system—and that therefore not only is there more to be done, but until your political practice bumps

up hard against that limit, what changes you *have* managed to bring
about are not as radical as they might look. You have not yet tackled
the "acting," the forms of material practice, whose transformation is
a necessary if not sufficient condition for the transformation of our
very categories of thought. If a future society claimed to have deconstructed our current notions of unity, identity, equivalence and reci-
procity, and still retained commodity production, then we could be sure
it was self-deluded.

Academic scholarships is most interesting, from the viewpoint I am
adopting, not where it is most obviously laden with ideological interests, but where it is most obviously not. What is considered most disinterested, in any society, is the most revealing and transparent model
of what interests it is most significantly unconscious of. The "disinterested" is, so to speak, the purest lens through which such interests may
be focused, untinted by more instantly recognizable modes of subjective bias. Such less self-evident interests may be identified, for example,
in the very structure and mutual articulation of knowledges in the academic institution: it is in the disposition and definition of intellectual
frontiers, rather than in what is produced within them, that the "political unconscious" of academia can be most illuminatingly mapped. In
the case of literature, what is perhaps most definitive is not the palpably
ideological modes of discourse commonly uttered by literary critics, but
that founding historical moment or *coupure* when, within a complex
constellation of social, political, and intellectual pressures, "literary"
discourse as such emerged slowly into being, as a language appropriate
to a now separated, demarcated body of privileged writing. The most
fundamental questions which could then be addressed to this body of
writing—which would, so to speak, act as the concealed problematic
or unconscious underside of all the particular, apparently "technical"
queries which could be directed to it—were already set in place by this
act of definition itself, this historic carving out of a new discursive object. Questions or methods which transgressed the terms of this primor-
dial definition, this founding institutional contract, were then invalidated
at a stroke.

That contract was able to survive and reproduce itself for as long
as the "general ideology" of bourgeois society treasured the assumption
that there was indeed a "general common humanity," of which "literature" was paradigmatic. Below or beyond all local ideological conflict,
literature could provide the pure lens which brought our deepest common interests into focus; and it was in this sense at odds as an object
with the techniques used to examine it—literary scholarship—for while
these were felt to be disinterested, literature itself was not. Literature

was the place where we could recognize, dramatically, that our social and personal lives were "interested" to their roots; but such a recognition could not be extended to the languages in which this object was articulated. The couple "literature/literary scholarship" reproduced within the academies the contradictory unity of humanism and positivism deeply embedded in the dominant bourgeois ideology under whose aegis "literature" as a distinct object first emerged. The literary-academic institution has always been riven by this more pervasive ideological contradiction, and if it is currently in crisis it is because it has proved quite incapable of resolving it. In the heyday of bourgeois society, literary studies could be certificated as a valid area of knowledge only if they strictly conformed to the dominant positivist criteria of what counted as knowledge in the first place; but by choosing this path they were pitched into conflict with their very object of knowledge, which powerfully resisted such definitions of knowledge. The alternative strategy, then, was to elaborate, within literary-academic discourse, the form of knowledge of the object "literature" itself, thus trading the secure if modest status of professional discipline for the precarious but potent function of humanistic critique. Ironically, however, the development of late-bourgeois society threw this humanistic alternative into deep crisis: under the pressures of a proliferating division of intellectual labor, intensifying social conflict and fragmentation, and the increasingly bureaucratic regulation of economic and political life, the terrain of a "general common humanity" began to dwindle, and with it the ideological rationale of liberal humanist literary studies. Stranded between a discredited positivism and an increasingly implausible humanism, the literary-academic institution was progressively stripped of its traditional apologias.

We can recast this dilemma in terms of the two levels of "interests" which I have examined. On the one hand, literary studies could view themselves as an "ideological" project in the narrower sense of the term, impassionedly engaged with more general questions of social value and cultural vitality. This strengthened their role within society as a whole at the same time as it threatened to undermine their status within the academy; for by such a project they swerved too far from the accredited criteria of what counted as academic knowledge, risking their dissolution into an unformalized amateur humanism. On the other hand, the more literary scholarship strived for accommodation within such criteria and procedures of academic learning, the more it crippled its own capacity to speak relevantly to the society as a whole. Increasingly, its only relation to that larger society lay in the preservation and reproduction of certain more fundamental categories of interest: objectivity, verification, impartiality, the weighing of evidence, and the rest. These, however, failed to provide literary scholarship with a *raison d'être* for its object, its specific "literariness"; what defense it could muster for itself lay almost wholly at the level of method, where it was effectively indistinguishable from other academic pursuits.

The reproduction of such fundamental categories of interest as "impartiality" is certainly one of the ways in which academic "disciplines" (the term is revealing) contribute to the reproduction of social life as a whole. Academic discourses are "disciplines" because they are a rehearsal of the mind, within a largely synthetic space, in those conceptual habits which are constitutive of the ethical, juridical, and political institutions of the social formation. This is why the British Civil Service tends to draw its top recruits not from social administration but from ancient history. It is at this "deep" level that academia is "ideological"; it assists in the perpetuation of social hegemony. That academic institutions are also ideological in the more precise sense of deploying languages which are ideological is not to be undervalued; but critiques of academia couched in these terms tend to lapse into sociological functionalism, claiming an untenably direct relation (at least as far as the traditional humanities are concerned) between academic institutions and the state. The recent poststructuralist preoccupation with power as an end in itself, a final term or conceptual baseline which cannot be pressed beyond, is among other things an overreaction to such functionalist reductionism. If it is implausible to see universities as a direct instrument of the state, then perhaps their power is ultimately self-referential—an oppressive tautology in which authority reproduces itself for the sake of its own reproduction, in which power can in fact be defined as that which delights in its own autonomous exercise and self-expansion. It is certainly important to see that there are interests and practices in academia, as in any other institution, which are internally rather than externally referential—which exist for the sake of the untroubled reproduction of the academic apparatus itself, rather than for the direct perpetuation of class or patriarchal power. Such practices are nevertheless indirectly related to the state, for by reproducing the institution they provide the conditions for the reproduction of those "deep" categories of interest which are embedded in other more central ideological practices, and which, as I have argued, are always imbricated with ideology in its more precise sense. In the ideological analysis of academic scholarship, then, we would seem to be dealing with the articulations between at least three levels of interest: institutionally self-referential styles and protocols; categories of interest constitutive of an entire rationality; and more politically direct forms of partisanship and intervention.

Literary scholars are not, in the classical meaning of the term, intellectuals. I do not mean by this that they are sometimes a little dim;
and there are, of course, definitions of the term "intellectual" which
would easily encompass them. For Antonio Gramsci, a bank manager
would qualify as an intellectual; from certain other viewpoints all those
who trade primarily in ideas would be awarded the title. But the classical idea of the intellectual contains two crucial, interrelated components
which the great majority of literary critics and scholars today notably
lack. First, the classical intellectual is one who works at the frontiers
between the traditionally differentiated academic subject areas, drawing upon more than one such specialty for his or her work; second, the
intellectual deploys such knowledge as a way of "reading" the contemporary cultural situation. These two strands of the concept of "intellectual" are interwoven, since the second activity, given a complex and "re-
gionalized" culture, becomes impossible without the first. On both of
these counts, most workers in literature fail to qualify for the title, a
failure which many of them would no doubt view with considerable
relief. It is sometimes now thought, particularly in post-1968 Paris, that
this whole traditional category of the intellectual has been profitably
scuppered, since for one thing the claim that there can be some ethical
or political metalanguage (a discourse of the "human" itself?) which
might grandly subsume every regional intellectual practice is the mere
wistful fantasy of an outdated humanism, and for another thing nobody, in these postrepresentional days, has the title or authority to speak
out about a "whole cultural situation," even granted that the phrase has
meaning. Traumatized by the specters of Robespierre and Trotsky, even
the "left" intellectual has beat a modest retreat inside the enclosure of
his or her own area, self-castigatingly scornful of the authoritarian pre-
sumption of "speaking out." Speaking out to whom, on the basis of
what program or constituency? Before such "left" intellectuals disappear too completely into their own guilt complexes, however, it might
be worth reminding ourselves that there are still a range of possibilities
somewhere in between Lenin and David Lodge. To transgress the boundaries of a single academic specialty is not equivalent to positioning oneself at some transcendental vantage point, as the work in Britain of
Raymond Williams well enough exemplifies; and to connect one's academic work to the central political issues of one's time, in the manner
of an Edward Thompson or Edward Said, is not necessarily to assume,
in some unacademic access of megalomania, that one is the moral conscience of the nation.

Literary scholarship, it could be claimed, was for the most part born
in the service of an urgent ideological project: the construction and

refurbishing, in nineteenth-century Europe, of the various "national" cultures and lineages. Nobody today much admires this dismally unenlightened enterprise; but it surely remains the case that until literary scholarship once again becomes "ideological," in the nonpejorative sense of that word, it will remain shuttled between an ineffectual humanism and an indefensible hermeticism. Unless the literary institution discovers a need for "society," it might quickly discover that society has little need for it.

The Politics of English Studies in the British University, 1960–1984

John Sutherland

B Y WAY of foreword, the American reader (who will not be as excited over the matter as his transatlantic colleague) should be informed that livelier than usual debate has recently been joined in Britain on the future role of universities, and the future role of English studies
within the universities. The crude instigator of this debate has been the
policy of the Department of Education and Science, under the minister
for education, Sir Keith Joseph. Very simply, Joseph has set himself a
number of goals: (1) to reduce the size of the British higher education
system, so restoring it—by his doctrinal lights—to standards of "excellence" at lower overall running costs; (2) to emphasize studies of immediate practical or economic value (they do not include English); (3) to
make universities more docile to direct government management by abol-
ishing tenure for the serving academic. Joseph's assault, rationalization,
or restructuring (according to one's sympathies) is outlined in two recent books: Peter Scott's *The Crisis of the University* (London: Croom
Helm, 1984) and Maurice and David Kogan's *The Attack on Higher
Education* (London: Kogan Page, 1983). This perceived "attack/crisis"
is an extramural pressure impinging on English studies. It is matched
by a certain intramural collapse, which takes the form of a questioning
of the previously accepted priorities of the subject (as it was essentially
formed in the late nineteenth century), of its curriculum, and its canon.
These doubts are representatively expressed in the recent critical interventions of Colin MacCabe and Terry Eagleton. My contract with the
University of London is standard in form. The employer requires that
one-third of my salaried time be spent on research, leading to publication in my scholarly field. What do these contractual obligations mean
for the average English academic? It's necessary to qualify the question
with a harsh truth. Most of us gain entrance to the profession by virtue
of examined and certified excellence. We are, typically, first-class graduates of the system we join; successful products turned producers. Once
well into our careers, our under- and post-graduate "promise" fulfilled,
we most of us realize that by the extraordinary high calibrations in which
achievement is measured, we are nothing special. In any generation, al-

126

though many may do useful work in English scholarship, only a dominant few will change or affect the course of the subject by individual contribution. Once he has made the adjustment to the fact that "they also serve who publish an annual note in *N & Q*, put out a good edition every ten years, and write the odd *TLS* review," what if the academic has also to face a sudden demoralization; a threat to his job security; and official vilification of his subject? What then happens to his "research" and the energies which sustain it? This is essentially the issue which the following essay addresses.

As a historical fact, I take research in English to be superstructural, and its material base to be principally the university which has institutionalized the subject and professionalized its practitioners. (It has not, however, made them all "professors"—a sore point with British academics.) To a lesser extent, commercial and university publishers (notably the Oxbridge duopoly) produce and control research, if only by keeping so much out of print. But I want to start by briefly—and tendentiously—tracing the evolution of the university community in Britain over the period 1960–84. The tendency is personal indignation; but that will be obvious enough.

The historical picture is dramatic. In two decades, higher education has undergone twin convulsions exactly opposite in their effect. An explosive era of growth, interrupted by a suddenly imposed interval of Arctic freeze, has been followed by severe contraction in the body of British universities. We are currently in the throes of this last, painful phase. With chastened hindsight, it's instructive to recall the Pisgah era of the 1960s and savor the educational utopianism of its predictions. The bullish mood of the time was confirmed by the 1963 Robbins report, which established the right of every qualified school leaver to higher education. As a follow-up to the 1944 Butler Act (and aboriginally to the 1870 universal education acts), the Robbins principle (it was never, of course, enshrined in British law or constitution) represented a momentous enfranchisement. Higher education was now conceived of as a universal right, not a minority's privilege.

The Robbins survey was set up in 1960–61 by Harold Macmillan's government, in the Disraelian one-nation spirit then politically fashionable among Conservatives. Something, it was felt, must be done for the people's higher education, as something had recently and successfully been done for the people's housing. Robbins himself was a London School of Economics academic—in itself a measure of the new consensus. (In the demonology of the right, the LSE has, since Laski's time, traditionally been the most obnoxious of institutions.) The report observed that Britain had an excellent record as to output and quality of graduates, but a uniquely poor record as to intake. The end product was good; the educational draft lamentable. Robbins made 178 recommendations. The most consequential was that the number of entrants absorbed annually into university education be substantially increased. Quantitative not qualitative change was envisaged. The traditional nature of the British university (above all its small size, autonomy, pastoral relationships between staff and student, liberal Newmanesque ethos, and close tutorial teaching method) should be preserved. Moderate increase in the size of existing institutions, and the creation of a diversity of entirely new institutions (uneconomically small by European or American standards), were the outcome.

By previous British standards, the growth in enrollment was startling. By 1968, the full-time university student population was doubled, at 205,195. The report foresaw an expansion, to half a million by 1980. The Robbins expansion targets were, in fact, adhered to until 1973. (There are at the moment some 309,000 full-time students—a number which will at best hold steady over the next few years, and perhaps even shrink.) Since low staff-student ratios were sacrosanct, the 1960s saw a matching intake of newly appointed university lecturers. It's now neoconservative dogma that the abrupt demand over a short period resulted in a lowering of professional standards. More, as Kingsley Amis famously asserted, meant worse. As one who benefited, my personal view is that, for the first time, old patterns of recruitment—notably the traditional Oxbridge source of supply—were circumvented. For a brief interval the graduate from the unfashionable provincial university had equality before the appointment committees. And this egalitarian aberration accompanied a wholesale elevation of university teachers, and their institution. The beckoning postindustrial Britain would, it was generally thought, need them to produce the information-oriented citizens of the future.

The "new" universities took their epithet seriously, and worked hard to distinguish themselves both from Oxbridge and from old municipal and redbrick predecessors. In setting they were largely provincial and rural, and have come to be known by county names, redolent of green fields and old England: Kent, York, Sussex, East Anglia, Essex, Lancaster, Warwick. But it was not all new universities. There were plenty of higher-education pounds to go round, and established institutions grew, and in many instances diversified with the spirit of the time. A notable case is Birmingham's Centre for Cultural Studies. Originally this annex was formed around the proletarian advocacy of Richard Hoggart, its first director. When Hoggart left Birmingham to work for UNESCO (it was a heady time for the top echelon of academics), the center was taken over by Stuart Hall. Hall, in turn, emerged as the leading Marxist popularizer in the country. This sequence (liberal initiative-radical consolidation) is typical of what happened elsewhere in the late 1960s and early 1970s.

For all their distinctiveness, the new universities had a number of features in common. Most owed something to Keele, a small university in Staffordshire which played a pilot role in higher education in the 1950s, by supplying an alternative model to that of Oxbridge and the municipal redbricks. Keele founded itself on a radical departure from the traditional single-honors system. At Keele, all incoming students were subjected to a "foundation year," as it was called, where the learning was widely cross-disciplinary. Thereafter, Keele undergraduates followed a twin-track course of study, in which arts and science combined as a double degree. The aim was to create a new generation of Renaissance men, capable of reading Shakespeare while meditating on the second law of thermodynamics. In the new combinative patterns which originated at Keele, and which were elaborated in the new universities, soft arts and social science disciplines—notably English, sociology, and philosophy ("how to live" subjects)—enjoyed unquestioned priority. The study of English literature boomed. For years, the Leavisite fraction had argued the centrality of the English department, as the necessary humane nucleus of the university. That ideal was now fulfilled (though not, it should be added, in ways that always pleased the disciplinarians of *Scrutiny*).

Like Keele, the new universities stressed imaginative subject connections: Essex, soon to become the most controversial of the group, opted for concentration on physical sciences, social studies, and internationally comparative approaches to literature. It purposely neglected classical humanities elements (such as classics), and had no professional schools. Training for life, not work, was envisaged. Its mix was devised to accompany a new mode of university life which was to be that of neither the college nor the traditional campus. Essex students—housed in the famous tower blocks and strategically distant from the nearest town, Colchester—would be a microcosmic and self-sufficient society, Alphaville. What Essex actually fostered, though no one apparently clearly foresaw or intended such a thing, was the dreaded hotbed of Marxism—that omnipresent nightmare of the British establishment.

Less heady mixtures were brewed elsewhere. At Sussex, history and English merged into what Asa Briggs grandly called "a new map of learning." At Kent, following a blueprint laid down by Patrick Nowell-Smith, philosophy and English were combined. An aubade for the Robbins era is found in Albert Sloman's exhilarated 1963 Reith Lectures, "A University in the Making." (Sloman was the first vice-chancellor at Essex, where his Reithian fantasies were quickly shattered.) For English as a subject, the optimism of the period is found in David Daiches's *The Idea of a New University* (i.e., Sussex). To be a student in these days was bliss; to be a professor very heaven.

Alongside all the utopian scheming and dreaming, it was confidently assumed that the new forces generated by the new universities could be contained in the old, well-tried structures of authority and organization. (Peter Scott aptly calls this complacent frame of mind "Whiggish.") Generally, such was the case. The British compromise between innovation and tradition worked, as it usually does. But, notoriously, things boiled over at Essex, where the students expressed themselves less by a new generosity of mind than by direct political action on the campus and in the streets. At Essex, the mixture produced Marxism, sociology, and the nearest thing to insurrection ever seen on a British campus; a kind of never-ending political rag week. It was fine spectator sport. A running battle developed, between the university and the nearby burghers of Colchester (who had returned a Conservative MP regularly since 1951, and whose notions of what a British university should be were formed on vague recollections of *A Yank at Oxford*). The Tory establishment of England, represented by the *Daily Telegraph*, indignantly demanded that Essex be dechartered and converted to an agricultural college. It remains on the Tory party hit list, and I shall be surprised if it survives in the long term. As regards the study of English, Essex provocation took the form of international conferences where, for instance, Macherey and Balibar were invited to pronounce on English soil, injecting alien European intellectualism into a subject traditionally provincial and pragmatic.

The Essex affair was something new. In the UK, English has always been, like the royal family and the established church, conveniently "above" politics — outside the sphere of ideology, as it would like to think. One of the startling Althusserian formulations given currency (particularly in the early 1970s) was that the apolitical common sense in which the English mentality swaddled itself was politically tendentious. Like latter-day Messieurs Jourdain, English academics had been ideological all their lives, without knowing it. This subversion of the normal, together with deconstruction of the text and disruption in the streets, was an alarming new post-Robbins secretion at Essex.

Diversity was a fetish of the new universities, but none of the others was inclined to project as extreme an image as Essex. At the University of East Anglia, the stress fell on comparative literature. East Anglia also recruited leading British writers as English teachers (e.g., Malcolm Bradbury, Angus Wilson). The end result was unusual in British terms, but generally acceptable: namely, a stimulus to new-wave creative writing. A generation of currently top-ranked young novelists have come out of Norwich, of whom the figurehead is Ian McEwan.

By 1968, the hierarchy of university life, with its vertical mirroring of the British class system, had been drastically changed. Hitherto, universities had ranked themselves, like English soccer, into a first, second, and third division. Now a more complex and egalitarian constellation emerged. This was important, since a new dignity attached to the scholar — and the student — formed outside the Oxbridge orbit. At the level of ideas, the new universities — with their dedication to novelty and to comparativism — were cued to draw on critical theories originating elsewhere than at Cambridge, the traditional cradle of English studies. The long-term effect of these farther intellectual horizons has been striking. In routine professional exchanges, one tends to forget how much broader and international in its origins our working equipment now is. Everyday vocabulary provides a measure. Had one in 1963 talked in a classroom about deconstruction, about pluralism, about disruption, about laying bare the device, or defamiliarization, distanciation — such terms would have been apprehended, if at all, as wild metaphors. Now they are jargon, not everywhere accepted (we may, in David Lodge's phrase, live with structuralism; we don't necessarily make love to it), but certainly everywhere recognized, if only as higher froggy nonsense. The changed lexicon of everyday English studies indicates the sizable breach which twenty years have wrought in the hermetically English nature of English studies. (As a historical parenthesis, the role of Frank Kermode as a disseminator of new criticism in Britain of the 1960s and 1970s is, I would suggest, crucial.)

Arguably the most effective higher-education innovation of the 1960s was the Open University. Melodramatically subtitled the "University of the second chance," and planned by politicians, the OU was a more overtly socialist initiative than were the new universities. It drew heavily on the heritage of Ruskinian, Morrisian, and Workers' Education Association sentimentality which is deep-rooted among the British left. The OU embodied a Fabian faith in the politically virtuous consequences of a working class dosed with as much education as they can stand. Unlike any previous British university, the OU offered open entrance, a course-for-credit system (novel in Britain), and distance teaching for part-time mature students. The OU made universal higher education, briefly, a widespread (if illusory) goal for traditionally underprivileged Britons. And the OU's success with men and women who had (in the phrase of the day) slipped through the net confirmed that the former elitist universities had underestimated the ability of the population at large to benefit from higher education. As with many British reformist measures, the OU was initially somewhat condescending and "paternalistic" (another favored term of the day) in its manner. Students were denied the traditional wayward freedoms of the English undergraduate to develop their own intellectual personalities. And some felt that the OU chalice was poisoned, in that its bourgeois educational benefits were bought at the cost of authentic class membership (a theme comically developed in *Educating Rita*). But as an educational experiment, the OU had more acknowledged successes than failures. And like the new universities, the OU had English (together with history) as the obligatory "core" of its foundation course.

The expansionist phase of British education continued until the early 1970s when, with much else in British life, it was destabilized by the oil crisis. Sudden inflation made long-term (more particularly, quinquennial) planning impossible. The need for public spending cuts left higher education vulnerable. For an interim of about five years, universities were at a paralyzing standstill. Then, in the late 1970s and early 1980s, particularly under the ministry of Sir Keith Joseph, the era of cuts began. It was good Thatcherite housekeeping and better new-right doctrine. Academicism, so automatically revered in the 1960s, was now suspect. As the Tory ideologue saw it, the socialist ratchet was being turned back, at last. In 1981, Joseph, by decree, reduced the annual intake to seventy thousand new entrants, a full ten thousand less than the year previous.

The cutting is just now (1984) reaching its surgical crescendo. Things are happening in British higher education that ten years ago would have been unthinkable. A major London college (Bedford), for instance, has been simply swept off the university map. Coleraine looks certain to follow. One-fifth of the university teaching profession, it is estimated, have been shuffled into what is euphemistically called early retirement. (It is a peculiarly humiliating way to end one's career, since it entails being officially designated as surplus to educational requirements.) There are now, it is estimated, twenty thousand fewer university places for students. And the cuts continue. Since the black autumn of 1981 (when the need for a 15 percent saving was announced), universities have had to slash their budgets by some 10–13 percent. There is dispute over the actual inflation-adjusted figure, but general agreement as to the consequence. Year on year, savings must be made at the human top of the pyramid: in staff salaries and student places. This means that what seems like a relatively small figure can have devastating repercussions on the actual life of an institution. Other sectors of tertiary education in Britain — notably the polytechnics (which are funded by local authorities) — are just now coming on the butcher's block. The outlook for them is if anything bleaker than that for the universities. The Open University (directly funded by the government) is threatened with an amputation, no less, of its arts-teaching capacity. (A major blow is that OU students, drawn from the poorest sector of the population, will have to pay "full economic fees.")

With tacit ministerial approval, a British Ivy League is emerging. This will revive the old divisional rankings between institutions. All this is justified economically by reference to the government's campaign against public spending. It is justified ideologically by the doctrine of elitist "excellence." Contraction has severely reduced mobility between universities, at the staff level. The intellectually stultifying effect is predictable; especially with an aging profession cushioned by cast-iron tenure contracts, unleavened by the arrival of what educational bureaucrats —with their zest for dead metaphor—now label "new blood." The academic blood stream is indeed growing somewhat stale and sludgy. The circuits by which the bearers of new ideas would be absorbed, by the process of junior appointment, have been blocked. Other anoxic blockages are evident. The general reduction of library funds has tended to cut away the financial base of learned journals, and of the commercial publication of monographs. The new imperative of "economic" fees has curtailed the previous internationalism of British universities. In the mid-1960s, fees for postgraduate work were as little as £50 a year. In 1980, for overseas students, the overall cost is around £3,000. To put this in perspective, it now costs about as much to do research at—for instance—Cardiff as at Harvard (with obvious consequences for the Welsh university).

All this is drearily familiar. In summary, the British university in this period has undergone a boom-bust cycle. Forced, hothouse growth has been followed by retrenchment. There are no ivory towers immune to this process. Oxbridge has been sheltered by its endowed income, but its finances since the 1960s have become increasingly state-dependent through the portion of its income which it receives in the form of student fees. (These are largely provided by the state, in the UK.) I must, of course, be careful not to overstate. What one sees here is not a latter-day dissolution of the monasteries. Indeed, there are intellectually respectable lobbies within British universities themselves who welcome purge, pruning, trimming (the metaphors suggest themselves, if one pictures the speakers). There has been no wholesale dismantling or desecration. But neither is it mere "adjustment" to diminished income. What one is witnessing, I suggest, is an ideologically motivated reformation of the universities, by means of economic sanctions. As a more dramatic than usual event in educational history, it is interesting for the onlooker to contemplate. But academics are directly involved. And, it is fair to say, most of them are thoroughly out of sympathy with the government's program, and consequently demoralized. The demoralization is more intense than in America, where educational expansion took place earlier and lasted longer. It has been increased by the great effort which previously went into the formation of new syllabuses, and their application in the classroom. During the 1960s, many academics felt—naively as events proved—that they were pioneers building a new higher education for the country. Many sacrificed the third of their time due to research for teaching work and interminable wrangling in boards of studies and subject subcommittees.

What does all this mean for the serving British academic in 1984? If he has any historical perspective, he will observe that his position is anomalous. There was a huge intake of new university staff in the 1960s, and "lecturer" was established as the career grade. In the 1970s, the freeze and later the cutbacks stopped growth, long before it had reached the maturity foreseen by Robbins. There emerged a familiar crisis of rising expectations, as the majority of university teachers came to terms with the fact that they could no longer look forward even to promotion to senior lecturer (equivalent to associate professor), let alone to running their own departments. Career frustration was heightened, since in many cases academics had sacrificed research to get new universities off the ground. Energy had gone into the devising of syllabuses, into charismatic teaching, into student contact. Interuniversity mobility, a necessary factor in the circulation of new ideas, had come to a stop. The usual career fallback, a job in Canada or Australia, was blocked off by new national recruiting policies in those countries. Jobs were tight in the US. This sense of stagnation and enforced immobility went together with the uniquely secure nature of British university tenure, where no one, however unpublished, perishes. The bulk of the profession could not be let go (whether superfluous, unproductive, or downright delinquent), and the usual career inducements to dutiful conduct were removed. Protected from the American publish-or-perish ultimatum, but exposed to cosmic doubts as to significance in the scheme of things, the British academic might well feel himself a kind of academic remittance man. (The type is well represented in Philip Swallow, the hero of David Lodge's *Changing Places*.) British tenure loftily justifies itself as the necessary condition for the academic to publish what he wants, without fear or favor. But it also protects the freedom not to publish. Many availed themselves of the right to professional silence. The invitation to early retirement, "golden lever" severance payments were introduced. (Redundancy was too unacademically hard a word to apply, but that is what was at issue.) This ill-thought-out measure had the predictable effect of shaking out the best, and creating a government-sponsored brain drain.

For the practicing scholar, the 1970s were a time of instability. Most academics found themselves pressed in a vise. One of its jaws was how to come to terms with a career likely to go nowhere in an atrophied line of work. The other jaw was how to deal with the problems represented by the new and often alien intellectual forces eroding old pedagogic and scholarly certainties. What accommodation could be reached with Marxism, with structuralism, with deconstruction? Or even with students (particularly postgraduates) excited by these new ideas? English studies (in their home country) are never strong on theory. But this twin dilemma accompanied a slackening of what disciplinary coherence the subject does possess. Leavisism was, by the late 1960s, a spent force. Increased student choice had dissolved hard philological elements in the curriculum. (Undergraduates, given the choice, did not want to do Old English—they wanted to do new English).

In short, the academic found himself physically secure (assuming he was under the early retirement threshold of fifty), but troubled in mind. The structure of English intellectual life is famously unsuited for the kind of polemic exchange which could clear the air, and the standard patterns of polarization under stress emerged. Energy was drawn to marginal activities. A new, fiercely defensive conservatism formed itself. For a while, its typical expression was denunciatory and yah-boo diatribe-reviews in the *TLS*. The principal ideologue of this literary-critical rightism was George Watson, with his paradoxically entitled book *The English Ideology*. Some academics, like Malcolm Bradbury, admitted frankly to a condition of schizophrenia. With one-half of his public person Bradbury wrote advanced criticism, and with the other half he turned out fiction, ostentatiously nostalgic for the pre-1956 certainties of British liberalism. (See what is surely the best novel written about postwar British university life, *The History Man*, 1975).

In the ranks of the profession, a kind of torpid automatism was more the norm. Many academics, like parsons of a previous era, retreated into the comfortable private life permitted by the unburdensome regime of their profession (five hours' work a day, three days' work a week, thirty weeks' work a year, one sabbatical term in fifteen off for rest, unbreakable tenure). In some university departments of English a pressure-cooker effect was evident: the young staff were like battle-trained soldiers, with no war to go to. Soon, most of them would also sink into torpor. One now saw a situation where it was conceivable that a person spend the whole of his career in one institution. A working life sentence.

The point of this introductory tour of British universities has been to emphasize the point, sometimes lost sight of, that academics do not naturally secrete research, as bees do honey. As with any writing, it is always easier not to do it. For most, the effort is rationalized by a conviction of either its career benefit or its general cultural worth. No one, I presume, has ever thought an article in the *Review of English Studies* would change the order of things. For many, the effort is harder to justify in 1984 than it was in 1964 (especially when one's institutional library may have "temporarily suspended" its subscription to *RES*).

For a number of reasons, some historical, some institutional, British universities in the 1960s and 1970s became, for the first time, arenas of active dissidence. This dissidence took two typical forms. In the 1960s, the dominant impulse was to attack the now clearly visible university "system" that Robbins had (unwittingly) brought about. The cry was for the creation of newer antiuniversities; for the abolition of exams; for hanging the last don with the guts of the last vice-chancellor. If the university system could be reformed from above, it could as readily be revolutionized from below. (One needn't stress the romanticism of this view; it is vividly satirized, after the event, in David Caute's *The Confrontation: A Trilogy*.) No antiuniversity survived longer than a couple of seminars; exams survived; no vice-chancellors were disemboweled. In the late 1970s, targets switched. The radical aim now was more to disintegrate English as a discipline. This was what was at stake, one assumes, in the Cambridge MacCabe affair, in which a scholar's affiliation to poststructuralism was a main issue, and in the Oxford battle over incorporating feminism into English studies. Front-line action by the disaffected now tilts at "English" rather than at the English university. This switch of theater tacitly concedes that the government firmly controls (via purse strings and discipline by cuts) the physical structure of higher education. Activism has been forced back into the immaterial territory of doctrine, syllabus content.

In all material aspects, the forces of reaction (tradition, if one prefers) are triumphant. Not only are exams firmly reinstalled as the final ordeal of undergraduate life, but the experimental forms introduced by the new universities (take-home papers, various kinds of continuous assessment) have been generally discarded. The three-hour paper is now almost universal again. Excellence, alpha minds, first-class men: these loaded items of the old academic lexicon are again current at high tables, in common rooms, and in staff meetings. The resilience of the old ways of British higher education, its inert power to survive dormant, and reestablish itself, is extraordinary. In the face of this resilience, revolt seemed to reason thus: if we can't change the institution, if we can't reorganize the department, let's kill the subject at the level of its theoretic coherence.

To take a long backward look, the most interesting forces of dissidence in the early 1970s gathered around the *Screen* group. Originating in orthodox university circles (principally Cambridge), this coterie established itself at the academic margin. Its closely knit membership applied themselves to the cinetext rather than to literature for two reasons: (1) cinema was a virgin territory, critically speaking, and (2) the film had no automatically discernible author. Unowned, a film could be considered as untrammeled text. (Not too implausibly, this preference for film harks back to the 1930s Cambridge dream of a pure clinical or laboratory situation in which literature might be analyzed in "scientific" isolation). Having cleared its esthetic ground, *Screen* served as a diffuser of new French and German doctrines. It introduced (for instance) Althusser, Benjamin, Brecht, and Lacan into general play.

As a journal *Screen* was unusual. For one thing, it was highly technical, eschewing the fine writing traditions which assume the academic critic to be a descendant of the great English essayist, bound by Quiller-Couch's maxim that "style is good manners." *Screen* contributors foregrounded, as they would say, barbarous jargon, submerging their individual style in the language of the collective. In this, the journal was notably bad mannered. (And at times it was so high-flown in its technicality as to produce complaints even from its coideological subscribers). Second, *Screen* was unusual in being read (and largely written) by students and younger members of the academic community. This wedged open a division which British universities traditionally labor to close, that between intellectual generations. Not to overpraise it, *Screen* fostered the creative quarreling which Leavis had earlier seen as the natural intercourse of literary criticism.

In the mid-1970s, *Screen*'s position looked strong. It had a corps of major theoreticians (Stephen Heath, MacCabe, Ben Brewster, John Ellis). The magazine, in its mid-'70s heyday, also had a clear program. This entailed a graduation from doxa to praxis. After the new esthetics would follow filmmaking, political critique, and propaganda. (Inevitably, Brecht was enshrined as the ideal type of critic-politician-writer on whom the *Screen* contributor modeled himself.) And yet *Screen* gave out as a coherent critical organ in the late 1970s and early 1980s. Why? A main reason was schismatism (especially around the issue of feminism), the bane of all radical political groupings. The quarreling became uncreative and internecine. *Screen* thus broke down, I would suggest, in the heroic effort to contain its own dynamic forces. It was also handicapped by not having any solid institutional base. Fearful of any institutional state apparatus, it had created no apparatus of its own (and had failed signally to take over the state-funded British Film Institute). *Screen*'s unpatronized protégés were not easily absorbed into the main current of academic life. (This is yet another conclusion to be drawn from the MacCabe affair.)

For the conformist many, as opposed to the dissident few, the main research initiative in Britain, as in America, is the Ph.D. thesis. Successful completion sets the pattern for a career in which research is converted into learned articles, monographs, reviewing. Up to the 1960s, the Ph.D. was held by only a minority of British university teachers of English, most of whom distrusted it as an unnatural (and inherently foreign) wedge between scholarship and basic undergraduate teaching. Since then, in line with American practice, it has become a sine qua non for appointment, if not senior promotion (one of the historical ironies of academic life is that many professors would currently be ineligible to apply for junior posts in their own departments). The British Ph.D. is now a generator of new critical thinking and, more passively, a reflector of current orthodoxies. It has differences, in practice, from the American or German equivalent higher degree. In Britain, typically, the Ph.D. is a less-directed piece of work than elsewhere. The British postgraduate starts on his dissertation, the moment he first registers. And he is left largely to his own devices. There is no classwork for him. The candidate works usually under only the occasional inspection of a supervisor. The examination typically involves the supervisor, for the occasion converted into an examiner, and an external examiner, typically proposed by the internal examiner, i.e., the supervisor. The cosiness of this arrangement will be apparent.

The British postgraduate system detaches the postgraduate from the hurly-burly of communal intellectual life, privileging him with great freedom. But the privilege is paid for by isolation, a sense of intellectual irrelevance often crippling in its intensity. It is the freedom of Robinson Crusoe. So detached is the postgraduate that few notice how slim are their chances of success. At my university, the failure rate can go as high as 70 percent, if one takes nonsubmission of thesis into account.

It is important to register how state patronage for Ph.D. work is dispensed. Most home-based students are supported by full grants from the DES. These are awarded with virtual disregard for the subject proposed, and great attention to the class of degree achieved at undergraduate level. A candidate with a first and a feeble topic is almost certain to get a DES studentship. A student with an excellent subject, strong references, and a 2.2 will probably not. The man (or, in common metonymy, the mind), is in question, not the research proposal. There is no government agency in the UK to direct the larger trends of research activity. All this rewards and perpetuates the random and atomistic nature of British postgraduate work, which finds its appropriate expression in the individualistic monograph, containing "original" material or "insights." The academic thus becomes the end product of the scholarship-boy ethos. (Another feature of this ethos is the cult of intellectual boyishness, always prominent in British university life. Many academics have a sneaking envy, I suspect, of John Sparrow, who produced his major edition of Donne at seventeen. Even more admirable is Empson, who threw off *Seven Types* as undergraduate essays for I. A. Richards. It's a sad moment in the academic's career when he ceases to be "promising," and has to evaluate himself by what he's done rather than by his glorious potential.)

It is the mark of English studies in Britain that there is relatively little collaboration, on the level either of team writing or debate, or, more socially, of seminars or conferences. (David Lodge makes the point tellingly with his latest novel, *A Small World*, where he comically contrasts the MLA annual function with its paltry British UTE equivalent). There is not even the contact between minds that conflict generates. English in England supports an unhealthily low level of dispute, the product not of consensus, or intellectual harmony, but of the sealed-off nature of research and the tendency of scholars to see their work as intellectual property created in a private workshop. (Another factor symptomatic of the nerveless tempo of academic life is the glacial slowness of exchange which the normal channels permit. Learned journals take up to two years to accept, another two years to publish, a submitted article; a simple serve-and-return exchange of views can thus take the best part of a decade.)

I am conscious of having rediscovered certain platitudes. The scholar's life is lonely; he is rarely a valued or adequately rewarded citizen; he is prey to melancholy and anomie. It is also the case that academics are prone to see crises where others see merely difficulties, or the irreducible frictions of everyday professional existence. Nevertheless, it is a fact that momentous changes are currently being inflicted on us. These changes will repercuss throughout the whole British university system. And they will require (among much else) that the serving academic consciously reassess where he stands vis-à-vis his research. He can carry on in the same individualistic, artisanal way as before, seeing himself as a little Leavis or Empson (only not so famous). Dissidence, or antagonistic postures, would seem on the face of it a nobler response. In the most influential work of literary theory of the past decade, *Criticism and Ideology*, Eagleton sets himself to fill the ideological-political vacuum at the heart of English studies by supplying a Marxist esthetics, from which a reinvigorated critical practice might be conducted. If I understand his subsequent work, Eagleton seems since to have come round to the view that the institutions of British higher education simply cannot contain, or sustain, oppositional criticism. This may be right, in which case academics with radical aims will have to find marginal or extrainstitutional bases for their critical interventions. (This dilemma exactly mirrors the current argument among the British left as to the propriety of extraparliamentary political activity). It is unlikely that the majority of British academics will undenizen themselves. Their (I should more honestly say our) best course is the short-term one of understanding better the institutional apparatus, which is the infrastructure to research activity. When things fall apart, there's at least the small consolation that we can see better how they work.

III. Biographical Contexts and the Critical Object

Narcissus Jilted: Byron, *Don Juan,* and the Biographical Imperative

Cecil Y. Lang

M Y ESSAY falls under the rubric "Biographical Contexts," which is the subject nearest my thinking heart. A few moments of autobiographical recollection will show why. After college, and then a four-year stint in military service and a three-year stint at Harvard, both of which I found exhilarating (though in equal and opposite ways), I began my first teaching appointment, at Yale, in September 1949. It was a heady experience. Yale was then, as for many years to come, pinnacled dim in the intense inane of New Criticism. I had been trained wholly in something called "literary history" (though I do not think either term accurate). I was somewhat in the position of a nineteenth-century Anglican turned Roman. At Yale I might have been called a convert; at Harvard I certainly would have been called a pervert. As an initiation, it was both intoxicating and sobering: I found my consciousness raised, my intellect depressed.

The textbook that we used was the original edition (1938) of *Understanding Poetry* by Cleanth Brooks and Robert Penn Warren,[1] which for various reasons, extrinsic and intrinsic, acquired something like the status of Holy Writ. In this book, in a prefatory "Letter to the Teacher," the authors conceded that "study of the biographical and historical background [of a poem] may do much to clarify interpretation." The revised edition twelve years later (1950) added to this letter a "Postscript" which said: "A decade ago the chief need was for a sharp focus on the poem itself. At that time it seemed expedient to provide that focus, and to leave to implication the relation of the poem to its historical background, to its place in the context of the poet's work, and to biographical and historical study generally." They go on to recognize some of the objections raised by reviewers and users and conclude by assuring the reader that they have now "tried to relate criticism to other studies. Specifically, we have attempted to view the poem in relation to its historical situation and in relation to the body of the poet's work." Somehow, "biographical study" (not subsumed under historical situation) got left in the lurch. And not only biographical study.

In recalling all this I am of course flogging a dead horse (though

in view of the state of literary criticism today I wish I were instead curry-
ing a live one). Nevertheless, I want to cite one specific instance—Shelley's
poem then called "The Indian Serenade," one of the works Brooks and
Warren did a hatchet job on. (In the revised edition the analysis is un-
changed, except for the deletion of five lines). The first line of the discussion reads: "The lover is speaking to his mistress." The authors assume
that the speaker is Shelley himself, and they say also that the poet has
gratuitously given the poem "an exotic and remote atmosphere" by pret-
tifying "the love affair," adding that for the "mature reader" it is a sentimental poem.[2] (In 1938 they had labeled the speaker a 'flighty, hysteri-
cal sentimentalist.')

Now, there is not one syllable of evidence anywhere that the speaker
is male; indeed, outside the poem, and in a MS reading of the draft,
there is proof positive that the speaker is in fact female. The title given
the poem now, from Shelley's autograph fair copy, is "The Indian Girl's
Song"; in its first two appearances in print (*The Liberal*, 1823; *Posthu-
mous Poems*, 1824) the titles were "Song, Written for an Indian Air"
and "Lines to an Indian Air."[3] Thus, we know that the poem was called
a serenade not because of literary convention but because it was a song
written to be sung, and there is persuasive evidence that it was designed
to be not merely a song but a song in a drama. It is now praised as
one of Shelley's "most perfect lyrics."[4]

Ten years later (1960), the third edition dropped Shelley's poem altogether (and also Tennyson's "Come into the garden, Maud," another
poem hatcheted by misrepresentation). In addition, it replaced the "Letter
to the Teacher" and "Postscript" with a very brief "Preface," which said,
among other things: (1) "Poems are written by human beings and the
form of a poem is an individual's attempt to deal with a specific problem, poetic and personal." (2) "Poems come out of a historical moment,
and since they are written in language, the form is tied to a whole cultural context." Gradually, over twenty-two years, a sort of negotiated
peace has been achieved, a peace which passeth *Understanding Poetry*,
and to this the most appropriate response would seem to be Satan's "Long
is the way / And hard that out of Hell leads up to light." (I add, paren-
thetically, that the fourth edition, 1976, discarded this preface altogether;
but with such a handsome *amende* in the third, further comment would
amount to necrophilia.)

In the 1940s appeared another influential book of this sort, *Theory
of Literature,* by René Wellek and Austin Warren.[5] It was not aimed at
the same audience and did not serve the same purposes as *Understanding Poetry*. One is a textbook for undergraduates, the other a sort of
Book of Common Prayer for advanced students and professors of lit-

erature. One is covertly ideological; the other is overtly judicious. Both are committed to textual autonomy. Both are still in print.

Section 3 of Wellek and Warren, "The Extrinsic Approach to Literature," has a chapter entitled "Literature and Biography." Here, they draw the familiar distinction between objective and subjective poets, naming Keats and T. S. Eliot as "objective"—those who stress the poet's "negative capability," his openness to the world, the obliteration of his concrete personality, and they add that for "long stretches of history we know only the first type," objective poets, the "works in which the element of personal expression is very weak." Examples are cited. The authors then go on to concede that there may be "use in biographical study" but conclude with this: "Whatever the importance of biography . . . , however, it seems dangerous to ascribe to it any real critical importance. No biographical evidence can change or influence critical evaluation." (In later editions the phrase "any real critical importance" was revised to read "any specifically *critical* importance." Everything else remained.) Well, when I was one and thirty all this seemed to me unassailable; at three and sixty, with time closing in on me and without pausing to argue the matter, I simply deny the validity of every statement and implication in the several paragraphs.

There is a sense in which no man is an island, but as psychoanalysis, more than anything else, has shown us, there is also a sense in which every man is an island. Words are common property. Tradition is our collective inheritance. In our "whole cultural context," that "everlasting sameness of the never-ending plains," we are all faceless, nameless. Nowhere but in our own lives, private and public—the world within responding to the world without—are we truly indivisible, and for this reason biographical interpretation of literature, more definitively than anything else, shows us the uniqueness of human experience rendered in words. All this seems to me so self-evident that I would regard it as a truism if the testimony of my senses, my intellect, and my cultural milieu did not demonstrate daily that it is anything but a platitude. But since I want to talk about Byron's narcissism, not my own, the rest is silence.

It will surprise no one if I say that Byron was obsessed with Byron. It seems to be a fact, and I do not propose to cover such familiar ground more than is necessary for the sake of exposition. Exhibit A in this exposition is of course the four cantos of *Childe Harold's Pilgrimage*, and a major part of their appeal today, as on publication, is their unabashed egotism.

Byron sailed from England on his first foreign tour on June 20, 1809;

he returned, two years later, on July 14, 1811. We don't know any specific reasons for the journey, but we know that they were secret and urgent. Leslie Marchand, his biographer and the editor of his letters and journals, suggests that Byron "had a wish to escape his own proclivities towards attachment to boys, or perhaps he feared a closer connection with the Cambridge choirboy Edleston, who had wanted to live with him in London."[6] Doris Langley Moore, as sympathetic, knowledgeable, and judicious a critic as Byron has ever had, allows for the possibility that he was not merely fleeing "some particular temptation" but in fact "fleeing toward a temptation."[7]

In the first two cantos of *Childe Harold*, published in March 1812, the speaker leaves his ancestral home, journeys to Portugal, Spain, Gibraltar, Malta, and then to Albania, where he calls upon Ali Pacha, the virtually autonomous, powerful, ruthless gangster ruler, wooed by both the French and British governments, widely known as the Lion of Jannina, a title conferred upon him by the Sultan, who was in fact much less famous than Ali the Lion. In real life this visit to Ali Pacha began on October 19, 1809, and terminated on the twenty-third, when Byron and his friend John Cam Hobhouse departed. Some time in the next eight days, probably on October 31, Byron began writing *Childe Harold's Pilgrimage*. He also wrote at this time "a very exact journal of every circumstance of his life and many of his thoughts while young." He let "Hobhouse see it in Albania" and Hobhouse "persuaded him to burn it."[8] They quitted Albania on November 3, and on November 6 in Arta (Ambracia) we know that Byron was reading Spenser's *The Faerie Queen* (*Childe Harold* is written in Spenserian stanzas) and that he called Hobhouse's attention to an Albanian reference in Book 3, Canto 12. This reference is interesting and important. It is interesting because, together with other evidence, it leads us to proof that, contrary to received opinion, *Childe Harold's Pilgrimage* was directly and significantly influenced by Spenser's own poem as well as by the eighteenth-century Spenserians named in the Preface. It is important because it led Byron to a way of treating poetically, publicly, and cathartically a radical, intimate aspect of his nature without putting it into plain language. The specific episode in *Childe Harold* must be viewed as a kind of palimpsest with the specific episode in *The Faerie Queen* showing through. Together, these episodes in the palimpsest make possible a new reading of *Don Juan*, a reading that has "real critical importance" and will alter "critical evaluation."

Byron describes the visit to Ali Pacha at length, both in *Childe Harold*, Canto 2, and also in a marvelous letter to his mother written about a fortnight later. Let me quote from the letter:

In nine days I reached Tepaleen, our Journey was much prolonged by the torrents that had fallen from the mountains and intersected the roads. I shall never forget the singular scene on entering Tepaleen at five in the afternoon as the Sun was going down. . . . I was conducted to a very handsome apartment and my health enquired after by the vizier's secretary "a la mode de Turque." —The next day I was introduced to Ali Pacha, I was dressed in a full suit of Staff uniform with a very magnificent saber, etc.—The vizier received me in a large room paved with marble, a fountain was playing in the centre, the apartment was surrounded by scarlet Ottomans, he received me *standing*, a wonderful compliment from a Musselman, and made me sit down on his right hand. . . . His first question was why, at so early an age, I left my country? . . . He said he was certain I was a man of birth because I had small ears, curling hair, and little white hands, and expressed himself pleased with my appearance and garb.—He told me to consider him as a father whilst I was in Turkey, and said he looked on me as his son.—Indeed, he treated me like a child, sending me almonds and sugared sherbet, fruit and sweetmeats 20 times a day.—He begged me to visit him often, and at night when he was more at leisure— I then after coffee and pipes retired for the first time. I saw him thrice afterwards. . . . His Highness is 60 years old, very fat and not tall, but with a fine face, light blue eyes and a white beard, his manner is very kind and at the same time he possesses that dignity which I find universal amongst the Turks. (*LJ* 1:226–31)

Byron does not say, here or elsewhere, what we learn from Hobhouse's account forty-six years later, that at this audience they were attended by "four or five young persons very magnificently dressed in the Albanian habit, and having their hair flowing half way down their backs: these brought in the refreshments, and continued supplying us with pipes, which, though perhaps not half-emptied, were changed three times, as is the custom when particular honours are intended for a guest." Hobhouse also refers to the "monstrous sensualities, which were certainly not invented, although they were practised, by Ali as well as by Tiberius," and in a footnote to this footnote he quotes (in Latin) a passage from Suetonius's *Life of Titus Vespasianus* mentioning, among other things, the "swarms of catamites and eunuchs about him."[9]

In *Childe Harold's Pilgrimage*, Canto 2, stanzas 55–72, the same episode is narrated, with the addition of something new and vital—or, to phrase it more accurately, with the addition of something explicit that the letter invites us to infer. In stanza 61 Byron refers to Ali Pacha's harem (after the first four lines I cite the canceled reading):

> Here, woman's voice is never heard: apart,
> And scarce permitted, guarded, veil'd, to move,

> She yields to one her person and her heart,
> Tam'd to her cage, nor feels a wish to rove:
> For boyish minions of unhallow'd love
> The shameless torch of wild desire is lit,
> Caressed, preferred even to woman's self above,
> Whose forms for Nature's gentler errors fit
> All frailties mote excuse save that which they commit.[10]

The next stanza (62) echoes part of the letter just quoted:

> In marble-pav'd pavilion, where a spring
> Of living water from the centre rose
> Whose bubbling did a genial freshness fling,
> And soft voluptuous couches breath'd repose
> Ali reclin'd, a man of war and woes;
> Yet in his lineaments ye cannot trace,
> While Gentleness her milder radiance throws
> Along that aged venerable face,
> The deeds that lurk beneath, and stain him with disgrace.

Stanza 63 continues (in the published version):

> It is not that yon hoary lengthening beard
> Ill suits the passions which belong to youth . . .

But in the Murray manuscript this reads:

> It is not that yon hoary lengthening beard
> Delights to mingle with the lip of youth . . .

Canto 12 of Book 3 of *The Faerie Queen* begins with a "universall cloud" and then a "hideous storm of winde," with "dreadful thunder and lightning."[11] Byron's journey from Jannina to Tepelene to call on Ali Pacha was interrupted by a nine-hour storm, which is alluded to twice in his letter (*LJ* 1:227, 229) and was in fact the occasion for his poem "Stanzas composed during a Thunder-Storm." Spenser's storm is followed by the theatrical appearance of a "grave personage . . . Yclad in costly garments," standing, whose name, "on his robe in gold letters cyphered," was Ease—which, with the "gold-embroidered garments" four stanzas earlier in *Childe Harold*, is a fair suggestion of Ali. Spenser's fifth and sixth stanzas describe the merrymaking of this masque of Cupid:

> . . . a joyous fellowship issewed
> Of minstrales making goodly merriment,
> With wanton bardes and rymers impudent,
> All which together sung full chearefully
> A lay of loves delight, with sweet concent.

In *Childe Harold*:

> . . . when the lingering twilight hour was past,
> Revel and feast assum'd the rule again:
> Now all was bustle and the menial train
> Prepar'd and spread the plenteous board within;
> The vacant gallery now seem'd made in vain,
> But from the chambers came the mingling din
> As page and slave anon were passing out and in.

In *The Faerie Queen*, stanzas 7 and 8 describe a personified "Fansy," glossed as "the power of the imagination to deceive with false images of love" or as "love of a capricious, casual, and wanton nature":

> . . . Fansy, like a lovely boy,
> Of rare aspect and beauty without peare.

Fansy is likened to Ganymede, beloved of Jove, and to Hylas, beloved of Hercules, and stanza 9 describes his companion, whose appearance, like Ali's, was that of an older man and who, also like Ali, lit "the shameless torch of wild desire":

> And him biside marcht amorous Desire,
> Who seemed of riper years then th'other swayne
> . . . .
> His garment was disguysed very vayne [fantastically fashioned]
> And his embrodered bonet sat awry;
> Twixt both his hands few sparks he close did strayne,
> Which still he blew and kindled busily,
> That soon they life conceiv'd, and forth in flames did fly.

We don't know many particular details about Ali's dress, but Hobhouse, who was present, tells us that he wore a "high turban composed of many small rolls [that] seemed of fine gold muslin, and his ataghan, or long dagger, was studded with brilliants."[12]

What *really* happened at Ali's palace? We don't know, of course, but Byron may have left us a coded confession. In an "Addition to the Preface" published in the fourth edition of *Childe Harold's Pilgrimage* in September 1812 (six months after the first), he says that Harold has been called "*unknightly.*" In this connection Byron limits his brief discussion almost wholly to vows of chastity. The "good old times" of chivalry, he says, were "the most profligate of all possible centuries." For proof he refers us to a book by Lacurne de Sainte Palaye, *Mémoires sur l'ancienne chevalerie*, especially to volume 2, page 69. Well, what do we find there? This: "A Lady who receives in her home a Chevalier is not willing to go to sleep without sending him one of her women to keep him company." Following this are sixteen lines of medieval verse, with marginal glosses:

> The Countess practiced in courtliness is not unhappy to have her guest. Therefore, with great pleasure she had a splendid bed prepared for him in a room to himself. There, he falls asleep easily and rests well, and the Countess at length goes to bed, summons the most courtly and beautiful of her maidens, secretly tells her: "My dear, go at once, without worrying about it, and lie with this Chevalier. . . . Serve him, if need be. I would willingly go myself, I would not refrain out of shame, were it not for Milord the Count who is not yet asleep."[13]

Byron, who loved to live dangerously in many ways, loved most of all to sail close to the wind with words. I think he is doing so here. Specifically, I think he is telling us, with his cunning allusion, what *really* happened at Ali's palace.

I will return to this later with a postscript, but it is apparent already that *something* happened and that it transformed the young Byron in the same way that, twenty-four years later, the death of Arthur Henry Hallam transformed the young Tennyson. Each event endowed for the first time a young poet with subject matter, and in each case the subject was the same, himself. I *surmise* (1) that Byron's companion John Cam Hobhouse had the same experience; (2) that Byron described it in the journal that Hobhouse "persuaded him to burn"; (3) that Byron's reading of *The Faerie Queen* was the catalyst perhaps for the idea of writing *Childe Harold*, certainly for the narration of the Ali Pacha episode; and (4) that, finally, chickening out like Wordsworth in Book 9 of *The Prelude*, Byron so muted his language that, even with the publication of the telltale manuscript variants in 1899, the pivotal significance of the experience remained hidden, at least from all but a few contemporaries, until now.

So much for *Childe Harold* and 1809. I move now to a time thirteen years later and to another poem—to *Don Juan*, Canto 9, which (except for nine stanzas, stanzas 1–8 and 76) Byron composed in August and September 1822.

Before settling in on Canto 9, however, it may be helpful to rehearse briefly the narrative preceding it. Byron begins his renovation of the traditional story of Don Juan with an important, indeed crucial, innovation. All the others begin with Don Juan at the peak of his career; Byron begins with Juan's birth and upbringing. In the first episode we see Juan, "tall, handsome, slender," and "deem'd . . . almost man" by everyone except his widowed mother, who (all agree) is a portrait of Byron's wife. Juan is seduced by Donna Julia, who was "married, charming, chaste and twenty-three." They are surprised in bed by her husband, age fifty, and after a witty reference to the story of Joseph and Potiphar's wife, Juan flees naked into the night. (I think Stendhal in *Le rouge et le noir* patterned the similar episode of Julien Sorel and Mme de Renal on this one.) Juan's mother sends him away on a long tour, which is the framework of the remainder of the poem. The next episode is the famous storm at sea and shipwreck, scrupulously based on several factual accounts, and then the lovely idyll with Haidee. Her father, the pirate Lambro, returning unexpectedly, captures Juan. Haidee dies of a broken heart; Juan is sold into slavery. In Constantinople he is bought by the eunuch Baba for the lecherous Sultana, Gulbeyaz. Juan is required to masquerade as a harem girl, and in this disguise beds down with Dudu, in an episode even more comical than the mating with Donna Julia in Canto 1. Learning of this, the Sultana, already a woman scorned, improves on hell's fury by ordering Juan, Dudu, Baba, and the harem matron all to be sewn up in bags and deep-sixed. This fate might have been preferable to the homosexual rape that would have ensued had they remained (as Peter Manning has pointed out to me), for the Sultan himself had been ogling Juanna with a lubricity less conspicuous only than that of the Sultana.[14] Wonderfully, they manage to escape, and when we meet them again, two-thirds of the way into Canto 7, the manner and matter, the tenor, of the poem have changed sharply.

The poem changes sharply in four important ways.

1. For the first time the poem is grounded in history. All the other episodes could have taken place at any time. The shipwreck episode, for example, is one of fact piled upon fact, all amply documented, but it is nonetheless an amalgam of facts about several shipwrecks from several sources. It is not "history." Canto 7, however, thrusts us into the midst of the Russo-Turkish War and the siege of Ismail, which began on November 30, 1790. I will return to this.

2. Before Canto 7, along with all the delicious satirical commentary and pranking rhymes, the poem "kind of tells a story, so to speak . . . I like a story. Very bad taste on my part, no doubt, but I like a story. You can take your art, you can take your literature, you can take your music, but give me a good story . . . Yes, [it] tells a story. That is the fundamental aspect without which it could not exist." Beginning with Canto 7, however, it becomes "something different" . . . not exactly "melody, or perception of the truth," but emphatically no longer primarily "this low atavistic form." Story was precisely the aspect of the novel that Forster wanted to be rid of, and it is precisely the aspect of this poem that now begins to diminish. Byron was well aware of this, and the change of emphasis was deliberate. "It is necessary," he said, "in the present clash of philosophy and tyranny, to throw away the scabbard. I know it is against fearful odds; but the battle must be fought; and it will eventually be for the good of mankind" (*LJ* 9:191). Story yields to "philosophy." Narrative wanes; narrative voice waxes. And not only that. Even more significant, the narrative and the narrative voice begin now to sustain each other symbiotically. Both are concerned with the same thing. Each exemplifies the other.

3. The quintessential theme of the poem here moves to front and center. That theme, generally stated, is the corrosive effect of life and time on innocence, the ephemerality of ideality; particularly stated, it is the dehumanization of Juan, Juan's becoming "gradually gâté and blasé," as Byron put it (*LJ* 8:78), the perversion of Juan into Don Juan. Byron himself experienced such a transformation in Venice, and, just when finishing the first canto of *Don Juan*, he became his own Leporello, perhaps deliberately: in two years, he assures a friend, more than twenty-five hundred pounds sterling had been "laid out on the Sex—to be sure I have had plenty for the money—that's certain—I think at least two hundred of one sort or another—perhaps more—for I have not lately kept the recount" (*LJ* 6:66).

The traditional Don Juan or Don Giovanni (as in Molière and Mozart and earlier) is an antihero because of two traits of character—blasphemy and sexuality, which are in some ways the same thing, since the assertion of sexuality over all other values is in itself not only an offense against God but the ultimate offense: absolute flesh is a denial of absolute spirit. In Byron blasphemy and sexuality are translated into equivalent terms, as he makes plain in one of his wonderful letters.

> As to "Don Juan"—confess—confess—you dog—and be candid—that it
> is the sublime of *that there* sort of writing—it may be bawdy—but is it

not good English? it may be profligate—but is it not *life*, is it not the *thing*? Could any man have written it—who has not lived in the world? and tooled in a post-chaise? in a hackney coach? in a Gondola? against a wall? in a court carriage? in a vis a vis?—on a table? and under it? I have written about a hundred stanzas of a third Canto—but it is damned modest—the outcry has frightened me.—I had such projects for the Don— but the *Cant* is so much stronger than *Cunt*—now a days,—that the bene- fit to experience in a man who had well weighed the worth of both mono- syllables—must be lost to despairing posterity. (*LJ* 6:232)

Byron's poem, as I have said, revolutionizes the tradition by begin- ning with Juan's birth and upbringing. Don Juan is corrupt; Juan cor- rupted. It is also revolutionary in transferring sexual aggression to the female figures, who (with the single exception of Dudu in the harem scene but including Haidee) are all sexual predators. In Canto 7 the first lines are: "O Love! O Glory! what are ye who fly / Around us ever, rarely to alight." And Byron here effects another translation: as, in the letter, blasphemy and sexuality are translated into Cant and Cunt, so in his poem they are translated into "Glory" and "Love." The next two cantos, 8 and 9, a sort of verbal diptych, exemplify first one and then the other. Canto 8 exemplifies glory in the person of the leader of the Russian forces against Ismail, Marshal Suvarow. Canto 9 exemplifies Love in the person of the Russian empress Catherine the Great. Suvarow is a fighting machine; Catherine is a fucking machine. Juan becomes both.

I said that Canto 7 marks the beginning of four important changes in the poem—the first three of which I can sum up as History, "Phi- losophy," Dehumanization. The fourth change I will call *parody*. In Canto 7 Byron begins to turn his poem into an implied parody of *Childe Harold's Pilgrimage*. The parody accelerates and intensifies until, in Canto 10, what is implicit becomes explicit, and we begin to see Byron at his most narcissistic.

Childe Harold's Pilgrimage, as is well known, is a work of myth- making. *Don Juan* is a work of myth unmaking. What *Childe Harold* mythologizes, *Don Juan* demythologizes. The promise of glory held out in *Childe Harold* is literally ridiculed in *Don Juan*, Canto 7. The Penin- sular War, more or less observed by Harold the Pilgrim, *in spite of* all the irony and satire, is nonetheless romanticized, partly by the narra- tor's ideological bias (one side is wrong, the other is right), partly by the inflated rhetoric. The Russo-Turkish War, observed *and participated in* by Don Juan, *because of* the irony and satire, is exposed as brutal and vain, partly by the *absence* of ideological bias (the Christian Russians are as barbaric as the Moslem Turks), partly by the deft control of tone, and partly by the factual background on which Byron so prided himself. (He used volume 2 of Gabriel de Castelnau's *Essai sur l'histoire ancienne et moderne de la nouvelle Russie*, which incorporated several pages of an eyewitness account by an anonymous Russian lieutenant-general.)

The Russo-Turkish War of Juan is a revision of the Peninsular War of Harold, and in this way Byron begins now his *recherche du temps perdu*. He begins to merge present and past, to transform Harold into Juan. The first overt sign of this comes in Canto 5, written in October–November 1820, exactly at the time when Byron had "begun a continuation" of his memoirs (*LJ* 7:207, 219). Canto 5 marks the first appearance of a strange, laid-back character—strange because he is totally irrelevant and equally unimportant. He is an Englishman, and with Juan he is sold in the market to the Sultan. He escapes with Juan and the others and with Juan takes part in the siege of Ismail. He is older than Juan, whom he regards as "a mere lad" (*DJ* 5.89), and, though he appears and is described in Canto 5, he is not named till Canto 7 (he does not appear at all in Canto 6), and then we learn that his name is Johnson (*DJ* 7.473), indeed, "John Johnson" (*DJ* 8.769). In fact, Byron once calls him "*Jack*" (*DJ* 8.769), once refers to him as "Jack Johnson" in a canceled reading (*DJ* 8.350), and once (*DJ* 8.305–6) coyly mentions his name in connection with Ajax. Jack Johnson is an affectionate portrait of Byron's boxing master, Gentleman John Jackson, who was "boxing champion of England from 1795 to 1803, when he retired" from the ring.[15] He was born in 1768, twenty years before Byron, and died in 1845. There is a portrait of him in Henry Downes Miles's *Pugilistica: The History of British Boxing*, together with a fine description and discussion, and in Pierce Egan's *Life in London* one of the Cruikshanks' drawings shows "Tom and Jerry receiving instruction from Mr. Jackson, at his rooms in Bond Steet." "Integrity, impartiality, good-nature, and manliness," according to Pierce Egan, "are the corner-stones of his intellect."[16] Byron knew him well and, along with many others, genuinely liked and admired him, as we know from the Byron letters, including five to Jackson himself, all greeting him as "Dear Jack." Nothing we know of their relationship contradicts the description in *Don Juan* (*DJ* 5.78–88), and other details, especially of personal appearance, coincide. Byron says Johnson was "stout and hale" and "square In make"; Miles says he was the "beau ideal" of "perfect manhood" and speaks of the "happy combination of muscular development with proportionate symmetry in his frame."[17] *Fights for the Championship; and Celebrated Prize Battles*, by the editor of *Bell's Life in London*, also speaks of his "symmetrical" frame.[18] Byron writes of the "resolution in [Johnson's] dark grey eyes" (*DJ* 5.79); Miles says Jackson's eyes "were full and piercing, and formed a great portion of his power as a pugilist —with them he riveted his men."[19] Byron speaks of Johnson's "*sang-froid*" (*DJ* 5.87) and says

> Seldom he varied feature, hue, or muscle,
> And could be very busy without bustle.
>
> (*DJ* 8.311–12)

Miles says Jackson "was always on his guard; there was no chance of rushing suddenly in and taking Jackson by surprise—he could not be flurried," and also speaks of his extraordinary power as a "runner of a short distance";[20] Byron's Jack Johnson, in a fine pun,

> Knew when and how "to cut and come again",
> And never ran away, except when running
> Was nothing but a valourous kind of cunning.
>
> (*DJ* 8.278–80)

And, finally, in a note in Canto 11 (stanza 19), Byron paid a particular tribute to Jackson: "my old friend and corporeal pastor and master, John Jackson, Esq., Professor of Pugilism; who, I trust, still retains the strength and symmetry of his model of a form, together with his good humor, and athletic as well as mental accomplishments."

It is generally acknowledged that beginning with the English cantos *Don Juan* takes on something of the character of a memoir—this is at a time when Byron was no longer at work on his own memoirs. I have already suggested that this memoir quality is prefigured in a general way by the Russo-Turkish War and in a specific way by the introduction of the character of Jack Johnson. I suggest now that the real memoir begins, not with Canto 10 and the visit to England, but with Canto 9 and Juan's visit to the court of Catherine the Great.

Canto 9 was composed in August and September 1822. In the eighteen months or so preceding this date a number of events conspired to turn Byron's thoughts to the past. Three persons variously impinging on his life died—John Scott, an Aberdeen schoolfellow, early in 1821 (*LJ* 8.99 n.); Napoleon in July; John William Polidori, who accompanied Byron to Switzerland in 1816, committed suicide in August. In mid-October 1821 Byron recorded in his "Detached Thoughts" Walter Scott's phrase about his features—"An Alabaster vase lighted up within"—a description he drew upon, nine or ten months later, in *Don Juan* (8. 768).

(E. H. Coleridge's gloss on this allusion connects it with the sculptor Bartolini, with whom Byron corresponded in November 1821, who began his bust of Byron on January 3, and who had designed "marble vases" for Napoleon's "terrace at Elba, which were to be illuminated at night 'from within.'" Byron could see Elba from his home, Villa Dupuy, at Montenero.)[21] In October 1821, by pure chance, he met on the road his old Harrow friend Lord Clare and later alluded several times to the chance encounter. "I never hear the word '*Clare*' without a beating of the heart—even *now*, as I write it—with the feelings of 1803–4–5–ad infinitum," he wrote in "Detached Thoughts" (*LJ* 9.44). And a couple of weeks or so later he wrote again: "This meeting annihilated for a moment all the years between the present time and the days of Harrow— It was a new and inexplicable feeling like rising from the grave to me. . . . We were but five minutes together—and in the public road—but I hardly recollect an hour of my existence which could be weighed against them" (*LJ* 9.49). And four months later he said: "I have always loved him better than any *male* thing in the world (*LJ* 9.117).

On January 2, 1822, Byron heard from Murray of Polidori's suicide in August.[22] On January 28, 1822, his mother-in-law, Lady Noel, died. (Byron had said she was "immortal"—"that an ill-tempered woman turned of Seventy—never dies—though they be buried sometimes" [*LJ* 9.72].) Byron heard the news on February 15 (*LJ* 9.105 n.). Her death was profitable to him financially as well as psychically, and from then on he became Noel Byron, well aware that his initials were the same as Napoleon Bonaparte's. On April 20 his daughter Allegra (by Claire Clairmont) died, at the age of five. This too took him back in time, for Allegra had been conceived three or four days before he left England, once and for all, in April 1816.

On May 22 the American George Bancroft (then a young man of twenty-two, later a distinguished statesman and historian) called on Byron, by invitation, at the Villa Dupuy, and in the course of the conversation Byron referred "to his last journey from England to Switzerland" in May 1816, and "described his tour on the Rhine as having given him unmingled pleasure."[23]

Less than a fortnight later Lord Clare called on him at the Villa Dupuy and Byron wrote: "A few days ago my earliest and dearest friend Lord Clare came over . . . on purpose to see me before he returned to England. As I have always loved him (since I was thirteen, at Harrow) better than any (*male*) thing in the world, I need hardly say what a melancholy pleasure it was to see him for a *day* only, for he was obliged to resume his journey immediately" (*LJ* 9:170).

This letter is even more interesting in another respect, but before going on I want to mention, in reverse order, three more deaths—that of Viscount Castlereagh (Marquis of Londonderry), of whose suicide Byron learned on or by August 27, 1822; second, that of Shelley, who drowned in the Bay of Spezia on July 8 and whom Byron described as "the *best* and least selfish man I ever knew. I never knew one who was not a beast in comparison" (*LJ* 9:190).

The first of these three deaths was that of probably the *worst* man he ever met, and with this death the wheel comes full circle. It is not mentioned in any of the books on Byron, and yet it may be the most significant of them all. It was the death of Ali Pacha. At the end of December 1821, Ali was under siege in an island citadel. All his sons and one of his grandsons, several of them known to Byron, had been beheaded, and his mad last days were not unlike those of Hitler in the Berlin bunker. Ali was shot by trickery and treachery on February 5, 1822, and then, by the Sultan's orders, he was beheaded and the head was embalmed and sent to Constantinople.[24]

Now, in the letter to Tom Moore, June 8, 1822, in which Byron speaks of Lord Clare's visit, he also wrote in a postscript, about his inspection of the American warships which occasioned his meeting with George Bancroft. "I have been invited on board the American squadron," he wrote, "and treated with all possible honour and ceremony. . . . These American honours arise perhaps, not so much for their enthusiasm for my "Poeshie," as their belief in my dislike to the English— in which I have the satisfaction to coincide with them. I would rather, however, have a nod from an American than a snuff-box from an emperor" (*LJ* 9:171).

"Snuff-box from an emperor"! This seems to put us back to October and November 1809, Byron's visit to Ali Pacha, and the great letter to his mother describing the visit (*LJ* 1:226–31). "Bonaparte," said Byron in that letter, "sent him [Ali] a snuff-box with his picture." Napoleon's snuffboxes were as numerous as fragments of the true cross, but the timing here suggests Ali Pacha's. We don't know when Byron heard the news of Ali's capture and decapitation on February 5. It was confirmed in London in the *Times* of March 22 (p. 2b), which got the news from Corfu in a dispatch dated March 5. Byron therefore must have known it sooner, and in any case it seems probable that the news boiled in his "being's inmost cells, the fountains of his deepest life, / Confused in passion's golden" impurity.

Canto 9 of *Don Juan*, to which I turn now, was composed in August and September 1822, thirteen years after the visit to Ali Pacha, three months or so after the inspection of the American Mediterranean squadron and the telling allusion to Ali's snuffbox. The subject of Canto 9 is Juan at the court of Catherine the Great. He has been sent there by Marshal Suvarow, who seems to have been attracted to Juan much as the Sultan had been—and in the same way (*DJ* 7.526–27), with the dispatch announcing, in rhyme, the capture of Ismail, with thirty thousand slain. Catherine rejoices (in this order) over the news, over Suvarow's rhymes, and then over Juan. She is of course enchanted by his youth and beauty. She has him vetted—indeed, *tested*—by Miss Protasoff, the Eprouveuse—and Juan becomes the royal favorite, a morsel for a monarch, in the line of Lanskoi, Potemkin, and all the others, about whom Byron knew all there was to know.

This is powerful stuff, but Byron handles it perfectly—as deftly and expertly as Mozart. He had achieved a similar success in Canto 8, in the battle of Ismail, where Juan, "pervaded" by "the thirst Of glory" (*DJ* 8.412–13), becomes an efficient instrument of war, becomes a killing machine. Juan's heroism is diminished, precisely, by his courage; his moral stature is degraded, precisely, by his valor. He is redeemed from squalor by a major instance of "humanity" (*DJ* 8.1114)—his rescue of little Leila, the Moslem orphan, who accompanies him throughout the rest of the poem. No such redemption is possible at the court of Catherine. Juan, like Tom Jones with Lady Bellaston, becomes a male whore.

Let's look now at details. The year of the siege of Ismail is 1790, when Catherine, born in 1729, as Byron knew perfectly well, was sixtyone or sixty-two years old. She probably had her husband, Peter III, murdered, and her lechery, even to the end of her life, age sixty-seven, was and remains legendary. Her motto ought to have been: "Trespassers will be violated." She had a succession of official favorites, all of them known to history, all of them young and handsome, and all discussed in Byron's source, Charles François Philibert Masson's *Mémoires secrets sur la Russie pendant les règnes de Catherine II et de Paul Ier* (1800). But I do not think it is true, despite all the commentators, that Don Juan here is a composite portrait made of three of the favorites. Byron is far more subtle, far more profound, far more ironic, far more devious, and far more interesting.

"Man is least himself," said Oscar Wilde, "when he talks in his own person. Give him a mask and he will tell you the truth." Don Juan here is Byron himself and, what is more, Catherine here is Ali Pacha. Juan is clothed in the "full suit of Staff uniform," with magnificent saber, that Byron had had made, for fifty guineas, by a tailor in Gibraltar, in August 1809, two and a half months before he saw Ali. "I have a most superb uniform as a court dress," Byron wrote to his mother, "indispensable in travelling" (*LJ* 1:221). Hobhouse had one also, and they were the uniforms of an aide-de-camp, according to John Galt, who saw them in Gibraltar and later in Sardinia,[25] and of such a "gaudy red"[26] that Galt thought them a ridiculous affectation.

Here is the description of Juan when Catherine receives him:

> Suppose him in a handsome uniform;
> A scarlet coat, black facings, a long plume,
> Waving, like sails new shivered in a storm,
> Over a cocked hat in a crowded room,
> And brilliant breeches, bright as a Cairn Gorme,
> Of yellow cassimere we may presume,
> White stockings drawn, uncurdled as new milk,
> O'er limbs whose symmetry set off the silk:
>
> Suppose him sword by side, and hat in hand,
> Made up by Youth, Fame, and an Army tailor—
> That great Enchanter, at whose rod's command
> Beauty springs forth, and Nature's self turns paler,
> Seeing how Art can make her work more grand,
> (When she don't pin men's limbs in like a gaoler)—
> Behold him placed as if upon a pillar! He
> Seems Love turned a Lieutenant of Artillery!
>
> His Bandage slipped down into a cravāt;
> His Wings subdued to epaulettes; his Quiver
> Shrunk to a scabbard, with his Arrows at
> His side as a small sword, but sharp as ever;
> His Bow converted into a cocked hat;
> But still so like, that Psyche were more clever
> Than some wives (who make blunders no less stupid)
> If she had not mistaken him for Cupid.
>
> (*DJ* 9.337–60)

For the audience with Ali Pacha, Byron's uniform was certainly that gorgeous confection made up by the army tailor in Gibraltar, and there can be no doubt that in his audience with Catherine Juan was wearing the same outfit, though except by necessity Byron would not have appeared in knee breeches. Let me quote Doris Langley Moore, as great an authority on costume as on Byron: "For ceremonial occasions abroad he had a cocked hat with plumes, and a scarlet suit embroidered with gold which was the full dress uniform of an aide-de-camp. I believe it was an admissible dress for peers being presented at foreign courts, and certainly it had a tremendous effect on certain Pashas in Albania and Turkey."[27] One detail, however, is significantly different—the yellow cashmere breeches. Court protocol required breeches, all right, but why yellow? Once more, Hobhouse may have given us the answer. Albanian custom, he reported, required the removal indoors of the "outward shoes." "The rich," he said, "have a thin boot without a sole, reaching a little above their ankles, which, when worn by a Turk or privileged Greek, is yellow or scarlet, but in all other cases blue, or some dark colour."[28]

Ali, in Byron's accounts, was "60 years old, very fat and not tall, but with a fine face, light blue eyes," and with a "very kind" manner (*LJ* 1:228); "Gentleness" throws a "milder radiance" along his face (*CHP* 2.556–57). Catherine is sixty-one or sixty-two, she is plump, has "blue eyes, or grey," and "though fierce *looked* lenient" and "Glanced mildly" on Juan. "Her face was noble, her eyes were fine, mouth gracious" (*DJ* 9.570, 562, 498–99, 464).

Ali was certain that Byron was "a man of birth" because of his "small ears, curling hair, and little white hands." Byron tells us that on Juan's "unembarrassed brow / Nature had written 'gentleman'" (*DJ* 9.661–62). Byron, with Ali, found his "pedigree more regarded than even" his title (*LJ* 1:228), and Juan, with Catherine, owed much "to the blood he show'ed / like a race-horse" (*DJ* 10.228–29). Ali told Byron "to consider him as a father . . . and said he looked on me as his son" (*LJ* 1: 227–28); Juan's mother, in a letter, praised Catherine's "*maternal* love" (*DJ* 10.256). Byron and Hobhouse saw, and indeed spent their first evening in Ali's palace in the company of, his two physicians; Juan is attended by Catherine's physician (*LJ* 1:227; *DJ* 10.304–52).[29]

The "shameless torch of wild desire is lit," chez Ali, we recall, for "boyish minions." Catherine, we are twice told, "sometimes liked a boy," and preferred "a boy to men much bigger," and Juan is referred to as her "minion" (*DJ* 9.375, 571; 10.348). Ali "Delights to mingle with the lip of youth" (*CHP* 2.506 vl.); Catherine "liked to gaze on youth" (*DJ* 9.486). Ali, with his kind manner and "dignity," has the "appearance of anything but his real character, for he is a remorseless tyrant" (*LJ* 1:228); Catherine, "though fierce *looked* lenient" (*DJ* 9.499).

Catherine thinks of Juan as "the herald Mercury / New lighted on a 'Heaven-kissing hill'" (*DJ* 9.521), and Byron, in the same episode, says, "we have just lit on a 'Heaven-kissing hill'" (*DJ* 9.676). The allusion is to *Hamlet* 3.4.58, where Hamlet is bitterly berating his mother for her unnatural act, and Gertrude replies: "Thou turn'st mine eyes into my very soul, / And there I see such black and grained spots / As will not leave their tinct." Juan, at second *Hamlet* reference, "retired" with Miss Protasoff, the "Eprouveuse," and it is interesting that Byron should have used the same word when terminating his initial interview with Ali: "I then after coffee and pipes retired for the first time" (*LJ* 1:228).

("In England," Byron observed in a letter six months later [May 3, 1810], "the vices in fashion are whoring and drinking, in Turkey Sodomy and smoking, we prefer a girl and a bottle, they a pipe and a pathic. They are sensible people," he continues without a break, "Ali Pacha told me he was sure I was a man of rank because I had *small ears* and handsome *curling* hair" [*LJ* 1:238].) In Albania, by Ali's order, Byron was "supplied with every kind of necessary, *gratis*," and "was not permitted to pay for a single article of household consumption" (*LJ* 1:226). In Russia Juan, as his mother's letter says, "brought his spending to a handsome anchor" and reduced his "expenses" (*DJ* 10.244, 248).

Juan and Ali talked of "war and travelling, politics and England," and when Byron left Ali's court, he says, Ali gave him "letters, guards and every possible accommodation" [*LJ* 1:228]. At the Russian court Juan falls ill and Catherine

> . . . resolved to send him on a mission,
> But in a style becoming his condition.

He is sent as her emissary to England, to negotiate

> Something about the Baltic's navigation,
> Hides, train-oil, tallow, and the rights of Thetis,
> Which Britons deem their "uti possidetis."

So she fitted him out "in a handsome way" and sent him to England "laden with all kinds of gifts and honours" (*DJ* 10.361, 367).

The English cantos that follow are praised by everyone, and in due course I will have something to say about them, but there is more to be said about the episode with Catherine the Great, in which there is yet another stratum: once more *The Faerie Queen*.

Let me turn once more to biographical fact, to July 1822, at the Casa Lanfranchi, Byron's palace in Pisa. There, Leigh Hunt and his family arrived about July 1, living in the "ground-floor apartments."[30] All this is a story in itself, and a well-known one, but I am concerned now with only one fact. I quote a paragraph from Leslie Marchand's *Byron: A Biography*:

> Hunt, who had lived among books since his earliest years, thought Byron's collection lopsided and rather poor, consisting chiefly of new ones and English works published on the Continent. "He was anxious to show you that he possessed no Shakespeare and Milton; 'because,' he said, 'he had been accused of borrowing from them!'" Byron said he could not

read Spenser. Hunt recalled: "I lent him a volume of the 'Fairy Queen,' and he said he would try to like it. Next day he brought it to my study-window, and said, 'Here, Hunt, here is your Spenser. I cannot see anything in him:' and he seemed anxious that I should take it out of his hands, as if he was afraid of copying so poor a writer."[31]

In view of what we know about *Childe Harold's Pilgrimage*, this remark is, to say the least, interesting. It is certain that *The Faerie Queen* had recently been in his consciousness to some extent, for in Canto 7 of *Don Juan*, completed on June 28, a couple of days before Hunt's arrival, Byron had wittily distorted a familiar line from the Introduction (line 9) to *The Faerie Queen* to read, "Fierce loves and faithless wars," which, as we have seen, is precisely the subject of Cantos 8 and 9.

In Canto 9 in stanza 42, immediately preceding Juan's appearance at court, Byron says:

> So on I ramble, now and then narrating,
> Now pondering:—it is time we should narrate:
> I left Don Juan with his horses baiting—
> Now we'll get o'er the ground at a great rate.
> I shall not be particular in stating
> His journey, we've so many tours of late:
> Suppose him then at Petersburgh; suppose
> That pleasant capital of painted Snows.

The usual—indeed, the only—gloss of "painted snows" is that of E. H. Coleridge, who quotes a passage from William Tooke's *Life of Catherine*, which does not mention either paint or snow and of which the very point is that the Petersburg winter is only too real.[32] For Byron the snow *is* painted, but it is painted with blood, and the source of his phrase is *The Faerie Queen*, Book 2, Canto 12. And it is this book, and most particularly this canto, that underlies this whole episode. Book 2 of *The Faerie Queen* is "The Legend of Sir Guyon, or Of Temperance," and it is primarily upon Canto 12, with the Bower of Bliss, that Byron draws. Even in Canto 1, however, Guyon rescues an infant orphan in a manner entirely comparable to Juan's rescue of little Leila, the Moslem orphan, in the siege of Ismail. And in Canto 7 (stanzas 53 ff.), the golden apples in the Garden of Proserpina contributed to the wonderful dream of Dudu in the harem scene in *Don Juan* (6.593–616). Guyon is of course beset with every temptation conceivable, all of which are warded off by the Palmer accompanying, and though it is not necessary to identify Guyon and the Palmer with Byron and Hobhouse, the points of resemblance, muttatis mutandis, are striking, and it would be humorless to dismiss the possibility of this delicious nuance.

Guyon and the Palmer enter the Bower of Bliss through a gate of ivory, intricately carved with the story of Jason and Medea and the voyage of the Argo. The ivory of the waves and billows is called a "snowy substance sprent / with vermell," sprinkled with vermilion, "like the boys blood therein shed" (*FQ* 2.12.43–45), and a little later (stanza 58) Spenser refers to the "painted flowers"— all this, of course, the essence of the Bower of Bliss, created by the "faire enchanteresse" (stanza 81), where, Spenser tells us several times, art imitated nature and "Art at nature did repine [fret]" (stanzas 42, 59), mentioning also "Art, as half in scorne / Of niggard Nature" (stanza 50). The Bower of Bliss is in a plain (which Byron seems to have drawn on in *Childe Harold*, 2.442–59, en route to Ali Pacha), in the midst of which "a fountain stood" (stanza 60).

In Juan's introduction to Catherine, he is in his resplendent uniform, "made up by . . . an army tailor" who is called

> That great Enchanter, at whose rod's command
> Beauty springs forth, and Nature's self turns paler.

Spenser had earlier (stanza 23) referred to "Dame Nature selfe" and in the same stanza to the "Great Whirlpoole" that even the fishes flee, which becomes in *Don Juan* "the whirlpool full of depth and danger" (9.507) about all women, especially Catherine. Before the gate of the Bower of Bliss the Palmer brandishes his mighty staff, made up of the same wood as the Caduceus, the "rod of Mercury" (stanzas 40–41), just as Byron, when Juan kneels before Catherine, speaks of the "herald Mercury / New lighted on a Heaven-kissing hill" (9.521).

Guyon and the Palmer penetrate to the depths of the garden and there view Acrasia lying "upon a bed of roses" (stanza 77) with her young lover, Verdant. Here is Spenser:

> The young man sleeping by her seemed to bee
> Some goodly swayne of honourable place,
> That certes it great pittie was to see
> Him his nobilitie so foule deface;
> And sweet regard and amiable grace,
> Mixed with manly sternnesse did appeare
> Yet sleeping, in his well-proportioned face,
> And on his tender lip the downy heare
> Did now but freshly spring, and silken blossoms beare.

Here is Byron:

> Juan was . . . slight and slim,
> Blushing and beardless; and yet ne'ertheless

> There was a something is his turn of limb,
> And still more in his eye, which seemed to express
> That though he looked one of the Seraphim,
> There lurked a Man beneath the Spirit's dress.
>
> (*DJ* 9.369–74)

And six stanzas later:

> Juan, I said, was a most beauteous Boy,
> And had retained his boyish look beyond
> The usual hirsute seasons . . .
>
> (*DJ* 9.417–20)

Following this is next to the bawdiest passage in Byron's works, the apostrophe to the vulva, especially Catherine's. And after *that*, in stanzas 67 and 68, she looks down at him, "and so they fell in love—She with his face, / His grace, his God-knows-what," and Juan—this marks his decisive transformation into Don Juan—Juan fell into "Self-love." Then, in the next stanza, the ne plus ultra of Byron's bawdry, we are told that all cats are gray in the dark—especially for a lusty young nobleman of twenty-one, handsome, rich, well dressed, willful, far away from home for the first time in his life and in an obscure, remote, exotic, barbarous part of the world, and, what is more, tempted to indulge "to the full," as Hobhouse wrote of Ali, "all the pleasures that are licenced by the custom of the country."[33]

> [Juan] was of that delighted age
> Which makes all female ages equal—when
> We don't much care with whom we may engage,
> As bold as Daniel in the Lion's den,
> So that we can our native sun assuage
> In the next ocean, which may flow just then,
> To make a twilight in, just as Sol's heat is
> Quenched in the lap of the salt Sea, or Thetis.

In the episode at the Sultan's palace Byron had already twice referred to Daniel in the lion's den (*DJ* 5.477, 646). "Assuage" has the sense of "abate, lessen, diminish (esp. anything swollen)" (OED). "Lap" for female pudendum is familiar in Hamlet's "country matters" bawdry with Ophelia (3.2.116 ff.). "Quenched in the lap of the salt sea, or Thetis" seems to be an allusion to *Hudibras*, 2.2.29 (a poem that Byron knew intimately and quoted at will):

> The sun had long since in the Lap
> Of Thetis, taken out his Nap,
> And . . .   the Morn
> From black to red began to turn.

In the Bower of Bliss Guyon and the Palmer come upon Acrasia and Verdant:

> That wanton Ladie, with her lover lose [loose or wanton]
> Whose sleepie head she in her lap did soft dispose.
>
> (*FQ* 3.23.76)

Byron had already defined "cunnus" (from Horace's *Satire* 1.3.107) as "Thou sea of life's dry land" (*DJ* 9.448). And to this I add two things: (1) as Byron wrote to his mother, he entered Tepelene, where Ali resided, "at five in the afternoon as the Sun was going down," and (2) in the same letter he remarks: "I bathed in the sea, today" (*LJ* 1:227, 229).

One does not want to be too ingenious, and I do not think I have erred in that direction. There is a conspicuous difference between the received interpretations of this episode and the interpretation you have just heard, a difference as conspicuous and as vital as the difference between night and day. Everyone can tell the difference between night and day, but no one can say exactly where one ends and the other begins, and in the case of this stanza it seems necessary to cite *all* the evidence. The paraphrasable prose meaning, in any event, is beyond dispute, and it is bawdy. The stanza is unquestionably a cryptogram. The context and the resonances imply something beyond plain prose and, this being true, one should not overlook the implications of the fact that the number of the stanza is 69.

Let me return now for the postscript to *Childe Harold* that I promised earlier. Don Juan has slept with Miss Protasoff before sleeping with Catherine, and in the harem he had slept with Dudu rather than with the Sultana (not to mention the Sultan!). Childe Harold, on the other hand, sleeps with nobody at any time, but Byron thought it desirable to discuss the charge of unknightliness in terms of a medieval French poem (from a book by Ste. Palaye, vol. 2, p. 69) in which a Chevalier sleeps with a maiden deputized by his hostess, the Countess. There *is* a pattern and the outlines are clear, so clear that it would require a scholarship of uncommon severity to resist the inference that it tells us something about Byron's experience chez Ali Pacha.

This reading of Canto 9 has shown definitively that biography has critical importance and can influence critical evaluation. "It has fre-

quently been suggested"—I am quoting Leslie Marchand—"that the Russian cantos of *Don Juan* are the weakest because Byron was writing
about what he had not seen and experienced, and by his own confession that always put a damper on his genius."[34] The editor of Byron's
poetry calls Juan's affair with Catherine "the poem's least interesting
episode."[35] On the basis of the biographical evidence presented here,
I myself would call it the poem's *most* interesting episode, and I would
affirm additionally that Canto 9 is the very climax of the poem viewed
as a whole, with the same structural importance that Canto 9 has in
several books of *The Faerie Queen* (especially Books 1 and 2), that
Book 9 has in *Paradise Lost* (the temptation and fall), and that Book 9
has in *The Prelude* ("Residence in France"). Moreover, Byron's Canto 9
shares with Book 9 of *Paradise Lost* and of *The Prelude*, and also with
Tennyson's "Pelleas and Ettarre," the ninth of the *Idylls of the King*, the
same crucial significance, sexual awareness.

The remainder of *Don Juan*, though no less interesting, is clear sail-
ing, for a clear reason. Juan is sent to England as Catherine's emissary
—by way of Warsaw, Konigsberg,

> And thence through Berlin, Dresden, and the like,
> Until he reached the castellated Rhine.

Juan reverses Byron's journey of April–May 1816, when he left England
for the last time. It is an extraordinary phenomenon and an extraordinary tour-de-force, and the progress of the poem can be measured, easily and in detail, in the letters of that period, in the third canto of
Childe Harold read backward, so to speak, and in other documents.
Mindfully and wittily, Byron draws upon the scenes, the language, and
even the inflated rhetoric of *Childe Harold's Pilgrimage*:

> Ye glorious Gothic scenes! how much ye strike
> All phantasies, not even excepting mine:
> A grey wall, a green ruin, rusty pike,
> Make my soul pass the equinoctial line
> Between the present and past worlds, and hover
> Upon their airy confine, half-seas-over.

These few lines in themselves are stunning echoes. The "rusty pike" is,
in *Childe Harold*,

> . . . the sword laid by
> Which eats into itself and rusts ingloriously,
>   (CHP 3.395–96)

symbol of Napoleon in defeat and exile as of Byron himself and all others who are the vampires of their own hearts. The "grey wall, green ruin" reflect the

> . . . chiefless castles breathing stern farewells
> From gray but leafy walls, where Ruin greenly dwells.
>
> (*CHP* 3.413–14)

Another allusion just as specifically evokes the "castled crag of Drachenfels" lyric in *Childe Harold*, and in this evocation (which also draws upon a letter to Hobhouse of May 16, 1816) Byron is remembering in 1822 his remembering in 1816 of Augusta Leigh:

> But Juan posted on through Mannheim, Bonn,
> Which Drachenfels frowns over like a spectre
> Of the good feudal times for ever gone,
> On which I have not time just now to lecture.
>
> (*DJ* 10.488–89)

After Drachenfels Juan

> . . . was drawn onwards to Cologne,
> A city which presents to the inspector
> Eleven thousand Maidenheads of bone,
> The greatest number flesh hath ever known.

From the diary of his physician and companion, Polidori, we know that Byron saw the "11,000 virgins' bones,"[36] but it is from the same letter to Hobhouse that we learn of the "German chambermaid—whose red cheeks and white teeth . . . made me venture upon her carnally." But there is another stratum to this letter. In September–October 1822, Byron, writing of Juan's Rhine journey, recalls his own Rhine journey of May 1816. In May 1816, the Rhine valley scenery reminded him of his 1809 journey in Portugal and, much more significant, the Albanian valley on the route to Tepelene, where he saw Ali Pacha (*LJ* 5.76). In Holland Juan embarks for England in language that echoes the departure in *Childe Harold* from England, and also the very seasickness of that voyage described in a letter: "As a veteran I stomached the sea pretty well—till a damned 'Merchant of Bruges' capsized his breakfast close by me—and made me sick by contagion" (*LJ* 5:71). The customhouse at Dover is in both *Don Juan* (10.567) and the letter to Hobhouse (*LJ* 5:71). Canterbury was a tourist stop, outward-bound in 1816, inward-bound in *Don Juan*.

At Shooter's Hill, eight miles south of London, the poem resumes the psychological development of the character of Juan and no doubt betrays some nostalgia on the part of the author. The dehumanization of Juan proceeds apace. The very smog seemed to Juan a "magic vapour," and, though it "put the sun out like a taper," to him it was "but the natural atmosphere" (*DJ* 10.657–64). In Canto 11 he is ambushed by four pads, and, too "hasty" in his own defense, draws his pistol and kills one of the assailants. The killing was unnecessary, as Juan admits.

Juan enters London society and is of course there, as elsewhere, a great success. He is invited to Norman Abbey, the countryseat of Lady Adeline Amundeville and Lord Henry, which is of course Byron's own Newstead Abbey, and it is described in some of the very words used to depict that home in the opening stanzas of *Childe Harold*, before the pilgrimage began. In other words, Byron has sent Juan back to the very beginning of *Childe Harold*.

In a couple of stanzas in Canto 14, as nimble witted as anything in all literature, Byron gaily warns us that he writes in code, and even this warning has been ignored or misconstrued by the commentators:

> "*Haud ignara loquor*": these are *Nugae*, "*quarum*
> *Pars parva fui*," but still art and part.
> Now I could much more easily sketch a harem,
> A battle, wreck, or history of the heart,
> Than these things; and besides, I wish to spare 'em,
> For reasons which I choose to keep apart.
> '*Vetabo Cereris sacrum qui volgarit*'—
> Which means that vulgar people must not share it.
>
> And therefore what I throw off is ideal—
> Lower'd, leaven'd like a history of Freemasons;
> Which bears the same relation to the real,
> As Captain Parry's voyage may do to Jason's.
> The grand Arcanum's not for men to see all;
> My music has some mystic diapasons;
> And there is much which could not be appreciated
> In any manner by the uninitiated.

This multilayered passage is the richest lode in all *Don Juan* and the most explicit for our purposes here. The first Latin phrases, cleverly adapted from the *Aeneid* (2.91, 6), "Haud ignara loquor" and "these are Nugae, quarum Pars parva fui," can be rendered as "I know whereof I speak" and "'these are trifling matters [which I myself saw and] in which I played a small part." This is not exactly straightforward and viewed in context can induce vertigo, for in the passage in Virgil Aeneas is relating to Dido the story of the Trojan horse. And what *he* said was "These are piteous sights which I myself saw and in which I played a great part." Byron thus warns us that he knows what he is talking about, that he took part in the events related, and that he is deliberately deceptive. But there is yet another layer of biographical evidence, for Byron had quoted the same Virgilian phrase some years earlier (1813–14) in connection with his poem "The Bride of Abydos." This tale, originally conceived as a love affair between brother and sister, everybody (including Byron himself) recognizes as a reflection of his love for his half-sister, Augusta, and his affair with Lady Frances Wedderburn Webster. Byron continues his waggish obfuscation in the next Latin phrase: "Vetabo Cereris sacrum qui volgarit," from Horace's *Odes* (3.2.26), is "I will forbid him who has divulged the sacred rites of mystic Ceres [to abide beneath the same roof or to unmoor with me the sacred bark]." The next stanza says that no one is supposed to penetrate all of what he writes; it has some mysterious ranges of meaning ("diapasons"), and therefore

> There is much which could not be appreciated
> In any manner by the uninitiated.

At Norman Abbey Juan meets a muster of society's darlings, invited from the four thousand 'for whom the world was made' (*DJ* 13.386; 11.355). Everyone agrees that these brilliant sketches are drawn from life, and several convincing identifications have been suggested and are generally accepted. Juan is of course pursued by the ladies as in real life Byron himself was pursued. In real life Byron was conspicuously *not* pursued by one woman, Annabella Milbanke, but for a complex of reasons, which did not include romantic love, Byron proposed marriage to her. She, for her part, for a complex of reasons, which included the absence of romantic love, rejected him. As Leslie Marchand puts it: "When half of the women of London society wore their hearts on their sleeve wherever Byron appeared, and dozens of others who had never seen him were willing to profess their love, Miss Milbanke refused his offer of honorable marriage because she could not feel a sufficiently "strong affection" for him."[37] A couple of years later he proposed again, and after a fair amount of skirmishing she accepted and they were married on January 2, 1815. She left him in January 1816 and they never saw each other again.

In *Don Juan*, at Norman Abbey, one lady conspicuously does not pursue Juan. Her name is Aurora Raby and, except for two small details

—Aurora Raby is an orphan (as Byron wished Annabella!) and, like Juan, Catholic (and Annabella had to be satisfied about Byron's religion [*LJ* 4:177])—her description coincides in every particular with what we know of Annabella Milbanke: of good birth, an only child, bookish, cold, prim, priggish, pensive, pretty, reserved, rich, and silent. In *Don Juan* (16.883) Aurora Raby's "pure and placid mien" is noted; and Byron, speaking of Annabella Milbanke in a letter remarks on her "placid countenance" (*LJ* 2:175) and in another letter on the "serenity" of her countenance.[38] Of Aurora Raby it is said that she had

> . . . a depth of feeling to embrace
> Thoughts, boundless, deep, but silent too as Space.
> (*DJ* 16.431–32)

Of Annabella, Byron wrote to Lady Melbourne: "She seems to have more feeling than we imagined—but is the most *silent* woman I ever encountered" (*LJ* 4:228). And Annabella Milbanke wrote to Byron: "It is my nature to feel long, deeply, and secretly."[39] A full stanza and a half can be documented so completely, phrase by phrase, that there can be no doubt as to the actuality of Byron's recollections:

> Juan was something she could not divine,
> Being no Sybil in the new world's ways;
> Yet she was nothing dazzled by the meteor,
> Because she did not pin her faith on feature.
>
> His fame too,—for he had that kind of fame
> Which sometimes plays the deuce with womankind,
> A heterogeneous mass of glorious blame,
> Half virtues and whole vices being combined;
> Faults which attract because they are not tame;
> Follies trick'd out so brightly that they blind:—
> These seals upon her wax made no impression,
> Such was her coldness or her self-possession.
> (*DJ* 15.445–56)

Annabella Milbanke wrote a "Character" of Byron,[40] which Byron read and described as "more favourable to her talents than to her discernment" (*LJ* 2:229). The first time she saw Byron, she praised—more accurately, *appraised*—his beauty: "His features are well formed—his upper lip is drawn toward the nose with an impression of impatient disgust. His eye is restlessly thoughtful." And, she goes on, "I did not seek an introduction to him, for all the women were absurdly courting him, and trying to *deserve* the lash of his Satire. . . . I thought that *inoffensiveness* was the most secure conduct. . . . So I made no offering at the shrine of Childe Harold."⁴¹ A few months later (October 1812), she drew up a sort of character of herself for Lady Melbourne, enumerating the qualities she wanted in a husband, one of which was: "I do not regard *beauty* . . . "⁴² Later still, in a letter to Byron, she wrote: "Early in our acquaintance . . . I studied your character. . . . My regard for your welfare did not arise from blindness to your errors; I was interested by the strength and generosity of your feelings, and I honored you for that pure sense of moral rectitude, which could not be perverted, though perhaps tried by the practice of Vice. I would have sought to arouse your own virtues to a consistent plan of action, for so directed, they would guide you more surely than any mortal counsel."⁴³ Moreover, Annabella Milbanke's coldness and self-possession were conspicuous and famous. The duchess of Devonshire called her "cold, prudent and reflecting": "She is really an icicle."⁴⁴ In a letter to Byron, she herself refers to the "formality and coldness" observable in her "manners" as well as in her "writing" and admits to "having been repulsively cold towards" Byron each time they had met the year before in London.⁴⁵ And earlier, when his first proposal was rejected, Byron, congratulating himself on his "escape," said: "That would have been but a *cold collation*, and I prefer hot suppers" (*LJ* 2:246).

Stanza 45, in this respect, is even more revealing:

> Early in years, and yet more infantine
> In figure, she had something of sublime
> In eyes which sadly shone, as seraphs' shine.
> All youth — but with an aspect beyond time;
> Radiant and grave — as pitying man's decline;
> Mournful — but mournful of another's crime,
> She look'd as if she sat by Eden's door,
> And grieved for those who could return no more.

Byron, speaking of Annabella's "disposition," said, "She is like a child in that respect — and quite *caressable* into kindness and good humour" (*LJ* 4.231). But the remainder of the stanza is a puzzling reference, glossed by no one. (In a manuscript variant, by the way, the seventh line, instead of "sat by Eden's door," read "sat by Eden's gate.") The source is, in fact, a poem by one of Byron's oldest and closest friends, Tom Moore: the second tale, "Paradise and the Peri," in *Lalla Rookh* (1817), which Byron read soon after publication and admired (*LJ* 5.252). The reference is to the opening eight lines:

> One morn a Peri at the gate
> Of Eden stood, disconsolate;
> And as she listen'd to the Springs
> Of Life within, like music flowing,
> And caught the light upon her wings
> Through half the open portal glowing,
> She wept to think her recreant race
> Should e'er have lost that glorious place!

This explanation of a difficult allusion would, in itself, justify a paragraph in *Notes and Queries* but not space and time in this essay. What, then, qualifies this stanza for inclusion in a discussion of biographical interpretation?

Two things. One is that in the climactic episode of Moore's story (lines 398 ff.) a Byronic hero, transparently the Giaour or Conrad, comes upon a young boy chasing "damsel-flies" (as in *The Giaour*, lines 388–95, a young boy chases an "insect queen"). The lad tires (as in *The Giaour*), rests, and then prays. That "man of crime" (line 430), whose brow is haggard and fierce and in whose eye can be read "dark tales of many a ruthless deed," whose "memory ran / O'er many a year of guilt and strife," observes the kneeling lad, "lisping th' eternal name of God," and—I'm embarrassed to go on with this—weeps and then joins him, "kneeling there / By the child's side, in humble pray'r" (lines 487–88), and thus experiences the redemption denied all Byronic heroes, save one. I suggest, without further discussion, that in this episode Byron saw himself and his daughter Ada.

The second reason for discussing the allusion to Aurora Raby mourning by Eden's gate is more complicated. Annabella Milbanke had turned down a proposal of marriage from a man named George Eden. The Edens, like the Milbankes, were a Durham family, and George Eden, according to Ethel Colburn Mayne, "was a friend of Annabella's childhood."[46] Now, nothing in Byron's life is simple, and this episode isn't either. For her own reasons (bad ones, as it turned out), Annabella Milbanke "let Byron think she was engaged to [George Eden], and then was embarrassed as to how to undeceive him without admitting to a lie" (*LJ* 2:202 n.). She and her parents visited Eden's parents, at Eden Farm, in Kent, on several occasions. Byron was told by Annabella Milbanke's "great friend" that Eden "would be the *best husband* in the world" and himself its "*Antithesis*" (*LJ* 2.217), and he said that "she deserves

a better heart than mine" (*LJ* 2.222). And immediately after the ceremony that joined him forever to Annabella Milbanke in unholy matri-
mony, Byron said in the carriage as they drove away on their honey-
moon: "You had better have married ———, he would have made you
a better husband." (This comes from the book *Lord Byron's Wife*, by
Malcolm Elwin, who supplies, in square brackets, the name "Eden.")[47]
He certainly would have made her a better husband, for he was in all
respects her male counterpart. And that is how Byron describes him as
Lord Henry, husband of Lady Adeline Amundeville.

George Eden succeeded his father as second Lord Auckland in 1814,
was created earl of Auckland in 1839, and had a "brilliant political career, being successively President of the Board of Trade, First Lord of
the Admiralty, and Governor-General of India."[48] When Byron knew
him, he was a Whig member of Parliament and, according to the *DNB*,
noted for his "constant attendance" and "plain commonsense." On his
death in 1849 Fulke Greville, diarist of the nineteenth-century political
world, wrote: "He was a man without shining qualities or showy accomplishments, austere, almost forbidding in his manner, silent and reserved in society, unpretending both in private and public life." Greville
also mentions his placid temper, his "apparent gravity," and his "cold
exterior."[49] That he was indefatigable the letters of his sister Emily Eden,
the novelist, clearly reveal. "George went to the opening of some medi-
cal college," she writes. "It is the oddest thing, and shows what he was
predestined for: but he never feels tired. . . , and he goes on working
away, filling all the hours fuller than they can hold, and sleeps like a
top at night!"[50] That Lord Henry was the same is equally clear from
the catalogue of his multifarious activities in the country (*DJ* 16.485–
656), for Norman Abbey is not merely Newstead Abbey, but also (I
believe) Eden Farm.

Lord Henry, according to Byron, was "cool, and quite English, im-
perturbable" (*DJ* 13.108), cautious, proud, reserved (*DJ* 13.115, 121–22),
and a "cold, good, honourable man" (*DJ* 14.553):

> In birth, in rank, in fortune likewise equal,
> O'er Juan he could no distinction claim;
> In years he had the advantage of time's sequel.
>
> (*DJ* 13.153–55)

George Eden succeeded his father as Baron Auckland in 1814. His rank
was thus the same as Byron's, and he was four years older. Lord Henry
was handsome (*DJ* 14.566), knew horses, rode well (*DJ* 13.181–82;
16.487, 489), and hunted (*DJ* 16.586), and we know from the letters

of his sister, who was with him in India, that Auckland was handsome, a connoisseur of horseflesh, and an expert horseman and hunter.[51] In fact, his death occurred "on his return from shooting."[52] Byron says that Lord Henry was a privy councillor (*DJ* 13.537–38) and

> A figure fit to walk before a king;
> Tall, stately, form'd to lead the courtly van
> On birth-days, glorious with a star and string;
> The very model of a Chamberlain —
> And such I mean to make him when I reign.
>
> (*DJ* 14.556–60)

George Eden was also a privy councillor,[53] though certainly not in Byron's lifetime. But clearly he was the stuff of which privy councillors are made. In the endless round of formal receptions in India in ceremonial dress, "stiffly uniformed and cockaded, gold-laced and gold-sworded," we are told, he "was an imposing figure."[54] "Our first and best energies are devoted to making a *clinquant* figure of his Excellency," wrote his sister from India, "in order that he may shine in the eyes of the native princes; and I take it he will make a pretty considerable figure"; on another occasion, a native dignitary at the Queen's Ball "was very much struck at George's entry, which is always a pretty sight."[55] Greville wrote of his "calmness and dignity" and of his "laborious and conscientious administration" in India, and of his "diligence, his urbanity, his fairness and impartiality" while in office in England.[56] Byron says of Lord Henry:

> Courteous and cautious therefore in his county,
> He was all things to all men . . .
>
> (*DJ* 16.609)

In *Up the Country*, by Eden's sister Emily, there is a portrait of him that could well be of Lord Henry himself. Eden never married and, the parents having died early on, several of his sisters always shared his home, in India as in England. Indeed, when he sailed for India in October 1835, accompanied by two of his sisters, he had a farewell letter from King William saying "he had always given George credit for his exemplary attachment to his sisters."[57] In this respect, therefore, it is worth noting that Lord Henry kissed Lady Adeline "Less like a young wife than an aged sister" (*DJ* 14.552). Byron, in fact, may imply that Lord Henry is not merely passionless but sexually neuter (*DJ* 14.567–68,

606–7), and though our sources are limited and partisan, one has no difficulty forming the same opinion of George Eden. And, finally, I think Annabella Milbanke must have had Eden in mind when she wrote to her aunt, Lady Melbourne: "So far from supposing that I could be attached by a character of *dry* Reason, and *cold* Rectitude, I am always *repelled* by people of that description."[58]

One thing remains to be said on the subject of Aurora Raby. Everybody senses her importance and everybody misreads the evidence. Nearly everybody misreads it utterly—including T. S. Eliot, T. G. Steffan, Andrew Rutherford, and E. D. Hirsch, Jr., who, pairing her with Haidee as one of "the two pure spirits" of the poem, says she is introduced "to preserve the possibility of the ideal and to renew the imagination of the hero and the narrator as well."[59] There are two partial exceptions. Leslie Marchand surmises that Aurora might be what Byron "had imagined and hoped Annabella might be when he first saw her" but says no more on the subject.[60] Thomas L. Ashton quotes Marchand's shrewd insight, ignores it, and then goes one step further. The name "Aurora" of course suggests not only beauty, youth, and innocence but also, in this poem, their incarnation in Haidee, and it is this suggestion that has led commentators astray. Her name, however, is not only Aurora, it is also Raby, which in no way evokes images of beauty, youth, innocence, and Thomas Ashton, alone among the commentators, has taken note of this.[61]

The Milbankes were from Seaham, County Durham. The lord lieutenant of Durham and "the center of the Durham society patronized by the Milbankes," as Ashton observes, was William Henry Vane (1766–1842), later (1833) first duke of Cleveland but in Byron's lifetime earl of Darlington and—what is more to the point—Baron Raby, of Raby Castle, Durham. Raby was a high liver and a low lifer, and even the *DNB* says he "was more important as a sportsman than as a politician." Thus, in naming her Aurora Raby Byron was once more writing about the impossibility of sustaining an ideal.

> Even Petrarch's self, if judged with due severity,
> Is the Platonic pimp of all posterity.

As a biographical sketch of Annabella Milbanke, the portrait of Aurora is even more ruthlessly honest than any of the others in *Don Juan*, except perhaps that of George Eden. She appeared to be a "Rose with all its sweetest leaves yet folded" (*DJ* 15.344), but that is only half of the portrait. And the only puzzling aspect of it all is why anyone described in some of the language used of her could possibly be regarded as "ideal": prim, silent, cold, indifferent. Moreover, Byron is quite explicit at one point:

> Juan knew nought of such a character—
> High, yet resembling not his lost Haidée;
> Yet each was radiant in her proper sphere:
> The Island girl, bred up by the lone sea,
> More warm, as lovely, and not less sincere,
> Was Nature's all: Aurora could not be,
> Nor would be thus;—the difference in them
> Was such as lies between a flower and gem.
>
> (*DJ* 15.457–64)

And that is all we know—perhaps more than we know—of Aurora Raby. She appears only in Cantos 15 and 16, and the poem breaks off with the fourteenth stanza of Canto 17. No one knows how the poem would have continued or how it would have ended. Byron suggests, in a letter and elsewhere, that Juan might have finished in the French Revolution, guillotined like Anacharsis Clootz.[62] I myself think, from evidence in the same letter, that a different (and better) conclusion is indicated. Byron said he had "not quite fixed whether to make him end in Hell—or in an unhappy marriage,—not knowing which would be the severest.— The Spanish tradition says Hell—but it is probably only an Allegory of the other state."[63] I think Byron would have married Juan to Aurora and that they would have lived unhappily ever after—in the hell of an unhappy marriage.

Narcissus has been punished. The love affair with himself that began with *Childe Harold's Pilgrimage* has led to his jilting in *Don Juan*, and as in mythology he remains as a beautiful flower, the greatest poem of the nineteenth century. Byron spent his professional life trying to learn the truth about himself and trying to tell it. Hobhouse persuaded him to destroy the beginnings of a journal in Albania in 1809, and he aided and abetted the destruction of the final one in May 1824. *Don Juan*, yet another attempt, traces the growth not of the poet's mind, à la Wordsworth, but of the poet's psyche. In *The Prelude* we know that our Redeemer liveth and that his name is Wordsworth, who tells us in thirteen or fourteen books how he achieved that awesome responsibility. The point is that we can all be like Wordsworth. Byron, in *Childe Harold's Pilgrimage*, hyped himself into believing that he had redeemed himself only, but in *Don Juan* he took back even that. Wordsworth's poem is exemplary, Byron's cautionary. *Don Juan* is his memoir in verse, and it would be difficult to conceive of any more direct and forceful contradiction of the idea that "no biographical evidence can change or influence critical evaluation."

Notes

1 Cleanth Brooks and Robert Penn Warren, *Understanding Poetry* (New York: Henry Holt, 1938; rev. ed., 1950; 3d ed., Holt, Rinehart and Winston, 1960).

2 Brooks and Warren, *Understanding Poetry*, rev. ed., pp. 174–76.

3 *Shelley's Poetry and Prose*, ed. Donald H. Reiman and Sharon B. Powers (New York: W. W. Norton, 1979), p. 369 n.

4 Judith Chernaik, *The Lyrics of Shelley* (Cleveland and London: Case Western Reserve University Press, 1972), pp. 150–54.

5 René Wellek and Austin Warren, *Theory of Literature* (New York: Harcourt, Brace, 1942).

6 Leslie A. Marchand, ed., *Byron's Letters and Journals*, 12 vols. (Cambridge: Belknap Press of Harvard University Press, 1973–82), 1:233 n.; hereafter cited in text as *LJ*.

7 Doris Langley Moore, *Lord Byron: Accounts Rendered* (New York: Harper and Row, 1974), pp. 103–4.

8 Leslie A. Marchand, *Byron: A Biography*, 3 vols. (New York: Knopf, 1957), Vol. 1, Notes p. 22.

9 Lord Broughton [John Cam Hobhouse], *Travels in Albania and Other Provinces of Turkey in 1809 and 1810*, New Edition, 2 vols. (London: John Murray, 1855), 1: 97–98, 112 n.

10 Lord Byron, *The Complete Poetical Works*, ed. Jerome J. McGann (Oxford: Clarendon Press, 1980), vol. 2. All quotations from Byron's poetry are taken from this edition. Texts of poems not yet published in McGann's edition, like *Don Juan*, have been kindly supplied by the editor.

11 Edmund Spenser, *The Faerie Queen*, ed. A. C. Hamilton (London and New York: Longman, 1977); hereafter cited in text as *FQ* with book, canto, and stanza number.

12 Broughton, *Travels in Albania*, p. 97.

13 "Une dame qui reçoit chez elle un Chevalier, ne veut point s'endormir qu'elle ne lui envoye une de ses femmes pour lui faire compagnie:

> La Comtesse qui fut courtoise,
> De son oste pas ni li poise,
> Ainsi li fist fere à grant delit,
> En un chambre un riche lit.
> Là se dort à aise & repose,
> Et la Comtesse à chief se pose,
> Apele une soue pucelle,
> La plus courtoise & la plus bele,

A consoil li dist, belle amie,
Alez tost, ne vous ennuit mie,
Avec ce Chevalier gesir,
· · · · · · ·
· · · · · · ·
· · · · · · ·
Si le servez, s'il est mestiers.
Je i alasse volentiers,
Que ja ne laissasse pour honte;
Ne fust pour Monseigneur le Conte
Qui ne pas encore endormiz.

14 *Don Juan*, Canto 5, lines 1233–48; *Don Juan* and *Childe Harold's Pilgrim-age* hereafter cited in the text as *DJ* and *CHP* with canto and line number.
15 See *DNB*.
16 Henry Down Miles, *Pugilistica: The History of British Boxing* (London, 1860), facing p. 89; Pierce Egan, *Life in London* (London: Hotten, 1869), p. 254.
17 Miles, *Pugilistica*, p. 92.
18 Editor of *Bell's Life in London*, *Fights for the Championship*; and *Celebrated Prize Battles* (London: Bell's Life Office, 1855), p. 16.
19 Miles, *Pugilistica*, p. 98.
20 Ibid., p. 96.
21 Ernest Hartley Coleridge, ed., *Poetry*, vols. 1–7 in *The Works of Lord Byron*, revised and enlarged edition (London: John Murray; New York: Charles Scribner's Sons, 1898–1905), 6: 360.
22 *Medwin's Conversations of Lord Byron*, ed. Ernest J. Lovell, Jr. (Princeton: Princeton University Press, 1966), p. 105.
23 George Bancroft, "A Day with Lord Byron," *History of the Battle of Lake Erie, and Miscellaneous Papers* (New York: Robert Bonner's Sons, 1891), pp. 190–210.
24 Broughton, *Travels in Albania*, pp. 114–15; William Plomer, *The Diamond of Jannina* (1935; rpt., New York: Taplinger, 1970); *Annual Register*, 1822, "History of Europe," pp. 270–71; Stoyan Christowe, *The Lion of Yanina* (New York: Modern Age Books, 1941).
25 John Galt, *The Life of Byron* (New York: Fowle, 1900), pp. 65–68.
26 Marchand, *Byron*, 1: 197, and Notes, p. 20.
27 Doris Langley Moore, "Byronic Dress," *Costume* 5 (1971): 1–13.
28 Broughton, *Travels in Albania*, p. 46.
29 See also ibid., 1: 94–95.
30 Marchand, *Byron*, 3: 1008.
31 Ibid., 3: 1014.
32 William Tooke, *Life of Catherine II, Empress of All the Russias* (Philadelphia: William Fry, 1802).
33 Broughton, *Travels in Albania*, p. 113.

34 Leslie A. Marchand, *Byron's Poetry: A Critical Introduction* (Boston: Houghton Mifflin, 1965), p. 206.
35 Jerome J. McGann, *Don Juan in Context* (Chicago: University of Chicago Press, 1976), p. 65.
36 Marchand, *Byron*, 2: 618–19.
37 Ibid., 1: 370.
38 Malcolm Elwin, *Lord Byron's Wife* (New York: Harcourt, Brace and World, 1963), p. 166.
39 Marchand, *Byron*, 1: 405.
40 Elwin, *Lord Byron's Wife*, p. 119.
41 Ibid., pp. 105–6.
42 Mabell, Countess of Airlie, *In Whig Society* (London: Hodder and Stoughton, 1921), p. 138.
43 Elwin, *Lord Byron's Wife*, p. 167.
44 Countess of Airlie, *In Whig Society*, p. 138; Elwin, *Lord Byron's Wife*, p. 116.
45 Elwin, *Lord Byron's Wife*, p. 198.
46 Ethel Colburn Mayne, *The Life and Letters of Anne Isabella Milbanke* (New York: Charles Scribner's Sons, 1929), p. 15.
47 Elwin, *Lord Byron's Wife*, p. 250.
48 Ibid., p. 93.
49 Ibid.
50 Emily Eden, *Letters from India*, 2 vols. (London: Richard Bentley and Son, 1872), 1: 107.
51 Eden, *Letters from India*, 1: 56, 286; Emily Eden, *Up the Country*, ed. Edward Thompson (London: Curzon Press, 1978), passim [first published in 1866].
52 *The Greville Memoirs*, ed. Henry Reeve, new edition, 8 vols. (London and New York: Longman's, Green, 1896), 6: 260; *DNB*.
53 G. E. Cokayne, *Complete Peerage*; obituary in the *Gentleman's Magazine*, February 1849, p. 201; not mentioned in *DNB*.
54 Janet Dunbar, *Golden Interlude: The Edens in India* (London: Murray, 1955), p. 167.
55 Eden, *Letters from India*, 2: 81, 239.
56 *Greville Memoirs*, 6: 262.
57 Eden, *Letters from India*, 1: 3.
58 Countess of Airlie, *In Whig Society*, p. 140.
59 E. D. Hirsch, Jr., "Byron and the Terrestrial Paradise," in Frederick W. Hilles and Harold Bloom, eds., *From Sensibility to Romanticism* (New York: Oxford University Press, 1965), pp. 483, 477.
60 Marchand, *Byron's Poetry*, p. 229.
61 Thomas L. Ashton, "Naming Byron's Aurora Raby," *English Language Notes* 7 (1969): 114–20.
62 *LJ* 8: 78; *Medwin's Conversations of Lord Byron*, p. 165.
63 *LJ* 8: 78.

Life, Death, and Other Theories

Lawrence Lipking

IF THE author has died, his spirit is still unquiet. Not many readers are willing to let it alone. Yet few issues of current literary studies
have aroused so much passion or drawn such a line between opposing
schools as the quarrel between Vitalists and Morticians, those who revive the author and those who condemn him to death. Contemporary
critical warriors tug at the body with all the disregard for personal safety
of Homer's Greeks and Trojans scrapping for spoils. Like many such
contests, this one may be seen as a struggle not only for glory but cash.
On the one hand, the standard currency of literary talk as it appears
in newspapers, popular or semipopular magazines, television, the commercial press, the citations of book clubs and prize awards, or even the
daily conversation of intellectuals continues to revolve around the notion that books are the products of authors, that reading books is a sort
of substitute for talking to authors directly, and that once an author
has died the only reason for writing about him is to open his life for
inspection. Literary biographies seem to satisfy a public hunger; literary criticism and literary theory do not. On the other hand, much of
the effort of advanced literary thought in this century might be understood as a campaign to get rid of the author. Practical criticism began
by divorcing poems from poets, theories of impersonality then came to
hold sway, and the growth of literary theory in the past twenty years
has been predicated largely on one method after another of denying the
relevance of authors' lives to authors' works. Nor is this response esoteric; most professors of literature share it. The typical review of a literary biography, at least in journals of limited circulation, will often
complain that all its information serves only to alienate us from the one
thing that counts: the orphaned, perdurable Text. Vulgar people like
to talk about authors. Educated people prefer them dead.

All my readers, of course, are educated people. But one virtue of
an education should be to instill us with some distrust of melodramatic
conflicts and caricatures of what vulgar people think. Is the line between
schools of critics really so firm? Many good critics have lately begun
to doubt it. In retrospect, even the best-sounding slogans, like Roland

Barthes's, sound hollow when often repeated. "The birth of the reader must be at the cost of the death of the Author."[1] Surely I am not alone in hearing a calculated ruthlessness in this pronouncement, which orders a final solution to the author problem. Is the world of letters not large enough to contain room for both authors and readers? Barthes's rhetoric forces a choice, and flatters his readers by seeming to speak for their rights. The loaded word "birth" (as if, before our time, no readers had existed), the aggressive "must" (foreclosing all options), the threat of mental murder promise us power. They are also highly coercive. Such prose does not inspire trust. If ever a false opposition needed to be deconstructed, this slogan is one. Nor do I need to claim that its author is dead in order to assert my right as a reader to disagree with him.

Why then are so many intelligent critics and theorists uncomfortable with the notion of the Author and so ready to terminate it? One reason, surely, is the association of the word with authority, the authoritative, authoritarianism. Anybody who knows how to write can be a writer, the term is democratic. But authors comprise an elite. They are those, by definition, who *originate* a work and therefore own it, by copyright law or simply by fixing their names. Many are called writers, but few are chosen authors. Hence it is easy to regard authorship as a sort of conspiracy against the freedom of writing and reading, an arrogation of power, an attempt to control the proceeds and interpretations of texts.[2] No one has ever endowed authors with more authority than those authors, or writers, who find something sinister in the whole process. Reading such accusations, one might almost forget the sordid reality of publication, how little power most authors exert in the world, how difficult it is to find, let alone to dominate, a reader. Some of the most popular authors, in fact, consider themselves the slaves of their readers, who always have the power to break the work with simple indifference. From this point of view the connection of authors with authoritarianism appears more a wish than a statement of fact. It derives from a longing for some past time when books threw weight in the world, or some earlier time when anonymous texts came into being as if by magic, without the agency of any human hand. The vision of an authorless text almost invariably culminates in a utopia of unlimited discourse, the free sharing of texts that nobody signs or owns.

Yet a world without authors would not be a world without power. Quite the contrary: those who wield the most power prefer not to commit anything to writing. The act of signing a text makes authors vulnerable. They expose themselves in print, and anything they are may be used against them.[3] By contrast, the most authoritative texts tend to be anonymous, like bibles or laws or committee reports. Refusing to reveal their origins, they distribute their authority to the highest bidder, the institutions that use them. We can never hope to limit their applications by finding out what the author may have meant. Shakespeare, in this respect, is like the Bible. Part of his authority derives from our inability to pin him down as an author. That is, he hides so well behind his texts (removing himself even from the circumstances of their publication) that we cannot charge him with responsibility for what they mean. Though Shylock may be hateful and a Jew, we cannot say that the play's expression of anti-Semitism is to be accounted for by anything *personal*. The age itself has authored the offense. That makes it more authoritative. Similarly, anonymous Homer's attitude toward Trojans disturbs critics far less than Roman Virgil's attitude toward Carthaginians. We know whom to blame for the ruin of Carthage. A rule might be constructed from such examples: The authority of a text varies in inverse proportion to its function as the product of an author.

The equation of the author with authoritarian ways of thought, therefore, seems glib if not invalid. Do better arguments exist for condemning the author to death? I do not think so.[4] But so many theorists assume the case to be proved that we need to take a longer look at their reasoning. In lieu of surveying every aspect of this complicated question, I must use as my example only the single best-known polemic, "The Death of the Author." Barthes states his point with the confidence of a master.

> In his story *Sarrasine* Balzac, describing a castrato disguised as a woman, writes the following sentence: "*This was woman herself, with her sudden fears, her irrational whims, her instinctive worries,her impetuous boldness, her fussings, and her delicious sensibility.*" Who is speaking thus? Is it the hero of the story bent on remaining ignorant of the castrato hidden beneath the woman? Is it Balzac the individual, furnished by his personal experience with a philosophy of Woman? Is it Balzac the author professing "literary" ideas on femininity? Is it universal wisdom? Romantic psychology? We shall never know, for the good reason that writing is the destruction of every voice, of every point of origin. Writing is that neutral, composite, oblique space where our subject slips away, the negative where all identity is lost, starting with the very identity of the body writing.[5]

After such an eloquent and (one might say) authoritative dismissal of the author, which now, in the wake of hundreds of similar statements, may sound like a truism, to go back to the beginning induces a mild shock: "In his story *Sarrasine* Balzac . . . writes the following sentence." *His* story? *Balzac* writes? Just who is this Balzac who writes, and why is he not dead? The answer, of course, is that Barthes never thought that he was, as a *writer*. The whole argument depends on a systematic confusion among writing, authoring, and speaking, on the modulation from "Balzac writes" to "Who is speaking thus?" Barthes deliberately phrases his questions so as to discourage an answer. "Who is speaking thus? Is it the hero . . . ? Balzac the individual . . . ? universal wisdom?" But this proves only that print on a page does not talk. In the context of the story itself, no reader feels any uncertainty, since Balzac's sentence clearly expands on the sentence preceding it. "That morning fled too quickly for the enamored sculptor, but it was filled with a host of incidents which revealed to him the coquetry, the weakness, and the delicacy of this soft and enervated being. This was woman herself . . ."[6] Restored to the narrative, the sentence Barthes isolates obviously represents the sculptor's train of thought (never spoken at all, in the conventions of fiction). The voice of universal wisdom has nothing to do with the case, nor do "Balzac the individual's" opinions about women. Indeed, insofar as the catalogue of "woman's attributes" does accurately describe La Zambinella (rather than her lover's illusions about her), one might argue that the narrator, or Balzac, ironically disengages himself from them, since the phrase that introduces them, "This was woman herself," cleverly plays on the fact that La Zambinella is *not* a woman. If the author were "speaking thus," he would surely know better than to mean it. But in practice, in reading, the question does not arise. The point is not what women are, but what Sarrasine takes them to be.

Some readers may think, however, that my analysis dodges two issues, the propositional aspect of literature and the question of the author's responsibility for what the text says. In fact it seems to me Barthes's formulation that dodges those issues. By identifying writing with "that neutral, composite, oblique space where our subject slips away," he makes it impossible to draw any conclusions at all about what Balzac intended. Worse yet, by arguing that "writing is the destruction of every voice, of every point of origin," he reduces writing to a secondary activity, an attempt to destroy voices and origins that preempt and threaten the writer's response.[7] Barthes's logic discounts the possibility that indications of voice and origin might be features of the text itself, features for which the author's own conscious decisions are responsible. In this respect the example is cleverly chosen. Focusing on an "opinionated" sentence whose sexist implications ought to disturb any sensitive reader, Barthes gives us a way out by transferring responsibility from the "speaker" to the neutral space of textuality. We can like our Balzac and also condemn his text. Yet the ironic effect of this particular sentence hardly characterizes every example of writing.

Consider Barthes's own interpretation, in *S/Z*, of another sentence on the same page of *Sarrasine*, where the hero professes his love: "I think I would detest a strong woman, a Sappho, a courageous creature full of energy and passion." "Sarrasine," Barthes comments, "could hardly identify more clearly the woman he fears: the castrating woman, defined by the inverted place she occupies on the sexual axis (*a Sappho*)."[8] A Sappho is an inverted and castrating woman. *Who is speaking thus?* Certainly not Sarrasine, who has voiced no such thought. And not Balzac, whose other writings testify his attraction to many kinds of women, both weak and strong. Is it the text itself? I see no castrating woman there. Or perhaps the speaker is Jacques Lacan, who created the fashion for exposing phalluses in texts like this in order to whet his instruments on them. That answer does have some merit; one sees the hand of Lacan. But a better answer is plain. It is *Barthes* who speaks thus, who identifies Sappho with inversion and castration (an identification that I myself, by the way, consider far more reprehensible and damaging to women than anything in Balzac's story). Barthes has perpetuated a myth, popular with French misogynists since Baudelaire, and he deserves full responsibility for it. He is its author, and as its author he is not dead.

But the point should not be belabored. For one defense must be offered for all those authors who have lately insisted that the author is dead, who disclaim any interest in intentions and careers, who have replaced subjects with spaces and writers with traces: they say it, but they do not mean it. No instance is more spectacular than Barthes himself. Many of us consider him the best author France has produced in the past twenty years. During much of his life, to be sure, he pretended to be a mere writer. But that fiction began to break down long ago, when other writers and readers noticed that every piece that came from his hand could be recognized, not by its ideas (which changed every few years) but by its distinctive, individual style. Barthes was forever Barthes; and to a large extent that was what he wrote about. Almost from the instant of his death, such admirers and disciples as Tsvetan Todorov and Susan Sontag gathered to tell us about his achievement.[9] His particular texts were less important, they thought, than the example of his career. The spontaneity of this author, his polymorphism, his capacity for breaking the dialectic and going against the grain, his refusal to fit in a school had liberated French criticism from its doxa and exalted the paradox. Barthes had always been consistent, if only to the principle of self-contradiction. He would be remembered for that. And though no one could rival the originality of his writings, their spirit would live on in others.

A similar theme informs Jonathan Culler's recent study of Barthes, which circles around "a figure of contradiction." "This enemy of authors is himself preeminently an author, a writer whose varied products reveal a personal style and vision. Many of Barthes' works are idiosyncratic. . . . Peculiar yet compelling, these works are rightly celebrated as the imaginative products of an *author*, a master of French prose with a singular approach to experience."[10] Culler seems uneasy with his own analysis, which suggests a sort of apostasy in Barthes's journey from a renegade spinner of texts to a traditional man of letters. But one might as well blame the genre in which Culler is writing, since anyone who undertakes a book called *Roland Barthes* for a series on modern masters can hardly avoid representing his subject as an author who has had a career. A book on Jacques Derrida or Luce Irigaray or Jonathan Culler, though perhaps premature, would inevitably assume the same shape. Not even Barthes could avoid writing about Racine and Michelet and Robbe-Grillet and himself as if they were authors. How else can an author survive?

If Barthes did not *mean* that the author was dead, however, why did he say it? Surely the answer to such a question must take account not only of theory but of the historical situation that the theory addresses. The end of Barthes's essay leaves no doubt of his intention: he wants to defend "the new writing" against its traditional enemy, the old humanism. "We are now beginning to let ourselves be fooled no longer by the arrogant antiphrastical recriminations of good society in favour of the very thing it sets aside, ignores, smothers, or destroys; we know that to give writing its future, it is necessary to overthrow the myth: the birth of the reader must be at the cost of the death of the Author."[11] Two historical occasions lie behind this pronouncement. One is Paris 1968, the age — or spasm — of iconoclasm, and the moment of Barthes's writing. The ripples from that wave of antiauthoritarian abandon have yet to die away in modern theory.

Yet the second occasion is broader and more important. For Barthes and many of his contemporaries, the attack on the author seems identical with a revolt against the dominant tendency of French criticism of the previous generation — above all, against Gustave Lanson. Lanson, Barthes wrote in 1963, "was the prototype of the French teacher of literature and, during the last fifty years, his work, method, and mentality, as transmitted by innumerable disciples, have continued to govern academic criticism." Those disciples prefer to believe that they deal with matters of *fact*. Yet "Lansonianism is itself an ideology," which "implies certain general convictions about man, history, literature and the relationship between the author and his work. For instance, Lansonian psychology is quite out of date, since it consists fundamentally of a kind of analogical determinism, according to which the details of a given work must resemble the details of the author's life, the characters the innermost being of the author, and so on. This makes it a very peculiar ideology."[12] Whether or not we consider this a fair description of Lanson, it clearly serves to situate Barthes and other French literary men of his time. They are the scourge of the author—at least in his academic incarnation. For too long the ideology of humanism and authorism have been suffered to quash rival theories. Now readers and texts take their turn.

I linger upon this background because, in retrospect and with some necessary modifications, it also seems to situate a good deal of recent American work, including my own. Why should anyone today want to write about authors? Lanson was already an old man when he died, in the year of my birth. Yet to many of us the history sketched by Barthes speaks of an unfinished project. Fifty years ago, in Germany, England, and America as well as France, the triumph of the author may well have seemed complete. To anyone now rereading those author-based texts—for instance, the Legouis-Cazamian *History of English Literature*, Lowes's *Road to Xanadu*, or the famous articles by Middleton Murry and Sir Ifor Evans on Keats's "On First Looking into Chapman's Homer"—the confidence they place in their method may come as a shock. Those critics actually think that they are right! That is, they believe themselves to have put literary criticism on a firm foundation for the first time in history, by tracking works of literature back to the original fragments and impulses in the author's mind prior to the moment of writing. Such criticism resembles archeology not only in its patient philological sifting but in its scientific claims. It depends on documentary evidence, and its results can be duplicated by anyone willing to go back to the sources and manuscripts. Hence the method confers a rare authority (in every sense of the word). It rewards the scholar by crediting his expertise with a unique access to the mind of the poet, an access unavailable to the mere reader of poems. And it also envisions a scientific future for criticism, when the patient biographical sifting of major authors will have opened the creative process itself to inspection.

What happened to these high expectations? A very sanguine literary scholar might say that they were fulfilled both by later advances in textual scholarship and by such superb biographies as Ellmann's *Joyce*, Painter's *Proust*, Staiger's *Goethe*, Bate's *Keats*, Frank's *Dostoevsky*, or Watt's and Najder's *Conrad*s. But very few critics and theorists believe that, and neither do I. Rather, it seems that the triumph of the author foundered and lost its confidence over an internal flaw, or what might be called the Humpty Dumpty effect: an inability to put works together again once they have been taken apart. Much of the best criticism of the twenties and early thirties follows the pattern of *The Road to Xanadu*, which spends hundreds of pages disassembling "The Ancient Mariner" and "Kubla Khan" but never provides a reading. Instead the last chapter, "Imagination Creatrix," offers a hymn to the mysterious power of "the shaping spirit which hovers in the poet's brain": "Out of the vast, diffused, and amorphous nebula, then, with which we started, and through which we have slowly forged our way, there emerged, framed of its substance, a structure of exquisitely balanced and coordinated unity—a work of pure imaginative vision."[13] One need not be a devout New Critic to object that, insofar as evidence can be given for the unity of the shaping spirit, it had better be shown not in the poet's brain or vision but in the poem. Lowes's rhetoric becomes superheated and esoteric just at the point when he needs to demonstrate how all his pieces fit. Thus we are left with the triumph of the author with a vengeance: the ineffable form in Coleridge's mind purified of the structures he wrought or the words he wrote. The process has swamped the product. As Murry says at the end of his study of the making of "Chapman's Homer," "Of the last act of poetic creation there is nothing to say."[14]

The history of practical criticism, as too many recent critics seem to have forgotten, is largely a response to that failure of saying (the anti-Lowes polemic of Richards's *Coleridge on Imagination* or Warren's reading of "The Ancient Mariner" suffices to make the point).[15] Clearly the methods of Lanson and Lowes had omitted too much. Yet the question remains whether the flaw was endemic to any attempt to base criticism on the author's point of view, or only to a special case of that attempt (what Barthes would call "analogical determinism" or I would call the Road to Humpty Dumpty). Has the author died or not yet been brought to life? I maintain that the latter is the case. To put a view of the creative process (or more lately, as in the work of the Lacanians or Harold Bloom, unconscious strategies of substitution) in place of the working-out of the poem does not seem required by any critical necessity of authorism. Authors are not only bundles of sources and impulses. They are also, primarily, makers: the contrivers of "close writing" to which all "close reading" responds. In that respect we have learned a great deal during the past fifty years. All the techniques of better reading also help us better to discern the "shaping spirit" whom Lowes had such trouble in seeing. That shaping spirit acquires its shape in the poem.

So conceived, however, the author is himself a creation—or, I would prefer to say, a "project"—of the writer. When Keats dreamed of his own high poetic vocation, his future as a great poet, he added, "But even now I am perhaps not speaking from myself; but from some character in whose soul I now live."[16] Some such transformation seems part of the experience of every significant author. As Keats and other writers know, authors are by no means identical with persons. Writing can lie about the person who is writing it, and some of the best authors, like Homer and God, may not exist except as skillful forgeries by some mere writer. Authors are always "implied"; they are made, not born. Thus the author of "The Ancient Mariner," let alone of its marginal gloss, cannot be identified with that poor fellow Coleridge. He is Coleridge writ large, Coleridge speaking in the character of an author. In this respect the modern conception of the author responds to fifty years of thought about the mysteries of identity—to such ideas as the existential phrasing of human life as a series of projects, Erik Erikson's stories of identity and the life cycle, the neo-Marxist doctrine that human beings make themselves, the feminist exploration of the ways that cultural myths determine character. These ideas have a common moral: we exist in what we do. And such ideas can help to redefine the author. I think that such a redefinition is now taking place, in books like Stephen Greenblatt's *Renaissance Self-Fashioning*, Richard Helgerson's *Self-Crowning Laureates*, and my own *The Life of the Poet*. Such books do not assume too quickly that the author-function can be taken for granted or divorced from the social and historical circumstances into which writers are born. But something—someone—informs the text, rereads and revises it, and takes responsibility for what it says. We are learning slowly to call that someone the author.

Why should there be resistance to that project? I have already spoken about the connection between attacks on the author and antiauthoritarianism (though in many intellectual circles, one should observe, to assert the life of the author requires a daring defiance of authority). But another reason is that an interest in authors goes counter to current fashions in theory. Most of all, it contradicts the convenient way that theorists prefer to regard history, as the expression of a single will or teleology. To ascribe an individual purpose or project of self-making to each author tends to interfere with an urge that almost no theorist can resist: the effort to define the moment of an irreversible change in human consciousness. Ever since Hegel, such turns in the universal mind have been what history means for philosophers. Not even the most skeptical and sophisticated of them, like Richard Rorty and Derrida, have been able to stifle the urge. If recorded history will not furnish the evidence, one can always place the moment between East and West or the pre-Socratics and Plato. And literary theorists have been even more inventive. Each of the so-called École de Yale, for example, has developed his theory largely from a version of the irreversible change in consciousness that occurred at the time of the romantics—e.g., the disappearance of God, the anxiety of belatedness, the crisis of representation —though none of them, to be sure, quite agrees with the others' versions. But surely they are moderate compared with the modern champion of irreversible change, Michel Foucault, every one of whose books conclusively proves that human self-definitions were modified once and for all in the 1780s—or was it the 1450s, or 1860s, or 400 B.C.?

I do not mean to mock the reality of historical change, or the fascination of that field we now call "mentalities." Yet one need not be an antiquarian to feel uncomfortable about the facility with which literary theorists package changes in consciousness. Even on strictly theoretical grounds, one might point out that the definition of the change usually implies an ability to enter the state of mind *before* the change—as Heidegger, for instance, seems not to doubt his own understanding of Heraclitus—thus demonstrating a compatibility between minds of different eras that the theory itself denies. But my major reservations stem from a more practical matter: the emphasis on change tends to distort readings by conferring a special significance on a few selected points—lamps, for instance, or aporias. These points have a great deal of glamour. By comparison with universal consciousness, the particular intentions of one complex author seem petty indeed. Hence, like Communists in the not-too-distant past, few contemporary critics can avoid the appeal of enlisting on the right side of historical inevitability. Revolutions in consciousness are less hazardous to join than barricades in the streets. But we had better beware of mistaking our theories of history for history itself. They are not without consequences.

Consider, for instance, one of the few works of modern theory to address the author seriously: Edward Said's *Beginnings*. After a rich and interesting discussion of poetic careers, Said concludes that sometime around the 1870s "the idea of a poetic or authorial vocation as a common cultural myth underwent severe change. . . . the poetic *vocation*, in the classical sense, had come to be replaced by a poetic *career*. Whereas the former required taking certain memorial steps and imitating a ritual progress, in the latter the writer had to create not only his art but also the very course of his writings."[17] This claim seems plausible. Curtius lies in the background, as well as the usual modern stress on the problematic, discontinuities, the sense of crisis. But in my view the argument is somewhat vitiated by the fact that the myth of which Said speaks had been, if not exactly dead, then at best a fabulous invalid ever since classical times. Just which poets can be said to have taken "certain memorial steps," imitated "a ritual progress," *not* created the very course of their writings? The examples that come to mind are distinctly minor.

Said suggests Virgil and Dante; but Virgil himself invented his ritual progress by splicing together Theocritus (eclogues), Hesiod (georgics), and Homer (epics); and Dante never proved his original genius more than by perceiving the *Vita Nuova*, the *Convito*, and the *Commedia* as following in the steps of the *Eclogues*, *Georgics*, and *Aeneid*. The truth is that *every* great writer has had to create "the very course of his writings," just as every author has been forced to balance ideas of vocation against the pressures of a career. To believe in a decisive moment of change from one to the other is to dwell on a dream of an earlier, unproblematic golden age. In that respect *Beginnings*, as its title suggests, may be said to represent Said's own dream of a golden vocation. We have a word for such works; we call them eclogues.

I have no quarrel with eclogues. But problems arise when we give them didactic force. That slippage occurs, for example, in Said's reading of Blake, who is taken as a prophet of the change, balancing the imprisoning texts of Experience against the nostalgia of Innocence. "The opening poem of Blake's *Songs of Innocence* represents the poet as using a reed—'a rural pen'—to write his happy songs for the joy of every child. His paper is the water which is stained as he 'writes': but one's inclination is to associate innocence in the poem with the impossibility of a permanent inscription in the water. The one line of the poem that suggests a troubling of innocence is 'And I stain'd the water clear.' Nevertheless, the ambiguously placed adjective 'clear' offsets the threat in 'stain'd,' so that one can read the line to mean either 'I stained the water until it became clear' or 'my pen stained the clear water': in both cases the conclusion is that because he writes on water, which even if momentarily stained would not retain the imprint, the poet composes happy (and clear) songs."[18] The innocence of the piper, in Said's ingenious Nietzschean version, reflects his status as a holy fool, a happy demented poet who writes on water. But Blake preferred firmer stuff. Descending from the child of inspiration, the verses give instructions in how to write.

> Piper sit thee down and write
> In a book that all may read—
> So he vanish'd from my sight
> And I pluck'd a hollow reed
>
> And I made a rural pen,
> And I stain'd the water clear,
> And I wrote my happy songs,
> Every child may joy to hear.

On internal evidence it is hard to see why the piper should have disobeyed the child's instructions to write *in a book*, and hard to see why the line about staining the water should be followed by the line about writing the songs, if staining and writing happen simultaneously. But of course the piper is *not* writing on water. Blake knew how to make a book, and he knew that between the pen and the writing comes the ink (or watercolor). To make ink one stains water; that is what Blake did, and what the piper does. The heavy, emphatic "ands" insist on the sequence: a song, a reed, a pen, some ink, writing, and a book—the book that every reader joys to hold.

My point is not simply that Said's reading is mistaken. It is that the misreading results from an active modern bias toward fluid texts. We like our bards better, it seems, when they write in the water. Such dunking proves their basic honesty, or at least their innocence from the guilt of imperial bookmaking, the charge of believing that a text can be finished once and for all, be controlled by its author, escape from time, death, chance, and contingency, enforce a single interpretation, imitate a known universe, communicate a voice, compose a form, or reach the high dry ground of immediate presence. If authors have believed such things, historically, then our job is to set them right, immersing their texts to baptize them into our creed. From this point of view, Keats's epitaph—"Here lies One Whose Name was writ in Water" —is not pathetic but definitive; it stands for the work of all writers without exception.

Some authors might prefer to leave something more solid. Yet the view of the skeptic reflects a certain truth. Not even the greatest writer has ever been able to finish his work so well or build his career so firmly as to shut it off from any later revision. The waters of time are always waiting to wash perfection away. Moreover, it is possible that the very conceptions of an author and a career depend on the chaos outside them, a principle of destruction that thwarts all efforts to wrap writing up. Death is the mother of beauty and also of authors. Rereading *The Life of the Poet*, whose title announces its opposition both to The Lives of the Poets and The Death of the Author, I become aware of how death-haunted it is. Despite its commitment to *life*, the book seems obsessed with famous last words and tombs. To put this schematically: insofar as it adopts the existentialist view of life as a series of projects, it closely conforms to the formulation of Karl Jaspers, who defines life as a project for death. Even Keats's beginning, with "Chapman's Homer," already takes its direction from the implied sense of an ending, as the ambitions of the young poet immediately remind him of his mortality. Hence, the elementary binary opposition life/death, which at first sight seems to shape my book, in retrospect seems slightly askew. In Derridean terms we might call death the *supplement* of life, not only balancing it but eventually replacing it. No matter how much my story defers this end, at last it inevitably recants life and succumbs.

Yet not many current theorists would accept that line of thought or its claims to inevitability. For a great deal of modern theory deliberately sets out to problematize the relation of life to death, to deny that the orderly passage from one to another obeys any law of necessity. Indeed, more and more that denial seems to me the hidden agenda of contemporary "advanced thought" and the secret of its attraction. I refer not to the "denial of death" so much as to the denial that life and death differ in any essential respect. The precocious death of the author protects him from fear of dying. Nor can life triumph over those who live only in texts. This line of argument runs through the work of Barthes (so obsessed with "the body writing") and many of his successors. It reaches a peak in that curious publishing venture called *Deconstruction and Criticism*. Three of the essays, by de Man, Derrida, and Hillis Miller, address one text by Shelley, *The Triumph of Life*—chosen, one suspects, largely for its title. Space is lacking to do those essays justice. But I would like briefly to think about one question raised not only by my argument but by a frequent animus in the tone of the essays: what are they *against*? That they are against *something*, a few quotations ought to illustrate.

Here, first, is Miller. "*The Triumph of Life* contains within itself, jostling irreconcilably with one another, both logocentric metaphysics and nihilism. It is no accident that critics have disagreed about it. The meaning of *The Triumph of Life* can never be reduced to any 'univocal' reading, neither the 'obvious' one nor a single-minded deconstructionist one, if there could be such a thing, which there cannot. The poem, like all texts, is 'unreadable,' if by 'readable' one means a single, definitive interpretation."[19] One need not linger on the circular, self-protective logic here. But what is Miller against? Evidently a group of critics who believe in univocal reading and readable texts—dogmatists that they are! The formula does not belong to Miller alone. It is a rare article or review in a little critical magazine, these days, that does not include at least one denunciation of univocal reading; we wait through them like commercials. But Miller also has a specific enemy in mind, M. H. Abrams. What then is Abrams's reading of *The Triumph of Life*? Here is its final sentence: "What was to have been the outcome of this crisis we can only speculate; the poet died before he could tell us."[20]

It does not sound dogmatic to my ears. But in fact such remarks (not the positivism of scholars like Donald Reiman)[21] are exactly the object of antagonism. It is not only that Abrams thinks that Shelley could have told us what his poem was about; it is that he considers the uninterpretability of *The Triumph of Life* a special condition of its being unfinished, rather than merely an instance of the uninterpretability of *all* texts. "We can only speculate," he concludes; to which Miller might counter that that is all we can do about any poem. The unfinished state and continuing crisis of *The Triumph of Life*, on this analysis, as well as its ambiguous perch between life and death, make it one of the most honest and typical works of world literature; it does not pretend to resolve its crisis or arrive at a terminal meaning.

Indeed, an extended interrogation of the very possibility of finishing, and therefore of unfinishing, fills page after page of Derrida's own "Living On." Even an apparently unified text, he argues, "can be *encroached* upon by an essential *unfinishedness* that cannot be reduced to an incompleteness or an inadequacy. I register, I record this remark on the shore of what is called the unfinishedness of *The Triumph of Life*, at the moment when Shelley is drowned. I do so without claiming to understand what people mean in this case by 'unfinished,' or to decide anything. I do so only to recall the immense procedures that should come before a statement about whether a work is finished or unfinished. Where are we to situate the event of Shelley's drowning? And who will decide the answer to this question? Who will form a narrative of these borderline events? At whose demand?"[22] One notices Derrida's charming if disingenuous habit of multiplying questions until the whole world of discourse seems one large question mark, where a poem that ends "Happy those for whom the fold / Of" may be no more or less unfinished than one that ends, for instance, "The soul of Adonais, like a star, / Beacons from the abode where the Eternal are." The latter ending, indeed, may well seem *more* unfinished, since it raises endless questions and ironies, whereas "Happy those for whom the fold / Of," once the first shock or irritation has passed, induces a restful stupor. Eventually, if we read enough such poems or enough Derrida, that stupor might become a permanent condition, replacing our ordinary habits of expectation or hunger for endings. That is, we should be trained for death. It is important to note that Derrida himself does not attempt to perform those "immense procedures" which he recommends. Rather, he exploits the pathos of a death-haunted universe, an *essential* unfinishedness able to contradict any gesture of life as soon as it arises. For all his questioning, this "affirmation" of unfinishedness is quite unequivocal and unconditional.

An even stronger claim to know the essence of death furnishes de Man's essay with its grand climax. "*The Triumph of Life* warns us that nothing, whether deed, word, thought or text, ever happens in relation, positive or negative, to anything that precedes, follows or exists elsewhere, but only as a random event whose power, like the power of death, is due to the randomness of its occurence."[23] To some extent this seems not only a mysterious but a self-contradictory statement. The claim that the power of deeds and words is caused by randomness, the suggestion that death is to be considered not an inevitable but a random occurrence can hardly be understood except through violating the express warning of the text and placing it in relation to the words, thoughts, and texts that precede and follow it and lend it a context. Yet whatever the statement may mean, de Man leaves us in no doubt what it is *against*: naive reading; or, more precisely, the naive belief that the strategy of reading which allows us to apostrophize the dead can be a source of value. Most criticism, in his view, follows this belief "along monotonously predictable lines, by the historicization and the aesthetification of texts."[24] Does de Man count himself among the naive? His own texts offer abundant evidence both for and against this proposition. But surely his attractiveness as a critic—and the power he still exerts in death— depends on persuading his readers, however momentarily and ironically, that they are not naive, at least in relation to others. This might be called a rhetorical strategy. But in my view the stakes are higher: it seems to me nothing less than a strategy for dealing with life and death.

For life itself is a series of strategies of reading, on this analysis: a way of positing the illusion of coherence on events that lack any coherence in themselves. Naive readers believe themselves at home in the world. But in fact our defenses, our sense of order, our networks of relation, are desperately thin. They can be broken in a moment by the smallest things: a dropped handkerchief, the thought of winding a clock, the loss of a wallet, some words on a page. In other words, some might say, death, which so pitilessly exposes our pathetic efforts to pretend that we are not involved in the arbitrary madness of random events or to cheer ourselves up ("I never fly to Omaha anyway; and besides, there were no Jews on the plane"). Yet the deconstructionist view would deny death that special status; since to confer inevitability on death would suggest the possibility of establishing some relation with it, as if, except for death, we might be free. A finished work implies some alternative to the state of being perpetually unfinished. But a sophisticated reader knows better. Death has no independent force; it is everywhere and nowhere, not life's eternal opposite but merely one more instance of the universal absence of meaning—Pope's uncreating Word, Forster's Ou Boum, or Blackmur's Moha. And all the rest is literature—most of all literature itself.

The reading or misreading I am suggesting, then, is that votaries of deconstruction find it Mithridatic or homeopathic: a drop of the abyss that inures us to the abyss around us. My main authority for that reading is that brilliant, premature deconstructionist, Goethe's Mephistopheles. In the first, false ending of *Faust*, the death of the hero coaxes the devil to repeat those words that lend death itself significance: "It is fulfilled" ("Es ist vollbracht"). But the choral murmur "It is over" ("Es ist vorbei") alerts Mephistopheles to his mistake; and he passionately deconstructs it.

> Over! a stupid word. Why over, why?
> Over and purely Not, the same thing perfectly!
> What use is all this limitless creation!
> Creating only brings annihilation!
> "It's over!" What is that supposed to mean?
> As good as saying it had never been,
> Yet it still runs around as if it were.
> The Ever-Empty is what I prefer.[25]

The Eternal Emptiness (das Ewig-Leere) is especially forceful as a proleptic deconstruction of the triumphant figure at the end of the play, the Eternal Feminine (das Ewig-Weibliche); and though Goethe himself obviously set out to punish Mephisto for his cynicism about the possibility of ending, later readers might point out that Faust did *not* die and that the author sealed his manuscript only by resorting to a miracle. The play continues to run; no critic will ever fix its meaning. "Over" implies "was," as death implies life (for the naive), but sophisticates can see through this binary logic. Texts neither live nor die, begin nor end; they keep going on. Some readers agree with Mephistopheles and think of themselves as texts. The Ever-Empty is what they prefer. Hence, never having given in to the illusion of life, they will never die—at least not naively.

How well does that strategy work? Obviously it has some limitations, in that human beings cannot live up to it. Even before the deaths of Barthes and de Man, their disciples had begun to find a source of value in apostrophizing them; and now that they exist only as authors, to hear their voices speak again in their texts affords an almost magical pleasure and consolation. Sometimes the birth of the author is helped by the death of the person, whose personality no longer interferes with a reading. Nor need one be ironic about this dis- or trans-figuration. Texts have no means of speaking except through a voice that is at once the author's and the reader's projection, a voice that belongs to the dummy as much as to the ventriloquist. The spirits of the dead, as Wila-mowitz pointed out, are able to talk to us only when we have moistened their lips with the blood of the living. For all of us, as literary people, spend a good deal of time speaking to the dead and encouraging them to speak through us. We cannot refuse to do this as readers; it is part of what reading means. If this be madness, then readers are always mad (as some deconstructionists maintain). What could be madder than talk-ing with the dead?

Yet credit must also be given to life. If authors survive, one reason is that no one has ever been able to construct a better way of cheating annihilation. The author will never die, so long as readers exist, be-cause what an author *is*, not only in metaphysics but in common ex-perience, is the sense of life in a text: the human voice or presence that outlasts all efforts to deconstruct it (even when that voice emanates from some deconstructionist). No theoretical argument will ever put a stop to this illusion, for imagining an author is required by reading itself. Perhaps it is time for a truce. The birth of the reader is also the birth of the author.

Notes

1 Roland Barthes, "The Death of the Author," in *Image — Music — Text*, trans. Stephen Heath (New York: Hill and Wang, 1977), p. 148. "La mort de l'auteur" originally appeared in *Mantéia 5* (1968).

2 According to Michel Foucault, "What Is an Author?" in Josué V. Harari, ed., *Textual Strategies* (Ithaca, N.Y.: Cornell University Press, 1979), p. 159, the author "is a certain functional principle by which, in our culture, one limits, excludes, and chooses; in short, by which one impedes the free cir-culation, the free manipulation, the free composition, decomposition, and recomposition of fiction."

3 "Texts, books, and discourses really began to have authors (other than mythical, 'sacralized' and 'sacralizing' figures) to the extent that authors became subject to punishment, that is, to the extent that discourses could be transgressive" (Foucault, "What Is an Author?" p. 148).

4 In addition to Barthes's argument, discussed below, there seem to be three main challenges to the traditional emphasis of criticism on the author. The first is philosophical: the existence of the author may be "put into ques-tion" by showing that authors are merely functional principles of texts, of readers' responses, of ideologies, of the assumption of a transcendent unity, etc. The second is technical: close analysis of texts reveals that the author is not a monolithic, single presence but a complex set of rhetorical possi-bilities such as "the persona," "the narrator," "the implied author," etc. The third is practical: elimination of the author allows the critic to adopt a

different vocabulary and to notice features of texts that were previously hidden in the author's shadow. Each of these challenges has some persuasive force; none is conclusive. If putting a concept in question were the same as destroying it, philosophers would soon be out of business (texts, readers, and ideologies may be questioned as strongly as authors). One notes that very few philosophers have been driven to doubt their *own* existence as authors. The technical challenge does complicate our notions of authorship, and in this respect may be welcomed not as killing the author but as improving our means of talking about him. The practical challenge does not pretend to refute the idea of the author but only to set it conveniently aside. Like any such practice, this new vocabulary must be judged not by its theory but by its results. I do not deny the proponents of any of these challenges the right to ask such questions as they choose. But none of them gives sufficient reason to believe that the author is dead, or to doubt that a hundred years from now critics and readers will still be discussing authors.

5 Barthes, "Death of the Author," p. 142. A student of Barthes might note that the last sentence predicts much of his later career, his paradoxical effort to *restore* the "identity of the body writing."

6 "Sarrasine" is printed as an appendix to Barthes's *S/Z*, trans. Richard Miller (New York: Hill and Wang, 1974), a work that builds on the principles of "The Death of the Author." The passage quoted appears on p. 248.

7 The denial that speech has priority over writing has been a prominent feature of the work of Jacques Derrida at least since *De la grammatologie* (1967). It might be argued, however, that Derrida like Barthes and Foucault tends to fluctuate between the position that writing is indifferent to matters of voice and origin and the position that writing is devoted to resisting or deconstructing voices and origins.

8 Barthes, *S/Z*, p. 175.

9 Todorov, "The Last Barthes," *Critical Inquiry* 7 (Spring 1981): 449–54; Susan Sontag, Introduction to *A Barthes Reader* (New York: Hill and Wang, 1982).

10 Jonathan Culler, *Roland Barthes* (New York: Oxford University Press, 1983), p. 11.

11 Barthes, "Death of the Author," p. 148.

12 *Times Literary Supplement*, Sept. 27, 1963.

13 John Livingston Lowes, *The Road to Xanadu* (Boston: Houghton Mifflin, 1964), pp. 396, 394. The book was first published in 1927.

14 John Middleton Murry, *Studies in Keats* (London: Oxford University Press, 1930), p. 32.

15 I. A. Richards, *Coleridge on Imagination* (London: Kegan Paul, Trench, Trubner, 1934), pp. 31–35; Robert Penn Warren, *The Rime of the Ancient Mariner* (New York: Reynal & Hitchcock, 1946), pp. 63–69.

16 *The Letters of John Keats*, ed. H. E. Rollins (Cambridge, Mass.: Harvard University Press, 1958), 1: 378 (October 27, 1818).

17 Edward Said, *Beginnings* (New York: Basic Books, 1975), p. 227.

18 Ibid., pp. 203–4.
19 J. Hillis Miller, "The Critic as Host," in *Deconstruction and Criticism* (New York: Seabury Press, 1979), p. 226.
20 M. H. Abrams, *Natural Supernaturalism* (New York: W. W. Norton, 1971), p. 442.
21 Though de Man and Miller adopt Reiman's text, *Shelley's "The Triumph of Life"* (Urbana, Ill.: University of Illinois, 1965) as "authoritative" (ignoring the editor's own revisions in *Shelley's Poetry and Prose*, 1977), de Man considers Reiman's "commitment to a positive interpretation" irrelevant (*Deconstruction and Criticism*, p. 71) and Miller does not consider it at all.
22 Jacques Derrida, "Living On," in *Deconstruction and Criticism*, p. 103.
23 Paul de Man, "Shelley Disfigured," *Deconstruction and Criticism*, p. 69.
24 Ibid., p. 68.
25 *Faust*, lines 11595–603. I have analyzed this passage at greater length in *The Life of the Poet* (Chicago: University of Chicago Press, 1981), pp. 109–12.

A Rose in Context:
The Daughter Construct

Barbara Clarke Mossberg

A mother's hardest to forgive
Life is the fruit she longs to hand you
Ripe on a plate. And while you live,
Relentlessly she understands you.
                    Phyllis McGinley, "The Adversary"

I don't write for you but know that one of the
reasons I do write is that you are my mother.
                    Anne Sexton, Christmas letter to her
                    mother accompanying a gift of poems

I am writing for myself and strangers. No one who
knows me can like it.
                    Gertrude Stein, *The Making of Americans*

HOW DOES Gertrude Stein mean "a rose is a rose is a rose is a rose"[1]—or is it a literary Oakland: there is no there there? Is it an unsympathetic, cavalier write-off of a rose,[2] or of what one can say about roses, or of what one can say about anything, for that matter? Does it say all that can be said; does it say something at all; or does it in fact reduce the *something* that can be said about *anything* to absurdity, to zero? Is it an expression of the limits of language, if not roses, which are limited and even incapacitated by the structure in which they find themselves in this sentence? Is it a case of teasing, a literary practical joke perpetrated upon the reader who should know better than to expect or to desire definitions, or a serious statement about the futility of definition? And if the latter were true, does Stein care?

Asked about its meaning during her lecture tour in the United States, Stein focuses on its import as a literary achievement: it was the first time a rose was red in literature for a century.[3] Stein was also the first person ever to have "completely caressed and addressed a noun."[4] Stein may have thought she made poetry in these eleven words, treated a noun tenderly and with respect, and restored color to the text, but these claims

199

do not address the meaning of this saying for her. She professes to value it out of context, but it is not only the statement for which Stein is most well-known, famous, or notorious, it is also the one with which Stein wanted to be identified. The statement has particular meaning for Stein; it recurs (in its variant forms of "Rose is a rose is a rose is a rose" as well) throughout her career, and in her life she adopts it as her signature. We see it first appear in 1913 in "Sacred Emily," then again in 1922 in both "Objects Lie on a Table" and "As Fine as Melanctha": "Civilization began with a rose. A rose is a rose is a rose is a rose." She discusses the saying in her lectures and her writing about writing. She writes "The Autobiography of Rose" (1936), and "Rose" becomes not only an autobiographical persona but a female character in her work, such as in "Melanctha" (1903) and *The World is Round* (1938). Shaped as a ring, the saying appears on the cover of *The Autobiography of Alice B. Toklas* (1933); it appears on Stein's stationery; and Toklas put the saying on their china.[5]

What is Stein saying about *herself*, then, in this dictum? If we turn to the sentence, we see that it does not set out a definition or even the impossibility of definition so much as it argues the lack of possibility for a certain being to exist in any form other than her original identity. There is something defiant about the second rose which subverts the definition process by its echo — a case of metaphoric boomeranging; but by the fourth rose, even as we see ourselves as readers entrapped by our expectations of definition, we see a case of the rose's entrapment. Other literary roses have suffered, but this rose — equally as allegorical as Blake's — is stuck. Each of the four roses represents successive moments in time, perhaps, but not progress nor growth in terms of identity; each linking verb constitutes a possible moment of freedom in which this rose can be or become something else, something *besides*, can be *understood* in terms other than herself. But there is a letdown as the rose reappears: rose again, always rose, rose forever. The case is hopeless if one values growth or change, consoling, if one sees what must be the rose's steadfast refusal to be anything but herself as a heroic, defiant, or stubborn stance against a constantly affecting world which threatens identity. In either case, the rose is fated to be herself, as she has always been. Structurally, the sentence makes this point: it is a circle (or ring) which feeds upon itself like a serpent its tail, a chain at once endless and confining; beginning and ending are indistinguishable. The sentence is a linguistic spider web in which the rose is not only the spider but the helpless, paralyzed fly; the intransitive verb cannot release the trapped "rose" but only can confirm her fate — that is, her identity.

Thus weighted with implications for a woman, the saying is no blithe *tour de force*. If we consider it in the context of Stein's life and literature, beginning with the literary and biographical context of the circular construction of the idiosyncratic axiom, we can understand more fully its significance and meaning for Stein as a self-portrait, an autobiography-at-a-glance, a parable of identity and destiny. Taken in a larger sociological and historical context of women in patriarchal culture, we can extend Stein's own not immodest claims for the historical significance of the sentence to construe it as the shortest tragedy in literature. The fact that it is the statement by which Stein is known appears particularly appropriate, for it not only illustrates and recapitulates Stein's aesthetics (such as her use of repetition and the continuous present) but what Stein is saying in her literary and life texts.

Rose's fate is of crucial import to Stein. The problem of identity at the core of Stein's work is exemplified in *The World Is Round* (1938), when the grammatic circularity of "a rose is a rose is a rose is a rose" structure becomes the theme itself. Rose is the heroine, a little girl (as she is in "The Autobiography of Rose," written two years earlier) oppressed and depressed by the circularity of the world, for the fact that it is "round" means that there is no escape from the self, from identity. Living in a "round" world, given her problems with her identity as a little girl, is complicated by the "round" (and also inescapable) female body, with the capacity to become pregnant, a threatening fate Stein herself plans to avoid. Her character of Rose has a foil, a boy named Willie, who is undaunted by the world's "roundness,"—"I would be Willie whatever arose"—even as his identity is questioned ("who are you who are you"). Rose is traumatized by the notion of inevitability in a world in which everything is determined ("a rose is a rose") specifically because she is a girl. She makes a series of allegorical journeys, including carving Stein's signature, "Rose is a rose is a rose is a rose" on a tree on her way to the mountain top which she thinks can "stop" the world's on-going continuity. Considering Stein's ambivalence to traditional expressions of female identity and destiny, which make female biology so burdensome to her, the story of Rose in a round world where "rose is a rose is a rose is a rose" assumes significance and an autobiographical context.

Similarly, *The Geographical History of America* (1936) sets forth Stein's identity problems as a woman in a structural as well as thematic way. In the first sentence, Stein linguistically puts herself into the same historical context as male American "fathers" Washington and Lincoln— a context from which she can reasonably expect to be omitted in "real" histories. She at once tells us her sense of identity conflict in a culture that makes identity—in her wittily understated words—"not a pleasure."

She then tells us she thinks of the dog who would "like to get lost, lost, lost, be where there is no identity." In the same "round" structure as "a rose is a rose" she ends the book where it begins, with "Chapter One" and her problem of identity, and the narrative in between consists of half-hearted nods to successive chapters; Chapter One repeats throughout the book. Thus just as a rose is a rose and the world is round, Chapter One cannot be escaped—that is, the identity problems this chapter embodies. The book's circular structure is reinforced with the ending, "I am not sure that this is not the end." Identity and its problems for the woman artist go on and on, but it is a closed system—there is no escape, even as there is the continuity of the wish to escape the self, at least the self as one is known, the self one is supposed to be, the self *in context*, the identity society gives you:

> Thank you for a name.
> Thank nobody for the same.
>
> Identity
> Is it well to know the end of any identity.
> . . .
> Human nature plainly worries about identity.
> . . .
> I was not careless about identity, oh no I was not and I was not no I
> was not careless.

In *What Are Masterpieces* (1935), Stein has explained,

> Identity is recognition, you know who you are because you and others remember anything about yourself but essentially you are not that when you are doing anything. I am I because my little dog knows me but creatively speaking the little dog knowing that you are you and your recognition that he knows, this is what destroys creation. This is what makes school.

In the same way, then, that Emily Dickinson distinguishes between poetry and prose as liberating and oppressive modes of expression, creativity for Stein is the antithesis of doing what we are taught and told, that which we do when we accept conventional notions about what we are able to do and should do, when we are dutiful and obedient. In other words, how people know you may limit your sense of possibility —particularly if the people doing the knowing do not expect anything great, as was the case with Stein's family who assumed she was a "rose" who was stupid.[6] But Stein's identity problems are conceived by her to be a function of being female. Her reference to the "little dog" whose knowledge of her threatens her ability to create is taken from the Mother Goose rhyme about the woman who sets out for town and is mysteriously assaulted. She wakes up in the roadway with her petticoats up about her waist, and torn. She is shaken and disoriented, but like the reader she does not know the exact nature of what has happened to her—the vague suggestion is that she has been sexually molested. The incident makes her doubt her own identity: how can this be me, she wonders, if *this* has happened to me; I must not be myself. In a spirit of scientific inquiry she decides to go home and see if her dog recognizes her. If he barks at her as he does at strangers, she will know she is not herself. On the other hand, if he recognizes her, Stein suggests she will no longer be able to create. In Stein's reading and use of this nursery rhyme—the little dog is a motif in her writings all her life—we see her value of an identity which is independent from other people's opinions of what she is and must be is crucial for her aesthetics.[7] Thus in her writing she tries—as she put it in "autobiography number one" (actually the thirteenth version of it)—to "renounce become." I will be using her biography as evidence that while she said it may be "well to know the end of any identity," she thought she knew the typical woman's destiny and deliberately sought to escape it in her lifestyle and through her writing.

In her autobiographies, Stein tells us about her identity problems as a woman in a patriarchal family and culture (she specifically uses the word "patriarchal"), determined to make her own destiny, to fight against the opinions of her father and brother and male teachers and editors of "rose," a woman, herself: who she is, will be, must be. In "How Could They Marry Her?" (1915), she begins, "I know what I want to do. I want to repeat all well." She then digresses, to get to her point, telling us that what follows is "not a description of Emily" (it is, of course, herself): she prays she might become worthy of an "ecclesiastical education" and that her address may become famous. Then: "She meant to make more noise than anything. / You have brothers. / "A busy life. I hoped to escape that. I think it is obliging." So concerned was Stein with fending off a dominating male world—escaping "obliging" as a traditional woman—that her view of history was affected by her sense of herself as a woman who was not going to continue to be dominated by a tyrannical father. On foreign policy, for example, she writes, "There is too much fathering going on just now and there is no doubt about it fathers are depressing. Everybody now-a-days is a father, there is father Mussolini and father Hitler and father Roosevelt."[8] Her aesthetics likewise reflect her self-consciousness as a woman writer. Parts of speech and punctuation have genders and sex roles: the comma is eliminated as being "servile," "dependent upon use and convenience and they are put there just for practical purpose"; "A comma by helping you along holding your coat for you and putting on your shoes keeps you from living your life as actively as you should lead it."[9] Thus the comma is objectionable because it plays a traditional female "obliging" role, even as a maternal figure, which compromises the writer who seeks independence in her use of language. Grammar is conceptualized by Stein as something she must rebel against, hold her own against: it is "coercive." In *How to Write* (1928) grammar is "Arthur" and a "vocabulary of thinking" is "George"; this work is composed after "Patriarchal Poetry" (1927) in which Stein celebrates her independent use of grammar and language.

Stein left her country, repudiated and eliminated her brother from her life and literary texts, set up house with another woman, broke conventions of patriarchal poetry and prose, created a lifestyle, clothes style, hair style, and literary style which sported with stereotyped feminine behavior and roles. Thus her identification with "rose" in "a rose is a rose is a rose" is all the more significant. Is she pessimistic about the chances for "rose" to "renounce become," escape her ordained identity? Is she optimistic about the ability to maintain a stable identity? Within a biographical context, her succinct parable of identity, destiny, and progress can be seen as a drama of the effort to escape oneself which she continuously articulated elsewhere; it can be seen as both comic and tragic; and it can constitute a paradigm of the dilemma in which Stein and other women writers found and kept themselves: as a daughter.

If we were to substitute the word "rose" with "daughter" and say in Steinese, "a daughter is a daughter . . ." we would be describing the mechanics of identity which Stein's life and autobiographical writing manifest "the daughter construct." Although the daughter remains a daughter, each one represents a stage in the writer's identity, from the first sense of beleaguered identity growing up in a patriarchy, through the rebellion stage ("she meant to make more noise than anything") through the recognition that she cannot escape this identity, to the insistence on being, being, and being this daughter in her life and art as an aesthetic strategy. It is the daughter in the fourth stage—the mature writer in the "daughter construct"—I will focus on in setting out the value of biographical context in studying the work of women writers. Understanding "a rose is a rose is a rose is a rose" in the context of Stein's life, literature, and in the context of other women writers in "the daughter construct" will enable us to flesh out the meaning and significance of Stein's brilliant parable of identity.

"The daughter construct"[10] is essentially a biographical context from which to understand a particular mode of self-representation, use of autobiography in symbolic and allegoric ways in texts diverse as Stein's "a rose is a rose is a rose is a rose," Carolyn Kizer's poetry, Sylvia Plath's novels, or the visual images of Swedish artist Lena Cronqvist. It manifests itself by a cluster of images, themes, personae, attitudes towards the self, the word, and the world, in women of different cultural milieus, nationalities, geographic areas, and even historical periods, from Amherst to Paris, Wellesley to Oakland, Guam to Sweden. These different women create and use the same personae, tell the same story, with the same images. The point of view is the daughter's, the persona is the daughter, or little girl, and the plot is about this daughter's experience as a little girl in relation to her parents and the world she conceives as a superparent.

This is not to say that these writers and artists always use this persona or theme but they use it consistently enough in their work so that it forms a pattern of connection in the course of their creative life. By "daughter" I mean to distinguish between the little girl or woman and the woman who expresses and defines herself as a daughter in relation to her parents all her life. Every woman is a daughter, of course, but not every woman, and not even every woman writer, maintains this primary identity at the expense of all others, making it dominate or exclude other identities that are the function of relationships with lovers, spouses, siblings, children, colleagues, friends. For most women, identities as mother, wife, lover, friend, can be thin veneers for the daughter identity no matter what their age or experience; but the "daughter" in the "daughter construct" forms relationships that perpetrate her identification as the "daughter" and her feelings as a little girl in her family and culture, convinced that her maintaining her daughter identity is necessary for her art.

A primary way the daughter maintains her identity is through her art itself. Parents are portrayed obsessively, compulsively, ambivalently. A daughter's point of view presides in the depiction of mother-daughter and father-daughter and child-patriarch relationships. Whether she is thirty-five or sixty-five, the mature woman artist shows herself as the young daughter, stranded as on an island, in a relationship she cannot escape with parents who are failures *as* parents — dominating, punitive, non-nurturing, absent. The writer dwells on childhood experience, either real or imagined. Her father is drawn as powerful yet ineffective, burdensome yet inaccessible, menacing yet mourned. He is a buffoon tyrant, whom the daughter shows herself defying, imploring, accusing, trying to please, trying to "get back, back, back to" and trying to get back *at*. The mother is pictured as literally and metaphorically "shut up," confined within her role and her house, silent, ghost or ghoul, a physical or temperamental invalid, childlike, withholding, helplessly ineffective as a mother. She is a weak presence, a powerful absence, denied, rejected, patronized, loathed, rebelled against, mourned, longed for, hungered for. And no matter what her age as she composes, the daughter shows herself as bratty, insolent, angry, defeated, defiant, full of rage, hunger, needs. She seeks to be independent but in crucial ways she never leaves home, literally or figuratively, dwelling there in her mind and art; for it is here, and on these terms, that she can create.

The works are autobiographical in format. Even if these self-portraits are distortions, exaggerations, complete fictions, and unfair lies, it is important to remember that this is the form and mode in which the woman artist chooses to express herself: these writings constitute a symbolic, allegoric portrayal of her life as an artist, struggling to speak up and out as a little girl in her culture. Emily Dickinson describes it thus:

> They shut me up in Prose—
> As when a little Girl
> They put me in the Closet—
> Because they liked me "still"—   613[11]

We get clues as to how to "read" a life from the way the fictive life is represented over and over again. Dickinson may never have been put in a closet when she was little, and we do not have to take it literally when she complains of efforts to "shut her up." But even so, the biographical context of such an image becomes crucial in understanding these texts and their significance: the actual experience of a daughter within a certain family and culture must account in large part for the self-image as daughter represented in the artist's work. We see identity conflict and madness related to the tension of being a dutiful daughter, conforming to traditional female roles, and growing up like the mother, at the same time desiring to rebel from the maternal role. The dutiful/ rebellious daughter images are so pervasive in these works that they constitute, I believe, a major mode of self-definition for the modern woman artist, an identity forged from the effort to escape the maternal matrix and the patriarchy which bounds it. In this escape, the woman finds herself in a civil war, vainly struggling to extricate her identity from her mother's; each autonomous identity, mother and daughter, threatens and defines the other. As little girl to her parents and society, the daughter portrays herself choosing between duty and rebellion: she wants to be loved but feels that what being loved entails—conformity—will compromise and defeat her own powerful identity; when she rebels, she alienates herself and forfeits parental approval and love, but gains power through the use of her mind and creative psyche in independent ways. As an artist, she is not and cannot be a good little girl.

We see the image of rebellion dramatically portrayed in the theme of identity conflict and madness, where civil war rages between woman and artist, mother and daughter. She is forced to fight against the woman within who can grow up and be "good": for these women, art requires the denial of adult female sexuality and the identity crisis resulting from being a contradiction in terms as woman artist: it requires being a rose, a rose, a rose—and saying "no" to anything else.

Thus we see the dilemma presented in this art of women who want to grow but not grow up—women who want to be different from their mothers; their aspiration to be great demands that they rebel. When a woman sees her same-sex role model as weak and devalued by society and family, or when she has a mother she cannot hope to be, even if she has a powerful father, an identity crisis develops.[12] Who is she to become, with whom to identify, if not her own mother? Even as she may reject what her mother stands for, her mother's role in society, the daughter finds herself inhabiting her mother's body. She opens her mouth and hears her mother's voice; she sees herself using her mother's mannerisms. She looks in the mirror and sees her mother's face. And yet this mother is teaching her how to be "good," how to get along in a patriarchal society, just like *her*. What does the daughter do?

She remains a daughter, in a paralysis; she stops where she is, like Peter Pan refuses to grow up, in order to be at a stage in life where sexuality is not quite as circumscribing. She becomes a career daughter, a "lifer," avoiding her mother's role, fate, destiny. Thus we see the paradox of the daughter who stays home, yet is rebellious there, angry, hungry, resentful. If she actually does leave the home compound, like Sylvia Plath, and marries and has children, she chooses a mate like her father and plays out the often fatal daughter role with him (the mother's role, after all):

> And then I knew what to do.
> I made a model of you,
> A man in black with a Meinkampf look
>
> And a love of the rack and the screw.
> And I said I do, I do.
>
> > Sylvia Plath, "Daddy"[13]

If she lives with a woman as Stein does, she becomes her "Baby." Even
when, as in the cases of Emily Dickinson and Flannery O'Connor, fate
conspires to keep her home, she elects to stay home in the one area of
her life where she does have a choice, an opportunity to leave: in her
writing. And home she stays, with a vengeance; she has an axe to grind
against both her parents. In subtle and openly rebellious ways, she cir-
cumvents her mother's fate, frees herself of the restrictions and confine-
ments placed upon women in her culture. In this light, the daughter
role is a strategy to transcend a sex-defined role in a culture in which
she is "shut up." If in her work she expresses the tension, ambivalence,
and anxiety about her social and artistic autonomy and efforts at creative "authority," it is a response to a patriarchal society, and the "daughter" thus becomes a metaphor of what it means to grow up as a little
girl in such a culture. As Stein says, she "renounces become" in order
to *be*: "rose *is*, rose *is*, rose *is*," existing in a continuous present in one
identity, so that the saying is a comedy. The power to ward off the future is conceived as a gift. As Stein says in *The Making of Americans*,
the people who can remain children "always have it in them to be very
lively, so as to keep adolescence from giving sorrow to them, they are
lively and they try all their living to keep up dancing so that adolescence will be scared away from them."

Perhaps the most dramatic manifestation of the daughter construct
is the protrayal of the consequences of keeping the mother-in-herself
at bay. Anything threatening her destiny to be great, whether it be men,
marriage, babies, home, society, her own sexuality, is conceptualized
by the daughter as a "food" or nurture a patriarchal society offers its
women through their mothers to grow up. Refusing this "food" is the
daughter's way to avoid being manipulated and betrayed into "becoming" her mother. Thus food is presented obsessively in the works, as
poison, something that is not eaten, garbage, something that must be
refused. But at the same time as we see food being offered and waved
away by the daughter in arrogant dismissal—she is above eating—we
see images of starvation, anorexia nervosa, food being withheld, empty
tables. In fact, mother and daughter in this literature are posed fronting
each other with open, empty mouths, bared teeth, hanging tongues,
pressed lips. She may fear ingesting whatever the mother offers, but the
daughter hungers for her mother herself, just as she imagines the mother
trying to devour her, consume her. Literally and metaphorically, the open
mouth is at the center of the daughter's work.

It perhaps makes sense, then, that the most recurrent image in this
literature is the hunger for the mother, for if the daughter must reject

her mother as a role model, she still needs a mother. But keeping her mouth shut—not eating—is an image with particular resonance for a writer who feels she should not use her voice, not speak out, not use her "mouth." Her rebellion as a writer is a function of the use of her "voice," so that her use of the word is something which bespeaks her own hunger for and rebellion against her mother. In this context, images of womb and stomach are intertwined, as from the child's point of view: the mother's belly expands with eating, so that must be the way a baby gets in there too—a baby must be something the mother *ate*. If one wants to avoid becoming a mother, logic suggests that one must not *eat*: thus the connection in these works between sexual reproduction and food, and the notion that pregnancy, the culmination of female biological destiny, is a function of taking in, in literal and metaphoric ways, cultural attitudes and doctrine about traditional roles for women. The daughter artist who wants to avoid being a mother cannot eat, cannot be so impregnated, and thus shows herself refusing such nurture and starving. But out of this self-imposed hunger comes her need to feed herself with words or images, and her art becomes a way to nurture herself, conceive herself as her own child.

The image cluster of food, word, and child is a function, I believe, of the psychosocial phenomenon of anorexia nervosa, wherein young girls of upper-class and middle-class families, are literally starving themselves to death, in an effort psychologists say is aimed at warding off becoming fully mature women.[14] If the woman artist adopts an aesthetic based on the notion that she cannot eat, she feels she can create only if her relationship with her parents remains infantile, unresolved, and inadequate. Then she "runs away" and feeds herself through her ability to create art. Thus her showing her parents in her work to be ineffectual or absent can be seen as the result of her need to nourish herself in her own way, in order to grow up into something she wants to be, to achieve an autonomy in the use of her voice, to say what she wants. If she shows herself living at home, lost and defiant, feeling both entrapped and abandoned by parental figures, it is because she can never be nurtured by them if she is to create.

In creating, she creates herself, in a sense becomes mother to herself, haunted by the image of the time when she was immersed in her mother's blood, drank her milk, was at one with her body in a nutritional way. Now, in the literary creation of herself, she swallows her mother whole, even as her mother preys on her from within. And her mother elicits her voice, the opening of the mouth to speak; she functions as a muse. The daughter construct may show how women feel

in their culture as women artists, how they feel about using their voice
—dependent, defensive, defiant, rebellious—but it also shows something
about the creative process itself.

I will sketch out a few examples of some well-known writers whose
life and works are at the heart of this construct. Emily Dickinson lived
out her life as a daughter enclosed ("shut up") in her "father's house";
during her life she maintained the habits and mannerisms of her young-
girl self, even her hairstyle; she played out the role of dutiful daughter
to her father and mother, and rebelled at night through her poetry. Looking at her life and works, taken together and individually, in the wider
context of the daughter construct illuminates features that otherwise
can be obscured.[15] The relation between her life and poetry makes
more sense; the relationships she established with men (and God) were
patterned after the one she had with her own father, and her letters
to her "Master" as well as her poems to a male lover, God, and father
reflect this sensibility. Dickinson led a privileged existence, although
she resented her brother Austin's opportunities as much as she pitied
him for being less free to be himself. But her writing describes a childhood of persecution, deprivation, abandonment, and, although such
a term sounds odd in connection with a nineteenth century writer,
discrimination:

> God gave a Loaf to every Bird—
> But just a Crumb—to Me—   791
>
> It would have starved a Gnat—
> To live so small as I—
> And yet I was a living Child—
> With Food's necessity
>
> Upon me—like a Claw—
> I could no more remove
> Than I could coax a Leech away—
> Or make a Dragon—move—
>
> Nor like the Gnat—had I—
> The privilege to fly
> And seek a Dinner for myself—
> How mightier He—than I—
>
> Nor like Himself—the Art
> Upon the Window Pane
> To gad my little Being out—
> And not begin—again—   612

Deprived of other Banquet
I entertained Myself—   773

I had been hungry, all the Years—   579

my lot . . .
Too hungry to be borne   801

We see the autobiographical mode of presentation: this happened
to me. In a literal sense, we are sure it did not; we know Emily Dickinson was plump and pampered, indulged in many respects. But the fact
that she casts her deprivation most often in terms of food—500, roughly
a third, of her poems contain oral imagery—suggests, especially to psychoanalytic critics, that Dickinson may be referring to inadequate
mothering, a reading the biography and poems themselves could be seen
to confirm.[16] The mother is absent from the poetry, and in her letters,
Dickinson denies having a mother: "I never had a mother"; "I always
ran Home to Awe when a child, if anything befell me. He was an awful
Mother, but I liked him better than none." During her forties, she complains of having no one to tell her right from wrong, or to dress her;
in her thirties she asks an editor she has never met "how to grow," and
in her fifties she complains about having to mind her mother all day.[17]
Thus all her life she was making a public issue about her fate as a dutiful daughter and her mother's inadequacy. But her mother was very
present—perhaps too present; she was an invalid cared for until her death
almost exclusively by Dickinson until Dickinson was fifty-one. They constituted each other's daily community.

Perhaps the elder Emily Dickinson is absent from the poems because
Dickinson already feels inhabited by her, close enough that she does
not have to make her an object, a subject outside of herself, whereas
she experiences her father as an "other." But another explanation is implicit in the context of the "daughter construct." Her mother, dominated
by Dickinson's father, was perceived as timid, dutiful, modest, pious,
weak; her family patronized her. As a role model she was inadequate
for Dickinson's plans to be "great, Someday," to gain "taller feet," to
make her family proud, to be "the Poet."[18] To establish herself as different from her mother, Dickinson has to repudiate her. The primary way
she can be different from her mother is through her aspirations to be
great, to be something else; since biologically this is impossible, she
distinguishes herself through her imagination, her capacity to fulfill her
intellectual aspirations; making this difference perfectly clear, she mocks
her mother's conventional habits of thinking and expressing herself. It

is through words that she is able to break away from her mother, in spite of the physical closeness they shared.

The "hunger poems" describe an anorexic's strategy: by not allowing herself to be nurtured, she can avoid her mother's fate, become something different, herself: thus her identity is one in relation to, in opposition to, her mother. She shows her persona deliberately not eating: that this is a strategy is made clear in "God gave a Loaf to every Bird—" (791), where she refuses to eat even the crumb that she *is* given, refuses not out of pride, but because it makes her superior:

> I wonder how the Rich—may feel—
> An Indiaman—an Earl—
> I deem that I—with but a Crumb—
> Am Sovereign of them all—

In "Art thou the thing I wanted?" (1282) Nurture is waved away; her hunger has grown too large now to be satisfied by anything the world can supply: she is now "like God," "dining without." In "I fit for them—" (1109), she declares that this "abstinence of mine produce[s] / A purer food." The literature about anorexia notes the conviction of afflicted women that in starving themselves they attain a higher morality, that in their discipline and control they are superior, powerful, purer, "perfect." For a writer, this sense of power of mind over body derives from what we could call a creative diet: Dickinson's obsession with food and hunger drives her to feed herself with the only food that will not make her into her mother—words, a "purer" food that does not decompose or "perish." As long as she is hungry enough to keep making words, she can be herself, that is, "different." This is how Dickinson herself explains it. In "I had been hungry, all the Years" (579), for example, she describes herself finally partaking in a communion-type ceremony, only to discover that she feels "odd"—"As Berry—of a Mountain Bush— / Transplanted—to the Road—." In other words, eating makes her common, part of normal human traffic; it is *difference* she is after, and writing is the way to achieve this difference.

Dickinson's poems celebrate her "different" identity: "I cannot dance upon my Toes" (326), "I'm ceded—I've stopped being Their's—" (508), "It was given to me by the Gods" (454), even as they also complain about the alienation she feels, as in "I never felt at Home—Below" (413) (where her alienation is described as a function of being a restless little girl during her life). "They shut me up in Prose" (613) and "Why —do they shut Me out of Heaven?" (248) articulate her sense of being punished for speaking out as an adult woman in terms of a little girl who uses her "voice" in unladylike fashion: she is "too loud," not "still" enough.

In her own life, Dickinson rejects the maternal matrix: her mother's religion, social world, marriage, children, houselife. "God keep me from what they call *households*"; "*My* kitchen I think I called it, God forbid that it was or shall be my own—," she writes; in another context, "you know how I hate to be common," and—in a bit of Steinese—"a mutual plum is not a plum."[19] She is a daughter, that fourth rose, by choice and necessity. But her poetry also reflects the strain that rejecting her mother (renouncing "become," as Stein says) causes:

> Me from Myself—to banish
> Had I Art—
> Impregnable my Fortress
> Unto All Heart—
>
> But since Myself—assault Me—
> How have I peace
> Except by subjugating
> Consciousness?
>
> And since We're mutual Monarch
> How this be
> Except by Abdication—
> Me—of Me?   642

To reject a mother is to reject oneself; battling the potential mother within herself, the daughter realizes that she is an integral part of her identity that cannot be banished without destroying herself in the process. The identity crisis is set out in such poems as "Rearrange a 'Wife's' affection!" (1737), "My Life had stood—a Loaded Gun" (754), "One need not be a Chamber—to be Haunted" (670), and "The first Day's Night had come" (410). Her voice is a weapon; her identity is fragmented; she is her worst, most terrifying enemy, like Stein in "Once upon a time I met myself and ran," encountering herself and fleeing. But as a daughter, she is always in such stasis.

Sylvia Plath's identity as daughter, speaking of stasis and terrifying enemies, is notorious, less metaphorical than Dickinson's, perhaps more self-conscious about the use to which she is putting her own biographical context, so that her readers are forced to seek out her biography as they read her work. This is the woman who took care of her father in "Daddy" (1962) and her mother in *The Bell Jar* (1962), prompting her embarrassed mother to go on the campus lecture circuit defending her maternal reputation, and even to become—at last—a writer herself, editing *Letters Home* (1975) and encouraging it being made into a play which would confirm the close mother-daughter relationship and her adequacy as a mother.[20] Plath's daughter chronicles—private, personal —become universal as readers project their *own* biographical context upon them; but Plath was aware of her motives in writing from the point of view of the fourth rose. In *The Bell Jar*, when Esther Greenwood, named, significantly, after Plath's mother's mother, decides to write a novel, she thinks, "that would fix a lot of people." Her mother at least tried to keep it from being published in the United States (Plath used a pseudonym, Victoria Lucas, in the British edition). What Mrs. Plath cannot understand is the relationship between the daughter's desire "to fix a lot of people" and the close relationship she assumed she and her daughter had experienced. Unlike Mrs. Dickinson, Aurelia Plath shared her daughter's aspirations to be great, to be a great *writer*; she even, I think, initiated them and certainly inspired them in every possible way—including typing, editing, and sending out manuscripts. Aurelia Plath was not a role model, but she could not have been more supportive; her daughter was living out her own interest in writing and literature which she had given up in order to be a dutiful mother to Sylvia and her brother Warren. Is this it? That she directed her daughter's dutiful use of language, put words in Plath's mouth? Served as midwife to "deliver" them up? If so, as a writer and in her writing, Plath is inhabited by her mother, expressing her voice, living a double life; but then how is she to establish her own identity through her use of the word? She can use language rebelliously, in secret, learn from "muses unhired by you, dear Mother" ("The Disquieting Muses," 1957).

In Plath, we also see hunger poems, intertwined images of food, mother, and mother love. Despite the difference in Dickinson's and Plath's mothers, Plath also uses hunger—or at least its evocation in her poems —to keep her mother at bay. But Plath, who has been "fed" by her mother to a much greater extent, rather murderously demands what her mother can give her. Her early letters to her mother are filled with descriptions of what she has eaten in her mother's absence—records of gluttony as often as not—and begging for more maternal food: words. She wants letters that are "fat" and "meaty." But in *The Bell Jar* when Esther schemes to get more food, she is poisoned: what the *Ladies Day* magazine and the culture it represents has to offer is not good for little girls. Esther's poisoning scene is a prose equivalent of Dickinson's "I had been hungry, all the Years." But in between the time Plath is begging for her mother's words and writing *The Bell Jar* and the late poems, she is using language dutifully, with her father's thesaurus on her lap, trying to please parental judges, critics, editors, professors. It is when she throws off the thesaurus that she uses language in a more liberating, less "obliging" way to rebel, to get back to, and get back at—as in the famous "Daddy," which cries out at the end, "you bastard." But even before her breakthrough period, Plath's pen is aimed: in "Colossus" (1959) she tries to come to terms with her dead father, an oracle to her Mary Poppins; in "Poem for a Birthday" at the same time, she confronts the meaning of the day in which she was first separated from her mother—a separation that gave her life:

> The month of flowering's finished. The fruit's in,
> Eaten or rotten. I am all mouth.
> October's the month for storage.
>
> This shed's fusty as a mummy's stomach:
> .   .   .   .
> Mother, you are the one mouth
> I would be a tongue to. Mother of otherness
> Eat me. Wastebasket gaper, shadow of doorways.   "Who"
>
> Moley-handed, I eat my way.
> All-mouth licks up the bushes   "Dark House"
>
> Once I was ordinary:
> Sat by my father's bean tree
> Eating the fingers of wisdom.
> .   .   .   .
> The mother of mouths didn't love me.
> .   .   .   .
> A red tongue is among us.
> Mother, keep out of my barnyard,
> I am becoming another.
>
> Dog-head, devourer:
> Feed me the berries of dark.
> .   .   .   .
> I must swallow it all.   "Maenad"
>
>   I inhabit
> The wax image of myself, a doll's body.   "Witch Burning"
>
> When I fell out of the light, I entered
> The stomach of indifference, the wordless cupboard.
>   "The Stones"

And so on: mouths, stomachs, bellies, tongues, mother, father, fetus, "mouth-holes," food tubes, sucking "at the paps of darkness." In poem after poem Plath addresses and discusses not just specific childhood events, but herself as her parents' daughter, events, her psychology as an adult woman understanding herself and her relationship to the world. She concentrates on the earliest stages of the mother-daughter relationship, the fetus, the infant, as if her identity in these states continues through her adult life. These poems are written, we should remember, when Plath is a mother herself; but she seldom writes *as* a mother. She is a daughter, using language as a child does, both to get love and approval and to establish her own identity. But in spite of her efforts to break away from her mother, through her marriage, her having her own children, her going to live permanently in England (like Stein and even Dickinson in her seclusion, an ex-patriot), she knows these attempts to break this bond are futile, just as Dickinson knows it is useless to try to separate me "from Me." In her dutifully written, regular weekly letters gushing with love for the "best mummy a girl ever had" (signed with her childhood name, "Sivvy") Plath keeps the bond intact, assuring her mother after a miscarriage that she would make her mother another baby, and including her mother in all her plans, whether it is applying for a grant or having a baby. She seems never to be able to tell where her parents leave off and she begins. How trapped and yet defiant she feels in this bond, this identity as dutiful writer-daughter, is expressed in "Medusa" (1962) (and we note that even the landscape is conceived of as stony "mouth-plugs"):

> Did I escape, I wonder?
> My mind winds to you
> Old barnacled umbilicus, Atlantic cable,
> Keeping itself, it seems, in a state of miraculous repair.
>
> In any case, you are always there,
> Tremulous breath at the end of my line,
> Curve of water unleaping
> To my water rod, dazzling and grateful,
> Touching and sucking.
> I didn't call you.
> I didn't call you at all.
> Nevertheless, nevertheless
> You steamed to me over the sea,
> Fat and red, a placenta
> . . . .

Who do you think you are?
A Communion wafer? Blubbery Mary?
I shall take no bite of your body,
Bottle in which I live,

Ghastly Vatican.
I am sick to death of hot salt.
Green as eunuchs, your wishes
Hiss at my sins.
Off, off, eely tentacle!

There is nothing between us.

But of course, there is, all that's left after Plath has left her mother's body: the daughter and the mother who is now an external placenta, still nurturing the fetus daughter/self in a symbiotic relationship. In "The Rival" (1961), Plath again complains of her mother's interfering in her independent life:

Your dissatisfactions, on the other hand,
Arrive through the mailslot with loving regularity,
White and blank, expansive as carbon monoxide.

No day is safe from news of you,
Walking about in Africa maybe, but thinking of me.

But as "Medusa" makes clear, both mother and daughter are responsible for this bond being kept in a state of "miraculous repair." The daughter wants her, "winds to her"; her mind is attached to her mother, still bonded by the umbilical cord, in a clever analogy to the cable which makes communion, even between England and Wellesley, possible: now voices, not blood. But that connection of voice and "blood jet" is important in Plath's work, where she expresses herself as a fetus within her mother's belly, the lifeblood flowing between them. "The blood jet is poetry. / There is no stopping it," she writes, but there is, and she does, when she kills herself, shuts off that flow of maternal blood/ nurture once and for all. (But the mother cannot stop, and still interacts with her daughter's words which accuse her of being too interfering, of violating her, of devouring her, leaving her empty, hungry, "all mouth.")

For Emily Dickinson, poetry was liberating, since it established a different identity than the mother's; for all we know, her mother never knew Dickinson wrote poetry. Sylvia Plaths' mother nurtured her with *words*, and therefore Plath's problems in extricating her identity from her mother's are more complex, and illuminated by a contemporary poet's discussion of the role her mother played as muse. In "Muse," which she calls "how my mother made me a poet," Carolyn Kizer discusses her early poems as written for her mother, "partly from love, partly as a bribe. The implicit barter: My poems, a partial invasion of my privacy, in exchange for some control over the rest of my life. Naive hope!"[21] Pursued in college by "anxious, demanding" letters, Kizer describes herself leaving home, marrying, having children, all in an effort to separate herself from her mother. Then her mother died: "Then my serious life as a poet began. At last, I could write poems without blackmail, without bargains, without the heartbreak of her expectations. I wrote those poems for her. I still do." Perhaps as long as her mother was alive, Plath could never establish an autonomous identity. She could not separate words from mother. While her mother breastfed her brother—the one who had ruptured the mother-daughter matrix—she was given letters to play with. When Sylvia was sent away so that her mother could care for Warren, her mother sent her letters, asking her to respond with poems and letters. When Plath was six, her mother included a poem on maternal care; Plath is encouraged to write back, and a mode of their mother-daughter relationship is established. Aurelia Plath tells us she would leave words under Sylvia's plate at the dinner table, that she was always more comfortable expressing love in written form. At age eight, Plath is already disciplined in her writing, spurred by her father's death to seek the world's approval and notice; at sixteen she already feels inhabited by her maternal muse: "You ask me why I spend my life writing?" (she asks herself); "I write only because / There is a voice within me / That will not be still."[22] This voice urging her on is her mother's, her words are often produced by her mother, and as I have argued elsewhere, it is her mother I believe she is trying to get back, back, back to, and back at, in her writing.[23] Leaving aside the question of fairness, we can return to the issue of the logic of her describing herself as starving when she has so much maternal support. Given these circumstances, how can her writing be a means to establish an autonomous identity?

Plath appears to have the symptoms of the typical anorexic: the child who is brought up with privilege, the recipient of devoted, scrupulous attention and love; the daughter who is a superachiever, dutiful, nice, a pleaser, suddenly turning hostile, rebellious, a monster. Her refusal to eat is a weapon directed at her parents, as if she understands how her desire to kill herself is a murderous act aimed especially at the person who gave her birth and whom she resembles, becomes. Theories of anorexia argue that such women feel overmanipulated, pressured by the constant expectations of them to achieve, undeserving of the love

that rewards their "good" behavior. They are insecure, requiring perfection. Thus, Plath at seventeen: "Never, never will I reach the perfection
I long for with all my soul. . . . Oh, I love now . . . now *now* I still am
not completely molded. My life is still beginning."[24] What strikes me
about these diary entries is the connection Plath makes between wanting perfection, wanting to please, having impossible standards, and the
desire to stay where she is, to remain that first rose. Both remaining that
rose and acquiring perfection are functions of the daughter's aesthetics
of anorexia; we may remember Plath's lines: "Perfection is terrible. It
cannot have children" ("The Munich Mannequin," 1963). Not eating
keeps an anorexic from becoming a mother; using language keeps Plath
a daughter. Still, like Dickinson and Stein, her identity feels precarious.
As a teenager she writes that she feels "vacant and empty," "not here."
Though she "smiles and chatters," she is "Not here / Never / Though
they think it." Her body is "but a ruse / To make them overlook / The
absence of myself" (as later she will write, "I inhabit the wax image
of myself, a doll's body"). In an early poem, apparently written after
a mother-daughter argument relating to her father, she makes her stance
clear in regard to her dutiful demeanor:

> I do what you wish, but without abandoning the desire
> of finishing my wretched life by your hands;
> . . . .
> In reality, my passion fought long enough for you;
> against my father and myself.
>
> I tell you again, and although I were sighing
> with my last breath, I would say it.
> I have wronged you and I had to bear it
> In order to blot out my shame and serve you . . .
> But, quits with honor and my father,
> It is now you I come to satisfy;
> It is to offer you my blood that you see me here.
> I have done my duty, I am doing my duty.

In "Electra on the Azalea Path" (1959) Plath later asks her father for
forgiveness from his "hound-bitch daughter": "It was my love that did
us both to death." But a constant motif in her poetry is this image of
self-sacrifice to a mother's love: her blood is both a love present and
act of final extrication.

If Plath gives voice to the deepest and most complex levels of mother-
daughter conflict as a teenager, she at the same time was able to successfully wear a mask of pleased, pleasing normalcy, of achiever, All-
American Girl. She did not become physically anorexic. But she did kill

herself all the same, and we ask what it means, just as we ask of a text what it means, what kind of statement is intended, how it should be "read." Should the fourth rose carry a warning: Hazardous to your health; may be fatal? If we say, but Plath was mad, she had a psychological pathology unique to her, we must consider other works, taken in the context of the daughter construct:

> I'm going to murder you with love
> . . . .
> I will devour you, my natural food,
> My host, my final supper on earth.
> And you'll begin to die again.
> > Carolyn Kizer, "Food of Love"

> Let us go back, open your belly, take me inside you. . . . Let us go back, carry me as you used to carry me. Let us be afraid together. . . . Your blood, my mother, the stream of blood flowing down the stairway when I came out of you, the flow of blood was a dying person. Iron, forceps, I was your prisoner as you were mine.

> You inhabit me as I inhabit you.
> > Violette Leduc, *La Batarde*
> > (translated by Marilyn Yalom, 1964)

The daughter construct shows what a widespread phenomenon of culture this is.[25] Leduc was probably neurotic in terms of her erotic love for her mother; she felt no need to break away, but even Simone de Beauvoir, who terms her autobiography *Memoirs of a Dutiful Daughter* (1959), was led to a problem of identity similar to Plath's: "Any reproach made by my mother, and even her slightest frown was a threat to my security; without her approval, I no longer felt I had any right to live." When her mother died, she tells how she "had put maman's mouth on my own face and in spite of myself, I copied its movements. Her whole person, her whole being was concentrated there and compassion wrung my heart." When Anne Sexton's mother was dying of cancer, she wrote W. D. Snodgrass, "My mother says I gave her cancer (as though death were catching—death being the birthday that I tried to kill myself, Nov. 9, 1956). Then she got cancer . . . who do we kill, which image in the mirror, the mother, ourself, our daughter????? Am I my mother, or my daughter?" (1958). She was aware of her suicide attempt as a way to kill her mother as well as herself. For Sexton as well as for Plath, their liberation could only be carried out on the page. One of Plath's last poems is called "Words:" it begins, "Axes."

In spite of having different lives, women in the daughter construct express themselves with remarkable similarity and consistency. In the case of Kim Chernin for example, we see an autobiographical book entitled *In My Mother's House* (1980), rather unnecessarily subtitled, "A Daughter's Story." Unlike Dickinson and even Plath, her mother was esteemed by the outside world; in the family circle she was seen as courageous, vital. She was a leader in left-wing movements, a hero. But the daughter distances herself from her, holds herself back, both in admiration and resentment that she is not first in her mother's life. The daughter moves away from her mother and becomes a poet, rarely coming home. Significantly, while her mother rather correctly interprets her daughter's career as a poet to be a rebellion from her, and while she disapproves of the poetry career in general, she seeks out her daughter to write her story, to give her a voice; that is, to make herself become immortal through her daughter's words. Chernin agrees, with some ambivalence, only after deciding that it is her story too she will tell; and in fact, it is all her story. When we turn to her other books, we see *The Obsession: Reflection on the Tyranny of Slenderness,* which sounds like a tract on anorexia, and a collection of poems entitled *The Hunger Song.*

To indicate how widespread this pattern of self-representation is, I will mention one case in the visual arts. Swedish artist Lena Cronqvist had never read Dickinson or Plath, but her paintings seem to illustrate their poems, from showing "Parental faces on tall stalks, alternately stern and tearful" ("Insomniac," Plath), to a self-portrait wherein she holds a baby on her lap which turns out upon closer inspection to be her grey-haired wriggling mother, to a woman standing inside a bottle and glass jar, to a child's face peering at a table set "too high" for it ("Victory comes late," Dickinson, 690), to landscapes of empty tables, parents isolated from one another, ignorant of the crying daughter at their feet, to a father's death scene (in twenty-four oils), recalling Kizer's "Thrall" (formerly "Dutiful Daughter"): "You wait for his eyes to close at last / So you may write this poem." There are little girls holding doll images of themselves, tongues, fetuses, nursing/choking images, tables of garbage, and women in mental institutions making clocks out of plates of food.

In considering the cross-cultural biographical contexts of these works, it appears that writers in the daughter construct share a history typical of the anorexic's. Both anorexia and the daughter construct in art and literature appear to be phenomena of a modern, affluent culture, a product of an upper class or middle class existence, and of educational opportunities for women. Both daughter-writers and anorexics seem to be struggling with the meaning of growing up to be a woman in a patriarchal culture that educates its women, lets them see their natural possibilities for power, and yet has different expectations and demands for men; they are privileged and underprivileged at the same time, acutely aware of their predicament. Anorexics create themselves; their art work is a skinny persona of flesh; their special achievement, mind over body. Daughters create a skinny persona with their words, replaying the dynamics of their childhood in versions that show the necessity for feeding themselves. Again, the body is the enemy over which the mind must triumph, control, in order to keep it from being a mother, the mother one hungers for.

The writers in the daughter construct often conceive their own experience as a metaphor for women and oppressed classes in general, specifically allying the daughter with the politically and socially oppressed. Despite how it may diverge from the actual biography, the meaning and use of the little girl persona in a patriarchal society is based on psychological and physical realities of childhood: the sense of being small, inferior, lacking physical, mental, social power; dependence, insignificance, alienation, loneliness; the struggle to gain independence and autonomy. In this light, the deliberate cultivation of the little-girl persona has particular relevance among well-educated, middle-class, Western women. The obsessive depiction of their experience as daughters may be not only a case of the daughter trying to commune with and break away from her parents' formative influence upon her artistic development and autonomy and hence serving as a metaphor of her growth as an artist, but a paradigm of women's socialization, documenting and subversively enacting the inherent contradictions in how we raise our women. The little girl in this art repudiates a society in which women must conceive creativity as antithetical to the work of sexually mature women. But given such a culture, the daughter persona is an ingenious device allowing women linguistic liberties, an independent autonomy, a powerful, effective, artistic identity.

Adrienne Rich writes that "The cathexis between mother and daughter—essential, distorted, misused—is the great unwritten story" (*Of Women Born*, 1976). But it is a story we have in fragments before us, written by women who are at once forging and reclaiming an understanding of themselves in their culture. When we view it whole in context of their identities as daughters, we see ideas about growing up and being a woman and writer that have import on our understanding of what is going on in their texts and lives—and in ours. We say that criticism ideally returns us to the text; the text returns us to the life, to the biographical context in which the writers live and in which we live. I suspect, in fact, that *what* the daughters are telling us has been known long before this. In nursery rhymes, we see the absence of mothers and fathers; old women (mothers) are shown as incompetent, not knowing "what to do," sitting by the hill; they reveal a culture's sense of a childhood perspective. But consider "Old Mother Hubbard." She goes to the cupboard to get her poor dog a bone (think of Plath's "wordless cupboard" and Stein's "dog"), but the cupboard is "bare." She cannot nurture, but thereupon knocks herself out to provide for this poor dog, bringing him in successive and, I think, breathless trips, fruit, linen, hats, and so on. But each time she leaves the dog becomes more developed; he laughs, dances, in fact thrives on her absence in his behalf. At the end, she bows to him and says, "Your servant." He is fully grown. The fact that she is shown as originally having nothing to offer is significant. The writers in the daughter construct seem to be expressing a truth about the growth process that this nursery rhyme touches upon. Whether their mothers encourage them or not, what the woman needs who wants to achieve a powerful identity in a patriarchal culture is a mother who cannot nurture her, so that she is driven to nurture herself with her words and images.

As a theory accounting for the mode of self-representation and autobiographical themes in their works, the daughter construct offers ways to read a text and a life, both for what is there and what is not, from a broad perspective; the text it can illustrate can be one piece or an entire oeuvre. When "a rose is a rose is a rose is a rose" is considered in such a context, it is not exactly a tragedy; as I suggested earlier, it may be in fact a comedy wherein the daughter frees herself of restricting roles in ingenious fashion to achieve a powerful identity. Remaining where she is, she can grow in her own way. As Dickinson acknowledged, "I had the Glory— / That will do" (349).

The dog, of course, would bark.

Notes

1   Although the version "Rose is a rose is a . . ." appeared in 1913 in "Sacred Emily," "a rose is a rose is a . . ." appeared in 1922 in "Objects Lie on a Table" and "As Fine as Melanctha." This latter version is the one Stein adopted for her signature.

2   A recent example is an advertisement by Pande, Cameron and Company with the headline "Perhaps a rose is a rose is a rose / But there is no rose / Like Pande Cameron's Genuine Rose China."

3   Words had come to lose their meaning and were worn out. "Now listen! I'm no fool. I know that in daily life we don't go around saying "is a . . . is . . . is." Yes, I'm no fool; but I think that in that line the rose is red for the first time in English poetry for a hundred years." Quoted by Thornton Wilder in his introduction to Gertrude Stein, *Four in America* (1947).

4 "When I said. / A rose is a rose is a rose. / And then later made that into a ring I made poetry and what did I do I caressed completely caressed and addressed a noun." Stein, "Poetry and Grammar," in *Look at Me Now and Here I Am: Writings and Lectures, 1909–45,* ed. Patricia Meyerowitz (London: P. Owen, 1967), p. 138.

5 In addition to the self-conscious use of the "rose" saying, roses appear in "Prim Roses" (1918), "For-get-me-not. To Janet" ("Advice about Roses"), *Stanzas in Meditation* (1929), "A Play without Roses Portrait of Eugene Jolas" (1932), and there is the "Say It with Flowers. A Play" (1931). See also Richard Bridgman, *Gertrude Stein in Pieces* (New York: Oxford University Press, 1970), p. 138.

6 For example, Stein's closest brother, Leo, with whom she grew up and lived in Paris until their separation, wrote in response to *The Autobiography of Alice B. Toklas* (1932), "Imagine the stupidity of anyone sixty years of age who makes that remark. . . . I doubt whether there is a single comment or observation in the book that is not stupid." Leo Stein, *Journey into the Self* (New York: Crown, 1950).

7 "I am not I any longer when I see, that is, when I am conscious of the outside world, or audience. This sentence is at the bottom of all creative activity. It is just the exact opposite of I am I because my little dog knows me" (*Four in America* [1933], p. 119). In 1938 in *Picasso* she writes, "It is always astonishing that Shakespeare never put his hand to his pen once he ceased to write and one knows other cases, things happen that destroy everything which forced the person to exist and the identity which was dependent upon the things that were done, does it still exist, yes or no." See Janet Hobhouse, *Everybody Who Was Anybody: A Biography of Gertrude Stein* (New York: Putnam, 1975), pp. 170–71.

8 Stein, *Everybody's Autobiography* (1936), p. 113.

9 Stein, "Poetry and Grammar," pp. 131–32.

10 "The daughter construct," developed in my study, *Emily Dickinson: When a Writer Is a Daughter* (Bloomington: Indiana University Press, 1983), is being expanded into a study of art and literature; this essay is a condensation of that work-in-progress.

11 Emily Dickinson, *The Complete Poems of Emily Dickinson,* ed. Thomas H. Johnson (Boston: Little, 1960; originally published as *The Poems of Emily Dickinson* [Cambridge: Harvard University Press, 1955]). Poems are cited by Johnson number.

12 See, for example, Nancy Chodorow, *The Reproduction of Mothering: Psychoanalysis and the Sociology of Gender* (Berkeley: University of California Press, 1978), pp. 136–38.

13 Sylvia Plath, *The Collected Poems,* ed. Ted Hughes (London and Boston: Faber & Faber, 1981). Poems are cited by title.

14 See Hilde Bruch, *The Golden Cage: The Enigma of Anorexia Nervosa* (Cambridge: Harvard University Press, 1978).

15 For a fuller treatment of Emily Dickinson as a daughter, see Mossberg, *Emily Dickinson.*

16 John Cody, *After Great Pain: The Inner Life of Emily Dickinson* (Cambridge: Harvard University Press, 1971).

17 *The Letters of Emily Dickinson*, 3 vols., ed. Thomas H. Johnson and Theodora Ward (Cambridge: Harvard University Press, 1958): II, 475, 517–18, 508, 403–4; I, 241; III, 675, 687.

18 Ibid., II, 345; I, 144.

19 Ibid., I, 97–100, 10; II, 455.

20 The writer of this play, Rose Goldenberg, like Stein had a "fat" childhood, "so I could only read, I wanted to be a writer as a child." She identified with Plath: "I had a sweet mother who lived through me. She's dead. I miss her. I started in life as a poet. Like Sylvia, I won the *Atlantic Monthly* Poetry Prize" (*Los Angeles Times*, October 3, 1983). She also wrote a teleplay, *Mother and Daughter: The Loving War* (ABC).

21 Carolyn Kizer, *Yin: New Poems* (Brookport, N.Y.: Boa Editions, 1984).

22 Lilly Library, Indiana University Sylvia Plath Archive of Juvenilia, unpublished. Following quotations are also unpublished juvenilia from this collection.

23 For a discussion of the early mother-daughter correspondence housed at the Lilly Library, see Mossberg, "Back, Back, Back: Sylvia Plath's Mummy Muse" in *Coming to Light: American Women Poets of the Twentieth Century*, ed. Diane Middlebrook and Marilyn Yalom (forthcoming).

24 From her Journal, also at the Lilly Library.

25 See Marilyn Yalom, "They Remember *Maman*: Attachment and Separation in Leduc, de Beauvoir, Sand, and Cardinal," *Essays in Literature* 8, no. 1 (Spring 1981): pp. 73–90.

IV. Defining a Context: The Example of Women's Studies

Engorging the Patriarchy

Nina Auerbach

WHEN I hear feminist criticism praised for its "ideological purity" I find it odd, because I have always seen myself and my work as defiantly impure. As a writer and as a member of the academic community, I take strength from my sense of impurity—my own and the world's. Scholars of women's history are seismographs of taint, pointing their readers to the lie within the label, the aggression within the altruism, the murder within the marriage, the dark questions within the sleek answers. As a representative of purity—moral, ideological, intellectual, or anything else—I am a walking lie. My own work and that of the women I admire give their allegiance to the messiness of experience.

I have an uneasy feeling that we whose vision was once seen as dangerous are now authenticated because, like the Victorian woman, we are perceived as being beyond culture. The perceptions that once were taboo have become purifying and exemplary. "Reading as a woman" is currently an ennobling activity, exuding the sanctity of marginality. The ostracism and enforced self-discovery that taught us each, in our varied ways, to see as we do beckon those in power to learn our language, crack our codes, adopt our ways.

A few years ago, when we began to be feminist critics, it was fun to be a demon, and now—for all of us, I think—it is amusing being an angel. But there is a danger in our believing our own mythology too ardently. History and taste change so rapidly and so irrationally that we all may be disenfranchised at any time, abandoned to the quaintness of yesterday's iconography and the purity of yesterday's ideology. It is salutary to remember that I and my community are impurely human, and that our diverse ideologies have been soaked from the beginning in the impurities of experience. For each of us, I think, there was an epiphany, an era in our lives when we realized that our experience of the world had to pit us against that world as we experienced it, and then—to oversimplify—we became feminists. I should like to go back to some of those moments in our differing lives, in order to find the source of the kind of reading and writing we do. I hope to present these as powerful and durable as well as pure, because they are rooted in the mixed and changing conditions of the history that is our lives.

Since its genesis in the late 1960s, feminist criticism has absorbed effusions of Lacanianism, institutionalized anxiety, Marxist mentoring, and reader response theory. At heart, though, I think we are still engaged in "Life Studies," as Sandra Gilbert beautifully and simply dubbed our work in 1979. We are not criticizing life with Arnoldian detachment; we are bringing its inequities and perplexities to the bland restricting formulas that have told us what to be. An early anthology of feminist criticism was called *The Authority of Experience*;[1] this authority taught us texts and readings the academy ignored, taught us to live lives whose dimensions we had not learned, and I think it will shape our varied ideologies as these mutate into the future. Since the authority of experience first let us see as we do, we should remain true to it. In tribute to its authority, I want to return to two sorts of formative experiences and the ideologies they shaped. The first is not my own; the second is.

Sandra M. Gilbert's "Life Studies" describes her conversion to feminist criticism in rapturous religious language. Elaine Showalter's dissertation, which would become *A Literature of Their Own*, shook the scales from her eyes: "I had awakened, my consciousness had soared, all was changed, changed utterly: I was a born again feminist." Years of good studentship fall away as she awakes to the primary authority of her female life: "Most feminist critics speak—at least from time to time—like people who must bear witness, people who must enact and express in their own lives and words the re-visionary sense of transformation that seems inevitably to attend the apparently simple discovery that the experiences of women in and with literature are different from those of men."[2] The books we need convert us to their source in experience, an experience our tasks as good women had up to then taught us to betray and deny.

For Gilbert's autobiography gives her ideology its life. She begins as a good daughter of the patriarchy: she is a student while her husband teaches, and she is writing about D. H. Lawrence, that seductive guru of our generation, who told us in the lushest language what to be and not be. With dreadful psychic logic Gilbert moves from writing about Lawrence to studying death, but that saving dissertation intervenes, redeeming her from the drift toward death to the study of life. She is saved from the death wish of obedience by a female authority that permits undiluted and unmediated speech. Elaine Showalter's reclamation of woman writers galvanized Gilbert to reclaim her own writing life.

This interchange of lives and books continues. Elaine Showalter's talk at the 1983 English Institute was a happy footnote to "Life Studies."[3] In it, Showalter describes her own conversion from obedient good woman to enraptured feminist critic. As a caretaking faculty wife, she doubted whether she would finish the dissertation that was to illuminate Sandra Gilbert; she describes her own conversion to "born again feminism," to use Gilbert's language. In this community, lives are exchanged as freely as books and ideas, for feminist ideology is inseparable from the lived knowledge of subordination, just as reading and writing are part of our continual self-authorization and self-authentication. An unexpected substitution at the English Institute dramatized this interweaving of life studies with feminist criticism, as it did the communality of our lives: Elaine Showalter was ill, and so another feminist critic, Nancy K. Miller, read her paper. The easy conviction with which Miller wove Gilbert's words into Showalter's life epitomizes the choric, even boundaryless, quality of feminist criticism as a school. Lives are our medium of exchange. Books are inseparable from the private experiences that authorized them, while these experiences take on the semipublic and shared quality of our books. Finally, this conjunction is the only gospel we trust.

I emphasize the boundarylessness that joins our lives to our books, making experience our most avidly shared text, to demonstrate our mistrust of precept, of rule, of any abstraction not proved upon our pulses. Our ideology, if we have one, is fluid, mutable, continually taking on the shifting dimensions of our continually shifting lives. Gilbert and Showalter's "born again feminism," their conversions from good womanhood, shape their ideological method: though both welcome men, with some apprehension, into women's studies,[4] and though both have written incisively about male texts, their dominant allegiance is to gynocriticism, which, as Elaine Showalter defines it, asks the following question: "How can we constitute women as a distinct literary group? What is *the difference* of women's writing?"[5]

Gynocriticism is a quest for woman's "precious specialty," as George Eliot somewhat gushingly called it, distinguishing women as a group. It is not a biological inheritance, but a cultural creation, endowing us with distinction through subordination. This is the quest of women who redeemed their own authority, who reclaimed their writing selves, by differentiating themselves from their culture. The study of woman's distinctiveness converts oppression into a saving creed. Gynocriticism is probably the most influential and productive school of feminist criticism, but, because my own experience differs from that of its practitioners, it is not my method or my ideology. At the cost of admitting my complicity in a fallen world, I shun my "precious specialty" and seek access to the larger, if tarnished, culture that dictates our own and others' differences.

When I think back to the origins of my own feminism, I cannot remember a moment of conversion, because I cannot remember ever having believed what I was told to be. I was always sardonically resisting. I enjoyed thinking of myself as a bad woman; never until recently did I admit that it was never "bad" to refuse to be "good" in the self-mutilating way young women were raised to be in the 1950s. I never wanted to be a caretaker; I never saw myself as a wife or a mother, and I never was one; nor, as I remember, did I see myself as a man. As a sheltered graduate student, I did assume that I would write my dissertation on Jane Austen and George Eliot, and that I would be a faculty member rather than a faculty wife. These things did happen, but few such confident shelters survive growing up. Unlike Sandra Gilbert's, my conversions were generally Carlylean *un*-conversions from a grandiose sense of possibilities. My experience did not redeem my life; instead, it made me question the ego I imagined I had, the reception I imagined I would receive, the disinterestedness of the community I was eager to enter. My feminism, then, is less a quest for my own saving difference from powerful men than a compromise with my idealism about the male-dominated community which looked to me like Camelot.

I never cared about being a good woman, but when I moved from New York to Los Angeles to become an assistant professor at California State College, I was fueled by belief in myself as a good pilgrim. Looking back to that sprawling, car-choked school between two freeways on the fringe of the barrio, I am abashed at my own expectations for it. Cal State was then, and I think still is, a university for the unacknowledged people of this very urban city. Our students were blue-collar workers, blacks, Chicanos, foreigners, and housewives; many of them drove fifty miles across spirals of freeways to make their early-morning or late-afternoon classes without jeopardizing their jobs. At that time, 1970, their average age was twenty-seven, my own age. For a large percent of them, men and women, college was stigmatizing. Their families resented their new, forbidden dreams of professions instead of jobs, choices instead of routines, anger instead of acquiescence. In their dangerous illumination, I saw my own. Teaching *Great Expectations* at Cal State transformed it from the boring little homily I had always privately thought it to a celebration of—just what its title says. The great expectations came alive, the cautionary moral, which only the privileged accept, receded. The bullied poor boy, hungry for glorification, whom my present middle-class students condemn with sanctimonious ease, was heard by his own. Perhaps Jonathan Culler would call it "reading as a woman"—the passion with which class after class adopted *Great Expectations*—but I doubt whether you have to be a woman to read that way. All you have to be is despised.

No doubt all beginning teachers identify with their students rather than with their colleagues, and I did too. Trying to negotiate the den of vipers which the Cal State English Department looked like to me at that time, I saw myself in my students, and I saw myself for the first time. In general, my colleagues approved neither of challenging teaching nor of any kind of scholarship; there were hidden rewards for mediocrity, suppressed sanctions against ambition. The most aspiring students, male and female, were put down when they tried to learn too much, see too far. Original work was punished by derision and bad grades; mindless work was rewarded by comradely smiles and by A's. Like my students, I tried to learn to be blandly affable and to keep my mind in the closet, my unorthodox scholarly writing a secret. My disdain for good womanhood had carried me to a place where I was made to behave like a good woman at last. I was converted into subservience.

The bad climate of Cal State was largely a seepage from California's political climate. The administration of then Governor Reagan had programmed the state colleges to be drearily functional and nothing more: our administrators feared retaliation if we overweened intellectually. The California state system as a whole was suffering backlash from the Berkeley, San Francisco State, and UCLA uprisings. We had our unspoken mandate: to educate our streetwise students with great expectations into a self-contempt that would keep them in their place. No individual was at fault for the servility that pervaded our classes and strangled our most energetic faculty and students. Like patriarchy, it was the air we breathed, a fear that became an article of faith.

No doubt people breathe more freely now at Cal State than they did in those revolutionary years, and no doubt I was a thin-skinned pilgrim who saw sharper moral contrasts than I might find now; but my two years there were a political baptism. Books would never be transcendent again, nor would I be able to escape into them: they were only vehicles of oppression or the fight against oppression, as they had been for my students and my studentized self. When Kate Millett claimed in *Sexual Politics* that the Western cultural tradition was a weapon against women, the indictment that shocked so many people seemed to me tame and limited compared with the weapons I was living with at Cal State.

My conversion, then, is not Sandra Gilbert's. For one thing, I was *un*-converted—into a loss of faith—forced to see (and sometimes to implement) the ways in which books betrayed experience. Moreover, though

my unconversion illuminated my later work as a feminist critic, it was
only tangentially related to my life as a woman. My first job was a lesson
in feminist methodology: there is no haven of the mind, no art is pure
of ideology and politics, books are powerful weapons because they transform our sense of reality, how we read is a political self-declaration.
But I did not learn these things in relation to women alone.

I became a feminist critic at the University of Pennsylvania because
my department assumed I already was one. A predominantly male university was being forced to mend its ways; in 1972, a burgeoning wom-
en's program was bringing feisty life to the Faculty of Arts and Sciences.
My unconversion from eastern loftiness, my new awareness of culture
as a battleground, literature as torn with this battle, all made feminist
reading and writing my natural medium. But unlike my feminist colleagues, I embraced this discipline obliquely. Putting aside my private,
lifelong, and often enjoyable rebellion, I accepted my oppression as a
woman after living with a class and a racist oppression that included
men as well. I recognized myself as a victim when I saw others victim-
ized. In the best female, caretaking tradition, I learned to fight for myself by fighting for others.

My experience as good pilgrim rather than good woman shaped an
ideology that differs from gynocriticism. I do not look for, or see, *"the
difference* in women's writing"; I hear no "different voice," in Carol
Gilligan's resonant phrase; I do not observe a female morality that is
more humane, less abstract, than that of men, as Gilligan does.[6] I may
be blind to these differences because I found feminism, not through my
uniquely female experience, but through a broader experience of injustice that helped me see injustice to women. Oppression has made the
women I know and study resilient rather than discrete; my emphasis
in *Woman and the Demon* on a disruptive, mutable female force, and
my present research on the power of actresses, spring from my awareness that victims learn to assume many selves. I do not think oppression
has given us a sole self, however humane we claim we all are; it has
given us instead a variety of personae with which to blend into a society that threatens us. The resilience, not the uniformity, of the oppressed strikes me; it is those in power whom I hear speaking in the
same different voice.

Extravagantly as I admire the work it has produced, then, I find I
must avoid gynocriticism for myself. My interest lies less in the muted
culture of women than in woman's mutable role in the history of the
main culture as a vehicle of disruptive, dispossessed energy. When I write
about it, that energy is female, but it could stand for *all* "hunger, rebellion, and rage."[7] Such energy has no "precious specialty," but only

its own, self-generated, power. All the voices of the outcast energize my concern for women.

My feminism is equally diluted by a dangerous nostalgia for the gorgeousness that has traditionally been part of our oppression. This nostalgia for the victimization we study so assiduously is one of the many impurities in feminist criticism as a whole: if all our battles were won, where would the female tradition be? Unlike some recent feminist theorists, though, I have no nostalgia whatever for woman's separate sphere.[8] Feminism has traditionally tended to attract advocates of a self-glorifying separatism so extreme that it meets the extremes of patriarchy, purging women of all violence and ego until we become a gush of sheer nurturance in an angry world. This sort of sentimental hygienic mythmaking is a dangerous strategy, apart from being false to all human women. Its removal of woman from the rapacious, morally complex human species bestows on men a power that was never theirs. When a woman attributes all aggression, all thrust for power, to men alone, she gives her own potential violence to her oppressor, making him more loomingly omnipotent than any actual man ever was. Such self-denying feminists create a gargantuan oppressor who never existed in life. It seems wisest for women to forfeit dreams of purity—which are generally patriarchal in origin—in order to gain for ourselves the best possible lives in an imperfect world.

We early feminist critics in the academic world invested men with just this mythic, dehumanizing power. Our first impulse toward separatism would lead, we feared, to patriarchal apocalypse, revolution, repression, some sort of fire from heaven. The last thing we expected from men was their envy. Recently, though, powerful men have yearned to speak in what they conceive of as our voice: the compromised conditions of the 1980s have brought them to women, no longer as angels or whores, but as vessels of a lost integrity. Jonathan Culler has devoted a key chapter of his *On Deconstruction* to the art of "reading as a woman"—that is, with all the skeptical purity of an outcast from culture.[9] In our student days, male professors forbade us to read "as women," that is, as they called it then, "subjectively." Lee R. Edwards's eloquent essay on *Middlemarch* reminds us of the classroom taboos that forbade our despair over Dorothea Brooke's final, married anonymity, which the jargon of that time called "maturity."[10] Now, such luminaries as Jonathan Culler, Jerome McGann, Lawrence Lipking, Wayne Booth, Terry Eagleon, and J. Hillis Miller laud the ideological purity of feminist reading, but I fear that this acceptance will lead to our being locked into a new prison. If a woman's reading of a novel is perceived as insufficiently "womanly," will her fresh perceptions be tabooed as our feminist ones were in the old days? Separatism is always a double-edged sword; women are praised for having qualities that are then forced on them; and if "reading as a woman" becomes an institutionalized enterprise, I fear that its hegemony will crush our power to read as it has been crushed so often before.

Moreover, vertigo sometimes overwhelms male critics trying to read as women. Some of them do not read as anybody: their scholarly contours dissolve with frightening rapidity, leaving them thrashing around in limbo trying to be virtuous. As I watch this, my early wariness returns, and I fear that the embrace of patriarchy means our own disappearance as well as the man's. My paranoia may be right. Some, though not all, of these men have written of their conversion as if feminism were an act of grace freely given to them: lauding their own illumination, they fail to cite the names of any actual, female feminist critics. This shyness about acknowledging female authority probably springs from an attempt to reproduce the evangelical feminist voice, but when they abandon conventional scholarly decorum to embrace life studies, they abandon the female lives which inspired our writing, and then their own, in the first place. Wayne Booth un-reads Rabelais with the same antinomian zeal with which Sandra Gilbert read Elaine Showalter, but Booth's unacknowledged tribute to her method obliterates her authority.[11] Is the wheel coming full circle now that we are being heard? Like those of Dorothy Wordsworth, Zelda Fitzgerald, and other exemplary helpmates, our experiences are continually threatened by absorption in the self-proclamations of male truth. The next generation's Anon. may be ourselves.

As a strategy, the monolithic potential within gynocriticism may make us vulnerable to this sort of invasion. If we turn in on ourselves to isolate "the difference" between our voice and that of supposedly powerful men, our voice will become easy to mimic. Our stress on our uniformity and uniqueness in culture may make us look frailer and more boring than we are. Lawrence Lipking reduces us to a single plaintive note: affirming that women are not "a subspecies of men," he isolates our corporate focus on "love and its discontents," on "needs rather than forms." "Hence," he concludes, "[woman's] poetics obeys another law of nature, the unsatisfied craving of children who cry to be held."[12] Is that really what we've been saying through the ages? It has not felt that way to me, nor have I heard that particular cry in our complex history and varied voices. Lipking is also the author of *The Life of the Poet: Beginning and Ending Poetic Careers*,[13] a rich and moving study of a medley of male lives as these create themselves through poetry. Surely no child's cry could encompass for Lipking the lives of Keats, Dante,

Whitman, and the rest: his wonderful book takes its life from the subtle differences among these men as they transfigure themselves into art.

I had always thought our own life studies were about these self-creating differences as well, but I see us increasingly reduced by the tendency to segregate women from the dominant culture—which is construed as relentlessly male—by the tendency to immure us in a culture and tradition that are solely our own. Our own complicity in this isolation may invite scholars to define us in reductive formulas they do not apply to more intimately known material. Our "precious specialty" may make us feel, and appear, too special for the gross machinery of scholarship. It also may shut us away from the full range of the world. My own sort of writing, at least, requires the flexibility which studying men as well as women allows me. I do not want to give up writers I love because my allegiance to women tells me to do so: we have been told for too long that being a woman means giving things up. I am resigned to giving up the papacy, but I am not prepared to give up *Moby-Dick* — or, for that matter, *The Life of the Poet*—in the name of some greater good. I do not want to abandon the energy, the achievements, of patriarchal culture any more than I want to be abandoned by these things.

Many of us feel the same warm appreciation of the culture which has made us feel outcast, but we justifiably fear its invasion of the sole territory we have made our own. The alternative, of course, is for us to become invaders. This is what I have tried to do in my writing and, in the best of times, in my life. Instead of dwelling on an inviolate female tradition, I have looked at men along with women through a female prism. It may be, as some feminists claim, that writing about men and women as if they were a single species reinforces the patriarchy, but I like to imagine my writing self as well as my living self as a pilgrim in a new country. For me, writing about something is an imperial act: it is my way of claiming power over it. Its magic is dispelled by being understood; it loses its awesome otherness as it is absorbed into the shape of my consciousness and my language. Probably I share the primitive superstition that by writing about the patriarchy, as by eating it, I engorge its power. Carlyle is my sanction: "To reduce matters to writing means that you shall know them, see them in their origins and sequences, in their essential lineaments, considerably better than you did before."[14] To know and to see are essential steps toward conquest.

In *The Madwoman in the Attic*, Gilbert and Gubar write brilliantly about the anxiety of authorship many woman writers still feel. Their title, and the Gothic thrill which courses through their book, associate this anxiety with pathology. But our anxiety is self-knowing and justified: since writing is an exercise of enormous power, it is not mad but

sane to fear an assertion of that power over the decomposed substance
to which you have reduced the subject of your book. Whether we are
women or men, reading is a similar engorgement and appropriation:
an intensely read text circulates through our body and mind. If we make
men our property in this way, we can absorb the patriarchy before it
embraces — and abandons — us into invisibility.

When I wrote *Communities of Women*, men were the grain of sand
in my oyster. I did not know quite what to do with them, but I knew
I could not leave them out, and so I included a long chapter on Henry
James and George Gissing which allowed me, through James's *Bostoni-
ans*, to confront a venerable tradition of patriarchal criticism. This integration that was the essence of *Communities of Women* hints at the
impossibility of my book's own subject, but its method gave me the as-
surance to write my next book, *Woman and the Demon*, which is my
attempt to embrace Victorian patriarchy: I looked into its face and a
coldly triumphant mermaid looked back. Under her gaze, *The Madwoman*'s pen/penis lost its authority for me. Adopting the mermaid
as my totem, I hoped to write the patriarchy in such a way that it would
lose its appearance of power. Writing *Woman and the Demon* exorcised
my sense of the otherness of "high" culture. No longer did I, as a Victorian scholar, inhabit a world that was noble, humanistic, central —
and barred to my marginal self.

I began by affirming our impurity because the best of our writing
is entangled in the messiness of our experience. I conclude by suggesting that the varied ideologies we evolve arise in large part from the imperial experience of writing. Dispossessed women throughout history
have used writing to possess forbidden experiences, forbidden knowledge, forbidden powers. Writing for us expresses not so much "the unsatisfied craving of children who cry to be held" as the will to satisfaction of adults who refuse to be held — and who try to swallow the world
that holds us. The evangelical voice that announced women's life studies
echoes now in literary prophecy and in the prophetic visions of science
fiction. Women's new visionary literature aims to transfuse an oppressive world into its own mythmaking substance, creating spaces large
enough to fit our dreams of invasion.

Writing suffused in experience, and literary visions suffused in the
expansive experience of writing, may not compose a pure ideology, but
they do, I hope, compose one that is durable, able to demystify, diminish, and finally engorge the power that subordinated us; and, what is
most important, able to change each time our experience changes. For
women's ideologies, like men's, have always been less pure than passion-

ate because they reflect the humiliations and the compromised victories of all of our lives.

Notes

1 Arlyn Diamond and Lee R. Edwards, eds., *The Authority of Experience: Essays in Feminist Criticism* (Amherst: University of Massachusetts Press, 1977).

2 Sandra M. Gilbert, "Life Studies; or, Speech after Long Silence: Feminist Critics Today," *College English* 40 (April 1979): 850.

3 Elaine Showalter, "Writing the History of Feminist Criticism," English Institute, 1983.

4 See Gilbert "Life Studies," pp. 864–65, and Elaine Showalter, "Critical Cross-Dressing: Male Feminists and the Woman of the Year," *Raritan: A Quarterly Review* (Fall 1983), pp. 130–49.

5 Elaine Showalter, "Feminist Criticism in the Wilderness," *Critical Inquiry* 8 (Winter 1981): 185.

6 Carol Gilligan, *In a Different Voice* (Cambridge, Mass.: Harvard University Press, 1981), passim.

7 This is the suggestive phrase Matthew Arnold used to denounce Charlotte Brontë's *Villette*. See his letter to Mrs. Forster, April 14, 1853, in *Letters of Matthew Arnold*, collected and arranged by George W. E. Russell, 2 vols. (New York and London: Macmillan, 1895), 1: 33–34.

8 Susan Gubar diagnoses this nostalgia shrewdly in the *New York Times Book Review*, February 19, 1984, p. 26.

9 Jonathan Culler, *On Deconstruction: Theory and Criticism after Structuralism* (Ithaca, N.Y.: Cornell University Press, 1982).

10 Lee R. Edwards, "Women, Energy, and *Middlemarch*," *Massachusetts Review*; *Woman: An Issue*, ed. Lee R. Edwards, Mary Heath, and Lisa Baskin (Boston and Toronto: Little, Brown, 1972), pp. 223–38.

11 Wayne Booth, "Freedom of Interpretation: Bakhtin and the Challenge of Feminist Criticism," *Critical Inquiry* 9 (Sept. 1982): 45–76.

12 Lawrence Lipking, "Aristotle's Sister: A Poetics of Abandonment," *Critical Inquiry* 10 (Sept. 1983): 62, 76, 78.

13 Lawrence Lipking, *The Life of the Poet* (Chicago: University of Chicago Press, 1981).

14 Quoted in Fred Kaplan, *Thomas Carlyle: A Biography* (Ithaca, N.Y.: Cornell University Press, 1983), p. 486.

"Forward into the Past":
The Complex Female Affiliation Complex

Sandra M. Gilbert and *Susan Gubar*

> You leave me sad and self-distrustful,
> For older sisters are very sobering things . . .
> No, you have not seemed strange to me, but near,
> Frightfully near, and rather terrifying.
>
> Amy Lowell, "The Sisters."

FOUR YEARS after Virginia Woolf's death, the American poet-novelist May Sarton addressed her English precursor in a poem entitled "Letter from Chicago." Remembering what Woolf's death had meant to her ("Here where you never were, they said, / 'Virginia Woolf is dead.' / The city died. I died in the city . . ."), Sarton goes on to describe the transfiguration of a once alien Chicago by a mysterious moment of recollection and resurrection: "yesterday I found you. / Wherever I looked was love. / Wherever I went I had presents in my hands. / Wherever I went I recognized you." Finally, declaring that "I speak to you and meet my own life," she concludes, "I send you love forward into the past."[1] As we shall argue here, her gesture of amorous salutation is—and has long been—an exemplary one for many modernist women of letters. Also paradigmatic, however, are the feelings of abandonment, anger, and alienation expressed by Sarton's confession in the middle of the poem that she was "Witness of unreal tears, my own" and that "I met your death and did not recognize you." For turn-of-the-century and twentieth-century women writers, finding themselves for the first time in possession of a uniquely female literary history, have frequently sought to ensure the viability of their own literary future by paradoxically sending love "forward" into the past, "forward" into the arms of powerful esthetic foremothers. At the same time, though, such writers have at last begun to experience an anxiety about the binds and burdens of the past comparable to, but not identical with, what Harold Bloom has called "the anxiety of influence." Confronting the lives and deaths of sometimes problematic foremothers, they have had to ask, "How usable, how energizing is a tradition of our own?"

That Sarton should have chosen Woolf as *the* pivotal precursor in whom she lost and found herself is singularly appropriate. Some years earlier, in a poem called "My Sisters, O My Sisters," Sarton had reviewed the difficulties of a range of other female artists—Dorothy Wordsworth, Emily Dickinson, Christina Rossetti, Madame de Staël, Madame de Sévigné, Sappho—and worried that "writing women" are "strange monsters." Meditating on Woolf, however, appears to have forced her to surface an even more deadly anxiety about "writing women," even while it allowed her to find the "place where time flows again."[2] For indeed it was Woolf herself who mourned what she claimed were the distortions, deflections, and deceptions of the female literary tradition even while she signaled a way for women to perceive time as flowing rather than static, purposefully historical rather than monstrously random. In *A Room of One's Own*, after all, Woolf worried that "anger [had tampered] with the integrity of Charlotte Brontë the novelist" and argued that "the whole structure . . . of the nineteenth-century novel was raised, if one was a woman, by a mind which was slightly pulled from the straight." Given her identification of integrity with esthetic excellence, she seemed—perhaps surprisingly—driven to insist that many of the novels of her precursors had a "flaw in the centre that had rotted them."[3]

Yet, as early as 1922, the author-to-be of *A Room of One's Own* had written in a celebratory letter to the *New Statesman*: "When I compare the Duchess of Newcastle with Jane Austen, the matchless Orinda with Emily Brontë, Mrs. Haywood with George Eliot, Aphra Behn with Charlotte Brontë, the advance in [women's] intellectual power seems to me not only sensible but immense."[4] Describing an unprecedented cultural situation, Woolf was sharply distinguishing herself—as Sarton and others later would—from such an ancestress as Elizabeth Barrett Browning, who had grieved in 1845 that "I look everywhere for [literary] grandmothers, and find none."[5] In a passage from *A Room* (1929) more positive than the one we just quoted, moreover, Woolf would clarify her perception, noting that "toward the end of the eighteenth century a change came about which, if I were rewriting history, I should describe more fully and think of greater importance than the Crusades or the Wars of the Roses. The middle-class woman began to write."[6]

To be sure, when middle-class women began to write and thus to create, for the first time, what Elaine Showalter (following John Stuart Mill) has called "a literature of their own," literary men began to experience considerable anxiety about male authority over an esthetic marketplace that men had traditionally dominated. As we have suggested elsewhere, turn-of-the-century and modernist male writers in particular often responded to the unprecedented accomplishments of female precursors and the threatening achievements of female contemporaries with defensive rage, passionately attacking the ambitions of the authoresses whom Hawthorne, as early as 1855, had excoriated as a "damned mob of scribbling women."[7] Not surprisingly, however, women themselves experienced the dynamics of maternal literary inheritance differently. Looking everywhere for grandmothers and at last finding them, they entered upon a new relationship with the past, one that, like Bloom's model, can be extrapolated from Freud's writings about psychosexual development. As we shall show, the complexity of this model, as well as its often painful implications, forces us to revise our earlier argument, in *The Madwoman in the Attic*, that "contemporary women [can] attempt the pen with energy and authority" because they have been empowered by the struggles of their "eighteenth- and nineteenth-century foremothers."[8]

Specifically, we now wish to argue that Freud's model of the family romance—particularly as it is outlined in "Female Sexuality" (1931)—becomes a suitable paradigm for the analysis of literary history at just the point when the woman writer confronts both a matrilineal and a patrilineal inheritance, that is, in the twentieth century. Then, whether the female artist, in what Freud would see as a "mature" renunciation of the mother, turns to the tradition of the father, whether in what Freud might see as a "frigid" rejection of both allegiances she attempts to extricate herself altogether from her own esthetic desires and ambitions, or whether in a move that Freud might define as "regressive" she claims the maternal tradition as her own, she has at last to struggle with what we would provisionally define as a complex female "affiliation complex."[9]

Considering the Freudian paradigm of female psychosexual development, it is not surprising that the woman's struggle for literary identity should be more complicated than that of the man in patriarchal culture and especially in the twentieth century. Certainly, as Freud describes it, the girl's path toward maturity is far more difficult than the boy's because marked by imperatives of object renunciation and libidinal redirection that require enormous investments of psychic energy ("FS" 208). Thus, if we view a woman's attitude toward her literary inheritance as structured by an "affiliation complex" modeled on Freud's account of female psychosexual development, we inevitably find the woman writer oscillating between her matrilineage and her patrilineage in an arduous process of self-definition. Even as we use Freud, however, we must swerve from Freud, specifically from his valuation of the different options available to the growing girl (and, by implication, to the developing artist).

To begin with, the turn toward the father that the father of psychoanalysis sees, in "Female Sexuality," as the most mature move possible in female psychosexual development seems to us to be, at least for the modern literary woman, just as problematic as any other solution to the riddle of (literary) femininity, and our sense of this problem accounts for our use of the phrase "affiliation complex." In Freud's view, after all, the appropriate female developmental strategy entails a repression of the "pre-Oedipal" desire for the mother and an elaboration of the wish for the phallus (which possesses the mother) into a desire for the father, the man who possesses the phallus (and hence the mother). In the nineteenth century, as we argued in *The Madwoman in the Attic*, such a maneuver was the principal option available to the daughter-writer; inheriting a male-dominated literary tradition, she was generally forced to write out of a desirous (even if agonistic) interaction with that tradition. For women from Maria Edgeworth to Charlotte Brontë, George Eliot, and Emily Dickinson, such a revisionary erotic transference produced great art. Wrestling with the master/muse even as they sought an invasion of his influence, these writers worked out, and out of, a powerful father-daughter paradigm. In the twentieth century, however, Freudian concepts like the girl's "secondary Oedipus complex," as well as Freud-derived Bloomian paradigms like the "anxiety of influence" and our own "anxiety of authorship," must inevitably give way to a paradigm of ambivalent affiliation, a construct which dramatizes women's intertwined attitudes of anxiety and exuberance about (female) creativity.

Etymologically, the word *affiliation* derives from the gender-symmetrical Latin *filia* and *filius*, words which, if not legally at least linguistically, suggest an equality of inheritance. To be sure, both the *American Heritage Dictionary* and the *OED* explicitly emphasize sonship and fatherhood, defining "affiliation" as "the act of taking a son, the establishment of sonship" (*OED*) and "In law: to determine the paternity of an illegitimate child" (*American Heritage*). More generally, however, both dictionaries agree that to "affiliate" means to "associate oneself as a subordinate or subsidiary with" and, most interestingly, the *American Heritage Dictionary* traces the word back to the Indo-European *dhei,* meaning "to suck," a word etymologically connected with "she who suckles." Thus, though lexicographers have erased (by reversing) the female origins of "affiliation"—emphasizing sonship rather than daughterhood, paternity rather than maternity—the word itself preserves matrilineal traces, particularly the idea of a nurturing and nurtured female. Indeed, the contrast between the secondary but now dominant maleness attributed to the word and its female linguistic roots reiterates Freud's own paradigm of the psychohistorically constructed female

Oedipus complex, which obscures the girl's pre-Oedipal phase just as the relics of Greek civilization eclipse the remains of "Minoan-Mycenian" culture ("FS" 195).

In its definitional history, then, the term "affiliation" itself emblematizes exactly the problem with which many twentieth-century women writers were obsessed: not only do artists from Olive Schreiner to Edith Wharton, Willa Cather, Virginia Woolf, May Sarton, and Sylvia Plath analyze the relationship between male history and newly visible female origins, they also perceive themselves as (sometimes vertiginously) free to adopt the powers of paternal and/or maternal traditions. That the concept of adoption is ambiguously present in the definition of *affiliation* suggests, moreover, an evasion of the inexorable lineage of the biological family even while it also implies a power of decision in two historical directions: one may be adopted, and thus legitimized, as a literary heiress; but one may also adopt, and thus sanction others to carry on, the tradition one has established. Finally, therefore, unlike "influence," which connotes an influx or pouring-in of external power, and "authorship," which stands for an originatory primacy, the concept of "affiliation" carries with it possibilities of both choice and continuity. Choice: one may decide with whom to affiliate — align or join — oneself. Continuity: one is thereby linked into a constructed genealogical order which has its own quasi-familial logic.

In "Female Sexuality" Freud offered an extensive analysis of the growing girl's "positive" transference to her father (a move we would associate with the woman writer's affiliation with her male precursor[s]); in addition, he proposed an etiology of female frigidity (a phenomenon we would associate with the woman artist's enactment of a renunciation of esthetic desire). Yet he put forward only one model for the daughter's recuperation of the mother: "masculine protest." For Freud, the woman who refuses to acknowledge that her mother has not given her a penis is engaged in an act of "masculine protest": she pretends that she is a man and that, like a man, she can possess the mother or a mother surrogate. If we translate this maneuver into literary terms, we can see that it implies that the woman artist might gain esthetic potency through a form of male mimicry, a strategy that a number of twentieth-century literary women (like many of their nineteenth-century foremothers) in fact undertook, revising a mode that had been used in very different ways by their precursors. For though Victorian women writers from "Currer, Ellis, and Acton Bell" to George Eliot employed male pseudonyms to legitimize their authorship while implicitly acquiescing in male authority, many twentieth-century literary women have impersonated men in order to possess or usurp male sexual privileges by fantasizing about the possession of female figures, and specifically female muses. In large part, however, the female figures they strove to possess remained — as the mother is in Freud's model — fictive objects of desire rather than independent images of desirousness. Such lesbian writers as Gertrude Stein, Amy Lowell, and Willa Cather, for instance, sometimes passionately and sometimes parodically locate themselves at the center of male culture in a position from which they can scrutinize and praise not autonomously energetic cultural precursors like Sarton's Virginia Woolf but mythic mistresses or mothers (Alice Toklas, Ada Russell, Ántonia Shimerda), about whom and for whom these writers do all the speaking.[10]

But what daughterly devotions and what maternal labors might deliver artistic maturity to those daughters who do not want to become quasi-sons? As we begin to try to define the complex of hostility and love that women writers have sent "forward" into their female past, we enter an area uncharted by Freud. Historically, the great psychoanalyst's model was tragically accurate, at least until the end of the nineteenth century. But, significantly, he began to formulate this model at a time when the structure of the patriarchal nuclear family was changing radically and rapidly because of the rise of the so-called New Woman (a figure richly represented among Freudian analysands and disciples ranging from H.D. to Karen Horney and Helene Deutsch). It may be possible, then, that Freud's theories were themselves symptoms of a reaction formation against the sociocultural instability generated by women for whom female anatomy did not necessarily imply an intellectually impoverished destiny. Thus, although Freud refused or evaded the task of tracing the psychosexual implications of such a massive transformation of the family romance, it is impossible — at least for literary historians — to ignore what we might call the rise of the autonomous mother. Specifically, what does it mean for a literary daughter to confront the existence of foremothers who define themselves as authors rather than objects of desire? As we shall show, Freud's model must be revised to account, as he does not, for twentieth-century women's anxieties about and visions of autonomous female creativity as well as for their fantasies about participation in a literary matrilineage which represents maturity rather than regression.

We believe that the existence of a series of autonomous authorial mothers has inspired feelings of intense ambivalence in turn-of-the-century, modernist, and contemporary women writers. On the one hand, as some feminist critics have suggested, and as we ourselves (perhaps with a certain measure of nostalgia) once argued, female artists, looking for grandmothers whose achievements certify the female imagination, have been inevitably pleased and empowered to recover and celebrate the writings of such figures as Woolf's "four great novelists"—Jane Austen, Charlotte Brontë, Emily Brontë, and George Eliot—along with the poems of Elizabeth Barrett Browning, Christina Rossetti, and Emily Dickinson. On the other hand, although we may appear to be abrogating the politics of sisterhood, we are now convinced that female artists, looking at and revering grand mothers, are also haunted and daunted by the autonomy of such figures.

In fact, we believe that the love women writers send forward into the past is, in patriarchal culture, inexorably contaminated by mingled feelings of rivalry and anxiety. Though there is no mythic paradigm of Jocasta and Antigone which would parallel Bloom's archetype of Laius and Oedipus, "strong equals at the crossroads," most literary women do—with Sylvia Plath—ask "who rivals," partly because, as Margaret Atwood explains, "members of what feels like a minority" must compete for a "few coveted places" and partly because those coveted places signify, as Freud's model tells us, the approbation of the father who represents cultural authority.[11] But the woman writer who engages with her autonomous precursor in a rivalrous struggle for primacy suspects or quickly learns that the fruit of victory is often bitter: the approbation of the father is almost always accompanied by his revulsion, and the autonomy of the mother is just as frequently as terrifying as it is attractive, for—as Woolf's comments about Charlotte Brontë suggest—it has been won at great cost.

Far from being unequivocally energized by the example of her female precursor, then, the literary daughter finds herself in a dire double bind. If she simply admires and adores her grandmother, she is diminished by the originary power she locates in that ancestress; but, if she struggles to attain the power she identifies with the mother's autonomy, she must confront what Emily Dickinson called the "Losses [that] make our Gains ashamed"—that is, the peril of the mother's position in patriarchy, the loss of male emotional approval paradoxically associated with male approbation—as well as the loss of the intimacy with the mother that would accompany daughterly subordination.[12] To have a history, therefore, may not be quite so advantageous as feminists from, say, Virginia Woolf to Adrienne Rich have traditionally supposed. Whether it represents what Laura Riding Jackson has scornfully referred to as a sort of literary powder room or whether it seems to offer a way toward a men's club whose doors are ultimately closed, the past proposes a series of severe ironies.[13] When there was no past, it was indeed possible for women from Mary Shelley to Elizabeth Barrett Browning and Christina Rossetti to dream of, in Dickinson's words, "a different dawn," a "morn by men unseen" (J. 24) that would lead to a different future;

but, once history has occurred, its ironies proliferate as its documents multiply, so that vision and reality split radically apart. In fact, paradoxically, the autonomous literary mother becomes the subject of both matrophilial utopian and matrophobic dystopian meditations, a figure at whose primal relation with tradition the daughter obsessively directs her consistently ambivalent attention, at just the moment when it would seem that maternal potency ought to have healed daughterly dis-ease.

As we have suggested that Sarton intuited, no modernist literary woman wrote more tellingly than Virginia Woolf about both the problems and the possibilities of what we might call matrilineal (literary) affiliation, in part because no modernist woman of letters was more intensely conscious of the influential existence of esthetic foremothers. To be sure, Woolf meditates in her fiction on all the different phases that we have traced in the "affiliation complex," studying the literary implications of transference to the father and of quasi-sexual "frigidity" as well as the artistic dynamics of "masculine protest" and of "mature" desire for the mother. In her critical essays, however, she most clearly reveals both the anxiety and the exuberance which she and many of her contemporaries experienced as for the first time they confronted a female literary inheritance. Indeed, for Woolf—as for a number of other modernist women of letters—it was the comparatively new enterprise of feminist or protofeminist literary criticism that made possible a voyage of dread and desire, a voyage "forward" into the geography of an unprecedented female past.

It is not irrelevant that Woolf can be said to have summarized her exploration of the past by depicting a writer's voyeuristic gaze at another writer. From early in her career she herself continually looked with mingled admiration and aversion at the lives of her precursors. Indeed, long before she was a novelist Woolf was a literary critic working in a new genre pioneered by women writers of her generation. Significantly, her reconstruction of her esthetic heritage, like the reconstructions attempted by many of her contemporaries and descendants, frequently involved a visualizing of the primal scene of writing, a kind of spying on the past. In particular, Woolf exemplifies how women of letters indulged in such erotic peering when approaching the forbidden precincts of the female tradition. A 1924 essay with the telling title "Indiscretions: 'Never Seek to Tell Thy Love, Love That Never Told Can Be'—but One's Feelings for Some Writers Outrun All Prudence" perhaps most dramatically demonstrates her sensual pleasure as well as her daughterly satisfaction at the visions her voyeurism reveals (*WW* 72–76), even while it records her anxious ambivalence toward such visions.

To begin with, tiptoeing toward women's literary history, Woolf employs a striking metaphor to explain her illicit excitement: "Inevitably, we come to the harem, and tremble slightly as we approach the curtain and catch glimpses of women behind it, and even hear ripples of laughter and snatches of conversation" (*WW* 75). Then, tearing aside the veil, she exposes the newly defined female family she discovers behind the swathings of time. Male readers, she observes, have never understood the truth about female authors: "A hundred years ago [women writers] were stars who shone only in male sunshine; deprived of it, they languished into nonentity— sniffed, bickered, envied each other— so men said" (*WW* 75). Now, as she looks for herself, Woolf announces that, contrary to received wisdom,

> it is by no means certain that every woman is inspired by pure envy when she reads what another has written. More probably Emily Brontë was the passion of her youth; Charlotte even she loved with nervous affection; and cherished a quiet sisterly regard for Anne. Mrs. Gaskell wields a maternal sway over readers of her own sex; wise, witty and very large-minded, her readers are devoted to her as to the most admirable of mothers; whereas George Eliot is an Aunt, and as an Aunt, inimitable. . . . Jane Austen we needs must adore; but she does not want it; she wants nothing; our love is a by-product, an irrelevance. (*WW* 76)

Gazing tremblingly into the harem of women's literary history, Woolf repudiates the idea of envy with willful irony as she transforms her precursors first into characters, then into ancestresses. Clearly, for this archetypal feminist critic the act of deciding to tear the veil and look freely at the past is prerequisite to and inextricable from a decision to adopt and be adopted by an alternative literary lineage. At the same time, however, the authorial pride with which Woolf herself recreates the "four great novelists" and Mrs. Gaskell in a fiction of her own making, while never making reference to their fictions, suggests some measure of at least impure "envy" or rivalry on her part.

As we shall see, such a combination of voyeuristic exploration, esthetic exploitation, and voluntary affiliation characterizes not only Woolf's critical oeuvre but also much of the criticism of women writers produced by her female contemporaries and descendants. As we shall also see, however, not only for Woolf but for other feminist critics this combination of exploration, exploitation, and affiliation is risky as well as rewarding. The passage we have quoted from "Indiscretions," after all, records a painful if eroticized vision of the female past: the foremothers Woolf espies were in their own lives sequestered and sometimes silenced; their greatest triumph—being "stars who shone only in male sunshine"—implied invisibility; they were said to be angry and envious, to sniff and bicker. Thus they constitute a problematic family indeed, and it is no wonder that immediately after symbolically adoring this matrilineal spectacle the critic withdraws from it. She has revealed her sisters, her cousins, and her aunts only to reveil them and return to the safety of her fathers. Her romantic engagement with these ancestresses pales, she nervously explains, "as the flirtations of a summer compared with the consuming passions of a lifetime," and she goes on to confess her enthrallment to Shakespeare, John Donne, and that "large, lame, simple-minded . . . great writer . . . Walter Scott" (*WW* 76).

Here, as elsewhere, Woolf's stance foreshadows a position most feminist modernists and their successors have taken toward the female past. To be sure, as its title suggests, "Indiscretions" is a deliberately imprudent and impudent essay, a *jeu* the critic seems simply to have dashed off for *Vogue*. Yet for all its comic hyperbole—or perhaps, as Freud might argue, because of such hyperbole—not only does this essay dramatize the love the woman writer sends forward into the past, it also begins to hint at precisely the binds in which the twentieth-century woman writer feels herself to be caught when she confronts the new reality of her female literary inheritance. First, she sees the pain her precursors experienced and wishes to renounce it: to become a woman writer may be, she fears, to become an invisible star in male sunshine—to be, in other words, marginalized, dispossessed, alienated. Or, worse, it may be to sniff and bicker—that is, to become a madwoman. In addition, though, she acknowledges the power her precursors achieved and worries that she may not be able to equal it: to become a woman writer may be to have to find a way of coming to terms with the accomplishments of other women writers. Finally, however, she fears the consequences of both renunciation and rivalry; to renounce her precursors' pain or to refuse to try to rival their power may be to relinquish the originary authority their achievements represent.

Paradoxically, it is this complex of binds that the voyeuristic stance addresses. By looking *at* her precursors, the female inheritor distances herself from her foremothers' struggle while at the same time participating vicariously in the originary moment of composition. Similarly, it is this complex of binds that the imperative of adoption seeks to correct. By looking *for*—seeking out, choosing, and thus achieving a kind of power over—precursors, the twentieth-century woman writer eases the burden of what Harold Bloom has called the "anxiety of influence" while resisting precisely the masculinist oppression and repression that she fears. Metaphorically speaking, as Bloom has shown, male literary history functions like a biological family, albeit a socially constructed one: it is impossible for Wordsworth to evade Milton's paternity, just as it is impossible for Stevens to evade Wordsworth's. For women, however, as we are arguing, female genealogy does not have an inexorable logic because the literary matrilineage has been repeatedly erased or obscured. Thus, when the woman writer "adopts" a "mother" like Mrs. Gaskell or an "aunt" like George Eliot, she is creating a fictive family whose romance is sufficient to her desire. What this means is that even in the unprecedented presence of female literary history, women do not engage in the kind of purely agonistic struggle that Bloom describes. Rather, after they have overcome what we have defined as the nineteenth-century woman writer's "anxiety of authorship" (the fear that because one is a woman one cannot be a writer), they have to confront other, equally distinctive and disturbing difficulties, problems associated with the "affiliation complex."

First, each must inevitably ask, "Have I chosen the right—the most empowering, the most authoritative—ancestors? Have I adopted the right name or names?"—meaning, in our terms, "Given the range of options available to me have I decided upon an appropriate affiliation?" Second, each must also wondur, "Have I betrayed my 'biological' family?"—meaning, in Bloom's terms, "Have I relinquished or been traitorous to the patrilineage which gave me a name in the first place?" Third, each must finally worry, "What is the bloodline that runs through me? What genealogy is really mine?"—meaning, in terms of women's literary history, "Do I really, despite my effort to certify myself with august ancestresses, descend from a line of silly scribbling ladies who write silly ladies' novels?" Fourth, each must speculate, "Will I be engulfed or obliterated by the primacy of the foremothers whose powers I need to invoke?" Given the almost vertiginous range of issues that the adoptive imperative or affiliation complex raises, looking both *at* and *for* must inevitably, again, become an essential survival strategy. For if voyeuristic looking *at* distances the woman writer from crisis even while it allows her to participate in creation, voyeuristic looking *for* enables her repeatedly to validate her selected past and her elected self.

From 1904 on, Woolf's critical essays epitomize such a complex process of looking at and for a matrilineal inheritance. Not insignificantly, the first piece she ever had accepted for publication—"Haworth. November 1904"—described a pilgrimage to Charlotte Brontë's Yorkshire parsonage and lingered lovingly on the display cases that contained "the little personal relics, the dresses and shoes of the dead woman" (*WW* 123) while confessing an anticipatory "excitement" at nearing Haworth, a pleasure which "had in it an element of suspense that was really painful, as though we were to meet some long-separated friend . . . so clear an image . . . had we" (*WW* 122). Some six years after she wrote this essay, when she was still struggling with the recalcitrant manuscript— *Melymbrosia*—that was to become *The Voyage Out* (1915), Woolf implied in a review of Mrs. Gaskell's works that the texts of a female precursor might be secondary substitutes for the personal presence of the author herself: "We who never saw her, with her manner 'gay but definite,' her beautiful face, and her 'almost perfect arm,' find something of the same delight in her books" (*WW* 149). Five years later, in a profile of George Eliot that she produced for *TLS*, the writer, now herself a published novelist, was still obsessed by the visual details one of her major precursors evoked: "One cannot," she confided, "escape the conviction that the long, heavy face with its expression of serious and sullen and almost equine power has stamped itself depressingly upon the minds of people who remember George Eliot, so that it looks out upon them from her pages" (*WW* 151).

Six years later still, moreover, meditating on Eliot's waning reputation, Woolf reiterated her concern with the relationship between face and page, noting that the novelist's "big nose, her little eyes, her heavy horsey head loom from behind the printed page" (*WW* 72). At around the same time, too, Woolf sought out and scrutinized an image of Jane Austen, imagining the scene of writing by meditating on the look and the looks of the writer. Compared with her vision of George Eliot's equine maturity, however, her glimpse of Austen as a prim yet powerfully sardonic schoolgirl was reassuring, and though she confessed that "Miss Cassandra Austen" feared that "a time might come when strangers would pry," Woolf reassured herself about Austen's powers even further by actually prying into a scene of composition.[14] Studying the unfinished text of *The Watsons*, she imagined how the novelist might have finished it. As she, figuratively speaking, watched Austen force her "pen to go through pages of preliminary drudgery" (*CR* 141), she exulted in her precursor's trimphant creation of a successful episode, confiding that her "senses quicken" at the "peculiar intensity which [this novelist] alone can impart" (*CR* 141).

Similar acts of literary voyeurism mark other essays Woolf published throughout her career. Her study "The Duchess of Newcastle" (1925) begins with a "curious student" who "quails before the mass of [the duchess's] mausoleum, peers in, looks about . . . and hurries out again, shutting the door" (*CR* 70) and culminates with a vision of people crowding the streets to look at "the crazy Duchess in her coach" (*CR* 78). In addition, Woolf's essay "Dorothy Wordsworth" (1932) continues the critic's emphasis on vision in three interestingly different ways.

First, Dorothy herself becomes a kind of heroine of perception. Distinguished by her expert powers of observation, "she scarcely," in Woolf's phrase, "seemed to shut her eyes," and, looking along the sight lines that the diary "points," Woolf sees precisely what Dorothy saw.[15] Second, Woolf dwells with voyeuristic fascination on the "strange love" between this woman see-er and her poet brother, quoting extensively from the diary passages in which Dorothy describes the pleasures of her relationship with "my Beloved" and transforming the romantic pair into a real-life version of Emily Brontë's Cathy and Heathcliff: "One could not act without the other. They must feel, they must think, they must be together" (*CR* 2 153). Third, Woolf sees Dorothy seeing, evoking her "cheeks . . . brown as a gipsy's . . . her gait . . . rapid and ungainly" (*CR* 2 155).

Finally, in an appreciation of Christina Rossetti that appeared in the same volume as "Dorothy Wordsworth," Woolf both used the voyeuristic strategies that she had employed throughout many other pieces and disrupted those strategies as she imagined the annihilation of the space that separated her from her foremother as well as an actual quasi-erotic engagement with the object of her admiration. Beginning with an image of Rossetti as an inhabitant of a "miraculously sealed . . . magic tank" (*CR* 2 214), Woolf confided that "one might go on looking and listening forever. There is no limit to the strangeness, amusement, and oddity of the past sealed in a tank" (*CR* 2 217). But as she explored "this extraordinary territory," she tells us, the figure of Christina Rossetti suddenly uttered a sentence which shattered the pane of time that divided the watcher and the watched, "as if a fish . . . suddenly dashed at the glass and broke it" (*CR* 2 217). The words that break the glass are spoken in a mysteriously surrealistic scene Woolf reconstructs from a biography of the poet. At a tea party, "suddenly there uprose from a chair and paced forward into the centre of the room a little woman dressed in black, who announced solemnly, 'I am Christina Rossetti!' and having so said, returned to her chair" (*CR* 2 217). Woolf's interpretation of the event further narrows the distance between her and the Victorian writer, for indeed the critic supplies the secret meaning of Rossetti's gesture: "Yes . . . I am a poet."

As she meditates on the meaning of such a statement from "a short elderly woman in black," moreover, Woolf enters into a passionate dialogue with her precursor—"O Christina Rossetti . . . your instinct was so sure, so direct, so intense that it produced poems that sing like music in one's ears" (*CR* 2 219) — and assures Rossetti that her miraculous lines will generate a new lineage replacing male monuments of unaging intellect: "Some of the poems you wrote in your little back room will be found adhering in perfect symmetry when the Albert Memorial is dust and tinsel" (*CR 2* 220). At last, then, the critic admits that had she been present at that tea party she "should certainly have committed some romantic indiscretion" comparable to the imaginative trespasses she confesses in the 1924 essay "Indiscretions": she would have "broken a paper-knife or smashed a tea-cup in the awkward ardour of my admiration when [the poet] said, 'I am Christina Rossetti'" (*CR 2* 221). Breaking the implements of gentility that would distance her from her own emotion, Woolf reenacts Rossetti's own smashing of the glass that intervenes between generations and particularly between generations of women, and indeed she even seems momentarily to identify with the originary woman, for the title of her essay—"I Am Christina Rossetti" —is so notably ambiguous as almost to turn the piece into a dramatic monologue.

That Woolf wished both to identify with Christina Rossetti and to adopt her as an empowering ancestress in order, among other things, to ward off the threat of involuntary participation in what she saw as a trivial and trivializing female tradition is made clear by her suggestion that Rossetti's self-defining proclamation was uttered in response to "something [that] was said in a casual, frivolous, tea-party way about poetry" (*CR 2* 217).[16] For this reason, Woolf shadows her voyeuristic visions of adoptive foremothers with a few virulent essays, virtually poison-pen letters, in which she definitively distances herself from "scribbling" women. In "A Scribbling Dame (Eliza Haywood)" (1916), for instance, she elaborated a conceit based on a comparison of the eighteenth-century romancer to a "domestic house fly" (*WW* 92), noting "that [Haywood] was a writer of no importance, that no one read her for pleasure, and that nothing is known of her life" (*WW* 93), and adding that the only virtue of Haywood's works was that one "could read 'with a tea-cup in one hand without danger of spilling the tea.'" A few years later, in a hilariously sardonic review entitled "Wilcoxiana (Ellen Wheeler Wilcox)" (1919), Woolf did an equally ferocious hatchet job on a woman poet. Pinning the "Madame de Staël of Milwaukee" (*WW* 173) to a wall of scorn, she described forty photographs of the American author who wrote "Laugh and the world laughs with you, / Weep and you weep alone"—lines at which Woolf herself obviously wanted to laugh—and she observed with voyeuristic revulsion that "rather than look like a blue-stocking [Wilcox] would have forsaken literature altogether" (*WW* 174).

But the hostility that so triumphantly surfaces in these revisionary versions of George Eliot's "Silly Novels by Lady Novelists" also more subtly haunts even the most laudatory of Woolf's other works of proto-feminist criticism. "Haworth. November 1904," for instance, focuses on the relics of an emphatically *"dead* woman" and "The Duchess of Newcastle" similarly italicizes the demise of the precursor, whose mausoleum causes onlookers to "quail." George Eliot has a "heavy horsey head," while Christina Rossetti is "a short elderly woman in black" whose religious, social, and sartorial eccentricities embody the "oddity of the past sealed in a tank." As she transforms these precursors into characters in search of an author named Virginia Woolf, the author of *A Room of One's Own* often verges upon caricature. Moreover, concentrating on their bodies rather than their books, she frequently seems to be evading a serious consideration of texts whose powers might make her tremble even more than does the "awkward ardour" of her admiration for Christina Rossetti.

Indeed, Woolf's treatment of her grand mothers' writings is at times more than implicitly dimissive. When we turn to some of this critic's "appreciations" of texts, we find overt ambivalence. *"Aurora Leigh,"* she explains in a *Common Reader* essay, "is not . . . the masterpiece that it might have been," which is perhaps "why it has left no successors" (*CR* 2 188, 192). Similarly, but more famously, she complains in *A Room* that "an acidity . . . a buried suffering . . . a rancor . . . contracts" *Jane Eyre*, although—as she notes with what may be an equally subtle manifestation of hostility—even her beloved Jane Austen had "less genius for writing than Charlotte Brontë."[17] More generally, she asserts elsewhere that "the effect of . . . repression is still clearly to be traced in women's work, and the effect is wholly to the bad," even though "the effort to free themselves . . . has also told disastrously upon the writing of women."[18]

In psychoanalytic terms, Woolf could be said in these passages to be expressing not only rivalry with the mother but also exactly the daughterly complaints that Freud outlined in "Female Sexuality" as "the strongest motive[s] for turning away from" the mother: the "reproach that her mother has not given her a proper genital, i.e., that she was born a woman" (and hence with only second-rate literary powers), and the lament "that the mother gave [her] too little milk and did not suckle her long enough" (in other words, that the mother did not nurture her emergent creativity) ("FS" 202–23). In this regard, Woolf's generalized feelings replicate the even more general revulsion articulated by Willa Cather when, implying that all or almost all women writers were scribbling women, she declared in 1897 that "when I see the announcement of a new book by a woman, I—well, I take one by a man instead" and by Rebecca West when she mused in 1912 that "it would be hard to say why women have refused to become great writers."[19] In addition, they summarize the gist of Amy Lowell's brilliantly sardonic self-analysis in a poem entitled "A Critical Fable" (1922):

"My dear Sir," I exclaimed, "if you'd not been afraid
Of Margaret Fuller's success, you'd have stayed
Your hand in her case and more justly have rated her."
Here he murmured morosely, "My God, how I hated her!
But have you no women, whom you must hate too?
I shall think all the better of you if you do,
And of them I may add." I assured him, "A few.
But I scarcely think man feels the same contradictory
Desire to love them and shear them of victory?"[20]

Lowell's fear—expressed in our epigraph—that her literary "sisters" leave her "sad and self-distrustful" also foreshadows Louise Bogan's rivalrous yet reproachful confession that the works of Victorian "poetesses in the parlor" elicit from her "howls, I can assure you," as well as Margaret Atwood's claim that "woman-woman rivalry" is "likely to take the form of *wanting* another woman writer to be better than she is" and Adrienne Rich's admission about the "Heroines" of the nineteenth century that, triumphantly "deviant" though they were, their "exact / legacy as it is" was "not enough."[21] Moreover, the attitudes that Woolf often expresses when she thinks back through specific mothers look back to Alice Meynell's scathing scorn of Harriet Martineau as a "woman of masculine understanding" who "could not thread her way safely in and out of two or three negatives" and to her contempt for Fanny Burney's *Evelina* as "an unabashed manifestation of waste thoughts."[22] At the same time, they look forward to Louise Bogan's anxious and angry sense that Woolf herself "is frequently intellectually pretentious and always emotionally immature" as well as to Sylvia Plath's feeling that Woolf's "novels make mine possible [but] I shall go better than she."[23] Furthermore, they look forward to Anne Sexton's "secret fear" of being "a reincarnation" of Edna St. Vincent Millay, a poet she considered soggily sentimental, as well as to Plath's determination not to be "quailing or whining like [Sara] Teasdale or [to write] simple lyrics like Millay" and to Edith Sitwell's anxiety that women's poetry is as a rule "simply *awful*—incompetent, floppy, whining, arch, trivial, self-pitying" except for "a few poems" by Christina Rossetti, Emily Dickinson, and Sappho.[24]

By reminding herself of Rossetti, Dickinson, and Sappho—notable and notably brilliant women writers—yet diminishing their achievements to "a few poems," Sitwell is of course not only expressing her feelings of rivalry with powerful precursors but also defending herself against her anxiety about what we have elsewhere argued is a male modernist mythology that all women writers are scribbling women writers. Thus, as she grapples with what male (and female) writers assert about literary women, Sitwell explains why so many female modernists began writing protofeminist criticism at this time, for they too sought to assert their own authority in part by drawing on the authorship of their precursors, and in part by disentangling themselves from their own reproachful attitudes toward their foremothers as well as from the damaging charges leveled by masculinist contemporaries. In a sense, then, the turn-of-the-century emergence of literary criticism by and about women is an anxious but healing response to wounding male assaults against women as well as to female fears about contaminated bloodlines. At the same time, however, as we have speculated, this criticism is often specifically characterized by its obsession with a timeless moment during which the female precursor is inspected, respected, suspected.

Such a transcendent interval of voyeuristic inspection not only bypasses chronology and history, but annihilates sequentiality, a point which explains why so many of these women artists chose to validate their heritage through critical essays rather than narrative fictions. In the novel (or indeed the short story), after all, each event inexorably leads to another and is therefore always threatened by ironic qualifications, by the metaphysics of causality. Woolf's critical portraits of women artists, however, concentrating on the scene rather than the sequence of creativity, can ecstatically celebrate or sardonically castigate moments of pure literary being along with moments of literary mutuality. Furthermore, although criticism is perhaps inherently voyeuristic and thus implies a belatedness toward or dependency upon its subject, literary criticism was a new field of endeavor for twentieth-century literary women, one which their precursors had not fully explored, so that it allowed female writers to be truly original while still fantasizing about the true originary act.

To be sure, nineteenth-century and turn-of-the-century women of letters from Geraldine Jewsbury, Mrs. Gaskell, and Margaret Fuller to Mary Elizabeth Coleridge and Alice Meynell did compose various and variously ambivalent tributes to the tribulations of their contemporaries, and in a few cases their foremothers.[25] In the twentieth century, however, the pace of such critical activity quickened, with writers from Willa Cather to Eudora Welty, from Adrienne Rich to Alice Walker producing biographies, appreciations, and analyses of the lives, works, and difficulties of female contemporaries and foremothers. Whether biographies, appreciations, or analyses, all these efforts function to help the critic-writer affiliate herself with a heretofore undiscovered past. When Vita

Sackville-West explained about Aphra Behn that "her work may not be read, but it is as a pioneer that she should, to her eternal honour, be remembered," she articulated both the hostility (Behn's "works may not be read") and the reverence (she is "a pioneer") informing countless feminist biographies.[26]

Another way of relating to such a lineage, though, is through the creation of parodic and allusive texts, novels or plays that function quasi-critically, and refer to or revise female pre-texts. While both confronting and questioning the logic of narrative causality, these works can never of course discover the timeless moments that critical appreciation reveals. Nevertheless, they work off and out of such moments, implicitly critiquing and explicitly paying a tribute to the plots fashioned by precursors. From May Sinclair to May Sarton, from Jean Rhys to Joyce Carol Oates, twentieth-century women novelists have played variations on the themes of their foremothers in order to strengthen themselves by restoring and revising the past while restructuring the future. Jean Rhys's *Wide Sargasso Sea*, for example, both celebrates and interrogates Charlotte Brontë's hegemonic *Jane Eyre* by retelling the tale from the silenced perspective of Bertha Mason Rochester and can therefore stand as the paradigm for many other works, including Margaret Drabble's *The Waterfall* and Joyce Carol Oates's *A Bloodsmoor Romance*.

Perhaps, however, the most notable and dramatic way of confronting a matrilineage is through the composition of lyric poetry. Though both criticism and fictions based on critical revision attempt to recover timeless instances of female literary authority, even criticism is to some extent constrained by causality. To contextualize a text, after all, is to historicize it. The lyric, however, can evoke and enact fantastic (utopian or dystopian) moments of being in which the female precursor may quite frankly function as a muse or an anti-muse for the daughter artist. Emily Dickinson in the nineteenth century, for instance, celebrated the achievements of foremothers like Elizabeth Barrett Browning, George Eliot, and Charlotte Brontë with a kind of ecstasy, while a certain rueful animosity seems to have animated Barrett Browning's two sonnets to George Sand, a writer whom the English poet praises for being "true genius but true women," yet censures for her "vain denial" of her "woman's nature."[27]

In the twentieth century, however, the production of such ambivalent eulogies to precursors almost became an initiatory ritual gesture for women poets, who now confronted the unprecedented existence of what Barrett Browning had called "grandmothers." From Amy Lowell's "The Sisters" to Erica Jong's "Alcestis on the Poetry Circuit" (on Sylvia Plath), modernist and postmodernist women have written verses defin-

ing the blessings and curses conferred on them by esthetic ancestresses
and peers.[28] A particularly magical paradigm of the poems that bless
the female precursor is offered by Elizabeth Bishop's subversive and celebratory "Invitation to Miss Marianne Moore."[29] Here, revising Pablo
Neruda's famously fraternal "Alberto Rojas Jimenez Comes Flying,"
Bishop appropriates a male-invented structure to call up the powers of
a woman who had been not only her literary but her literal mentor. More
specifically, in what resembles the classical poet's traditional invocation
of the muse, this admirer of Moore's repeatedly asks her older friend
to "please come flying" (as the ghost of Jimenez had come flying to
Neruda), and the woman she evokes at first seems a spirit of place, in
particular a spirit of Brooklyn, soaring over the Brooklyn Bridge—
perhaps, indeed, over the poetic tradition embodied by Hart Crane's
"The Bridge"—and over the rivers, skyscrapers, libraries, and museums
of Manhattan. But Bishop's Moore also seems to be a bit of a witch,
"with the pointed toe of each black shoe / Trailing a sapphire highlight"
and "with a black capeful of butterfly wings and bon-mots." Indeed,
the consummation Bishop devoutly wishes to achieve in her confrontation with this woman artist seems not only erotic but also apocalyptic:
erotic because Bishop envisions Moore coming and mounting "the mack-
erel sky / . . . like a daytime comet," apocalyptic because Moore's coming and mounting seem to suggest what Adrienne Rich calls "a whole
new poetry beginning here."

Pictured first as a sort of Old Testament deity "in a cloud of fiery
pale chemicals," and later "with heaven knows how many angels all riding / on the broad black rim of [her] hat," Moore flies over a Manhattan "all awash with morals," a society corrupted by "taxicabs and in-
justices at large." Transcending "the accidents . . . the malignant movies,"
she seems to presage an "uninvented" music that accompanies the dis-
integration of culture as her female poetic hierophant knows it. For, like
a woman Orpheus, Moore, says Bishop, will tame the lions "on the steps
of the Public Library" so that they will "rise and follow through the
doors / up into the reading rooms," presumably to range through the
shelves devouring unacceptable poetry. What Bishop wants to share with
Moore is a shopping spree or a good cry ("We can sit down and weep;
we can go shopping"); what she fears is that the two will be forced to
analyze their own alienation ("We can . . . play at a game of constantly
being wrong / with a priceless set of vocabularies, / or we can bravely
deplore").

But in any case, Moore offers Bishop a cleansing apotheosis of
destruction—"dynasties of negative constructions / darkening and dying around you / . . . grammar that suddenly turns and shines"—a vo-

cabulary of annihilation which implies that the union of the woman poet with her precursor might constitute a healing break with the past, a break motivated by "natural heroism." Moreover, in its combination of an ostensibly decorous tea-party title (*"Invitation* to *Miss* Marianne Moore") with an exuberantly transfigured landscape ("The waves are running in verses this fine morning"), Bishop's daughterly incantation suggests that the woman who comes bearing "a long unnebulous train of words" might be greeted at and with a reception that would definitively inspire not only Bishop's own poetic future but that of her readers. At the same time, it is impossible not to notice that perhaps precisely because Bishop's poem is about a real woman whom—as Bishop's friends have observed—Bishop both loved and resented, it is also a fantasy, a daydreaming fairy tale about a literary fairy godmother in witch's clothing who could never actually "come flying" across the Brooklyn Bridge as this wishful invocation asks her to do, and whose "soft uninvented music" may well have, as Woolf said of Barrett Browning's *Aurora Leigh*, "no successors." Moore's own faintly ironic reading of the piece as a "magic poem—every word a living wonder"[30] tacitly acknowledges this point. Here, as in so many of Woolf's essays and fictions, the modernist woman's female precursor, newly substantial though she may be, is still associated with the equivocal sorcery Emily Dickinson attributed to Elizabeth Barrett Browning in the nineteenth century.

A similar air of fantasy permeates Sarton's "Letter from Chicago," the poem with which we began this meditation on matrilineage. To be sure, where Bishop's poem is from the first an incantatory invitation and thus frankly wishful, Sarton's starts as an elegiac farewell, a piece that is openly wistful. Recording her abandonment in a "city of departures" by a dead literary mother, the poet sees herself as dead and surrounded by death, cut off from a maternal heritage which is itself morbid and moribund: "I met your death," she tells Woolf, "and did not recognize you." Interestingly, the poem's turn from lamentation to affirmation is manifested through a series of paradoxes and oxymorons which follow a four-year period that has passed since "the world [was] arrested at the instant of [the literary mother's] death." Becoming "the city of arrival," Chicago is transformed into a place where Woolf can be present—and can be given "presents"—precisely because she is absent. Because Woolf is "not, never to be again," she is "never, never to be dead, / Never to be dead again in this city." "Detached from time, but given to the moment," Sarton's English precursor makes time flow for the American poet even while she herself—like the objects of so many of her own critical essays—inhabits an eternal inspiring moment of being. Thus time itself is finally both transformed and transformative.

When Sarton concludes her love letter to Woolf with the line "I send you love forward into the past," she implies that for literary women redemptive time must flow oxymoronically: in order to move "forward" into one's own life, one must quest backward into the lives and lines of foremothers like Woolf.

That Sarton's excavation of Woolf's vitality begins not with the novelist's life but with her death — a death, indeed, which was self-chosen, self-inflicted — suggests that what the younger woman has specifically had to come to terms with is the older woman's inexorable autonomy and the pain associated with that autonomy. Thus, when we place this poem in the context of the affiliation complex we have been defining here, we can see that the literary daughter who turns for empowerment to a powerful mother must work through a sense of anxiety about the mother's independence to a recognition that just such independence both undermines and validates her own search for literary authority. More, that Sarton's account of her own (and her "mother's") metamorphoses is couched in a rhetoric of paradox, just as Bishop's invocation of Moore is filtered through fairy-tale metaphors, while Woolf's own critical essays often include elements of voyeuristic fantasizing, inevitably reminds us that all these writers did still, after all, inhabit a male-dominated culture, and specifically a culture in which it was still, as Freud's work implied, more "realistic" for a daughter to turn to the father than to the mother. If twentieth-century "writing women" — to go back to Sarton's "My Sisters, O My Sisters" — were no longer "strange monsters" without matrilineal options, they still had to struggle to find images and metaphors in which they could envision "the deep place where poet becomes woman . . . And that great sanity, that sun, the feminine power."

This point is strongly reinforced by the writings of such contemporary poets as Dorothy Livesay, Anne Sexton, Maxine Kumin, and Erica Jong.[31] Speaking of "The Three Emilys" — the poets Emily Brontë and Emily Dickinson along with the painter Emily Carr — Livesay observes that though she hears "these women crying in my head" she (defensively) possesses "another kingdom, barred / To them". Similarly, Sexton writes of the dead Plath that the author of *Ariel* died with her mouth "into the dumb prayer," while Kumin notes of the dead Sexton in "How It Is" that "it is hot and dry inside" her "old outline," and Jong rhetorically asks about Sylvia Plath as paradigmatic poet-suicide, "Who can hate her half so well / as she hates herself?" Finally, summarizing all of these feelings of ambivalent dread and desire, Carolyn Kizer remarks in a section of her ambitious "Pro Femina" that her precursors were "barbiturate-drenched Camilles / With continuous periods, murmuring softly on sofas / When poetry wasn't a craft but a sickly effluvium."[32]

Because some of these literary daughters' responses to esthetic mothers (and older sisters) appear so problematic, we must ultimately ask a series of serious questions not only about historical feminist constructions of female literary history but also about feminist criticism as it is practiced today. Why, when the women's studies division of the Modern Language Association mounted a centennial forum on the relationship between women's writings in 1883 and 1983, did they title their session with a quotation from Adrienne Rich—"Drawing Our Skirts across History"—which repressed an essential, twice-repeated word, "*deviant*," whose presence at the beginning and end of the source poem "Heroines" connoted just the pain that we have suggested infiltrates female literary history? Why, indeed, when Rich herself quoted Simone de Beauvoir's *The Second Sex* in "Snapshots of a Daughter-in-Law" (1958–60) did she decontextualize Beauvoir's vision of a woman who plunges "breasted and glancing through the currents," transforming the French writer's dystopic sense that "words issue from" the female figure's "breasts" because she is still a totemic icon of male desire into a utopian image of female salvation? And why does Rich's latest collection — *The Fact of a Doorframe: Poems Selected and New, 1950–1984* — erase even the footnote that would send readers back to Beauvoir's bitter meditation?[33] Why, too, do feminist critics so often dismiss as "male identified" or distort as "protowomanist" the texts of those ancestresses who do not easily inhabit what we would fondly call "positive-role-model city," a city of ladies who never experience pain or defeat? Why, finally, do many feminist theorists assume that women, even now, are so inexorably alienated from culture that "the feminine" has never been in any significant way "inscribed"? Perhaps we should begin to speculate that the denial of history implicit in the writings of some French feminists and the sanitizing of history explicit in the works of some of their American counterparts have been fostered by just the complex of rivalry and anxiety that we have been tracing here.

Thus, though those of us who work in this field have often mutually lamented the ways in which hegemonic scholarship has erased, neglected, or trivialized female contributions to history, and although we have also worried that perhaps for this reason we women suffer and have suffered from an odd communal amnesia, we cannot help wondering whether we ourselves have not contributed to the problem. For perhaps the very same rivalries and reproaches — along with the same needy desires — that we have traced in the critical essays and poems of turn-of-the-century and modernist women writers still afflict us today. We too — all we feminist critics — may desperately wish to find an adequate past, a family romance sufficient to our longing, and we too may fear the inadequacies of the past which we now unequivocally possess. Is it possible that we have rewritten and reappraised history in order to give it the positive inflections we desire and require? Are our angry vilifications and wishful falsifications any more accurate than those our foremothers addressed to their grand mothers? What can we learn from Amy Lowell's argument in "A Critical Fable" that "no one likes to be bound / In a sort of perpetual family pound / Tied by *esprit de corps*—to the wills of the dead?"[34] How can we, in fact, be educated by Lowell's belief that a poet "will find her own latitude," especially if we juxtapose that claim with her confession, offered in a passage from "The Sisters" which we have used as an epigraph here, that her female literary relatives are "near, / Frightfully near, and rather terrifying"? Perhaps we should congratulate Virginia Woolf for not having been the Sweet Singer of Rodmell but rather the Bloom of Bloomsbury; perhaps, indeed, it was the tender toughness with which she regarded, say, the "four great novelists" that allowed Woolf to acknowledge and adopt the "family pound" while appraising "the wills of the dead" so that she could "find her own latitude."

Notes

Epigraph: Amy Lowell, "The Sisters," *Selected Poems of Amy Lowell*, ed. John Livingston Lowes (Boston and New York: Houghton Mifflin, 1928), p. 56.

1 May Sarton, "Letter from Chicago," *Collected Poems of May Sarton* (New York: Norton, 1974), pp. 153–54.

2 May Sarton, "My Sisters, O My Sisters," *Collected Poems of May Sarton*, pp. 74–77.

3 Virginia Woolf, *A Room of One's Own* (New York: Harcourt, 1928), pp. 76, 77.

4 Virginia Woolf's response to "Affable Hawk" appears in the *New Statesman*, October 9, 1920; reprinted *Virginia Woolf: Women and Writing*, ed. Michele Barrett (New York: Harcourt 1979), pp. 55–56; hereafter cited in the text as *WW*.

5 *The Letters of Elizabeth Barrett Browning*, ed. Frederic G. Kenyon (New York: Macmillan, 1897), 1: 231–32.

6 Woolf, *Room of One's Own*, p. 68.

7 For the women's tradition, see Elaine Showalter, *A Literature of Their Own* (Princeton: Princeton University Press, 1977). We have discussed the reactions of literary men to the rising prominence of literary women in "Tradition and the Female Talent," in Herbert L. Sussman, ed., *Proceedings of the Northeastern University Center for Literary Studies*, Vol. 2 (1984), pp. 1–27, and in "Sexual Linguistics: Gender, Language, Sexuality," *New Literary History* 16 (Spring 1985).

8   Sandra M. Gilbert and Susan Gubar, *The Madwoman in the Attic* (New Haven: Yale University Press, 1979), p. 51.

9   See Sigmund Freud, "Female Sexuality" (1931), in *Sigmund Freud: Sexuality and the Psychology of Love*, ed. Philip Rieff (New York: Macmillan, 1963), pp. 144–211; hereafter cited as "FS."

10 Stein speaks with and for Alice in her portrait "Ada" in *Geography and Plays* (New York: Something Else Press, 1922), pp. 14–16, and in erotic poems like "Lifting Belly" in *The Yale Gertrude Stein*, ed. Richard Kostelanetz (New Haven: Yale University Press, 1980), pp. 4–54; Amy Lowell's poems to Ada Russell appear in the sequence "Two Speak Together," *Selected Poems of Amy Lowell*, pp. 209–18; Willa Cather's use of the male persona is best illustrated in *My Antonia* (1918; rpt. Boston: Houghton Mifflin, 1954).

11 Harold Bloom, *The Anxiety of Influence* (New York: Oxford University Press), p. 11; Sylvia Plath, *The Journals of Sylvia Plath*, foreword by Ted Hughes, Ted Hughes consulting editor and Frances McCullough editor (New York: Dial, 1982) p. 211; Margaret Atwood, *Second Words: Selected Criticism and Prose* (Toronto: Anansi, 1982), p. 202.

12 Emily Dickinson, *The Complete Poems of Emily Dickinson*, ed. Thomas H. Johnson (Boston: Little, Brown, 1960), no. 1562; hereafter cited as "J." with poem number in the text.

13 In an unpublished letter to the authors (summer 1984), Laura (Riding) Jackson made a statement to this effect.

14 Virginia Woolf, "Jane Austen," *The Common Reader* (1925; rpt. New York: Harcourt, 1932), p. 137; subsequent references to this volume will appear in the text with the initials *CR*.

15 Virginia Woolf, "Dorothy Wordsworth," *The Second Common Reader* (New York: Harcourt, 1932), pp. 148–55; further citations will be included in the text as *CR 2*.

16 Rossetti's novella *Maude* is discussed in the context of scribbling women in Gilbert and Gubar, *Madwoman in the Attic*, pp. 549–54.

17 Woolf, *Room of One's Own*, pp. 76, 80.

18 Virginia Woolf, *Contemporary Writers*, with a preface by Jean Guiguet (New York: Harcourt, 1965), p. 25.

19 Willa Cather, *The World and the Parish: Willa Cather's Articles and Reviews, 1893–1902*, selected and edited with commentary by William M. Curtin (Lincoln: University of Nebraska Press, 1970), 1:362; Rebecca West, "So Simple" (1912), reprinted in *The Young Rebecca: Writings of Rebecca West, 1911–1917*, ed. Jane Marcus (New York: Viking Press, 1982), p. 71.

20 Amy Lowell, "A Critical Fable," *Selected Poems of Amy Lowell*, p. 44.

21 Louise Bogan, *What the Woman Lived: Letters of Louise Bogan, 1920–1970*, ed. Ruth Limmer (New York: Harcourt, 1973), p. 126; Atwood, *Second Words*, p. 203; and Adrienne Rich, *Facts of a Doorframe: Poems Selected and New, 1950–1984* (New York: Norton, 1984), p. 295.

22 Alice Meynell, *Hearts of Controversy* (London: Pelican Press, n.d.), p. 82; Meynell, *Wares of Autolycus: Selected Literary Essays of Alice Meynell*, chosen and introduced by P. M. Fraser (London: Oxford, 1965), p. 169.

23 Bogan, *What the Woman Lived*, p. 375, and Plath, *Journals*, pp. 168, 164.

24 Anne Sexton, "The Uncensored Poet: Letters of Anne Sexton," *Ms* (November 1977), p. 53; Sylvia Plath, *Letters Home*, ed. Aurelia Schober Plath (New York: Harper, 1975), p. 244; Dame Edith Sitwell, *Selected Letters, 1919–1964*, ed. John Lehmann and Derek Parker (New York: Vanguard Press, 1979), p. 113.

25 See *Selections from the Letters of Geraldine Endsor Jewsbury to Jane Welsh Carlyle*, ed. Mrs. Alexander Ireland (London: Longmans, Green, 1892), pp. 347–49; Elizabeth Gaskell, *The Life of Charlotte Brontë*, ed. Alan Shelstron (Baltimore: Penguin, 1975); Margaret Fuller, "Miss Barrett's Poems" (1845), "On George Sand" (1839), and "On Meeting George Sand" (1847) in *The Woman and the Myth: Margaret Fuller's Life and Writings*, ed. Bell Gale Chevigny (Old Westbury, N.Y.: Feminist Press, 1976), pp. 57–58, 202–4, and 360–64; and Alice Meynell, "Charlotte and Emily Brontë," in *Hearts of Controversy*, pp. 77–100, as well as "A Woman of Masculine Understanding" (on Harriet Martineau), "Miss Mitford," "The English Women Humorists," "Elizabeth Barrett Browning," and "*Evelina*" in *The Wares of Autolycus*, pp. 8–12, 82–85, 111–26, 166–67, 167–74.

26 Vita Sackville-West, *Aphra Behn: The Incomparable Astrea* (New York: Viking, 1928), p. 13. See also Willa Cather, "The Best Stories of Sarah Orne Jewett" and "Katherine Mansfield," in *Willa Cather on Writing: Critical Studies on Writing as an Art*, with a foreword by Stephen Tennant (New York: Knopf, 1949), pp. 47–59, 107–20; Eudora Welty, "The Radiance of Jane Austen," "Katherine Anne Porter: The Eye of the Story," and "The House of Willa Cather," in *The Eye of the Story: Selected Essays and Reviews* (New York: Vintage, 1979), pp. 3–13, 30–40, 41–60; Adrienne Rich, "The Tensions of Anne Bradstreet," "*Jane Eyre*: The Temptations of a Motherless Woman," and "Vesuvius at Home: The Power of Emily Dickinson," in *On Lies, Secrets, and Silence: Selected Prose, 1966–1978* (New York: Norton, 1979), pp. 21–32, 89–106, 157–84; Alice Walker, "Zora Neale Hurston: A Cautionary Tale and a Partisan View" and "Looking for Zora," in *In Search of Our Mothers' Gardens* (New York: Harcourt Brace Jovanovich, 1983), pp. 83–92, 93–116.

27 Dickinson, *Complete Poems of Emily Dickinson*, nos. 312, 593, and 1562; Elizabeth Barrett Browning, "To George Sand: A Desire" and "To George Sand: A Recognition," in Louise Bernikow, ed., *The World Split Open* (New York: Random House, 1974), pp. 113–14.

28 See Amy Lowell, "The Sisters" and "On Looking at a Copy of Alice Meynell's Poems," *Selected Poems of Amy Lowell*, pp. 52–56 and 57–60; Kay Boyle, "The Invitation in It," *American Citizen* (New York: Simon and Schuster, 1944), pp. 6–7; Muriel Rukeyser, "For Kay Boyle," *The Collected Poems of Muriel Rukeyser* (New York: McGraw-Hill, 1978), p. 549; Lyn Strongin, "Emily Dickinson Postage Stamp," in Florence Howe and Ellen Bass, eds., *No More Masks* (Garden City, N.Y.: Doubleday Anchor, 1973),

p. 274; Diane Wakoski, "My Trouble," in Jeannette L. Webber and Joan Grumman, eds., *Women as Writer* (Boston: Houghton Mifflin, 1978), p. 165.

29 Elizabeth Bishop, "Invitation to Miss Marianne Moore," in *The Complete Poems of Elizabeth Bishop, 1927–1979* (New York: Farrar, Straus, and Giroux, 1983), pp. 82–83.

30 Moore to Bishop, August 24, 1948; quoted by Bonnie Costello, "Marianne Moore and Elizabeth Bishop: Friendship and Influence," unpublished paper delivered at the MLA Convention 1982; we are grateful to Bonnie Costello for sharing this paper with us.

31 Dorothy Livesay's "The Three Emilys," Anne Sexton's "Sylvia's Death," Maxine Kumin's "How It Is," and Erica Jong's "Alcestis on the Poetry Circuit" are reprinted in Sandra M. Gilbert and Susan Gubar eds., *The Norton Anthology of Literature by Women: The Tradition in English* (New York: Norton, 1985), pp. 1716–17, 1980–81, 1996–98, 2357–58.

32 Carolyn Kizer, "Pro Femina: Three," in *Knock upon Silence* (New York: Doubleday, 1965), p. 47.

33 The original footnote appears in *Adrienne Rich's Poetry*, selected and edited by Barbara Charlesworth Gelpi and Albert Gelpi (New York: Norton, 1975), p. 16. It cites Simone de Beauvoir, *The Second Sex*, trans. H. M. Parshley (New York, 1953), p. 729.

34 Lowell, "A Critical Fable," *Selected Poems of Amy Lowell*, p. 45.

Paradise Reconsidered: Edens without Eve

Susan Morgan

N ORTHROP FRYE has beautifully said about Blake's poetry that "the end of art is the recovery of Paradise."[1] Many nineteenth-century British writers were concerned with that recovery and, like Blake, revised traditional definitions about paradise in the process of depicting it. Eden, at least the Eden of present desire, would not be a matter of simple return, for recovery also meant redefinition. Central to that redefinition was a new sense of history, specifically as a recognition that paradise is lived in time and as a responsibility to understand the past if the future is to fulfill our dreams. Another element in that redefinition, at least as it was frequently explored in nineteenth-century British fiction, was the sense that paradise is not only a matter of history but also a matter of gender, and that the two are intertwined.

Why would notions of history and of gender be connected in the attempt to redefine and recover Eden? Recalling the biblical story provides at least a theoretical explanation. Having been successfully tempted herself by the hunger for knowledge, Eve became a temptress and seduced Adam into sin. Returning to paradise may well mean returning without her, replacing Eve with a less adventurous, less dangerous, partner, in order to reach a higher level of innocence which protects that achieved Eden from becoming the beginning of a new fall in a ceaseless cycle. Continuity replaces repetition, the temporal future replaces the eternal return. But to say all this is, of course, to presume the perspective of Adam. And it is also to locate where George Eliot's novels begin.

Eliot's first novel, like the short stories which precede it, centers on a man. *Adam Bede,* that beautiful book "full of the breath of cows and the scent of hay," is about Adam Bede in a way that *Daniel Deronda,* her last novel, is not about Daniel Deronda.[2] The "broad-shouldered man with the bare muscular arms, and the thick firm black hair tossed about like trodden meadow-grass," strides along the highroad of this novel, turning our heads as he turned the head of the elderly horseman passing through Hayslope who stopped to have a long look at this "stalwart workman in paper cap, leather breeches, and dark-blue worsted stockings."[3] We too will have a long look at Adam, the handsome carpenter who looms tall in the forefront of the novel. And we are happy to watch Adam, because he is intelligent and sensitive and good and because what he must learn, a "fellow-feeling with the weakness that errs in spite of foreseen consequences" (*AB* 214), is a noble and, at least as important, an achievable lesson for him.

Adam's story is deeply fulfilling, both for him and for the reader. A flawed but noble hero, with a "conscience as the noonday clear" (*AB* 2), but a narrow heart, Adam learns to accept sorrow as a permanent force which changes only its form, "passing from pain into sympathy" (*AB* 498). Here is the kind of sorrow which expands the loving soul twined round those who have done great wrong. First with his drunken father, then with Hetty Sorrel, and finally with Arthur Donnithorne, Adam accepts that "I've no right to be hard towards them as have done wrong and repent" (*AB* 480). He accepts that goodness means more than simply to be good himself. The strength which keeps him so easily from doing evil must go out to others less strong. Adam learns the lesson of suffering, and is redeemed in this world.

In that redemption he also learns one of the most familiar and most suspected principles in nineteenth-century fiction: the correspondence between a "sense of enlarged being" and a "fuller life" (*AB* 541), between what we dream of and whether our dreams come true. The sad story has a happy ending. We last see Adam in the midst of good work and quiet joy, surrounded by passionate love, brotherly bonds, heirs, and a warm community, all grouped harmoniously in a paradise this side of the grave.

Eliot's first novel is a vital nineteenth-century refutation of Richardson's essential premise that the "Writer who follows nature and pretends to keep the Christian System in his Eye, cannot make a Heaven in this World for his Favorites."[4] For Eliot, who salvaged the loving principles if not the system of Christianity, though there is "a sort of wrong that can never be made up for" (*AB* 551), good can and does come from evil: there is salvation through suffering. *Adam Bede* locates that salvation as a heaven in this world, in a thatched house in a timber yard in an obscure English village.

The difference here between Richardson and Eliot directs us to that frequent topic in nineteenth-century British literature, particularly in the first half of the century, its fascination with, its complex and skeptical exploration of, the idea of an earthly paradise. The homely timber yard is not so very distant from Shelley's "Isle under Ionian skies, / Beautiful as a wreck of Paradise." This is the same earthly paradise which ends *Emma* and *Persuasion* and *Waverley* and *Villette*, which forms the last long movements of *Pride and Prejudice* and *The Heart of Midlothian* and *Wuthering Heights*. Usually rural and domestic, it is a world of labor and familial relations which has been earned on this earth through a suffering which leads to mercy and to love. It is a paradise characterized by time, created by change and by death, the mother of beauty. As Keats put it—thus providing us with a happy explanation both of why a primary mode of nineteenth-century fiction is the novel of education and of how that mode embodies an interest in the earthly paradise —"Do you not see how necessary a World of Pains and troubles is to school an Intelligence and make it a soul?"[5]

Scott, Austen, the Brontës, all offer novels which create the vale of soul-making, novels which dramatize the process of developing a human sympathy. They are novels of education, committed to the power of experience to transform our souls for the better in a way that eighteenth-century works like *Clarissa* or *Tom Jones* or *Moll Flanders* (or, in a different sense, other nineteenth-century works) are not. Just as important as the redemptive power of experience is the reward. The representation of that reward is sometimes as brief as Austen's line at the end of *Emma* about the "perfect happiness of the union," sometimes as developed as the long final sections of *The Heart of Midlothian* and *Wuthering Heights*.

These last two novels, particularly Scott's, have been criticized for their final sections, as if the writers had lost their imaginative nerve, abandoned Satan's party, and turned in the end to detailed pictures of a mundane moral life.[6] But such criticism misjudges the structure of these novels because it mistakes their undertaking. *The Heart of Midlothian* would be a tidier but not a better or more unified book without the Isle of Roseneath. Nor would *Wuthering Heights* improve without young Cathy putting posies in Hareton's porridge. To imagine otherwise would be like believing that Wordsworth should have cut out the address to his sister which comprises the final section of "Tintern Abbey."

What these prolonged finales suggest is that paradise in nineteenth-century British fiction is, in essence, anticlimactic. This point may be accurate in a simple, structural way because true paradise (unlike the innocent, naive, or self-deluded state which may open novels) ends novels. However climactic a particular ending may be, that climax is always eroded, even undermined, by our knowledge that it means the action of the novel is effectually over.[7]

But our sense of letdown in the endings of the books I am looking at is more than a matter of the general structure of fiction. Particular endings press the notion that the large dreams and illusions of Emma, the brave adventures of Jeanie Deans, the highly wrought fancies of Lucy

Snowe, the wild passions of Heathcliff and Catherine, the tragic relations of Adam, Hetty, and Arthur, all are past. The earthly paradise these endings evoke must precisely be understood as less than what might have been if it is to be paradise at all. For the human ideal, the real heaven, which is to say the heaven on earth, can be lived only under Wallace Stevens's "friendlier skies," in a particular time and a particular place, and thus with the familiar limitations which bound all our lives. We must accept those boundaries, marked by the water that surrounds that "Highland Arcadia," the Isle of Roseneath, in order to realize the ideal in the reality.

This point is dramatized in particularly loving detail in *The Heart of Midlothian* and *Wuthering Heights,* in their visions of life after stories usually end. The slow progress of Jeanie and Reuben into a solid material future full of children and teapots and property asks that it matter to us. Cathy Linton and Hareton Earnshaw, to be married on New Year's Day, are united in a quiet happiness inaccessible to Heathcliff and Catherine. In a novel depicting one of the most tempestuous love stories of our culture we are asked finally to care about that quietness, that familiar kind of joy.

Yet these calm lives do not rest as the entire last word. Even in that new world, "under that benign sky," we, if not Mr. Lockwood, are asked also to "imagine unquiet slumbers," as Heathcliff and Catherine still walk the moors and disturb the peace. Roseneath too has its disturbances, its living ghosts, as Effie from time to time appears in secret, not only distressing Jeanie but filling that contented domestic ruler with jealousy.

Scott's novels influenced the work of many nineteenth-century British novelists. We have not begun to measure that influence because we have hardly begun to interpret Scott. But the immediate tradition Scott can be placed in is that of women writers. Two powerful inspirations for his own novels are Edgeworth and Austen, and his most direct impact is probably on Gaskell and on Emily Brontë, whose single novel borrows its structure from *The Heart of Midlothian.* The two books characterize the paradise of domestic realism both by the soothingly familiar details of good housekeeping and by disturbing visitations from another reality. These visitations serve to remind us that paradise truly is the "wreck of paradise," that the fictions we create and call realistic have their own illusions of completeness which we must recognize as illusions, if only by recalling another time. Heaven on earth is full of memory and regret, for a more intense life, a more painful, a more beautiful, and most important, a different world.

The vision of paradise as anticlimax has many manifestations in

nineteenth-century British novels. George Eliot's fiction adds a variation which redefines the nature of the vision. The by-her-time-classic
difference between an intense, sensual, but ultimately destructive present, becoming past even as we read about it, like the Edenic, "half-
neglected abundance" (*AB* 222) of the Poysers' garden in current time,
contrasted with a hopeful but less romantic future, is taken up with a
new tension in *Adam Bede*. The harmony with which the story concludes is again shown to be limited, to depend on its own illusions of
an ordered universe. But this final fulfilling world of domestic realism
is presented as a male dominion, while its limitations are highlighted
through the discontent of a female. There is a correlation between what
Adam learns, what he gains, and the fact that he is a man.

Behind the tall figure of Adam creeps another figure, dwarfed and
partially hidden by his striding presence, and shaded as well by its own
darkness and dreadful fate. Henry James, though always a suspect critic
of Eliot's work, given his own problems with influence, claimed about
Adam Bede as early as 1866 that "the central figure in the book, by virtue of her great misfortune, is Hetty Sorrel. In the presence of that
misfortune no one else, assuredly, has a right to claim dramatic preeminence."[8] James is looking through Eliot's book to the ones both he
and Eliot went on to write. The dramatic preeminence is Adam's, and
his story is great enough to hold that place. Yet James's insight remains.
Hetty does lure us away from Adam. Her hopes and misery, her beauty,
her emotional and mental and moral stupidity, her fate, all unite in a
tale which disturbs a humanistic reading of the novel. When I think
what we, as opposed to Adam, have learned, I think uneasily of what
to make of Hetty.

Hetty's soul making tells quite another story from the one we have
been taught through watching Adam. Transported as a criminal for
eight years, Hetty lives through the suffering in order to die on the way
home. As Arthur Donnithorne, her remorseful seducer, says, she "will
never know comfort any more" (*AB* 481). The essential attribute of an
earthly paradise, its quality of pain and reduced hopes and lost dreams,
is literally embodied in this first novel as the character of Hetty. Her
absence haunts the timber yard. The happy ending is primarily taken
up with Adam's and Dinah's responses to the awful news of her death.
A better future exists because, as the narrator puts it, Adam's "better"
love for Dinah "is an outgrowth of that fuller life which had come to
him from his acquaintance with deep sorrow" (*AB* 541). Another way
to put this might be that the better future with Dinah exists because
Hetty cannot be part of it.[9]

We trace here Hetty's relation to her fictional ancestors, those other two Cinderellas whose visionary gleam also vanished in the light of common day. Catherine Earnshaw metamorphosed into Cathy Linton; and Effie Deans, the pagan peasant with her Grecian-shaped head, became a lady and a Catholic. But because the point, as Wordsworth so memorably taught us, is that our sense of heaven in this world requires a sense of something missing, these characters are more than simply sacrifices or excluded figures. They measure the difference between what is and what might have been. And to be shut out of heaven, even an earthly heaven, blesses a character with a special appeal. Effie and Catherine and Hetty are the romantic judgment on the real. They are the outsider's judgment on the community. They focus loss, and remind the reader that in the end we cannot neatly say that losses have compensations.

The original step Eliot's first book takes, identifying a familiar and appealing moral vision of life's meaning and its rewards with male dominion, establishes a subject for the rest of Eliot's novels and transforms nineteenth-century fiction. But that step is not by itself liberating. Austen's novels, Scott's novels now and then, Emily Brontë's single masterpiece, all present female characters with an openness to their importance and their potential missing in *Adam Bede*. The immediate difficulty with offering a feminist reading of *Adam Bede* is that the novel, and by that I suppose I mean the narrative voice and the plot, is on the side of the men. Adam's story is important in a way that Hetty's or Dinah's is not, both because he is the lead character and because Loamshire is a man's world, a point which is offered not only as realistic but as affirmative. Arthur Donnithorne and his grandfather, Reverend Irwine, Martin Poyser, Bartle Massey, and Adam Bede, these are the leaders who direct the fate of the community. Adam matters because he is a man. Hetty is not only less valuable than Adam, a minor character. She is portrayed in strongly negative terms.

What distinguishes Hetty from the selfless Dinah and, more important for the development of the novel, from those previous flawed and selfish outsiders, Effie and Catherine, is that the moral perspective of the book so thoroughly condemns her. We see how that harshness functions by turning to Hetty's harshest judge, Bartle Massey. Bartle states the issue vividly enough: "As for that bit o' pink and white, . . . I don't value her a rotten nut . . .—only for the harm or good that may come out of her to an honest man—a lad I've set such store by" (*AB* 426–27). The schoolmaster is a misogynist. But his embittered dislike of women signals his own need to learn forgiveness. The moral judgment of the narrative about the heroine sides with the schoolmaster and the com-

munity. Unlike Mr. Stelling in *The Mill on the Floss*, who as a false
teacher represents the falseness of culture, Bartle Massey is a loving
though damaged soul who deeply cares about educational progress.
Hetty, intellectually as well as morally stupid, has the heart of a cherry
stone. Because Hetty is outside the human community, we share Bartle's
and the narrator's evaluation of her as subhuman, as most closely related in her sensual greed to Bartle's female dog, appropriately named
Vixen. The enemy of true community progress in *Adam Bede* is not
false culture.[10] It is a woman's dreams.

Hetty's crime against the community is a matter no more of sex
than of murder, though it is a matter of gender. Hetty cannot accept
an earthly paradise which celebrates the Poyser farm as the good life
and validates Mrs. Poyser as embodying the proper feminine role. Hetty
is bored in her dairy and cares little for making cheese. She wants someone beyond the option for fulfillment actually offered her, the tall, re-
strained carpenter with broken fingernails. Why give her loyalty to a
world where everyone else knows what is good for her better than she
does, where everyone tells her to be grateful for possibilities she doesn't
want, where her own wishes cannot even be spoken of? Hetty imagines
herself released from the givens which shape her days, able to shape
her days to her own desires. What tempts Hetty, her inexcusable excuse
for being seduced, is her own dreams. Given the chance to realize her
dreams, to live the romance and escape the reality, she takes it. She rejects
the masculine and culturally inherited vision of the earthly paradise.

But, of course, these are my terms based on my perspective, not that
of the narrator. What does Hetty's story mean apart from its relation
to Adam's story, the story that dominates the novel? Does the narrative
value her independently of the harm or good she does to the stalwart
lad we, as well as Bartle, set such store by? The answer the moral perspective of the novel gives is no. What we must answer in a feminist
reading of the novel, in any reading of the novel which does not choose
to ignore the issue of male/female significance and relative value at the
heart of the book, is what to make of that morality.

Adam Bede affirms two major aspects of the masculine vision shaping our culture. First, as I have been discussing, that vision defines reality as the earthly paradise of fulfillment and community progress whose
center is work and the home. There Adam lives, the tallest and most
important figure in the domestic paradise. And there Dinah lives, "the
sweet pale face" (*AB*, 548) of the full-time wife and mother who has
accepted the male Methodist Conference ban on women's preaching.
As Adam says approvingly, "She thought it right to set th' example o'
submitting" (*AB* 550).

The second aspect of that masculine vision, the aspect which has traditionally been so appreciated by critics of Eliot's fiction, is its fine moral sense, the firmness of judgment which knows the weight of our feelings and acts.[11] And it is according to that measure, with that firmness, that Hetty Sorrel is pardoned and condemned. Mercy proves as deadly as justice because both see Hetty's crime as reprehensible and Hetty as revealed to be beyond the human pale. The leading members of the community, no matter how sincere their forgiveness, cannot accept Hetty's dissatisfactions as anything but sinful; they do not even realize there is anything to understand. Adam does learn sympathy. But neither he nor Reverend Irwine nor Martin Poyser nor Arthur could understand Hetty, or could go on living anywhere near her. That is why Adam's final conversations during that dreadful time, his dramatic confrontations and struggles to understand, are with Arthur, the other man, who matters simply as a member of the community in a way that Hetty never did.

If the moral terms on which the narrative both judges and forgives Hetty are harsh, the greatness of *Adam Bede* is that the novel also, though readers have tended to ignore this, offers other, more expansive terms, providing a larger perspective which is itself a criticism of the community ideology. This perspective cannot be summed up under the broad liberal rubric of Eliot's religion of humanity. The rural carpenter's story called up from a sweeter, better, more harmonious past entwines notions of realism, of history, and gender so as to begin a feminist vision which is the heart of what is radical and historical and amoral in Eliot's fiction.

U. C. Knoepflmacher in 1968 suggested that the discrepancy between the author's presentation of Adam and of Hetty and her harsh disposal of Hetty reveals that "her moralism and the 'realism' with which she reveals an amoral natural order still are in conflict."[12] Adam is linked to Eliot's belief in the universe ordered by human conscience and love, while Hetty invokes the inhuman and unconscious natural landscape of Loamshire. Yet Adam and Hetty represent not so much the tensions between moralism and naturalism as a debate on the nature of reality.

Through Hetty, *Adam Bede* challenges its own representation of the schooling of an intelligence to make it a soul, and undermines its central conviction that "deep, unspeakable suffering may well be called a baptism, a regeneration, the initiation into a new state" (*AB* 436). The theme of Eliot's novel is the apparent sense or the randomness of life, the difficulty of presuming a moral universe when the order, the value, the morality are male. The community premise of the novel, upheld by the plot as well as by the residents of Loamshire, is that the desire to shape life according to the demands of self is antisocial, unrealistic, and deeply immoral. It is also, and this is the element which will shape Eliot's novels to come and radically invert their perspectives, a feminine desire.

Social concern, realism, and morality are not inherently linked. The major threat to Eliot's mid-Victorian realism turns out to be not class or nature or imagination but gender. Through Hetty's story *Adam Bede* fatally limits the boundaries of the moral universe, and undermines its own definition of the familiar realism of "Dutch paintings" (*AB* 180) and details of domestic life. The apparent contradiction of a realist art depicting a world of moral order, which has troubled readers of Eliot's fiction, dissolves when we step beyond Eliot's social liberalism, when we identify it as male.

Reality is not the world of earthly compensations and everyday contentment which replaces the romantic alternative. It is not the world of moral order, even, I would stress, of an order informed by mercy rather than mere justice. Forgiveness is a feminine value but, like Dinah, in the earthly paradise it is at the service of a better world for men. The true power of forgiveness, as both Blake and Gaskell knew, is to illuminate. It is Hetty, or, more probably, the feminist reader, who must learn to forgive Adam and the Loamshire community and the narrator for building a better world with the stones of a young girl's heart.

The larger perspective in *Adam Bede* which I am calling realism is neither naturalistic nor moral. Indeed, the traditional appreciation of Eliot's moral sense has encouraged us to accept the images of Hetty as subhuman, a cherry or a kitten, and to ignore the sexism of such image making. Realism becomes the perspective which can hold together the double fates of both Adam and Hetty and thus the double way we live in a quotidien existence: satisfied and yet dissatisfied; knowing the familiar pleasures of our real experience and knowing the imaginative inadequacy of that experience as well. In spite of Hetty's egotism, her ignorance, her stupidity, in spite of how effectively she is crushed, Hetty speaks to more historical, if less encouraging, truths than the notion of building better worlds can contain.

Eliot's fiction turns more and more to siding with the insights of the inarticulate and immoral dairymaid. We see the same hunger that cannot be fed in Eliot's next novel, *The Mill of the Floss*. The question of feminine fulfillment, or the lack of it, becomes an explicit subject of the book. Maggie Tulliver's longings are presented more sympathetically than Hetty's. And along with that sympathy is a plot which gives

Maggie, unlike Hetty, a fulfilling choice and has her reject it, presenting her as coming to realize that having your dreams come true by disregarding the world already around you doesn't finally satisfy. Maggie understands, and before it is too late, the sad truth that Effie Deans only experiences. The trouble with Hetty, and her great appeal, is that she would not, any more than Effie, and probably with no better results, have given up her chance. Maggie is smarter than Hetty and morally she is a mixed character rather than simply a blind ego in a pretty frame. With her death we are encouraged to feel some ambivalence about an idea of community progress which requires replacing her with Lucy of the golden curls. Female sacrifice is losing its appeal.

The issue is presented in an important new way in *Middlemarch*. Dorothea Brooke's strongest desire, the desire which cannot be fulfilled within the givens of actual life, is the selfless desire to help the world, and thus to change the givens of life. Dorothea is virtually the opposite of Hetty, but because her sense of dissatisfaction with the possibilities of her life as a woman and her longings have her author's moral blessing as Hetty's did not. Dorothea is given wealth, class, education, intelligence, generosity, and a major role in the plot. Most important, Dorothea is good. We can trace her flaws. But her lack of fulfillment cannot, as it could to a great extent even with Maggie Tulliver, be accounted for as the consequence of those flaws.

Middlemarch parallels the stories of Dorothea Brooke and Tertius Lydgate, but with the difference that has struck many readers, that in this book committed to the moral principle of consequences, of the inescapable results of our acts for ourselves and for others, Dorothea is allowed to escape.[13] Her marriage to Casaubon, like Lydgate's to Rosamond, is an act of blindness to others and deception to self. Lydgate pays for that blindness as long as he lives, giving up his professional dreams, accepting "his narrowed lot with sad resignation," and "carrying that burthen pitifully."[14] But Casaubon dies, not only first but immediately, by a deus ex machina that frees Dorothea from the consequences of her mistakes.

Dorothea's release from that oppressive marriage is a gift. But as with all gifts from the gods, we should suspect it. Freedom does give Dorothea a second chance to make at last the right choice, the choice of open eyes and admitted passion that leads to fulfillment. But the catch is that this gift of a second chance is not so fulfilling after all. Rather than teach us that individual moral failings will damage our lives—the lesson of the two first marriages—we learn through this apparently generous ending for Dorothea a harder and more general lesson. Our lives will be limited anyway. Moral failures may trap us, but it doesn't follow that moral victories lead to full lives. Becoming good doesn't save us. The fault may lie in ourselves. But it certainly, and this is the inescapable point, lies in our times.

Through the St. Theresa legend, through the social and political contexts which inform Dorothea's life, *Middlemarch* renders explicit the suggested point in *The Mill on the Floss,* that gender is a matter not of essence but of history, that women are at the mercy of their historical moment. And at the present moment, they cannot fulfill their dreams. Maggie and Dorothea, like Hetty and Catherine Earnshaw and Effie Deans before them, haunt the final lines and new worlds of their novels. At the Red Deeps "the buried joy seemed still to hover—like a revisiting spirit." And Dorothea Brooke's full spirit flows on with an effect "incalculably diffusive." Both remind us of what might have been, of aims not realized.

But male fulfillment is hardly an alternative. If Adam's story traces the male satisfaction in the Eden of domestic paradise, Lydgate's looks at the snake in the garden, the failure of reciprocal love in an Eden based on the illusion of masculine superiority. How can a man, how can anyone, find harmony with another human being when his education has denied her humanity, her very reality as an independent self? What chance has he to make a wise and loving choice? Lydgate does get his heaven in this world and discovers the real horror within that masculine myth. The perfect marriage of the girl all Middlemarch admires with the cultivated stranger so superior to the local suitors becomes a long agony of domestic woe, as even their furniture goes the way of their illusions. Heaven on earth is possible, can be realized, only in some other place, at some other time, for people other than ourselves. Lydgate's bare house marks the present. And Adam's timber yard exists in a past Eden that may never have been.

In Eliot's final book, Daniel Deronda's new East exists, not in the story at all, but in a future beyond his lifetime. Against these past and future Edens stand the dreams of women who insist that a reality which enslaves them in a "blessed protectiveness" remains an illusion, its falseness measured by the real fulfillment it excludes.[15] Change in Eliot's fiction may be measured by the change in the heroine from a powerless and amoral peasant who dies for her dreams to a young gentlewoman powerful enough to win over Grandcourt and to end her story insisting that "I shall live. I mean to live" (*DD* 879). However minimal such a claim may seem, it is a true victory, one literally not allowed to Eliot's first two heroines. That Maggie as well as Hetty dies, while Gwendolyn as well as Dorothea lives, emphasizes that we cannot match any of their fates with a meaning based on individual moral worth.

From Eliot's first novel to her last, the center of meaning, where reality lies, shifts from the insider to the outsider, the hero to the heroine.[16] Gwendolyn matters in a way that Daniel does not, much as Adam matters in a way that Hetty does not. If Hetty is outside her particular community, she is also outside the human community, hardly a person at all. But Gwendolyn, though also an outsider in her social world, represents the only human community the novel offers. Grandcourt is a devil and Daniel is a saint. Both are incorporeal, both extremes beyond the realm of mixed character which Austen long before told us composes realistic fiction and everyday life. In her immorality Gwendolyn is a return to Hetty, and the double story of Gwendolyn and Daniel has its sources in the original dichotomy of Hetty and Adam. The meaning of that dichotomy has changed.

As in *Middlemarch,* the central issue in this final book is what constitutes history, how the present can move into the future without recreating the past. We know what the idyll of Mirah and Daniel will be. We have been there before with Adam and Dinah. The historical promise of *Daniel Deronda* is made not through Daniel but through Gwendolyn. Unlike Dorothea's, Gwendolyn's freedom to have a second chance is not used up through again becoming a wife. Her second chance is not realized within the story at all. We don't know, and perhaps we can't imagine, what Gwendolyn will do. But we do know that her unknown future will not repeat her past. And that is enough.

Buried in Eliot's gender distinction is a question: which reality, Adam's or Hetty's, Gwendolyn's or Daniel's, is the historical moment we live in now? And the implicit answer, in the nostalgia with which Adam's community is presented, in the distance in both time and place of Daniel's fulfillment, in the movement of the heroines from background to foreground, is that our historical moment, and in that sense our reality, is that of the heroines. They are the way we live now. And the way we live now is within a context we are not part of, and which cannot realize our hopes.

Once Eliot had linked the vision of a better world to valuing one gender more than the other, her idea of group progress carried its own negation, its moral claims canceled by its sexism. There is no historical advance into the future if Gwendolyn Harleth stays behind, no religion of humanity for a community that destroys Hetty Sorrel. If men try to escape repetition through a new Eden without Eve, they lose Eden and end up excluded along with her once again. Accepting that exclusion, identifying with that outsider, is the true break out of repetition into history. Art, at least the developing art of nineteenth-century British fiction, does not imagine the recovery of paradise. Men and women, all are Eves.

The case of Eliot's fiction provides a useful paradigm for describing the changes which have taken place in writing the literary history of nineteenth-century British fiction. It also, and this is my purpose here, provides a paradigm for rewriting that history in the future. Traditional critics of Eliot from the very beginning, with the publication of *Adam Bede,* stressed the masculine quality of Eliot's work, its breadth of characters and largeness of vision. Nor, with some exceptions, did the arguments change with the awareness that the author was actually a woman.[17] Indeed, traditional approaches to Eliot are characterized by the assumption that she is different from other women writers, from Austen, for example, with all her drawing-room talk about whom young ladies marry, about how to behave. Eliot is an intellectual, a philosopher, a writer who translated German and read Feuerbach, who scorned kittenish beauty and in *Middlemarch* defended telling the story of Lydgate's passion for "industrious thought" (*M* 107) against the preference for tales of love and weddings. Eliot has a masculine mind.

In recent years feminist critics have reclaimed Eliot, and have argued, to steal Blake's lines once again, that she is not of Adam's party but of Eve's.[18] We can see this clearly in new readings of *The Mill on the Floss* which stress the community's destructively oppressive effect on Maggie Tulliver's intelligence and sensitivity and desires, instead of admiring, as have so many previous critics from Leavis on, Maggie's power to renounce selfish fulfillment for the sake of a good larger than herself.[19] Within the general project of establishing a women's tradition in fiction, feminist readers have come to place Eliot as a major voice for the tensions between creativity and social complicity with the male culture which so haunt women writers. The ties between such opposites as Hetty and Dinah, Maggie and Lucy, or Dorothea and Rosamund point to the divided spirit which characterizes the art of women writing in a man's world. That spirit is shared with other women artists and creates its own tradition of influence and relationship.[20]

This approach, as I think we have all recognized, offers a powerful and profound insight into women's fiction. But the trouble with the older readings of Eliot's work and the newer feminist readings is that both sides underplay the changing narrative attitude toward women in her fiction and claim her exclusively as their own. The male view, of course, simply pretended that the issue of women wasn't important, that moments in the novels where the issue couldn't be ignored were flaws, that women stand for something else anyway, that what was important was Strauss and Feuerbach and ideas about history and the religion of humanity and the big picture.

But the female view has its own fictions, apart from preferring to skim past *Adam Bede* and begin with *The Mill on the Floss*. The idea of a separate women's tradition, when it stands as the whole truth about Eliot's work and not as what it is—the new truth—ignores one of the great insights in the old truth: that Leavis was right, that Eliot's fiction is part of the great tradition in nineteenth-century British fiction. Like Austen, Eliot had a more extensive reputation and impact than Gaskell or Charlotte Brontë. Regardless of Eliot's personal situation, when we consider her in terms of the fiction we should see that we are not talking about an outsider at all. No one was more influential, no one more mainstream, more actively a creator of the great tradition than the novelist for grownups with the man's name.

My point here is not to defend the critical fiction of a great tradition. It is to say that if we consider the life of Eliot's novels without reference to the life of their author, then the idea of a separate women's tradition is also seen to be a critical fiction. It dissolves the moment I ask, Separate from what? Is there a men's tradition which is mainstream and to which Eliot's novels did not or do not belong? Someone might argue that Gaskell's or the Brontës' fiction was outside a mainstream (although I have come to doubt that about Gaskell, at least for nineteenth-century readers), but what does that mean? Certainly, reviewers were biased against women novelists; no doubt readers and male novelists were biased against them as well. That is why the case of Eliot's achievement is so enlightening in feminist efforts to rewrite literary history.

Do we want to construct a line of development of nineteenth-century British fiction which, while acknowledging itself as a construct, tries to take account of influence and uses some of the well-known male authors and leaves Eliot out? Was the work of Dickens or Thackeray more important than that of Eliot to other writers or to the reading public in their time, or is it so in ours? Feminist critics have thrown out one of the basic insights of traditional readers of Eliot's fiction, the very insight which drove readers to insist on her masculine mind: in terms of subject matter, of scope, of narrative method, of what they borrowed from previous fiction and what they invented for the future, Eliot's novels define nineteenth-century fiction.

I am arguing that there is no separate women's tradition in nineteenth-century British fiction. I would not make the same claim for nineteenth-century American fiction or for twentieth-century fiction. It may well be that our present sense of the sharp line between male and female writing, Norman Mailer and Marilyn French, Robert Stone and Margaret Laurence, has distorted our readings of the nineteenth century. I do not undervalue the patterns of influence among women writers which the work of feminist critics is at last revealing. But too much has been left out. I suggest that feminist criticism take a new step in its project of revising literary history, one which, through the recognition of Eliot's absolute centrality, takes back from the masculine tradition not only Eliot and other women novelists but much of the work written by men as well. I propose a new literary history of nineteenth-century fiction which uses our awareness of the centrality of Eliot's work to say that the voice of the mainstream was, at this important juncture, what James remembered as the "voice soft and rich as that of a counseling angel."[21]

The pattern of development in Eliot's work which I have been discussing here illuminates a direction in which feminist criticism could move. Eliot's narratives begin by being of Adam's party, with Hetty as an outsider, excluded from the main line of cultural progress. That exclusion, as Eliot's book tells us about Hetty and as feminist criticism has revealed about a woman's place in fiction, makes dangerous lunatics of us all. Eliot's novels moved from the depiction of women as apart to one where women were central because that is where human values lay. Gwendolyn Harleth, culturally damaged and individually flawed as she is, remains the only human survivor in the community of *Daniel Deronda*, as Daniel accepts his true identity as a fantasy figure and sails away with Mirah to the dreamscape where they and Dinah and Adam and so many other figures belong.

The further insight of *Adam Bede* is that insisting on a literature apart and a separate voice is still to privilege Adam and, crucially, to fall for the largest critical fiction of all, that there is a main voice of nineteenth-century British fiction which belongs to men. Our own growth as feminist critics can be from the crucial step of establishing the existence of a women's tradition as a thing apart toward seeing it as a major force shaping the development of the British novel. Placing a woman's tradition as central would then include exploring the influence of women writers on men writers, and of men writers on women writers. It would acknowledge that Jeanie and Effie Deans are close relatives of Catherine Earnshaw, that Gwendolyn Harleth is well known to Clara Middleton and Isabel Archer, that Hetty Sorrel dreams and dies again in *Tess*. We have, at last, established a place for women in literature. But Eve's party is more extensive than we have imagined so far. It is time to move out from separatism to reclaim a larger place, the great women's tradition which informs nineteenth-century British fiction. During that time, in that place, women characters are the voice of the novel, the imaginative center of the genre during its greatest growth. Inheriting the endurance of their long-talking predecessors, Moll Flanders and

Clarissa Harlowe, these characters embody many of the issues and the methods of the British novel up to the modern age.

Notes

1 Northrop Frye, *Fearful Symmetry* (1947; rpt., Boston: Beacon Press, 1962), p. 41.

2 *The George Eliot Letters,* ed. Gordon S. Haight (New Haven: Yale University Press, 1954–78), 2:387.

3 George Eliot, *Adam Bede* (New York: Holt, Rinehart and Winston, 1965), p. 216, p. 9. All further references to the novel are from this edition.

4 *Selected Letters of Samuel Richardson,* ed. John Carroll (Oxford: Oxford University Press, 1964), p. 108.

5 *The Letters of John Keats,* ed. Maurice Buxton Forman (London: Oxford University Press, 1931), 2:363.

6 Among many others, see criticisms of *The Heart of Midlothian*'s structure by V. S. Pritchett, *The Living Novel* (London: Reynal & Hitchcock, 1946), and Dorothy Van Ghent, *The English Novel: Form and Function* (1953; rpt., New York: Harper & Row, 1967).

7 For a full discussion, see Frank Kermode's *The Sense of an Ending: Studies in the Theory of Fiction* (New York: Oxford University Press, 1967).

8 Henry James, "The Novels of George Eliot," in Gordon S. Haight, eds., *A Century of George Eliot Criticism* (Boston: Houghton Mifflin, 1965), p. 47.

9 The doubleness of Hetty and Dinah is interestingly discussed by Sandra M. Gilbert and Susan Gubar, *The Madwoman in the Attic: The Woman Writer and the Nineteenth-Century Imagination* (New Haven: Yale University Press, 1979), pp. 443–99, passim.

10 For a view of how Mr. Stelling represents false culture, see Mary Jacobus, "The Question of Language: Men of Maxims and *The Mill on the Floss,*" *Critical Inquiry* 8, no. 2 (1981): 207–22.

11 These appreciations pervade Eliot criticism. Some examples would be Bernard J. Paris, *Experiments in Life: George Eliot's Quest for Values* (Detroit: Wayne State University Press, 1965), or the essays by George R. Creeger and Thomas Pinney in George R. Creeger, ed., *George Eliot: A Collection of Critical Essays* (Englewood Cliffs: Prentice-Hall, 1970).

12 U. C. Knoepflmacher, *George Eliot's Early Novels: The Limits of Realism* (Berkeley: University of California Press, 1968), p. 122.

13 See Carol Christ, "Aggression and Providential Death in George Eliot's Fiction," *Novel* 9, no. 2 (1976): 130–40.

14 George Eliot, *Middlemarch,* ed. George S. Haight (Cambridge: Houghton Mifflin, 1956), p. 586. All further references to the text are to this edition.

15 George Eliot, *Daniel Deronda,* ed. Barbara Hardy (Baltimore: Penguin Books, 1967), p. 879. All further references to the text are to this edition.

16   Barbara Hardy has made a similar point in *The Novels of George Eliot: A Study in Form* (London: Athlone Press, 1959), p. 47.

17   The development of Eliot's reputation is traced in David Carroll, ed., *George Eliot: The Critical Heritage* (New York: Barnes & Noble, 1971).

18   Compare Zelda Austen's "Why Feminist Critics Are Angry with George Eliot," *College English* 37, no. 6 (1976): 549–61; and Elaine Showalter's "The Greening of Sister George," *Nineteenth-Century Fiction* 35, no. 3 (1980): 292–311.

19   Along with Jacobus, "Question of Language," see Nina Auerbach, "The Power of Hunger: Demonism and Maggie Tulliver," *Nineteenth-Century Fiction* 30 (1972): 150–71.

20   Some of the by now classic studies are Gilbert and Gubar, *Madwoman in the Attic*; Ellen Moers, *Literary Women: The Great Writers* (New York: Anchor, 1977); Elaine Showalter, *A Literature of Their Own: British Women Novelists from Brontë to Lessing* (Princeton: Princeton University Press, 1977); and Patricia Meyer Spacks, *The Female Imagination* (1972; rpt., New York: Avon, 1976).

21   Leon Edel, *Henry James: The Untried Years, 1843–1870* (Philadelphia: J. B. Lippincott, 1953), p. 294.

Conference Program
Index

Historical Studies and Literary Criticism
The 1984 Caltech/Weingart Conference in Humanities
Conference Director: Jerome J. McGann

Scholarship and Ideology

Lecture: Sunday, March 18, 4:00 P.M.
The Clinton K. Judy Memorial Library
Baxter Hall

"Scholarship and Ideology"
Hans Aarsleff
Professor of English
Princeton University

Seminar: Monday, March 19, 9:00 A.M.
Millikan Memorial Library

"Criticism and the Public Sphere"
Terry Eagleton
Tutorial Fellow in English
Wadham College, Oxford University

"The Politics of English Studies in the British University, 1960–1984"
John Sutherland
Reader in English
University College, London

Moderator
George W. Pigman 3d
Associate Professor of Literature
California Institute of Technology

Historical Methods and Literary Interpretations

Lecture: Monday, March 19, 4:00 P.M.
The Clinton K. Judy Memorial Library
Baxter Hall

"Against Tradition: The Case for an Antithetical Historical Method"
Dr. Marilyn Butler
Fellow of St. Hugh's College, Oxford University

285

Seminar: Tuesday, March 20, 9:00 A.M.
    Millikan Memorial Library

    "Reconstructed Folktales as Literary Sources"
    Bruce Rosenberg
    Professor of American Civilization and English
    Brown University

    "The 'Intimations Ode': A Timely Utterance"
    Marjorie Levinson
    Assistant Professor of English
    University of Pennsylvania

Moderator
    Leo Braudy
    Professor of English and Chairman of the Department
    University of Southern California

Biographical Contexts and the Critical Object

Lecture: Tuesday, March 20, 4:00 P.M.
    The Clinton K. Judy Memorial Library
    Baxter Hall

    "Narcissus Jilted"
    Cecil Y. Lang
    Commonwealth Professor of English
    University of Virginia

Seminar: Wednesday, March 21, 9:00 A.M.
    Millikan Memorial Library

    "Life, Death, and Other Theories"
    Lawrence Lipking
    Chester D. Tripp Professor of Humanities and Director of the Program in
        Comparative Literature and Theory
    Northwestern University

    "The Daughter Construct"
    Barbara Clarke Mossberg
    Associate Professor of English
    University of Oregon

Moderator
    Ronald Bush
    Associate Professor of Literature
    California Institute of Technology

Defining a Context: The Example of Women's Studies

Lecture: Wednesday, March 21, 4:00 P.M.
The Clinton K. Judy Memorial Library
Baxter Hall

"Engorging the Patriarchy"
Nina Auerbach
Professor of English
University of Pennsylvania

Seminar: Thursday, March 22, 9:00 A.M.
Millikan Memorial Library

"Tradition and the Female Talent"
Sandra Gilbert
Professor of English
University of California, Davis
and
Susan Gubar
Professor of English
Indiana University

"Paradise Reconsidered: Edens without Eve"
Susan Morgan
Associate Professor of English
Vassar College

Moderator
Ruth Yeazell
Professor of English
University of California, Los Angeles

Index

DESIGNED BY BRUCE GORE
COMPOSED BY METRICOMP, GRUNDY CENTER, IOWA
MANUFACTURED BY EDWARDS BROTHERS, INC., ANN ARBOR, MICHIGAN
TEXT AND DISPLAY LINES ARE SET IN SABON

Library of Congress Cataloging-in-Publication Data
Caltech-Weingart Conference in the Humanities
(4th : 1984 : California Institute of Technology)
Historical studies and literary criticism.
Proceedings of the conference.
Includes index.
1. Historical criticism (Literature)—Congresses.
2. Literature—History and criticism—Congresses.
I. McGann, Jerome J. II. California Institute of
Technology. III. Weingart Foundation. IV. Title.
PN98.H57C3   1984   801'.95   85-40374
ISBN 0-299-10280-7